Advertising

We work with leading authors to develop the strongest educational materials in business and finance, bringing cutting-edge thinking and best learning practice to a global market.

Under a range of well-known imprints, including Financial Times Prentice Hall, we craft high quality print and electronic publications which help readers to understand and apply their content, whether studying or at work.

To find out about the complete range of our publishing please visit us on the World Wide Web at: www.pearsoned.co.uk

Advertising

Fourth Edition

Frank Jefkins

BSc (Econ), BA (Hons), DipPR(CAM), ABC,
FIPR, FAIE, FLCC, FCIM, FInstSMM

Revised and edited by

Daniel Yadin

MA MCIM

FT Prentice Hall
FINANCIAL TIMES

An imprint of **Pearson Education**

Harlow, England • London • New York • Boston • San Francisco • Toronto
Sydney • Tokyo • Singapore • Hong Kong • Seoul • Taipei • New Delhi
Cape Town • Madrid • Mexico City • Amsterdam • Munich • Paris • Milan

To John Jefkins, Jon Yadin and Ros Ordman

Pearson Education Limited
Edinburgh Gate
Harlow
Essex CM20 2JE
England

and Associated Companies throughout the world

Visit us on the World Wide Web at:
http://www.pearsoned.co.uk

Fourth edition published 2000

© Pearson Education Limited 2000

ISBN-13: 978-0-273-63435-5

British Library Cataloguing-in-Publication Data
A catalogue record for this book can be obtained from the British Library.

10

07

Typeset by 35 in 10/12.5pt Palatino
Printed in Great Britain by Henry Ling Limited, at the Dorset Press, Dorchester, DT1 1HD

Contents

2 The advertising department 22

3 Types of advertising 33

4 The advertising agency   49

19 Planning and executing an advertising campaign   335

20 The advertiser and the Internet   345

Preface

This book is a practical guide to an important business discipline. Advertising is above all a practical affair. While marketing drives products and services towards the consumer, advertising helps to drive the consumer towards the product at the point of sale. Unless this happens, there can be no hope of making a profit from the product or achieving success for the business.

Like previous editions, this book has been revised and updated to meet the needs of advertising practitioners and students. As before, it covers advertising for the syllabuses of the LCCI and the CAM Foundation. It is also a practical guide to use when studying for Chartered Institute of Marketing examinations.

Because advertising is part of the progress of our society, it changes constantly. New media are created; some die. New products and techniques for reaching and motivating consumers are constantly emerging and developing. Even while you are reading this page, change is taking place. Every day, worldwide, hundreds more join the Internet, each one a potential customer for alert entrepreneurs and advertisers. Chapter 20 is a guide to this new arena of opportunity.

For busy practitioners, especially those of us who have minimum time for study, this book is a reference and a reminder of proven techniques and an overview of what's new. For the student, it represents what's possible in a career that can be both totally fascinating and extremely well paid.

1999   *Daniel Yadin*

Notes:
(1) *Advertising* is a companion to another professional book from the same publisher: *Public Relations*. They are an essential duo for those preparing for LCCI and CAM examinations.
(2) A reference such as (*see* 22) refers to numbered section 22 in that same chapter. A reference such as (*see* 5: 2–5) refers to numbered sections 2–5 of Chapter 5.

1

Advertising and the marketing function

HISTORY OF ADVERTISING

1. Introduction

Marketing is more than just distributing goods from the manufacturer to the final customer. It comprises all the stages between creation of the product and the after-market which follows the eventual sale. One of these stages is advertising. The stages are like links in a chain, and the chain will break if one of the links is weak. Advertising is therefore as important as every other stage or link, and each depends on the other for success.

The product or service itself, its naming, packaging, pricing and distribution, are all reflected in advertising, which has been called the lifeblood of an organisation. Without advertising, the products or services cannot flow to the distributors or sellers and on to the consumers or users.

A successful national economy depends on advertising promoting sales so that factory production is maintained, people are employed and have spending power, and the money goes round and round. When this process stops there is a recession. Similarly, prosperous countries are those in which advertising does its job. In Third World countries and in Russia, economies are poor and advertising is minimal, especially when a large proportion of the population are young non-earners.

2. Early forms

Advertising belongs to the modern industrial world, and to those countries which are developing and becoming industrialised. In the past when a shopkeeper or stall-holder had only to show and shout his goods to passers-by, advertising as we know it today hardly existed. Early forms of advertising were signs such as the inn sign, the red-and-white striped barber's pole, the apothecary's jar of coloured liquid and the wheelwright's wheel, some of which have survived until today.

3. Effect of urban growth

The need for advertising developed with the expansion of population and the growth of towns with their shops and large stores; mass production in factories; roads and railways to convey goods; and popular newspapers in which to advertise. The large quantities of goods being produced were made known by means of advertising to unknown customers who lived far from the place of manufacture. This process developed some two hundred years ago in industrialised countries.

Advertising grew with the development of media, such as the coffee-house newspapers of the seventeenth century, and the arrival of advertising agencies such as White's in 1800 to handle British government lottery advertising. Reynell and Son was another early agency, founded in London in 1812.

Charles Barker and George Street flourished in the early nineteenth century. Street, first employed as a booking clerk for classified advertising by a London newspaper, built up a substantial business as an independent advertising agent. Barker was originally a parliamentary reporter for *The Times*, operating teams of runners between Parliament Square and Printing House Square. Both companies eventually became the kind of full-service advertising and public relations agency we know today. Both helped to set the operational style, practice and ethics that the current crop of UK agencies benefit from. Sadly, Streets was swallowed up by various advertising groups during the 1970s and 1980s. Barkers are still in business, but in a different form and owned by different organisations.

4. Advertising and the modern world

If one looks at old pictures of horse buses in, say, late nineteenth-century London one will see that they carry advertisements for products famous today, a proof of the effectiveness of advertising. Nineteenth-century advertisers still with us today include Beecham, Cadbury (*see* Figure 1.1), Lever Brothers and Lipton.

Thus the modern world depends on advertising. Without it, producers and distributors would be unable to sell, buyers would not know about and continue to remember products or services, and the modern industrial world collapse. If factory output is to be maintained profitably, advertising must be powerful and continuous. Mass production requires mass consumption which in turn requires advertising to the mass market through the mass media.

The first advertising agencies were space-brokers, and their legal position as agents of the media remains today as with the legal precedent of the

STRENGTH, VIGOUR, AND PLUCK!

CADBURY'S Cocoa is world-renowned for its absolute purity, and its strengthening and sustaining properties, the Medical Profession and all expert judges according it unstinted praise. The highest compliments have been paid to it; and NANSEN and JACKSON had Chocolate of CADBURY'S manufacture for their famous Polar Expeditions.
CADBURY'S Cocoa is Absolutely Pure, and a "PERFECT FOOD."

Figure 1.1

'agent acts as principal' and is responsible for the payment of media bills even if the advertiser defaults. However, as printing processes improved and it became possible to illustrate advertisements the early agencies competed for business by offering creative services to advertisers. Thus, the service agency took over from the mere space-broker.

The British are apt to disdain advertising, claiming that they are not persuaded by advertisements. In spite of this homes are full of advertised

3

products, and if a product is advertised on TV there is a heavy demand for it in the shops. *Marketing Week* engaged The Human Factor to research the situation, and the results were published in the issue of 26 February 1993. One thousand adults were interviewed. The researchers reported, 'Overall, the study found a surprisingly high level of distrust and condemnation of advertising. Even people who claim to enjoy the ads on TV more than the programmes do not believe ads present a true picture of products.' Yet they buy them! The researchers identified three main and extreme groups. These were the moralists (41 per cent) who regard advertising as a bad influence on society; the advertising immune (46 per cent) who say they pay little attention to advertisements; and the enthusiasts (9 per cent) who pay great attention to advertising.

This is a curious situation in which advertising has to operate. It is like saying that passengers on an airliner have no belief that it will take them anywhere. Without advertising modern industrial society would not exist. So does this public disregard for advertising mean that its effects are subliminal? Does the eye tell the mind to act in a way it pretends not to do? Or is it just a kind of intellectual snobbery?

5. Advertising in the North and South

In the 'North' (i.e. the industrialised countries of the world) it is easy to take this process for granted. So used are people to buying well-known goods that they often criticise advertising. They sometimes complain that it is unnecessary, even a waste of money, and that prices could be cut if there was no advertising. This will be discussed later, but at this early point it is useful to remind the reader that the historical and economic process described in 3 is now taking place in the industrialising countries of the 'South'. The extent of advertising marks the development and prosperity of a country.

DEFINITIONS

6. Marketing

The (British) Chartered Institute of Marketing defines marketing as: 'the management process responsible for identifying, anticipating and satisfying customer requirements profitably'.

7. Analysis

From this definition it is clear that modern marketing is based on the concept of producing and selling at a profit what people are likely to buy.

Sometimes, as with new products like camcorders and home computers, it is necessary to anticipate what the market will accept. There is a difference, therefore, between a marketing-orientated company and a sales-orientated company. The latter seeks to sell what it has produced, without first identifying, anticipating and consequently satisfying customer requirements.

In developing countries the concept of 'marketing' is often misunderstood and wrongly applied to what is in fact 'selling'. In such countries there is a seller's market for imported, assembled or made-under-licence products which may have satisfied the original home markets but have not been designed for an identified buyer's market. Few foreign motor-cars, for instance, are specially designed to satisfy overseas markets, and they are advertised and sold, not marketed. Gradually, however, this situation is changing as marketing research is introduced and indigenous industry develops.

The Japanese were very clever marketers when they first introduced motor-cars like Datsuns to Britain. They exported motor-cars which were of a shape that was familiar to British motorists. The first Datsun to arrive in Britain in 1969 looked remarkably like the Ford Cortinas. That was good marketing.

8. Advertising

The Institute of Practitioners in Advertising definition says: 'advertising presents the most persuasive possible selling message to the right prospects for the product or service at the lowest possible cost'.

9. Analysis

Here we have a combination of creativity, marketing research and economic media buying. Advertising may cost a lot of money but that cost is justified if it works effectively and economically. A good advertising campaign is one which is planned and conducted so that it achieves the desired results within an acceptable budget. Many advertising campaigns cost millions of pounds, but that is relative to the size of the market and the volume of sales required to maintain constant output of a factory's production capacity, whether it be a detergent or a motor-car.

COSTS

10. Who pays for advertising?

In 5 criticisms of advertising costs were mentioned and in 9 reference was made to economic advertising. Where does the money come from to pay for advertising, is its cost justified, and would prices fall if advertising ceased? These questions can be answered as follows.

(a) The cost of advertising is met in the price paid by the consumer, and is but one of the many costs, e.g. those arising from research and development, raw materials, manufacture and distribution, which have to be recovered before a profit can be made. Advertising is one of the distribution costs which include salesmen, delivery, and retail profit. It is therefore an investment. If the product fails, the manufacturer has to pay all the costs including advertising. Normally, however, it is the consumer who pays for advertising.

(b) The cost of advertising is therefore justified in two ways: it enables the consumer to enjoy the product (and, where there is competition between rival products, to have a choice), and it also enables the manufacturer or supplier to enjoy a profit.

(c) Generally, prices fall as advertising increases demand. If advertising were to be stopped demand would also fall off. Either the product would fail to sell, or the price would have to be increased as it would be more costly to produce and distribute a smaller quantity.

11. Advertising expenditure figures

The total annual expenditure on advertising in the UK is just under £12 bn at current prices; at constant prices, just under £10 bn. This is according to the Advertising Association's *Advertising Statistics Yearbook.*

To the above must be added further expenditure on 'below-the-line' media, i.e. direct mail, exhibitions, sales literature and other forms of advertising, plus sales promotion. Reliable figures for these items are not available and a realistic grand total is not possible, except that about £530 million is spent on direct mail and £700 million on exhibitions and shows.

The figures in Table 1.1 reveal the dominance of press advertising.

The recession hit advertising but nevertheless people have to eat, as seen by the continuing growth of supermarket chains, and food advertising has been heavy with many new food products being launched. The figures in Table 1.2 signify this.

Table 1.1

	£ million	%
Press	6,413	60.60
TV	3,333	31.50
Outdoor and transport	426	4.00
Radio	344	3.25
Cinema	73	0.65
Totals	£10,589	100.00

Source: *Advertising Statistics Yearbook,* The Advertising Association 1996

Table 1.2 Adspends of selected food brands 1992/93

	£000s
Allinson wholemeal bread	1,190
Anchor butter	2,420
Batchelor's Cup-a-Soup	3,000
Birds Eye Steakhouse beefburgers	1,110
Hellman's light mayonnaise	1,950
Homepride sauces	2,040
McVitie's Hobnobs	260
Kellogg's Pop Tarts	4,380
Nescafé Cappuccino	2,840
Pringles snacks	1,510
Wall's Cornetto	1,410

ADVERTISING AND THE MARKETING MIX

12. The marketing mix

To continue with the account of the relationship between advertising and the marketing function, the approach taken to the marketing mix will not be the conventional one, but is less academic and more in line with what actually happens in the marketing world. It is designed as a chronological sequence of actions.

13. Definition

The *marketing mix*, or the marketing strategy, is the combination of stages or elements necessary to the planning and execution of the total marketing operation. It should not be confused with the *product mix* which is the range of products or services a company may market, such as a range of cakes, biscuits and confectionery. Nor should it be confused with the *media mix* which is the range of advertising media that may be used in an advertising campaign, e.g. national newspapers, women's magazines, posters and commercial television.

14. Four Ps

The 'Four Ps' concept of the marketing mix, as introduced by E. Jerome McCarthy, developed by Philip Kotler, and widely adopted by marketing teachers, creates four divisions of the mix, namely, Product, Place, Price and Promotion. Advertising comes under Promotion, but so does Publicity which is the American authors' narrow interpretation of public relations. The fault with this oversimplification is that it destroys the sequential linking of the numerous elements of the mix. Advertising is divorced from a number of elements to which it is related, e.g. price and distribution which are put under different 'P' headings.

The 'Four Ps' concept is a handy, elementary version of the marketing mix, but its apparent simplicity is misleading and a more logical mix is given below in **15**.

As will be stated in the next chapter on the advertising department, the appointment of an advertising agency should be made as early as possible so that it may advise on early stages of the mix such as branding, product image, pricing, and packaging. Unfortunately, this rarely happens and marketing people turn to advertising with a ready-made product which is not an ideal advertising proposition.

15. A logical marketing mix

A more sensible presentation of the mix is to start at the beginning and finish at the end. In this way advertising can be associated with other elements. Although not every product or service will include every element, the following is an omnibus marketing mix of 21 elements.

(a) Conception, invention, innovation or modification of product or service. This includes research and development.

(b) The standard product life cycle and its variations, e.g. the continuous, recycled, leapfrog and staircase versions (*see* Figures 1.2–1.6).

(c) Marketing research.

(d) Naming and branding.

(e) Creation and promotion of product image.

(f) Market segmentation.

(g) Pricing.

(h) Product mix, rationalisation and standardisation.

(i) Packaging.

(j) Distribution.

(k) Sales force operations.

(l) Market education.

(m) Corporate and financial public relations.

(n) Industrial relations.

(o) Test marketing.

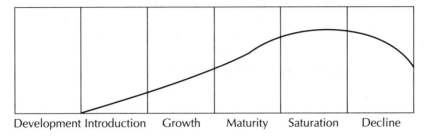

Development Introduction   Growth   Maturity   Saturation   Decline

Figure 1.2 Standard product life cycle

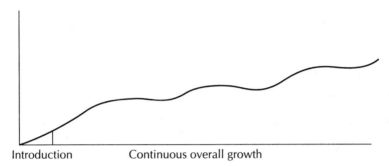

Introduction   Continuous overall growth

Figure 1.3 Continuous product life cycle

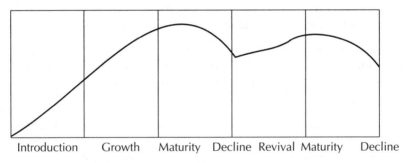

Introduction   Growth   Maturity   Decline Revival Maturity   Decline

Figure 1.4 Recycled product life cycle

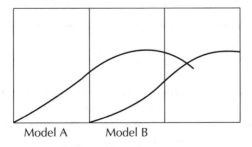

Model A   Model B

Figure 1.5 Leapfrog effect product life cycle

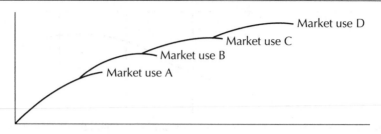

Figure 1.6 Staircase effect product life cycle

(p) Advertising

(q) Advertising research.

(r) Sales promotion.

(s) The after-market.

(t) Maintaining customer interest and loyalty.

(u) On-going PR activity.

16. Advertising involvement

Although advertising is listed as a single element it is associated with almost every other element, borrowing from them or interpreting them.

(a) The volume, emphasis and timing of advertising will depend on the product life cycle situation. For instance, at the introductory or recycling stages, the weight of advertising will be heavier than at the maturity or decline stages.

(b) Marketing research will provide evidence of motives, preferences and attitudes which will influence not only the copy platform or advertising theme but the choice of media through which to express it.

(c) Naming and branding may be initiated by the advertising department or agency, and clearly plays an important role in advertisement design.

(d) The product image will be projected by advertising and PR.

(e) The market segment will decide the tone or style of advertising, and the choice of media.

(f) Pricing can play an important part in the appeal of the copy. Is the product value for money, a bargain or a luxury? Pricing can be a very competitive sales argument. People are very price conscious. Even though legislation prevents the control of prices, indications of likely or 'list' prices, can be important aspects of advertising appeals.

(g) The product mix has many applications. In advertising, one product may be associated with another, or each brand may require a separate campaign.

(h) Packaging is a vital aspect of advertising, as when pack recognition is sought. It is itself a form of advertising, especially at the point-of-sale, as in a supermarket when the package often has to identify the product and literally sell it off the shelf.

Increasingly, Eco-labelling will be looked for as proof that a product is environmentally friendly. There are schemes in many countries for approving products so that they may carry E marks.

(i) Distribution involves trade advertising such as direct mail, in the trade press and at exhibitions.

(j) The sales force has to be familiarised with advertising campaigns which will support their efforts in the field.

(k) Market education is a public relations activity aimed at creating a favourable market situation in which advertising will work.

(l) Corporate and financial public relations often uses institutional advertising in the business press. The corporate image may be the theme of institutional advertising.

(m) Test marketing requires a miniature advertising campaign simulating the future national campaign.

(n) Advertising research includes copy-testing, circulation and readership surveys and statistics, recall tests, tracking studies and cost-per-reply and cost-per-conversion-to-sales figures.

(o) Sales promotion can augment or even replace traditional advertising.

(p) The after-market calls for advertising to make customers aware of post-sales services.

(q) The maintenance of customer interest and loyalty may be achieved by advertising which promotes additional uses and accessories, or simply reminds.

(r) On-going public relations activities help to bridge gaps between advertising campaigns, and help to maintain long-term brand recognition.

The marketing mix described above is true of industrialised countries, but even then varies in application between North America and Europe because of geographic, social, political and ethnic considerations. There are also subtle differences between North American/European marketing situations and those of Japan. For example, Japanese advertising places more emphasis on promoting the name rather than the qualities of the product.

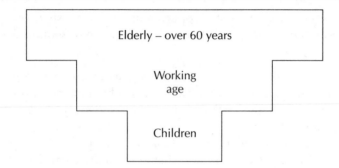

Figure 1.7 (a) Population triangle of an industrialised country

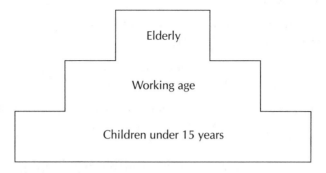

Figure 1.7 (b) Population triangle of a developing country

But the relevance of much of the marketing mix to developing countries is a matter of doubt since the conditions are so very different. This may not be obvious to readers who live in urban areas and see around them typical marketing mix elements which do not exist throughout their country as they do, for instance, throughout Britain. A supermarket may seem very sophisticated in Addis Abbaba or Penang, but does not compare with the numerous supermarket chains in Britain which each own hundreds of huge stores. The exception may be the emerging and newly industrialised countries (NICs) such as Malaysia, Hong Kong, Indonesia, Taiwan, Singapore and South Korea, but even here some of the larger stores, or complexes of shops like Sage, are Japanese.

A major problem is the nature of the population triangle (*see* Figure 1.7) which may be the reverse of that in the North, with large populations of young people under 15 years of age who have no spending power. The number of people in the cash economy will be small, and even well-educated people (e.g. graduates in India) may be unemployed or too poor even to buy a newspaper.

In countries with large rural populations and with countries of large area (e.g. Nigeria, Zambia) there will be poverty, illiteracy and numerous ethnic groups speaking different languages, who are difficult to reach by marketing communication techniques. Even in a country such as Indonesia where literacy is reasonably high, the country is so vast (equal to the width of the USA) that marketing is not easy outside cities like Jakarta.

Marketing research will be severely limited by the absence of elementary requirements such as official statistics like population figures and lists of addresses. There may be little customer awareness of modern packaging, except for its secondary use as, say, a water container. Pricing policies may depend on government legislation such as fixed prices. Advertising media may be scanty. Such advertising as there is will be mostly for imported goods or foreign goods manufactured locally and the names of American/ European multinationals such as Coca-Cola, Cadbury, Guinness, Heinz, Nestlé, Procter & Gamble, Reckitt-Colman and Unilever, will be more common than those of indigenous firms.

The Japanese companies (and increasingly the South Korean) will be promoting their motor-cars, electric and electronic goods. Throughout Asian countries Japanese companies predominate. Even the Malaysian-built Proton motor-car is a Mitsubishi in origin. With a typical bazaar or market stall instant-sale philosophy, native businessmen may be reluctant to accept marketing theory and advertising methods which require forward-planning and investment in future sales which may seem unpredictable. As for after-sales service, that could be mythical because of lack of trained staff, unwillingness to lock up money in spares, or because of a black market, not forgetting restrictions on foreign exchange so that funds are concentrated on new products rather than on spare parts. This is particularly true in black Africa.

In these circumstances, the likelihood of the marketing mix being relevant, except in a very modified form, is problematic in the average Afro-Asian developing country. Many of these countries are at an economic point reached by the North a century ago.

ADVERTISING AS A COMMUNICATION PROCESS

17. Marketing communication

Much of the marketing strategy is concerned with communication. Advertising is a specialised form of communication because in order to satisfy the marketing function it has to do more than inform. It has to *persuade* people to complete the marketing strategy which is designed to sell at a profit what the marketing department believes people are willing to buy. Advertising has to influence choice and buying decisions.

18. Another definition

This positive task is brought out in another definition which says that 'advertising is the means of making known in order to sell'. A name like Ford, Guinness or Texaco makes known – it identifies – but it does no more than, say, the name on a private house. The three examples above do not even explain what these companies make. In the case of brand names such as Stork, White Horse or Silk Cut, they do not say that the product is a margarine, a whisky or a cigarette respectively. Therefore, advertising takes the communication process a step further and makes these three companies or three products known in ways which will sell them. It may also be necessary for advertising to distinguish between products, services or companies with the same name, e.g. Tetley (beer or tea), Kellogg (breakfast cereal or business service), or Swan (electric kettles, beer or matches).

19. Effective communication

A graphic example of effective communication was the technique used by Thailand's Population and Community Development Association. The Association issued T-shirts bearing a picture of Winston Churchill giving his famous two-finger V-sign plus the words 'Stop at two'.

20. The VIPS formula

David Bernstein has explained the need for directness with his VIPS formula: Visibility, Identity, Promise, Singlemindedness. The advertisement must be visible, that is, easily noticed. The identity of the advertiser, or their product or service, must be obvious and not hidden by either too clever presentation or bad design. The offer (the promise) must be made clearly. To achieve all this the advertisement should concentrate on its purpose, and not be confusing by trying to say too many different things.

21. Value of simplicity

An advertisement can be so clever that all that is remembered is the gimmick or perhaps a very interesting picture, not the advertiser, the product or the offer. One of the most brilliant advertising campaigns was based on the simple saying 'Players Please' with its double meaning, the customer being encouraged to use those two words when buying cigarettes. Clever, but not noticeably so!

Advertisements are not always studied in detail, but are glanced at, seen in passing, or seen on television or heard on the radio very briefly. The message must have instant impact.

22. Changing attitudes

The object of advertising is usually to change or influence attitudes. It aims to persuade people to buy product A instead of product B, or to promote the habit of continuing to buy product A (they are unlikely to buy both product A and product B). For example in the case of a new ball-point pen, a simple selling *proposition* has to be converted into the idea that the pen makes an ideal gift or award. This principle can be seen in the advertising for Parker pens which contrasts with that for Tempo, including point-of-sale display advertising and the packing of the first in a presentation case and the second on a dispenser card.

Today, many products, services plus causes and social issues, are advertised which would not have been acceptable or even permissible not many years ago. The prime examples have been the official campaign to educate people about AIDS, and the commercial campaigns for condoms. There have also been environmental campaigns (often using direct mail) for Greenpeace and Friends of the Earth.

There is also a more intellectual attitude towards many products and some people are prepared to pay higher prices for purer, healthier or safer ones. With threats to the ozone layer and with fears about pollution, there has been the 'green' campaign, but sadly a number of manufacturers and retailers have exploited this issue. The Advertising Standards Authority has published warnings about this. *See* also 18: **38**, *A Shade Less Green*.

23. Inducing action

The example above shows that advertising is not just concerned with giving information. It must do so in such an interesting, original, characteristic and persuasive way that the consumer is urged to take action. This action may be to fill in a coupon, telephone an enquiry or order, go to a shop, or remember the product next time he or she needs to buy, say, a drink, a car, a holiday or an insurance policy. In the case of the ball-point pen, advertising can help the buyer to make the appropriate purchase.

24. Communication barriers

If readers, listeners or viewers misunderstand the advertising message, the campaign is a waste of time and money. The ease with which people misunderstand has been discovered during marketing research surveys. People who were asked whether they owned a car often said 'no' if they drove a company car. Similarly, when asked whether they owned a house they said 'no' if they were buying one with a building society or bank loan. In advertising, we have to be careful not to set up unintentional communication barriers. We may know what we mean – but do other people? We must never assume that people know what we are talking about, and this is where the market education work of public relations can help to make advertising effective.

25. Examples of misunderstanding

Here are some other examples.

(a) 'The Nigerian democratic system corresponded roughly with the American democratic system' could be misread to mean 'the Nigerian democratic system wrote rude letters to the American democratic system'.

(b) A communications problem in countries with cosmopolitan multi-racial societies – whether a large industrial city in the North or an Arab oil state – is that some words may either have different meanings or sounds or be pronounced differently. 'Lager' beer is often misspelt 'larger' beer, and 'poster' advertising is often called 'postal' advertising which is actually direct mail advertising.

(c) The letters 'i' and 'e' may be pronounced differently or even confused, so that a foreigner visiting London might unwittingly post letters in a litter bin instead of a letter box, and be surprised that his friends at home never received them. Similarly, advertisements can be misread. Perhaps, because there is no 'z' sound in a local language, the word 'prize' is commonly written as 'price' by Africans. A prize competition becomes a price competition, a very different matter.

(d) In one LCCI Advertising examination candidates were asked to write and design an advertisement for a baby car. In Europe, a baby car is a small motor-car – a Mini or small Fiat, for example – but to most overseas candidates a baby car was taken to mean a toy model or a child's pedal car!

(e) In another LCCI examination, 'in the public interest' was frequently misread to mean 'interesting the public', which resulted in many wrong answers.

(f) Yet another misunderstanding arose with a question about armchair selling (i.e. mail order) which was misread as selling armchairs.

(g) A fourth question referred to 'a saloon car' which was misinterpreted to mean 'a car showroom'.

(h) 'Sales points' have been misinterpreted as 'retail outlets' by some candidates.

These examples emphasise that advertising is a communication process which must be free of misunderstanding. The message will be absorbed quickly as when people walk by a poster, listen to the radio, watch the television screen, or glance at a newspaper. Advertising messages may be absorbed almost subconsciously. For instance it would be easy to confuse 'coke' (Coca-Cola) with 'coke' (the heating fuel), or battered fish with broken fish. This is very different from reading the instructions on a package, which is done more carefully and slowly, although clarity is still vital.

A lot of time may be spent on writing advertisement copy, but most readers are 'glancers' and get a quick impression from the large display lines. Only if these display lines interest them do they stop to read the more detailed copy in smaller type. Consequently, the shorter the copy the more likely will a correct message be conveyed – provided, of course, that it is written without ambiguities.

26. Words and pictures

One way to convey a message quickly is to use a jingle or slogan, e.g. 'British Airways Takes Good Care of You'. Another solution is a picture, e.g. the British Airways slogan is usually accompanied by a picture of a smiling BA air hostess. The Singapore girl has become synonymous with Singapore Airlines.

Both forms of expression have been used in television advertisements which have established catch-phrases such as the Woolwich's 'I'm with the Woolwich'; the American Express saying, 'American Express? That'll do nicely, sir'; and the more recent campaign slogan, 'Do more'. Another, which has survived for more than forty years, is 'Ah, Bisto!' with the two children sniffing the aroma of the gravy.

Thus, effective communication depends very often on a merging of words and pictures, as indicated in Figure 1.8.

Modern advertising makes very clever use of words. For instance, a typical use is to use words in an ingenious way so that the reader is challenged to stop and think about the meaning. Examples are:

'You can't get better than a Quick-Fit fitter' (car exhaust fitting service).

'All this wood from one branch' (Do-it-all do-it-yourself supplies).

'Admittedly the Audi S2 differs from its rally counterpart. It has a cigar lighter.'

'Finish Thirst' (Lucozade).

27. Problems of press advertising

Messages are said to be more readily seen than heard, and visual messages have greater impact than those which require the effort of reading. This

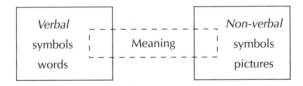

Figure 1.8 Interaction of words and pictures to convey meaning

tends to make written and read information the hardest to accept and recall. It implies that press advertising has to overcome many problems, especially in multi-ethnic societies or where there is a low level of literacy. Yet the press remains one of the most effective advertising media. There are multi-million circulation newspapers which are primary advertising media in the North, while the press expands in the South as literacy grows, Nigeria being an excellent example. The nature of press advertising is best understood when it is remembered that it is a static medium, lacking the benefits of sound and movement and often without the impact and realism of colour. It has the advantage that the message can be retained and read again.

28. Advertising skills

How are these problems of press advertising overcome, and why does the press remain such a dominant means of communicating advertising messages? These questions form the themes of later chapters about copywriting, layout and press media, but in this introductory chapter here are two simple answers. First, creative skills are used to make press advertising larger than life, e.g. big type, slogans, size of space, dramatic pictures. Second, newspapers and magazines reach either mass or specialist readerships relatively cheaply and efficiently.

29. Heart of advertising

These two reasons provide an insight into the heart of advertising and the special skills involved. Creativity to attract and win the attention, the interest and eventually the action of consumers, and the most cost-effective choice and use of innumerable media, are the characteristics of successful advertising. All this calls for interaction between the three sides of advertising: the advertiser, the advertising agency and the media owner.

30. Importance of ideas

The skills necessary in press advertising also apply to other media such as radio, television, outdoor, direct mail, exhibitions, point-of-sale display and sales literature. Ideas are needed in order to communicate marketing messages, and buying and planning skills are required to exploit communication media effectively. Campaigns have to be planned and executed as sales battles. They are a blend of strategy and resources.

31. Reconsideration of definition

This brings us back to a reconsideration of the definition in 8: 'advertising presents the most persuasive possible selling message to the right prospects

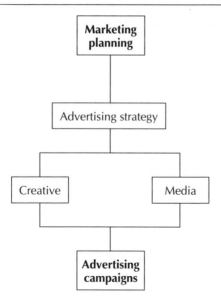

Figure 1.9 Advertising: creativity and media, the two essential requirements for effective campaigns

for the product or service at the lowest possible cost'. These two requirements – creativity and the best use of media – should be remembered throughout the reading of this book, the study of this subject, and the practice of advertising itself. (*See* Figure 1.9.)

32. Changes and developments

The 1980s and 1990s have seen more changes and developments in advertising than had occurred during the previous 200 years. Apart from the technological changes in newspaper production, and the transformation of British radio and television under the Broadcasting Act 1990, the advent of the single European market has made London a more important advertising centre than New York. Berkeley Square has replaced Madison Avenue. This is because London has become the advertising springboard for continental Europe.

There are, of course, many European companies which use other advertising centres, to mention only BMW, Buitoni, Benetton and even Unilever. But for many pan-European advertising agencies – often those of American origin – London is the premier base.

However, London's advantages are three-fold.

(a) The English language is the language of marketing communication.

(b) Creative expertise, especially in the making of television commercials, which is the envy of Europe.

19

(c) Britain's initiative in defining advertising interests, conducting research, and training executives.

Meanwhile, on the other side of the world Japanese industry is served by Tokyo's advertising centre, with large agencies like Dentsu. There has also been a growth in public relations consultancy practice in a country which had been slow to adopt public relations techniques to match its marketing skills.

As an example, the giant Japanese trading concern Mitsubishi, while retaining the Dentsu, Dai-Ichi Kikaku and Asatsu agencies for its motor and electric accounts, set up an in-house agency to handle the promotion of imports and international products.

Table 1.3 Top UK advertisers, all media, August 1998–July 1999

Rank	Advertiser	Spend (£000)
1.	British Telecommunications	£145,970
2.	Dixons Stores Group Ltd	£143,180
3.	Procter & Gamble Ltd	£123,970
4.	Vauxhall Motors Ltd	£98,194
5.	Ford Motor Co. Ltd	£92,089
6.	Golden Ltd	£83,814
7.	Renault UK Ltd	£83,139
8.	Unilever Elida Faberge Ltd	£74,883
9.	Unilever Lever Brothers Ltd	£73,581
10.	Mars Confectionery	£72,421

Source: A.C. Nielsen Media International

BASICS OF AN ADVERTISING CAMPAIGN

A campaign should follow a five-point plan:

(1) What exactly is to be achieved? Do we *aim* to achieve, say, a given sales target?

(2) When is this to be achieved? This week – over the year?

(3) What is the strategy? Will the extra sales come from new or existing customers or by switching customers from other brands?

(4) What tactics shall be used? What creative ideas and media?

(5) How much will this cost? It it a good investment?

Progress test 1

1. Why does an industrial society require advertising? **(2, 3, 4, 5)**

2. What is the (British) Chartered Institute of Marketing definition of marketing? **(6)**

3. What is the difference between a marketing- and a sales-orientated company? **(7)**

4. How does the Institute of Practitioners in Advertising define advertising? **(8)**

5. Who pays for advertising? **(10)**

6. Approximately how much is spent on advertising in Britain each year? **(11)**

7. On which medium is most money spent – press or television? **(11)**

8. On which medium do advertisers of popular consumer goods spend most money? **(11)**

9. Explain the marketing mix. **(13)**

10. What are the Four Ps? **(14)**

11. List some of the principal items in a marketing mix which plot the sequence of actions from product design to the after-market. **(15)**

12. As a form of communication what is the chief task of advertising? **(17)**

13. What is the VIPS formula? **(20)**

14. Explain how advertising converts a proposition into an idea. **(22)**

15. Give examples of communication barriers. **(25)**

16. How can words and pictures combine to give meaning? Give an example from recent advertising which you have seen. **(26)**

17. What are the two most important advertising skills? **(28, 31)**

18. Why has London become the European advertising centre? **(32)**

2

The advertising department

INTRODUCTION

1. Organisation

The organisation of advertising and public relations differ, so that most advertising personnel work in advertising agencies but most public relations personnel work in-house. Nevertheless, both do have internal and external services. Whereas in advertising it would be unusual not to use an agency, in public relations it is not absolutely necessary to use a consultancy. This is due to the very different natures of advertising and public relations, and to the very different personnel employed by each.

The result is roughly that the larger the volume of advertising the greater the need for an advertising agency and the ability to share the skills of many specialists. The greater the volume of public relations the greater the need for an internal public relations department to deal with the communication needs of numerous departments. If extra work (or specialised work such as financial or Parliamentary relations) occurs, a consultancy may also be used.

The in-house advertising department serves two purposes: to buy and supervise agency services and to buy and supervise services not provided by the advertising agency. This division of responsibilities coincides with above-the-line and below-the-line advertising, as will be explained shortly.

2. The advertising manager

In this chapter we shall call the man or woman in charge of the in-house advertising department the *advertising manager*. This person buys and supervises advertising for his or her organisation, and is the opposite of the *advertisement manager* who sells advertising media. Thus, there are three inter-relating executives – the client's advertising manager, the agency's account executive, and the media advertisement (or sales) manager who represent the three sides of advertising. (*See* Figure 2.1.)

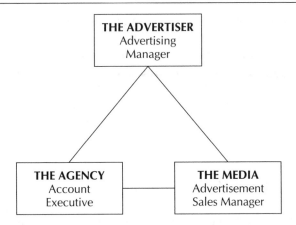

Figure 2.1 Advertising: the relationship control triangle

3. Other titles

The advertising manager may be known under a variety of titles such as publicity, product, brand or marketing services manager, and there may be other more fanciful titles such as communication, sales promotion or advertising and public relations manager. Sometimes the marketing manager will be responsible for advertising, and elsewhere the public relations manager may handle advertising. It all depends on the type of organisation and the volume of advertising it undertakes. The point is that someone has to be responsible for ordering and controlling advertising.

Although all these titles may apply to people with very similar jobs, there can be some particular meanings. A publicity manager may combine advertising and public relations as with the publicity manager of a holiday resort. A product or brand manager is responsible for the total promotion of a product, brand or group of brands, and this may embrace many duties from new product development, branding, packaging, advertising to sales promotion and after-sales service. A marketing services manager supports the marketing manager with many services such as marketing research, advertising and public relations.

The titles will also depend on the type of organisation and its promotional needs. A fast moving consumer good (FMCG) requiring frequent regular sales to take up factory output (e.g. most national brands found in supermarkets) will need heavy, repeated competitive advertising. A hi-tech product may need little advertising but considerable market education using public relations techniques such as feature articles, technical seminars and audio-visuals.

The large self-sufficient in-house department has acquired a new name in recent years, and it appeared in a recent CAM Advertising examination paper. This is the *in-house agency*. This is something of a misnomer since advertisers cannot obtain recognition for commission purposes. It would defeat two of the purposes of the commission system which are guarantee of prompt payment and no long-term credit, and reduction of the number of accounts from hundreds of individual advertisers to a small number of agencies. However, very big advertisers do have sufficient clout to be able to negotiate media purchases at favourable rates, and even to receive the same commission or discount as agencies. Everything is negotiable!

4. Above-the-line and below-the-line

Here we shall consider the advertising manager in relation to above-the-line and below-the-line advertising, how the in-house department differs from the advertising agency, and the special role, skills and responsibilities of the advertising manager.

The work of the advertising manager will range from a simple liaison with the agency, with a modest staff of perhaps no more than a secretary and an assistant, to a large self-sufficient department of maybe 200 staff which handles all planning, media and creative work. The latter is rare and applies to large firms which are advertising daily and, because of price changes and special offers, finds it better to deal directly and quickly with the media. Examples of such firms are large supermarket chains, some direct response companies, and package tour operators who are offering holidays all the year round. These are the ones which may be termed in-house agencies.

However, a typical in-house advertising department will be organised to direct both above-the-line and below-the-line advertising. Here we see the division of responsibilities when the agency usually handles the former (with its income from commission) and the in-house advertising department undertakes the latter which pay no commission. Reference to 'commission' is broad-based since some agencies renounce commissions and charge fees, while there are a few 'through the line' agencies which provide all forms of advertising.

Nevertheless, the advertising manager is ultimately responsible for both divisions. He or she does not simply give the agency a budget to spend as thought best. The agency will undertake press, television, radio, cinema and outdoor advertising. One full service agency (see next chapter) may undertake all the above-the-line advertising, but this may be divided between a media independent (which plans and buys media only) and an *à la carte* creative agency, and outdoor advertising may be bought through a specialist agency in that field. Sometimes media independents and poster agencies may be owned by a full-service agency or by a consortium of large agencies. The biggest media independent is Zenith.

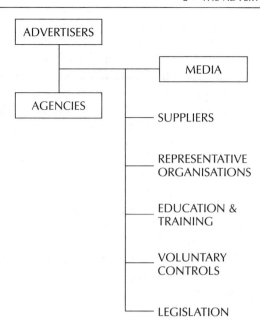

Figure 2.2 The organisation of the advertising industry

5. Appointing an agency

Although strictly speaking, and for legal reasons, the advertising agent is the agent of the media, and the 'agent acts as principal' and is legally responsible for the payment of space and airtime costs even if the client defaults, it is necessary for the advertiser to choose and appoint an agency to produce its advertising.

The advertising manager is therefore engaged in the search for an agency, its appointment and eventual re-appointment or otherwise. This will usually be done in association with superiors such as the marketing director and managing director who will sign the contract of service.

The appointment of the agency results from a number of agencies being short-listed. This is called 'shopping for an agency'. Arrival at this short-list will depend on having decided how much and what kind of advertising is required. Some firms like Rentokil and Marks & Spencer, which are highly successful businesses, spend very little on advertising compared with the millions spent by, say, Procter & Gamble, Ford, Cadbury or Heinz. Thus, the size of the appropriation or budget will merit a small, medium or large agency. Technical, industrial or business-to-business products or services are best served by a technical or business-to-business agency. A popular FMCG may require television advertising, and the agency will require ITVA recognition, a TV airtime buyer, and a TV commercial producer. A short list of, say, three suitable agencies will then be briefed on the client's needs, and proposed schemes will be assembled and presentations made to the client. The number of short-listed agencies should be as few as possible and they are entitled to charge a fee for the costly work of producing presentations.

There are several recognised ways of compiling the short-list. Advertising can be observed, and its creators identified. Recommendations may be made by business associates. Agencies advertise themselves in trade journals such as *Campaign*, *Marketing* and *Marketing Week*, and also in business magazines and newspapers. The Institute of Practitioners in Advertising (the agency trade body) will provide suggested short-lists. The Advertising Agency Register will, for a fee, arrange the showing of videos about appropriate agencies. *BRAD* and *Advertisers Annual* list agencies and give client lists, useful in indicating the firms they service and helping to avoid approaching an agency which already services a rival. Many agencies have websites. These can be used by intending clients for initial assessment of agencies' potential, without incurring any obligation and without expense, except for the cost of a telephone call.

6. Understanding agencies

The contract of service will stipulate what is expected of an agency, what shall be done on the client's behalf, the budget (usually decided in advance but could be discussed with the agency), the method of paying the agency, and the terms of cancellation. For instance, it will be necessary to state:

(a) whether the agency is mostly remunerated by commission from the media and other suppliers plus on-costs on other purchases;

(b) whether the agency renounces all commissions (discounts) and charges an hourly or daily service fee;

(c) whether credit is given, or payment has to be paid in advance (as occurs with small technical accounts which produce little commission);

(d) and whether the agency retains copyright of creative work and does not assign it to the client until the final bill has been paid.

The advertising manager, representing the client, has to understand the different financial and contractual systems operated by different agencies. They are not identical, and he or she will need to be able to advise management of the most favourable or suitable. They tend to favour the agency and they always favour the media which have the advantage of dealing with a small number of agencies instead of hundreds of individual advertisers, so that under the recognition system they are able to demand prompt payment.

However, the recognition and commission system (while not implying that the agency is recognised as being a good one!) does mean that the media subsidise the advertisers who would otherwise find it more expensive to operate independently of an agency. By 'more expensive' is meant that the advertiser receives the services of the account executive, media planning and buying, copywriting and general administrative costs free of charge out of agency commission from the media. The client pays only the cost of space or airtime, and for physical creative and production work.

Even so, there are occasions such as with a technical account requiring little media purchase (or when production costs exceed media costs), or overseas in those countries (e.g. in the Third World) where the total advertising expenditure by a client is too small to provide the agency with an adequate income. The agency may then need to charge a fee as well as accept commission from the media. The rate of commission may also vary according to the agency's accreditation rating based on turnover. In Britain it is also common to add a small surcharge to the commission. But under the non-monopolistic current recognition system, an agency is not guaranteed a standard rate of commission and is expected to negotiate with individual media owners.

So, the first thing the advertising manager has to know is how different advertising agencies work, what services they provide, how to buy these services, and how to work with them. The success of the company's advertising will depend to a large extent on his or her ability to co-operate harmoniously with agency staff. This is difficult because the agency staff will be enthusiastic about their proposals and ideas and will regard themselves as the experts, but the advertising manager, representing the client and its policy, has to evaluate the work and, if necessary, be critical. This can provoke a hostile situation because agency people such as media buyers, copywriters and artists may never meet the client yet, via the account executive, they may receive criticism of their work. There may be delays on the client's part, or impatience at the speed with which the agency works. It may not be appreciated that the agency has to serve other clients. A good client–agency relationship is therefore a big responsibility of the advertising manager.

Consequently, it is rare for an agency to retain a client for many years, even though this may be desirable. For one thing, personnel change on both sides, and the old saying about 'new brooms sweeping clean' often applies to client–agency relationships. It is difficult for an agency to go on having new ideas, and clients are apt to switch agencies in search of fresh ideas. Moreover, agency–client relationships are not unlike those between political parties and electors. At first there is the honeymoon period, but as the idealism gives way to the pragmatic the relationship sours. Many advertisers do not retain their agency for more than three years, and the process of changing agencies can be seen reported in the trade press every week. Even so, the advertising manager is as responsible for getting the best out of an agency as the agency is in keeping the account.

7. Working with the agency

Whether prior to proposals being prepared by short-listed agencies, or when renewing a contract, or when introducing new projects to be handled by the agency, the advertising manager must brief the agency as fully as possible. This applies not only to the product or service but also to the company's policy and the intended market. As examples of policy, Guinness have always maintained that its advertising should represent the company's corporate image, while Benetton's policy seems to be to shock the public with outrageous posters and press advertisements. One would not find images of a Chinese Pope drinking Guinness.

This briefing should be a continuous process, products, packaging and prices being supplied, works visits or product sampling or trials arranged, and the agency given every opportunity to know and understand what it has to advertise. The agency should also be given the benefits of any research conducted by or subscribed to by the marketing department, including the results of advertising.

This is the normal procedure, the agency coming in about midway in the marketing mix or strategy. It is not the ideal situation for it is too late for the agency to be concerned with the branding, packaging, pricing and choice of market segment. The closer the agency can be to new product development the better able it is to advise on a cost-effective campaign.

There are some agencies which specialise in new product development (NPD). The use of such an experienced agency at an early stage (e.g. prototype) can be worthwhile because the client may be good at manufacturing, designing or formulating, but poor at marketing. The right brand name, the most attractive packaging, the well identified price bracket, and so on can make all the difference. The advertising manager needs to be aware of the assistance which is available, and not simply throw a product at an agency as a *fait accompli*. However, this happens all too frequently.

One way or another, it is the business of the advertising manager to regard the agency as an extension of his or her department, to work harmoniously with the agency account executive, and to understand the roles of various agency departments and personnel. If he or she is unfamiliar with the workings of an agency it is a good idea to arrange to spend two or three days at the agency to see what goes on.

Too many products have suffered from bad marketing which has hampered the agency's ability to do a good job. It has been given a product with a bad name, poor packaging or aimed at the wrong market segment. This often happens when the client side is dominated by a marketing rather than an advertising manager. Advertising is a subject rarely understood by marketing people, and this is seen by the way in which it is relegated to a minor part of the Chartered Institute of Marketing examination syllabus. Ironically, advertising plays almost too big a part in the CAM syllabus.

8. Supervising the agency's work

Once the campaign is being prepared the procedure follows of receiving, approving and if necessary amending media schedules, copy, layouts, artwork, typesetting, proofs, TV storyboards, radio scripts, poster sites, rushes of commercials, and generally supervising the agency's work.

It will also be necessary to understand and be able to approve agency accounts. If the advertising manager disagrees with fee charges it will be necessary to ask to see time sheets for the work that is invoiced. There will be bills for media purchases, model fees, artwork, typesetting, photography, actors' fees, music fees, print charges and so on. These may be rendered in dribs and drabs so that they can be paid by the agency which needs to maintain its cash flow situation. The advertising manager has to attempt to associate all these isolated accounts with the originally agreed total budget.

9. Operation and results

During the run of the campaign the advertising manager will monitor advertisements, posters and commercials in order to check that they have reproduced well and appeared as scheduled. Finally, results will be assessed, either by physical results such as the number of enquiries or value of orders, which may be related to particular media on a cost-per-thousand basis (dividing the media cost by the response), or results in terms of awareness, or the durability of advertisements. This last item makes use of marketing research techniques such as tracking studies. These topics are dealt which in later chapters.

10. Below-the-line in-house responsibilities

Liaison with the advertising agency is only half the story because agencies usually concentrate on the media advertising from which commission is earned. Many agencies do not handle below-the-line advertising which has to be charged out to the client on a fee basis. There are exceptions, of course, where full service agencies do take on other work such as print and exhibitions, and there are a few 'through the line agencies' which handle everything. Recruitment advertising may also be undertaken. In addition there are specialist *ad hoc* agencies which supply sales promotion, direct mail, sponsorship and other services, but these are likely to be hired as part of the in-house advertising manager's below-the-line activities.

Here, then, is an outline of the variety of below-the-line activities in which the advertising manager will be engaged. Only a very large company would require them all, and some are of special interest to certain advertisers. For instance, a holiday tour operator would need to print brochures and conduct direct mail, a department store would need window and shop display material. A cooker manufacturer would need leaflets for retail showrooms, and a direct response marketer would need direct mail facilities as would a charity seeking donations.

Direct mail may be used by all sorts of companies, and not only by direct response marketers. The advertising manager can organise this in one of three ways. An outside direct mail house can be employed which can provide part or all of a company's direct mail requirements. 'All' would cover writing sales letters and enclosures; designing mailing shots; printing letters, enclosures, and envelopes; providing mailing lists (or maintaining client's lists); addressing envelopes; filling; and mailing. Alternatively, there could be in-house print shop facilities; mailing lists could be hired or held on a computer database, the entire job being handled internally. The economics of this depend on the frequency of mailings. A third way is to build a database of prospects, and this could embrace existing customer information which could be called up for the production of labels.

Database marketing can make use of computerised information held by a company for purposes such as account collection, membership lists, business follow-ups and may be used by more than one department. For instance, such a system can be used (as with gas and electricity companies and credit card operators) to 'piggyback' other people's mail shots with bills. Direct mail is explained in Chapter 9.

Sales literature. The advertising manger may be responsible for the writing, design and printing of leaflets, folders, price lists, order forms, brochures and catalogues, using inside staff or freelance writers and designers, photographers, and either an in-house print shop or outside printers.

Point-of-sale material may be produced in-house, or bought from specialist designers and manufacturers and may include show-cards, suspended mobiles, dump bins, wire stands, display models and many other devices. The advertising manager will also have to organise its distribution, perhaps offering a variety of items in a broadsheet mailed to shop-keepers. The full range of POS material is described in Chapter 6.

Exhibitions. The advertising manager will be responsible for booking stand space in public and trade exhibitions, and for organising stands at events and conferences, or portable or mobile exhibitions. If this is a frequent activity there will be in-house stand designers and constructors. Otherwise, outside designers and stand builders will be engaged. Stands will also have to be fitted out, equipped with whatever is being exhibited, and staffed by sales people or demonstrators. In all this he or she will usually collaborate with the sales manager, and also with the public relations manager regarding material for the exhibition press room. Chapter 10 deals with exhibitions.

Sponsorships may well be another responsibility of the advertising manager, often working closely with the marketing manager, public relations manager, specialist sponsorship consultancy and counterparts in the sponsored organisations. This subject is dealt with more thoroughly in Chapter 8, but there are important forms of advertising linked with sponsorships such as arena boards, placards at venues, banners, flags, advertisements in programmes, and promotional activities such as the production and sale of bodywear and various souvenirs.

Sales promotions may be conducted by a special sales promotion manager, especially if it is a standard marketing strategy as seen with a number of FMCGs such as some breakfast cereals, toothpastes and beverages. But it may be the responsibility of the advertising manager, who may use an outside agency to organise a promotion or buy sales promotion material such as games from creative producers. Advertising will need to coincide with the distribution of packages produced for the promotion. The handling of response will need to be organised, either in-house or through a fulfilment house if applications have to be serviced. All this calls for meticulous planning. In the case of a game with lucky numbers, security printing is vital to avoid fraud, while a fulfilment house must be able to despatch offers without delay. Timing is often important, as when tokens have to be collected. For instance, Nescafé sometimes offer cash awards for tokens from a certain volume of purchases. It may take weeks to collect and submit the tokens, and weeks elapse before consumers receive their cheques. Sales promotion is discussed more fully in Chapter 7.

11. Qualities involved

It will be seen from the above outline of an advertising manager's below-the-line responsibilities that he or she must possess many skills and much experience. Essentially, it is an organising, buying and supervising management role. This demands the ability to direct specialist staff, and to deal with a variety of outside agencies and suppliers. It calls for knowledge of artwork, photography, printing and an awareness of the ever-changing technologies which are available.

In fact, the advertising manager has to be more knowledgeable than advertising agency personnel who are mostly confined to one speciality such as media buying or copywriting. Even the agency account executive is less broadly knowledgeable and skilled than the advertising manager with a comprehensive in-house department.

Progress test 2

1. What is the difference between the advertisement manager and the advertising manager? (**2**)

2. What is an in-house agency? (**3**)

3. How does the advertising manager select an advertising agency? (**5**)

4. How do the media subsidise advertisers? (**6**)

5. What client–agency problems are likely to affect their relationships? **(6)**

6. What agency work and services does the advertising manager have to supervise? **(8)**

7. What are the below-the-line responsibilities of the advertising manager? **(10)**

8. What professional knowledge and qualities does the advertising manager need to have? **(11)**

3

Types of advertising

INTRODUCTION

1. Scope of advertising

Advertising serves many purposes and many advertisers, from the individual who places a small classified advertisement in the local newspaper to the big spender who uses networked TV to sell popular brands to the nation's millions. Anyone can be an advertiser and advertising touches everyone. Even some company newspapers contain sales and wants ads.

2. Types

It is possible to identify seven main categories of advertising, namely:

- *consumer,*
- *business-to-business,*
- *trade,*
- *retail,*
- *financial,*
- *direct response,*
- *recruitment.*

Each category is described in detail below (except direct response, which is discussed separately in Chapter 9).

It will be seen that each requires its own treatment in creative presentation and use of media, i.e. the twin skills described as the 'heart of advertising' (*see* 1: **29**).

CONSUMER ADVERTISING

3. Different kinds

There are two kinds of goods bought by the general public, *consumer goods* and *consumer durables*, which together with *consumer services* are advertised through media addressed to the appropriate *social grades*. These four terms are best explained now as they will be used from time to time throughout this book.

4. Consumer goods

These are the vast range of goods to be found in the shops, those which enjoy repeat sales like foods, drinks, confectionery and toiletries being called Fast Moving Consumer Goods (FMCGs). Pharmaceuticals which are packaged, branded and retailed are called Over The Counter (OTC) medicines, to distinguish them from the ethical pharmaceuticals which are sold to pharmacists for dispensing doctors' prescriptions.

5. Consumer durables

Usually more expensive and less frequently bought, consumer durables are of a more permanent nature than consumer goods. These include clothes, furniture, domestic appliances, entertainment goods like radio, television and video, and mechanical equipment from lawn-mowers to motor-cars. They include 'brown goods' such as TV sets and 'white goods' such as washing machines.

6. Consumer services

The service industries (including leisure industries) have shown remarkable growth in recent decades. They include services for security and well-being like banking, insurance, investment, repairs and maintenance, and those more to do with pleasure such as entertainments, hotels, restaurants, travel and holidays.

7. Social grades

The IPA definition of advertising referred to the 'right prospects' and 'lowest possible cost'. The social grades system makes it possible to identify certain groups of people – prospective buyers – and then to pinpoint the media which will reach them most effectively. In developing countries where only a minority of people are literate, and they are mostly the ones reached by the media, the idea of selecting media to reach certain groups may seem strange. In such countries it may be more appropriate to talk about income or socio-economic groups.

Table 3.1 Social grades in Britain (National Readership Survey)

	Grade	Members	Percentage of population
A	Upper middle class	Top businessmen, other leaders	about 2.7%
B	Middle class	Senior executives, managers	about 15.2%
C^1	Lower middle class	White-collar, white-blouse office workers	about 24.1%
C^2	Skilled working class	Blue-collar factory workers	about 27.1%
D	Working class	Semi- and unskilled manual workers	about 17.8%
E	Lowest level of subsistence	Poor pensioners, disabled, casual workers	about 13.1%

However, in Britain the social grades, based on *occupation* and not income, are as shown in Table 3.1.

The reader should not confuse socio-economic groups (based on income) and social grades (based on occupation). The latter replaced the former in the UK more than 20 years ago, being introduced for use in the National Readership Survey.

In former decades it was reasonable to link the class breakdown of British newspaper readership with statistics and social grades. Because of changes in demographics and media it is no longer possible to do this; and no longer the subject of media research. *The Times*, although world famous, has a small circulation of about 760,000 while the *Sun* sells more than three million copies daily. Both happen to belong to the same company but each has a very different readership. The kinds of goods or services advertised in the one would not be advertised in the other.

Thus, while 760,000 is a modest circulation figure in the UK, and has a predominantly A social grade readership, it is the same as the biggest circulation newspaper in Nigeria which is read by literate people of many socio-economic groups. Most Nigerian newspapers are in English, but vernacular newspapers are also published.

In some countries, newspapers may not appeal to class differences so much as to different political, religious, language, nationality or ethnic groups of readers. For instance, there are English language newspapers in many parts of the world but also many others in local languages. In Hong Kong, for example, there are famous English language newspapers like the *South China Morning Post*, but also some hundred Chinese language newspapers.

In the Middle East and Gulf states there are Arabic and English language newspapers, the latter being read by the hundred or more nationals who have adopted English as the universal language, and are unlikely to learn Arabic. Indonesia attracts many English, American, Australian, Canadian and New Zealand people, and two English language papers are published in Jakarta. Most educated Indonesians also speak English. Famous newspapers such as the *Straits Times* in Singapore, and the *Times of India* are printed in English, but there are also newspapers in local languages.

The idea of social grades has to be regarded as something peculiar to British society where it is possible to have curious class distinctions as when the workers in the factory may be C^2 with typical trade unionist attitudes while the clerical and secretarial workers in the offices may be C^1 with more independent social attitudes. Hence the expression 'blue shirt' and 'white blouse' workers. This has nothing to do with what they earn, and they may be neighbours in the same street, but it affects what they buy. For example, the former may tend to spend as they go, while the latter may prefer to save and invest. For advertisers they represent very different markets. The 'affluent worker' is not very socially mobile as a London University study conducted in Luton revealed. However, both social grades belong to the mass market which buys the majority of FMCGs and form the mass audience for popular TV, even if they may read different newspapers.

When planning an advertising campaign it is therefore necessary to define the social grade or grades of likely buyers, and to select the media which will reach them in the largest numbers at the lowest cost.

8. Media of consumer advertising

The media of consumer advertising will tend to be those with wide appeal, and even when more specialist journals such as women's magazines are used they will still have large circulations. There are some 70 British women's and home interest magazines. In fact, the term 'consumer press' is applied to the publications which are displayed for sale in newsagents' shops, on news-stands and on newspaper vendors' pitches.

Most of the trade, technical and professional journals have other forms of distribution such as special orders placed with newsagents, postal subscription or free postal controlled circulation. Controlled circulation (cc journals) are not to be confused with membership or subscription magazines. They are mailed (free of charge) to selected readers plus those who have requested copies.

In Britain there are also hundreds of 'free' local newspapers which are delivered door-to-door every week. With saturation coverage of urban areas they provide good advertising media for many local businesses.

The primary media of consumer advertising are the press, radio, television, outdoor and to a limited extent cinema, supported by sales literature, exhibitions and sales promotion. We should not forget sponsorship, especially the sponsorship of many popular sports which in turn can be supported by arena advertising at the sports venue.

There is now the sponsorship of actual TV and radio programmes as permitted by the Broadcasting Act 1990 and sponsors have included consumer product advertisers such as Lyons (bakery), Egg (financial), Douwe Egberts, Midland Bank, Stella Artois, Mars confectionery, Tetley tea and Diet Coke.

Note: Primary media are first choice media and may be above-the-line or below-the-line, depending on the individual campaign being conducted. Traditionally, above-the-line media are press, radio, television, outdoor and cinema, which pay commission on media purchases by recognised advertising agencies.

BUSINESS-TO-BUSINESS ADVERTISING

9. Purpose

The purpose of business-to-business advertising is to promote non-consumer goods and services. These may include raw materials, components and accessories; plant and machinery; services such as insurance; office equipment and supplies.

Hardly any of these products and services will be bought by consumers, except as replacements as when a car needs a new battery or tyres. Unless the formula or specification is stated, consumers will be unaware of most of these products.

Many finished products are produced or assembled from materials, parts or components made by numerous suppliers. Few manufacturers are self-sufficient, supplying everything themselves. A building will consist of steel-work, cement, glass, timber, bricks, roofing materials and all the internal furnishings, together with special equipment such as escalators and services, e.g. water, gas and electrical systems. Secondary suppliers and subcontractors will be involved, together with consultants, although a main contractor or a consortium of contractors will be responsible for the final construction.

10. Media of business-to-business advertising

The suppliers of services, equipment, raw materials, components, office machines and supplies will usually advertise in media seldom seen by the general or consumer public. The media used will consist of trade and technical journals, technical literature and catalogues, trade exhibitions, direct mail, technical demonstrations and seminars. Technical journals will have smaller circulations than the consumer press. Trade exhibitions will have fewer exhibitors and smaller attendances than public exhibitions open to the general public; in fact, admission is usually by ticket or business card. The amount of money spent on advertising will be far less, and there may be more reliance on market education using public relations techniques such as video documentaries, external house journals and technical feature articles.

Business-to-business advertising media are very much a feature of the industrial North and are fairly rare in developing countries except large ones such as India which has a substantial industry ranking ninth in the world. The industrialising South depends very much on European and North American trade and technical journals which have international circulations. Some of these journals are so specialised that unless they did have international circulations they would not survive in their country of origin. Other press advertising may appear in business newspapers and magazines which may, for example, run regular features on computers, word processors and facsimile machines. Trade exhibitions, for the same reason, usually rely on international interest.

11. Special characteristics

Business-to-business advertising differs in yet another way. Whereas consumer advertising may be emotive, this kind of advertising has to be more detailed and informative, although not unimaginative. Trade journals provide valuable international market-places for thousands of products and services, maintaining sales of long-established ones and introducing new ones.

Business-to-business advertising is mainly produced by advertising agencies which devote themselves to industrial or technical clients. Agencies which handle clients or 'accounts' who market cranes, electronic equipment, chemicals or industrial insurance rarely handle accounts for mass consumer goods such as tea, petrol, beer or soap. The kind of creative staff are different, e.g. artists who can produce 'exploded' drawings which reveal the interior of an engine, or copywriters who can write meticulously and persuasively in technical language.

The costs of such advertising are different, too. The artwork may cost more than the space, while the space purchase will yield little commission and agency income may be derived from service fees charged to clients rather than from commission received from media owners.

There may be little advertising, or to be effective expenditure would be prohibitively expensive. Public relations activities, while not to be regarded as free advertising, may be more effective and economical, especially when the need is to educate the market and create knowledge and understanding. This is not to 'knock' advertising but to highlight an equally effective form of marketing communication.

TRADE ADVERTISING

12. Definitions

Trade advertising is addressed to distributors, chiefly wholesalers, agents, importers/exporters, and numerous kinds of retailers, large and small. Goods are advertised for resale.

The term 'trade press' is sometimes used loosely and misleadingly to include all non-consumer publications. Strictly speaking, and the distinctions are sensible, the trade press is read by traders, the technical press by technicians (as described in the previous section on business-to-business advertising), and the professional press by professionals such as teachers, doctors, lawyers and architects. There are some journals which are difficult to define as sharply as that, and their readership may spread over more than one group. A building magazine, for instance, may be read in both the building industry and the architectural profession.

13. Purpose

The purpose of trade press advertising is to inform merchants and traders about goods available for resale, whether it reminds them about well-established brands, introduces new lines or, as is often the case, announces special efforts to help retailers sell goods. For example, price reductions, better trade terms, new packages, consumer advertising campaigns or sales promotion schemes. Such advertising invites enquiries and orders and also supports the advertiser's field salesmen when they call on stockists.

14. Media of trade advertising

The trade press may or may not be used for this kind of advertising. There could be a mix of two or three media addressed to the trade. Direct mail is often used, especially when it is necessary to provide a lot of information such as consumer advertising campaign schedules giving dates and times when and where advertising will be taking place in the press or on radio and/or television. Replicas of advertisements may be reproduced, perhaps full-size, e.g. 'broadsheet' – the size of a large newspaper page – which folds down to a convenient envelope size for posting. This direct mail shot may also include pictures and details of display material which is available, together with an order form. It may also include the details of 'co-operative' advertising schemes in which the manufacturer contributes in some way (artwork, part payment) to the retailer's own advertising in local media.

Another useful medium is the trade exhibition, sponsored by a trade magazine or trade association, which will be attended by distributors. Some of the larger exhibitions may also be open, or open on certain days, to the general public as well, e.g. car and furniture exhibitions.

Occasionally, commercial television time may be bought to tell retailers about new lines, or retailers may be mailed to tell them that consumer advertising campaigns are about to appear on TV. In the television regions, a number of joint schemes may be organised with the aid of television companies such as the provision of special sales teams to visit retailers, or studio visits when retailers in the region are invited to preview forthcoming commercials.

15. Special characteristics

Since the object of trade advertising is to encourage retailers (whether large chains or one-man businesses) to stock up the product (especially to achieve *adequate distribution* in advance of a consumer advertising campaign), emphasis will be placed on the advantages of so doing. The advantages will be higher sales and more profits, and the appeal will be to the retailer's desire to make money. In so doing, trade advertising will also have to compete with the 'selling-in' activities of rival manufacturers.

Trade advertising will be seen as part of the total advertising campaign for the product and so will be produced by the same advertising agency that handles the consumer advertising. However, whereas consumer advertising aims to persuade the consumer about the benefits to be gained from buying the product, trade advertising aims to persuade the retailer about the benefits which will result from *selling* the product. Trade advertising supports distribution. It prepares the way. There is no point in advertising products and encouraging consumers to buy them if the goods are not in the shops. The demand created by consumer advertising must be satisfied by the availability of the goods in the shops. That is what is meant by 'adequate distribution'. If the advertised goods cannot be bought, customers will buy either nothing or, worse still, a rival product!

16. Selling-in and selling-out

It will be seen from **15** that trade advertising is part of the selling-in process while consumer advertising is part of the selling-out process. This is also known as the 'push-pull' strategy meaning that efforts to urge the retailer to buy in and promote stocks 'push' the product to the trade while efforts to urge the consumer to buy 'pull' the goods through the distribution system.

RETAIL ADVERTISING

17. Introduction

Here we have a form of advertising which lies between trade and consumer advertising. The most obvious examples are those for department stores and supermarkets, but it can include the advertising conducted by any supplier including a petrol station, restaurant or insurance broker.

This will be dealt with separately in Chapter 9, but a major form of retailing nowadays is direct response marketing or retailing without shops. This is today's mail-order trading which has moved from the traditional club catalogues to sophisticated off-the-page and direct mail campaigns for products and services. Financial houses and department stores have become leading practitioners of these techniques.

18. Purpose

The purpose of retail advertising is threefold:

(a) To sell the establishment, attract customers to the premises and, in the case of a shop, increase what is known as 'store traffic', that is the number of people passing through the shop. If they can be encouraged to step inside they may possibly buy something which they would not otherwise be tempted to buy. This was the original philosophy of Gordon Selfridge who encouraged people to enjoy a visit to his London store, or Jesse Boot who laid out the goods for all to see on the counters of his chemist's shops. They were pioneers of modern shopping.

(b) To sell goods which are exclusive to the store. Some retail distributors are appointed dealers for certain makes, e.g. the Ford dealer. Others, such as supermarkets, sell 'own label' or 'private label' goods which manufacturers pack in the name of the retailer. There are also small symbol group shops which sell goods from one wholesaler, such as Mace or Spar, and carry their brands which are advertised on behalf of the retailers.

Large department and variety stores such as Debenhams, Woolworths and Marks & Spencer have a special brand name for all their products, e.g. Marks & Spencer's St Michael brand.

Most of the chain stores such as Boots, Sainsbury and Tesco sell many own label lines. They will be cheaper than and compete with national brands. Thus Sainsbury and Tesco will have their own baked beans but also sell Heinz. However, Nestlé, Kelloggs and some other makers of famous national brands make it very clear that they do not pack own label goods. Competition between national and own label brands is intense, and there is always the risk that the national brand will be de-listed in favour of a store's own label. About 31.5 per cent of grocery products are own or private label in Britain according to AGB Superpanel & TCA, and as many as 50 per cent of Sainsbury's lines are own label.

Own label products are usually made to the retailer's own specifications or recipes, and are not simply existing national brands sold under a retailer's label at a cheaper price. Sometimes, because the retailer is negotiating a special price, it is an inferior product. For example, the baked beans are sometimes in watery sauce compared with the national brand in rich tomato sauce. There are some manufacturers which are 'contract packers', e.g. jam makers, who supply own labels only.

This is a very old system which dates back to the corner shop family grocer who existed long before the arrival of chain stores like Boots or the supermarkets which emerged after the Second World War.

According to AGB Superpanel, the largest private label share by value are paper goods (43.6 per cent), frozen foods (42.4 per cent), dairy products (41.0 per cent), bakery products (35.0 per cent), beverages (35.0 per cent), sauces and ketchups (27.2 per cent), canned foods (27.0 per cent), packet foods (23.5 per cent), cleaners (22.8 per cent), toilet soap (22.1 per cent), toiletries (21.9 per cent), dentifrice (16.2 per cent) and pet foods (8.0 per cent).

However, not all stores are large or belong to chains, and many are small businesses selling a variety of goods as might be found in a confectioners, tobacconists and newsagents shop. Others will be speciality shops selling, say, flowers, photographic goods, meat, fish, fruit and vegetables, or fashion goods. Then there are the niche shops which sell, say, socks, ties or shirts. Mixed retailing has also become popular whereby a speciality shop may sell complementary lines as when a butcher sells canned vegetables, or a fish and chip shop sells soft drinks. The latest development has been the general store, often open 24 hours a day, at the petrol station, and BP, Shell, Esso and other petrol distributors have spent fortunes rebuilding their service stations to include such shops.

All these retail outlets are likely to use advertising to promote sale of their stock.

(c) To sell the stock in the shop, perhaps promoting items which are seasonal, or presenting a representative selection, or making special offers. The latter could be regular policy, or could be organised as shopping events such as winter or summer sales.

19. Media of retail advertising

Except in the cases of big London stores which advertise in the national press (and then mostly to sell by post), or chains which advertise in regional newspapers covering large areas or on regional television, most retail advertising is confined to local media. One other exception is when the shop is in a major city centre which attracts shoppers from a large area. Even then, a regional evening newspaper will serve both a city and its suburbs and outlying towns and villages. The principal media for retail advertising are:

(a) local weekly newspapers, including numerous free newspapers which gain saturation coverage of residential areas by being delivered from door to door;

(b) regional daily newspapers, of which most are 'evenings'. There are about 100 such newspapers outside London;

(c) public transport external posters and interior cards, and arena advertising at sports grounds;

(d) direct mail to regular or account customers, and door-to-door mail-drop distribution;

(e) regional commercial television;

(f) independent local radio;

(g) window bills and point-of-sale displays within the shop;

(h) window and in-store displays;

(i) catalogues.

The shop itself is a considerable advertising medium, and it may well be a familiar landmark. Marks & Spencer rarely advertise, but their shops are so big they advertise themselves. With retail chains, the corporate identity scheme will quickly identify the location of a branch. Some of the out-of-town superstores have their own bus stops which feature in bus route notices and timetables.

20. Special characteristics

Retail advertising is characterised by four main aspects:

- creating an image of the shop,
- establishing its location,
- variety or special kind of goods offered,
- competitive price offers.

Nearly always, the object of the advertising is to persuade people to visit the shop, although telephone ordering and the use of credit accounts and credit cards is a growing feature. Many stores have developed postal sales, but these really come under the heading of direct response marketing (*see* Chapter 9), the modern name for mail order advertising (whether 'off-the-page' with press advertising, or by direct mail). Increasingly, many larger stores are using the Internet.

21. Co-operative advertising

This was mentioned in **14** when discussing the media of trade advertising. Advertising support given by manufacturers to retailers is also termed 'vertical advertising'. Co-operative advertising is an important facet of retail advertising, and can take many forms, including the following.

(a) The use of logotypes. A logotype (or 'logo') is a specially designed distinctive symbol used to identify a company or a brand. It may be a sign, shape or trade character like those for Michelin, Mercedes-Benz, Shell and White Horse whisky; or a name written in a certain way as used by Halifax Bank, IBM, b^2, Intel, Coca-Cola, Ford and Wella. Retailers can identify themselves as stockists by using their suppliers' logos on letter-headings, in catalogues and in press and other visible advertising. Owners of logos supply retailers with the necessary artwork.

(b) Shared costs. The cost of buying advertisement space in the press or airtime may be shared by a supplier if his or her product is promoted by the retailer.

(c) Supplied artwork. Manufacturers may supply retailers with camera-ready artwork for press advertisements, to which the retailer has merely to add their name, address and telephone number. Camera-ready copy means that it is ready for photographing when plates are being made for offset-litho and flexographic printing. Most newspapers are printed by this process.

(d) Suppliers share costs. Large retail advertisers, such as big supermarket chains and variety chain stores like Woolworths, may take advertisement space in national, retail or local newspapers, the whole cost being shared by different suppliers whose goods are sold in the advertiser's branches.

(e) Stockists' lists. These are another form of co-operative advertising, usually at no cost to the stockists who are listed in press advertisements or in cinema or TV commercials placed by the manufacturer. Thus, customers are directed to a source of supply.

Note: The expression co-operative advertising is applied here to *retail* advertising. There are also two other forms: joint promotions such as bread and butter; or trade or industry schemes based on levies on supporting firms, e.g. glass manufacturers (known as horizontal advertising).

FINANCIAL ADVERTISING

22. Introduction

It is probably difficult to put a limit on what can be contained under this heading, but broadly speaking financial advertising includes that for banks, savings, mortgages, insurance and investments. In addition to advertising addressed to customers or clients it can also include company reports, prospectuses for new share issues, records of investments in securities and other financial announcements.

Some, like building society and National Savings advertisements, may be addressed to the general public while others will appear in the financial and business press only, e.g. the *Financial Times*, *The Economist* or the *Investors Chronicle*. It is interesting that while trade and technical magazines may be scarce in developing countries there is often a business or financial weekly, sometimes distinguished by pink paper for which the British *Financial Times* is famous.

23. Purpose

The object of financial advertising may be to borrow or lend money, conduct all kinds of insurance, sell shares, unit trusts, bonds and pension funds or report financial results.

24. Classes of financial advertising

The main categories in this field are as follows.

(a) Banks advertise their services which today are not confined to traditional bank accounts but include deposits, loans, insurance, house purchase, wills and executorship and advice on investment portfolios. Some banks specialise in certain areas of banking, and others concentrate on certain kinds of business. For instance, one may finance business loans or underwrite new share issues, while another may seek to attract university students or specialise in servicing the farming community. A number are associated with credit or charge cards.

(b) Friendly societies and private medical care organisations like PPP and BUPA offer schemes to provide insurance in time of illness.

(c) Building societies both borrow money from savers and lend money to house-buyers. Most of their advertising is directed at not only raising funds but keeping funds so that they have sufficient money to meet loan applications. Competitive interest rates are important sales points, and today in Britain there is rivalry between building societies, banks and insurance companies for the same kind of business. Some supermarket chains have also now entered this arena.

The Building Societies Act 1986 permits building societies to broaden their business base to include personal pensions, insurance services, estate agency services and loans, thus competing with the banks. The Abbey National Building Society has become a listed PLC with shareholders and is one of Britain's largest banks.

(d) Insurance companies exist to insure against almost any risk from big commitments like ships and aircraft worth millions, to covering the risk that rain may stop play. Some insurance not only covers risks but provides benefits to savers or pensions in old age or to cover funeral expenses. In the cases of fire and theft, insurance companies are also selling peace of mind should damage or loss be suffered.

(e) Investments are offered, not only in share issues but in unit trusts and other investments in which smaller investors can share in the proceeds of a managed portfolio of shares.

(f) Savings and banking facilities are offered through post offices, which sell National Savings certificates and various bonds and operate the Giro and Post Office banks.

(g) Brokers and financial advisers offer insurance, pension and investment schemes and advise their clients on how to manage such financial commitments. The Automobile Association acts as a broker for motor insurance.

(h) Credit and charge card companies, such as Mastercard, Barclaycard, American Express and Diners' Club, promote plastic money facilities, often on an international scale.

(i) Local authorities borrow money from the public, usually on short-term loans which are advertised.

(j) Companies announce their intentions and final dividends, giving summaries of annual reports, and often offering copies of annual reports and accounts.

25. Media of financial advertising

Choice of media will depend on the target audience. Building societies appeal to small savers and therefore use the mass media of the popular press and television. The big national banks with branches everywhere also use the national press and television. Investment advertising will appear in the middle-class and business press. Prospectuses for share issues, which usually occupy two or more pages, appear in newspapers like *The Times*, *Daily Telegraph* and *Financial Times* but those for government privatisation schemes appear in more popular newspapers since the small investor is sought. Banks may take stands at exhibitions. They also produce sales literature about their services, as do insurance companies, especially proposal forms.

Financial houses have adopted database marketing, and have become one of the biggest users of direct mail and 'off the page' direct response techniques. The availability of huge share registers of investors in privatised industries (e.g. British Gas and other utilities, and British Telecom), plus the services of list brokers who rent mailing lists, and sociographic systems of social grading the postcoded population, have made potential investors accessible to promoters of financial services.

So common, and sometimes annoying, has become this practice of mailing small investors who appear on accessible share registers that warnings are printed in annual reports. Shareholders are advised to notify the Mailing Preference Scheme if they wish to be spared such mailings.

26. Special characteristics

Financial advertising in the press, and especially the business press, tends to occupy large spaces and contain detailed information necessary to explain schemes and achieve confidence. The emphasis is generally on benefits which are usually represented by figures such as interest rates and returns on investments, together with warnings that the value of investments may go up or down. The law also insists that such warnings are given in TV and radio advertising. Profit, benefits, security, confidence, credibility and reputation are the keynotes of the copy appeals.

RECRUITMENT ADVERTISING

27. Introduction

This form of advertising aims to recruit staff (including personnel for the police, armed forces and other public services) and may consist of run-on classified advertisements or displayed classified. Other media such as radio and television are sometimes used. Before recession and mass unemployment occurred, recruitment advertising had become an important source of revenue for the media and there were many specialist recruitment advertising agencies or divisions of advertising agencies devoted to handling this kind of advertising. Famous ones like Austin Knight Advertising have survived.

Today, recruitment advertising makes good use of smaller circulation newspapers. AB (middle and lower middle-class) readerships such as the *Guardian* and the *Independent* recruit highly skilled, specialist, sales, marketing, managerial or executive staff. There are certain days of the week when recruitment advertisements appear for particular trades or professions such as accountancy, computers or teaching.

28. Different kinds

Recruitment advertising is mainly of two kinds: that inserted by employers whether identified or using box numbers, and that placed by employment or recruitment agencies which have been commissioned to fill vacancies.

29. Media of recruitment advertising

Except for the occasional recruitment advertisement on radio and television, the media are mainly made up of the following categories of press.

(a) **National newspapers**. Different newspapers appeal to different target groups, e.g. the managerial advertisements in the *Daily Telegraph* and *Sunday Times* and the teacher advertisements in the weekly education feature in the *Guardian* and the *Independent*. Very few jobs are advertised in the popular tabloids.

(b) **Trade, technical and professional journals**. These are the more obvious market-places for recruitment advertising addressed to those with special skills, qualifications and experience. For example, jobs in advertising are advertised in *Campaign, Marketing* and *Marketing Week*, and those in public relations in *PR Week*.

(c) **Regional press**. Local dailies and weeklies are used to advertise jobs offered by local employers.

Note: Many of the publications listed in (a)–(c) are bought and read solely for the purpose of seeking work or changing jobs.

(d) Free publications. A number of freely distributed publications gain their revenue chiefly from recruitment advertising, e.g. *Metro* and *Nine to Five*, which are distributed in the street to office workers such as secretaries. Recruitment advertising is also featured in the free newspapers delivered weekly to homes.

30. Special characteristics

The art of recruitment advertising is to attract the largest number of worthwhile applications at the lowest possible cost. The advantage of using a recruitment or selection agency is that applications can be solicited discreetly and they can be screened to provide employers with a short-list of the best candidates. Two skills have to be applied. The advertisements must be so worded that they both sell the job and attract the best applicants, while correct choice of media will bring the vacancy to the notice of the largest number of good applicants as economically as possible. The readership as well as the rates call for media planning and buying skills which is why this is a specialist agency service. Frequent users of recruitment advertising usually have a standard style of advertisement complete with company logo.

These advertisements must be worded so that they do not exclude applications for reasons of sex or ethnic group, and must conform with the Sex Discrimination and Race Relations Acts.

Progress test 3

1. What are consumer goods? Explain FMCG and OTC. **(4)**

2. What are consumer durables? **(5)**

3. What are consumer services? **(6)**

4. What are the six social grades, and what kind of people does each grade represent? **(7)**

5. How do the media of consumer advertising differ from those for industrial advertising? **(8,10)**

6. Why is trade advertising necessary? **(13)**

7. What is the purpose of retail advertising? **(18)**

8. How can co-operative advertising help both the manufacturer and the distributor? **(21)**

9. What kind of advertisers are included under financial advertising? **(24)**

10. What are the special characteristics of recruitment advertising? **(30)**

11. Which two Acts of Parliament have to be obeyed in recruitment advertising? **(30)**

4

The advertising agency

INTRODUCTION

1. Servicing the client

An advertising agency is a team of experts which services clients who are known as 'accounts'. This use of the word 'accounts' has nothing to do with accountancy. An account is simply an advertiser who uses the agency's services. In the trinity that forms the advertising business – the advertiser, the advertising agency and the media owner – the agency occupies the middle position between those who wish to advertise and those who provide the means of doing so.

2. History

The first advertising agencies were set up at the beginning of the nineteenth century and Britain's first agency, White's, was founded in London about 1800. It began by producing advertising for government lotteries, and then went on as advertising agent for the War Office, Admiralty, HM Commissioner for Prisons, the Colonial Office and later the Crown Agents. Mostly, it handled recruitment advertising.

The first agencies were no more than space brokers, selling press advertising space on a freelance basis for newspapers. As newspaper production improved with greater variety in the sizes and designs of type and the introduction of illustrations, the space brokers began to compete by offering copywriting and design services. Before this, only one type size was used throughout a publication, and the only alternative to a run-on classified-type advertisement was to repeat the same line of copy which drew more attention to the message but was not very imaginative. In this way, the creative advertising agency was born. Advertisers bought advertising space through the agencies which offered them the best ideas. The early account executive was known as the 'contact man'. After the Second World War the modern service agency developed with additional services such as marketing, marketing research and media planning as media statistics became available. The first media statistics on readership were those of the Hulton Readership Survey in the 1950s, although the Audit Bureau of Circulations had been certifying net sale figures since 1931. With the advent of commercial television in 1955, another agency service was added so that the biggest advertising agencies, the ones handling mass market goods, became those which bought airtime and produced TV commercials.

3. Agencies today

In Britain there are now some 750 advertising agencies ranging from studios, which specialise in industrial advertising, to large and often international full service agencies.

Many of the latter, like J. Walter Thompson, are American in origin. More than 260 agencies representing 50 per cent of agency business

Table 4.1 Leading UK agencies ranked by billings

Agency	Billings (£m)	Employees	Tel: 020 7-	Fax: 020 7-
Abbott Mead Vickers BBDO	£355	290	616 3500	616 3600
Ogilvy & Mather	£355	295	345 3000	345 9000
Saatchi & Saatchi	£340	525	636 5060	637 8489
Bates Dorland	£305	280	262 5077	258 3757
J. Walter Thompson	£250	350	499 4040	493 8432
DMP DDB	£245	410	258 3979	402 4871
Lowe Howard-Spink	£230	230	584 5033	584 9557
Publicis	£220	200	935 4426	487 5351
Grey Advertising	£215	400	636 3399	637 7473
Leo Burnett	£215	320	591 9111	591 9126
DMB&B	£205	225	630 0000	630 0033
Bartle Bogle Hegarty	£200	390	734 1677	437 3666
M. & C. Saatchi	£195	200	543 4500	543 4501
McCann Erickson	£180	300	580 6690	323 2883
Euro RSCG Wnek Gosper	£170	170	240 4111	465 0552
WCRS	£150	190	806 5000	806 5099
WWAV Rapp Collins	£135	260	727 3481	221 0520
TMP Worldwide	£130	250	872 1500	487 4374
HHCL & Partners	£125	180	436 3333	436 2677
Young & Rubicam	£120	140	387 9366	611 6570
Delaney Fletcher Bozell	£100	150	836 3474	240 8739
FCA!	£90	80	314 2600	314 2601
Leagas Delaney Partnership	£90	105	836 4455	240 9005

Note: because some agencies may issue billings figures more than once a year, it is important to check the latest for each agency you are researching. The telephone and fax numbers listed above help to simplify this procedure.

Source: CMC Research and agency statements

are members of their trade association, the Institute of Practitioners in Advertising.

The main types of agency are discussed in **11–25** below.

4. Location

While the majority of agencies are located in capital cities such as London or New York, they are also to be found in most industrial cities, especially if such cities are media centres with publishing houses and radio and television stations. Large agencies often have their head office in the capital and branches in the regions. In Britain, there are important agencies in major cities such as Birmingham, Edinburgh, Bristol, Glasgow, Leeds, Liverpool, Manchester and Newcastle.

5. Public relations

In this chapter public relations is not included as an advertising agency service or department, although it is true that in small agencies (especially in developing countries) public relations services are often provided (probably limited to press relations in association with advertising campaigns), while a number of large advertising agencies do have subsidiary public relations consultancies. Because advertising and public relations are two different forms of communication with different purposes, and public relations is actually a far bigger subject than advertising, it is discussed separately in Chapter 14. For a fuller study of the subject the reader is referred to the authors' companion handbook, *Public Relations*.

From time to time some agencies try to expand their business by setting up public relations services, and this was seen when recession tended to hit advertising rather than public relations expenditures. One reason for this was that while the consumer market shrank, companies often had a lot of explaining to do and that called for public relations techniques. While some advertising agencies may be able to offer a broad communications service, advertising and public relations do tend to make uncomfortable bedfellows, and are best operated separately.

ROLE OF THE ADVERTISING AGENCY

6. Agent acts as principal

The role of the advertising agency is to plan, create and execute advertising campaigns for clients. However, the extent to which it does so varies today according to the kind of agency it is. There are agencies which offer every kind of service, those which only buy media, those which only create, and others which offer special services.

Generally, however, the old idea holds that the advertising agency is strictly speaking the agent of the media (like the original space broker). The agent's legal status remains that 'the agent acts as principal' and is responsible in law for payments. This legal precedent or 'custom of the trade' means that, if an advertiser defaults, the agency is responsible for paying debts incurred on the client's behalf. Agencies can be financially vulnerable and some have gone bankrupt when their clients have failed. Thus the agency business is a risky one, and the maintenance of cash flow is essential. As will be explained in **10**, creditworthiness is the basis of agency recognition by the media owners.

7. Middle position

Operating in this middle position – almost like a wholesaler – between advertiser and media owners, the role of the advertising agency can be summarised in two ways.

(a) It offers the client a team of highly skilled experts which can be shared with other clients. It would not be economic for the majority of clients to employ such a team full-time. The agency is also skilled at buying ancillary services such as film and video production, artwork, photography, print, typesetting and marketing research.

(b) It offers the media an economic way of buying and selling space and airtime since the media owners have to deal with a relatively small number of agencies compared with thousands of individual advertisers. The quality of advertising production will be high and will match the standards and requirements of the media, and the advertisements will comply with the law and the British Codes of Advertising and Sales Promotion, and the Independent Television Commission (ITC) and Radio Authority (RA) Codes in respect of television and radio commercials.

RECOGNITION AND THE COMMISSION SYSTEM

8. Recognition

Recognition does not mean that the agency is approved or has special qualities, nor is recognition granted by the professional bodies such as the Advertising Association or the Institute of Practitioners in Advertising. Recognition is granted by the bodies representing the media owners. These are the Newspaper Publishers Association (NPA), the Newspaper Society (NS), the Periodical Publishers Association (PPA), the Independent Television Association (ITVA) and the Commercial Radio Companies Association (CRCA).

Figure 4.1 The advertising agency and its world

A client should not therefore seek a recognised agency because it is believed it is better than an unrecognised one. An unrecognised agency would simply have no source of media income, and would have to charge the client for all its services. Consequently, it is difficult for a media-buying agency to operate unless it is recognised.

9. Office of Fair Trading ruling

Before April 1979 only a 'recognised' agency could claim commission on its purchases of advertisement space in the press or of airtime on commercial television or independent local radio. Standard rates of commission were agreed for different kinds of media, e.g. 15 per cent for nationals, 10 per cent for regionals and the trade press.

However, in 1979 a ruling of the Office of Fair Trading under the Restrictive Trade Practices Act 1976 held this to be an illegal, restrictive and monopolistic practice in that it did not permit agencies and media owners to negotiate competitive commission rates. Moreover, since a new agency could be set up only if it was recognised and so able to get commission, and to do so it had to have clients worth a certain volume of business, another monopolistic situation existed. Prior to the OFT ruling it was extremely difficult for a new agency to operate, unless perhaps directors broke away from an existing agency and took clients with them. (*See also* 18: **21**.)

10. Effect of ruling

The current system of recognition establishes the creditworthiness of agencies so that they are entitled to buy space and airtime on credit, provided that they adhere to the British Codes of Advertising and Sales Promotion. A direct result of this has been the setting up of 'à la carte' agencies which are creative only, and do no media buying. They do not require 'recognition', and are not hampered by the requirement to have a certain volume of business.

Commission is still important to the larger agencies which handle the bigger campaigns. It is their main source of income. Because of this income, the client enjoys many services free-of-charge (e.g. the advice of the account executive and agency marketing manager, campaign planning, and all the expertise and clerical work involved in media, print and other buying). The client pays for all space, air-time, artwork, and production costs, on which the agency also earns discounts or charges a percentage or on-cost. When the volume of billings provides inadequate commission income, as occurs with small and especially industrial accounts or in overseas countries where the scale of advertising is smaller, a service fee based on time is charged. However, there are some large agencies which prefer to rebate commissions, and charge fees for their time and expertise.

The commission system suits the media, but it is an anomalous and unprofessional system. It does not permit the agency to be paid according to the volume and quality of its work, as with public relations consultants which enjoy a more professional system of remuneration. No doubt fees will eventually replace commission, although this may be resented by advertisers who will be obliged to pay for all the agency services they receive.

SERVICE AGENCIES

11. Full-service agencies

These are large or medium-size agencies capable of conducting a complete advertising campaign. They may have subsidiary companies or have associations with other companies dealing with marketing research, public relations, recruitment advertising, or sales promotion. A number of these big agencies, e.g. Saatchi & Saatchi, Abbott Mead and Lopex are public companies with shares quoted on the Stock Exchange. The big agencies handle the campaigns for top advertisers such as Lever Brothers, Procter & Gamble, Kellogg, Ford, British Telecom, Nestlé, Vauxhall, Mars, Kraft, Birds Eye, Brooke Bond, Cadbury-Schweppes, Boots and Tesco who spend between £22 and £63 million each, Lever Brothers topping the list in 1991. Of the top 100 British advertisers, those at the bottom of the list spend about £8 million each and in 1991 this was Walkers Crisps. These figures exclude outdoor, cinema, industrial and overseas publications. The big agencies are therefore responsible for a vast proportion of the total annual expenditure (over £7.5 billion) on British advertising, covering press, TV, outdoor, cinema and radio, but not direct mail and other below-the-line advertising.

Unilever, the largest British advertiser, has many subsidiaries such as Lever Brothers, Elida Gibbs, Birds Eye, Brooke Bond and others, and its total expenditure in 1991 was £173,469,000. Similarly, all the Procter & Gamble companies spent £107,245,000. HM Government's ministries, National Savings and other agencies spent £75,518,000.

12. Medium-size agencies

There are many other medium-size service agencies which are responsible for more modest accounts, augmenting their regular staff with freelance and specialist services as and when required. There are, for instance, many first-class freelance copywriters and visualisers who prefer to work independently. The future is likely to see an expansion of home-based creative staff who can produce layouts on computers, write copy on word processors, and transmit their work electronically to terminals in agency offices. This is one way in which agencies can reduce the high cost of renting city offices.

13. Business-to-business agencies

As the name implies, these agencies specialise in advertising industrial and technical goods, which are generally combined as business-to-business advertising mainly in the trade and technical press, at trade exhibitions, and by means of printed materials such as sales literature, catalogues and technical data sheets. Payment is usually on a fee basis. Often, the principals of the agency will have worked in industry, perhaps as advertising managers. The creative staff will be familiar with the technology and its jargon, and capable of writing and designing authentically. This kind of advertising calls for meticulous attention to detail. Although the accounts are smaller in value, they tend to be more stable compared with big consumer accounts where clients change agencies more frequently in search of fresh ideas.

The growth of hi-tech products such as computers, Internet software and services, mobile telephones, video games, word processors, copiers and fax machines has seen considerable development in the hi-tech agency business.

MEDIA INDEPENDENTS

14. Development of media independents

During the 1970s agencies which concentrated on buying media – and did so very competitively – became a new feature of the agency world. In 1981 the Association of Media Independents was formed. The existence of these agencies emphasises the second of the two aspects of advertising described in 1: **29**. In the ten years 1974–1983 their billings (*see* **53**) increased nearly six times. They are usually 'recognised' by the ITVA, NPA and PPA. The AMI became a member of the Committee of Advertising Practice in 1993.

Table 4.2 Leading UK media independents ranked by billings

Agency	Billings (£m)	Employees	Tel: 020 7-	Fax: 020 7-
Zenith Media	£615	250	224 8500	706 2650
Carat	£465	190	430 6000	430 6299
MediaVest	£405	105	233 5678	233 5677
MindShare	£405	200	969 4040	969 4000
BMP Optimum	£350	75	893 4893	893 4111
Universal McCann	£270	65	436 7711	915 2165
Mediapolis	£270	80	393 9000	393 2525
New PHD	£260	125	446 0555	446 7100
MediaCom UK	£250	75	872 9928	872 9631
CIA Media Network	£230	105	633 9999	803 2086
Media Business Group	£230	100	408 4400	499 7279
Initiative Media	£230	125	663 7000	663 7001
Optimedia International	£220	60	935 0040	486 1985
BBJ Media	£210	75	379 9000	497 1177
Western International Media	£135	55	581 1455	823 7115
Motive Communications	£130	55	453 4444	437 2401
Manning Gottlieb Media	£100	30	470 5300	412 0244

Note: because some independents may issue billings figures more than once a year, it is important to check the latest figures for each one you are researching. The telephone and fax numbers listed above help to simplify this procedure.

Source: CMC Research and agency statements

Of these 'Indies' or media shops, by far the largest is Zenith. Some advertisers divide their campaigns between media independents and 'à la carte' creative agencies in order to get the best of both worlds, while some of the large service agencies use media independents.

15. Reasons for success of media independents

The reasons for their success are threefold as follows.

(a) The breakdown of the former fixed commission system.

(b) The media explosion, including new publishing techniques and alternative television (see 5: 23–35).

(c) The inflated cost of media. Media buying had become more critical regarding cost-effectiveness, and wider knowledge was required of new or changing media. The influence of free newspapers, colour supplements, new specialist international journals, independent local radio, teledata and Viewdata, Channel 4 TV and breakfast TV had revolutionised media planning and buying. Now there are other media fields such as satellite and digital television and the effects of the Broadcasting Act 1990, such as sponsored TV programmes.

Nevertheless, since the previous edition of this book, there have been a number of changes in the agencies listed in Table 4.1. Some have gone out of business, while others have merged. While some large agencies use media independents, others have sought to strengthen their media buying facilities.

16. Media breakdowns

The breakdown of media buying by media independents is roughly:

Cinema	2%
Outdoors	2%
Radio	2%
Newspapers	21%
Magazines	20%
Television	53%
	100%

17. Remuneration

The method of charging varies according to the size of client and the kind of media used. Media independents buy media as keenly as possible and negotiate the best rates of commission they can get. Under the old system recognised agencies were either assured of or limited to standard rates of commission paid by all the members of the recognising media body. The media independents may be remunerated by commission from the media, or by a mixture of commission received and additional fees charged to clients. Commission may be rebated (clients being charged net instead of gross media rates, then charged a fee according to the workload).

Fees are a realistic way of charging (or paying for media), with clients benefiting from buying skills and paying for them accordingly. No longer do the media subsidise the advertiser by allowing agencies commission with which to give clients free services. It also maintains the usefulness of agencies to the media since fewer accounts are involved and prompt payment is assured.

18. Relationship to creative agencies

Media independents also place much of the advertising produced by 'à la carte' agencies (see 19–25) which, since they are purely creative, do not buy media direct. They do not need to be 'recognised' nor are they handicapped in setting up business because of recognition requirements about minimum number of clients and volume of billings or media turnover.

À LA CARTE AGENCIES

19. Development

À la carte agencies, often working on *ad hoc* assignments, have developed from what used to be (and may still be referred to) as 'hot shops'. They are wholly creative agencies which undertake a variety of work such as new product launches, rejuvenated products, packaging ideas, corporate identity schemes, sales conferences, exhibition stands or the creative aspects of a total advertising campaign. Some are so individual in the services they offer that they are considered under separate identifying headings in **20–25** below.

20. Creative agencies

These produce copy platforms or themes and create campaigns for different media, perhaps inventing characters and writing jingles and music for TV commercials. They complement the media independents who are then responsible for buying space and air-time. We are back to our two basic skills of creativity and media buying. The client has to consider whether the larger full service agency can satisfactorily provide both skills, or whether it is better to use the buying and creative expertise of two separate agencies. It may seem more complicated to do this, but the highly competitive recession situation has made client requirements more demanding.

It is claimed that the newer agencies are a response to the inadequacy of the traditional full service agencies. The answer may be in the size of the campaign and the predominance of TV usage. It is significant that agencies associated with some of our major advertisers in the multi-million expenditure bracket are handled by agencies like Saatchi & Saatchi and Bates Dorland which have grown into very big agencies. Others, e.g. Ogilvy & Mather, have themselves set up specialist subsidiaries in fields like direct response. It will be seen that the agency world has been adjusting itself rapidly to the demands of the times.

21. New product development agencies

These agencies claim superiority over the traditional agencies because they get involved very early on in the various stages of the marketing mix (*see* 1: **12–15**). They may influence the original concept of the product, and certainly participate in naming products, packaging designs, pricing and market segmentation, distribution, test-marketing, and selling-in to the trade operations as well as the main consumer advertising campaign.

Since the majority of new products fail, and probably some 50 per cent fail even after apparently successful test-marketing, clients will take up the advantages of using new product development agencies; they have a keener approach to everything likely to influence a successful launch. These agencies have a substantial record of success, and they offer proof of this in their advertisements in *Campaign*, *Marketing* and *Marketing Week*.

22. Direct response agencies

Campaigns for mail order traders, including the promotion of magazine subscriptions, business travel, package tours, credit cards, savings and investments, and other services sold by mail, as well as the off-the-page offers frequently seen in the weekend colour magazines, are handled by direct response agencies. Many campaigns are conducted entirely by direct mail, using sales letters, sales literature and catalogues. Again, these agencies have responded to demand, and direct response in all its forms, including the use of commercial television as a medium, has become a very skilled and powerful marketing operation. Among the biggest users of direct response are financial houses and department stores, eclipsing the mail-order catalogue clubs which used to dominate mail order.

The technique is to sell direct, by post, telephone, fax and the Internet. Devices such as Freephone and Freepost, plus invitations to give credit or charge card details on coupons or order forms, are all part of the effort to attract direct sales. Sometimes there may be addresses where goods can be inspected and bought, but usually direct response means retailing without stores. (*See* also Chapter 9.)

23. Incentive scheme agencies and premium houses

Two kinds of agencies have been put together here because they have similarities. Both buy and supply goods and services which are offered as gifts or premiums to customers or as incentive awards to employees. Incentive scheme agencies offer packaged schemes which can be awarded to the staff whose ideas improve productivity or who are top salespeople. The schemes may range from weekend holidays to the award of points which can be accumulated in order to claim items from a catalogue. Some direct response catalogues normally used by mail-order clubs are adapted for this latter purpose.

Premium houses buy and supply the numerous items which are used for sales promotion purposes. These include self-liquidating premium offers when customers send in so many tokens from packages together with cash to purchase goods at less than normal shop price. Most of these goods, both incentive and premium, are standard lines, but some are purpose-made. The reader of trade press advertisements for incentives and premiums, will find many familiar products on offer. The manufacturers employ special sales executives to promote this class of business which can produce considerable volume sales.

In the case of premium offers to consumers, and mail-ins which are free offers, another side of the business is the redemption of tokens and payments. This requires warehouse and packing facilities, and it is important that goods are despatched promptly even though offers usually stipulate that delivery may take twenty-eight days. The premium house may handle everything, but a *fulfilment house* may be employed to deal with the response only. Fulfilment houses also service the sales promotion agencies which are described in **24**.

24. Sales promotion agencies

Some of these are subsidiaries of full service agencies, others are independent. Sales promotion (which has largely replaced the former expression 'merchandising') consists of marketing activities, often at the point-of-sale, which lie between consumer advertising and retail selling. This will be discussed more fully in Chapter 7. Here, we are concerned with agencies with the expertise to organise such activities. Unlike the offer of well-known goods as incentives or premiums, a modern sales promotion scheme is very often an original exercise created for short-term operation.

Typical examples:

- big prize competitions,

- in-store demonstrations,

- various collecting schemes based on the trading stamp idea,

- money-off flash packs,

- cross-couponing schemes whereby a token on a pack can be used as a price-cut on another product,

- high street redemption schemes allowing discounts on purchases at certain stores,

- charity promotions,

- promotional games.

To some extent the more sophisticated promotions, requiring considerable originality, planning and execution, have come about because of economic changes during the early 1980s. The new demands have justified the existence of the sales promotion agency or, when it already existed, its greater value to the marketing strategy. The subject now occupies many pages in magazines such as *Marketing* and there are also the specialist magazines *Ideas* and *Sales Promotion*.

There are two reasons for this: the inadequacy of traditional consumer advertising media (including television), and the inadequacy of traditional sales promotion such as self-liquidating premium offers and mail-ins for free offers. Dissatisfaction with media is partly to do with its demassification and disproportionate or increased cost, while disenchantment with schemes requiring customer effort stems from the price competition which now exists in the shops for similar goods. It is no longer an advantage to send away for a set of premium offer saucepans when they can be bought as cheaply in a local shop. As a result, the sales promotion schemes have had to be more ingenious.

25. Sponsorship agencies

Sponsorship may be for marketing, advertising or public relations purposes, and quite often may embrace all three (*see* also Chapter 8). Sponsorship is big business and vital to the marketing of some companies. It is not the pretence at public relations which one finds in developing countries where steel bands, basketball teams and football teams are sponsored as if that was all public relations was about. There are two sides to sponsorship: people, activities and events which need financial support, and companies which are prepared to invest money in whatever will aid the marketing strategy. Sponsorship agencies bring the two together.

One of the most costly sponsorships is motor racing which requires the means of maintaining teams and machines at international grand prix, which is why the cars may bear evidence of co-sponsorship. Motor racing enjoys hours of TV coverage. The trend is towards sponsorship of big events, including ones such as football and cricket which are so long established that their adoption by sponsors has caused astonishment (*see* 8: **2, 4**).

A sponsorship agency not only brings sponsor and sponsored together, and does so in ways which are mutually satisfactory. It is responsible for all the associated activities such as arena advertising, media coverage and its monitoring, sale of concessions (e.g. T-shirts), hospitality for journalists (e.g. lunch boxes for cricket commentators) and for the sponsor's guests who are invited to attend events. It will also be involved in organising prizes and prize presentations.

The Broadcasting Act 1990 has made possible the sponsorship of TV and radio programmes, a major innovation in broadcast advertising. This has brought about agencies such as Media Dimensions which create the very clever sponsor's announcements in trailers, introductions and bumper breaks. This new topic is described in fuller detail in Chapter 8.

AGENCY PERSONNEL

26. Diversity of agency personnel

In this section a wide division of labour, and a number of specialist jobs, will be described. All of these will be found in the largest full service advertising

61

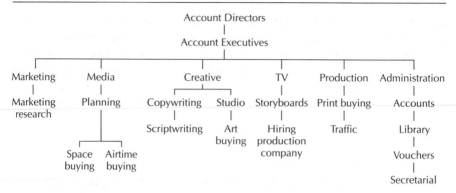

Figure 4.2 Departments and functions of a large full service advertising agency

agencies (*see* also Figure 4.2). However, in the smaller agencies to be found in the regions and especially in smaller or developing countries, many of these jobs will be carried out by the same person. (For a fuller discussion of the role of agency personnel in planning and executing an advertising campaign, *see* Chapter 19.)

27. Role of the advertising manager

A common mistake is to assume that the advertising manager works in the agency. He or she is in fact in charge of the *client's* advertising department. The agency–client relations and negotiations will be conducted between the agency account executive and the company advertising manager (or whoever is in charge of advertising on the client's behalf. This could be the marketing manager, sales manager, product or brand manager or even the proprietor).

28. Account director

Usually one of the partners or directors of the agency, the account director (and there may be several in a large agency) will be responsible for a group of accounts (clients). Working under the account director will be account executives who handle one or more accounts. The account director will be responsible to the board of directors and is concerned with profitability. He or she will lead negotiations for new and renewal business, and will direct policy matters such as whether or not to accept certain accounts especially if there is any risk that they may conflict with existing accounts.

29. Competing accounts

It is not unethical for an agency to handle competing accounts, and there may be some advantage if the agency has experience in a certain field, e.g.

banking or electronics, provided the rival firms do not object. They may, on security grounds, object and it might, for instance, be undesirable for an advertising agency to handle the accounts for two rival motor-cars in view of the intensity of this rivalry.

This can be a problem when an agency seeks to service a conglomerate only to find that it owns a subsidiary which would rival an existing client.

There is also the problem of conflicting accounts, when it would be undesirable to service both a brewery and a teetotallers' society, or a car ferry and Eurotunnel. There is a difference between a *competing* and a *conflicting* client.

30. Account executive

In the days of the early agencies which emerged from the space brokers, and right into the 1930s, the person seeking business was called the 'contact man' who was little more than a salesman, and it has become a derogatory term today. Even the title of account executive has been dropped by some agencies in favour of representative, just as advertising managers are more often known as brand or product managers. However, account executive remains in general use.

He or she maintains the liaison between the agency and the client, and that does not mean being merely a go-between. The account executive has to understand the client's needs, and the business and industry, and interpret these needs to the agency. Conversely, the account executive has to present the agency's proposals, ideas and work to the client. It is a delicate, diplomatic job and with responsibility to keep the account. The account executive should have a broad knowledge of advertising and be able to work with everyone in the agency, directing their efforts in the interest of the client. He or she may be a graduate who entered the agency as a trainee, and whose future lies in agency directorship, a better job with another agency, partnership in or ownership of his or her own agency, or advertising management with a company. The recognised professional qualification in Britain is the CAM Diploma.

31. Contact report

Essential to good management of an account is the contact or call report. After every client meeting the account executive quickly submits to the client a special form of minute. At the top is stated when and where the meeting was held, who was present, and to whom in the client's organisation and the agency the report is being distributed. The report will give a brief statement of items reported and decisions taken. A vertical rule is printed on the right-hand side, and in the margin are annotated instructions and the initials of those who are to carry them out. It should be distributed

PRO*AKTIV*
Practicians in Advertising, Public Relations
and Corporate Communications

CONTACT REPORT

Client: Cuspidor Containers Ltd
Date: 10 November 2001
Venue: The agency
Reference: CC12007

Present: For the Client: John Cuspidor, Martin Box, Anita Laver.
For the Agency: Derek Sharp, Jo-Ann Mattock, Ed Cutlass, Sylvie Blade.

Distribute to: All present + Mike Casement, Roger Binns (Client).
Sylvie Blade, Duncan Claymore (Agency)

		Action
Item 1.	**Business press campaign**	

AL reported feedback on the current press advertising campaign.
Each insertion in the Financial Times and Daily Telegraph has so far
produced a response rate of over 30 excellent leads, with little waste.
SB recommended continuing the campaign for another three months.
This was approved by the client, with immediate effect.

SB

Item 2.   **Radio campaign**

At the last meeting, it was suggested that a campaign on certain
independent local radio stations would be useful support for future
press campaigns. DS reported that research conducted over the past
two months indicated this to be a viable measure. Research findings
were handed to the meeting. Client asked for costings, to be
distributed to all concerned within three working days.

EC

Item 3.   **Sales brochure**

As the result of the successful advertising campaign now running,
more brochures are needed. Client approved the printing of another
twenty thousand, with appropriate discounts.

DC

Item 4.   **Next meeting**

All

Agreed, 20 November 2001, 10am, at the Agency.

Figure 4.3 Example of an advertising agency contact report

immediately after the meeting so that there is opportunity to make any necessary revisions, and misunderstandings are avoided. The reports are filed in a facts book which becomes a concise record for constant reference and also the basis of the agency's annual report to the client. Figure 4.3 is an example of an agency contact report.

32. Marketing manager

The modern agency is marketing conscious, and the agency marketing manager fulfils several functions. Marketing advice is offered to clients who do not have marketing managers, or it complements company marketing managers who are given more confidence if the agency is marketing-orientated. Unless there is a separate executive responsible for marketing research, this executive will also advise on the use of marketing research and commission surveys by independent research units. Advice will be given, for instance, on aspects of the marketing mix such as product development, naming and branding, packaging, market segment, test-marketing and distribution.

33. Contribution to campaign

The marketing manager's contribution may well affect the success of the advertising campaign, and the importance of adequate distribution is worth emphasising here. Distribution to meet demand provoked by advertising could depend on lead times determined by such factors as the length of journey cycle of the company's sales representatives, that is the time gap between their visits to retailers. Similarly, it is important that everyone is clear about the market segment which could affect brand name, packaging, price, kind of stockist, choice of advertising theme and choice of advertising media. The entire sequence of elements is of marketing significance, and an advertising campaign could be a disastrous waste of money if all these elements were not harmonised.

34. Limitations of 4Ps

This is also a practical example of the limitations of the 4Ps concept of marketing (see 1: 14) because the marketing manager of an advertising agency is not only concerned with the fourth P, Promotion. Advertising has to be related to the *sequence* or chronological order of marketing considerations. This, of course, is what the new-product development agencies are all about. They discount the idea of planning an advertising campaign for a given product: they want to be involved in the whole marketing mix. Under the old 4Ps principle so familiar to American marketing (or to those whose training is based on the American 4Ps marketing concept) advertising is brought in rather late in the marketing strategy. But if we dispense with the

4Ps, and start at the beginning, the eventual advertising campaign evolves throughout the stages of the marketing mix. This could mean that the account executive and the agency marketing manager should sit in on the advertiser's decision-making conferences from the earliest possible moment (*see* also 19: **4**).

That this does not happen often enough is further evidence of the poor understanding of advertising which some marketing managers have, and it is probably due to the limitations imposed on marketing by the 4Ps concept.

35. Marketing aspects

To take the definition of marketing again, it becomes possible – indeed necessary – to consider how advertising will be able to contribute to selling at a profit what people will buy. This brings the agency marketing manager in at the threshold of product design.

It has been known for a product to be killed at birth, or redesigned, or sent to an independent test house, because the advertising agency has been able to express opinions or doubts at a very early stage. This could also apply to such stages as:

(a) naming – does the name lend itself to good promotion?;

(b) packaging – would it be easier to promote the product if it were packaged differently?;

(c) distribution – would it be more economical to sell direct to retailers rather than through wholesalers?

Like other members of the agency team, the marketing manager, without divulging any trade secrets, will be able to advise clients on the basis of wide experience. For example, something which helped in the successful marketing of a sewing machine might also be applicable to a vacuum cleaner. Or a problem which occurred in the distribution of a soft drink to supermarket chains (e.g. lead time between obtaining orders and delivery) could apply equally to a new cheese spread, and affect the timing of the appearance of advertisements. Failure to reckon with such a lead time resulted in a disastrous marketing operation when an expensive television advertising campaign occurred *before* the product had reached the shops, and the advertising expenditure was a total waste of money.

36. Media planner

In large agencies there will be a division between media planning and media buying, but in a smaller agency one person will handle both. Media planning calls for an intimate knowledge of the range and values of available media. In Britain, as in most industrial countries, media are extensive.

There are thousands of national and regional newspapers and magazines; numerous television and radio stations; thousands of outdoor and transportation sites (including the London Underground railway); and many other advertising media. The media mix is usually carefully selected on the basis of a *minimum* use of media of *maximum* advertising value, and there will be primary spearhead media and secondary support media. A modern agency will use a computer to assess and select media.

37. Media statistics

The media planner is assisted by statistics both from independent sources, and from the media themselves as part of their sales campaigns (*see* also Chapter 17). Figures on circulation are provided by the Audit Bureau of Circulations (ABC). Figures on readership, and profiles of readers, are provided by National Readership Surveys (NRS). Television audience figures are supplied by the Broadcasters' Audience Research Board (BARB) and radio audience figures are supplied by the Radio Advertising Joint Audience Research (RAJAR). There are many surveys covering other media, while individual publishers, TV companies and other media owners conduct their own special surveys and supply agencies and advertisers with their figures.

38. Media rates

The media planner now has to marry statistics to costs. These are expressed as cost-per-thousand sales, readers, viewers, listeners, passengers, passers-by, households and so on.

The rate for a whole page in Journal A may be £1,000, but only £800 for Journal B. Which is really the best buy? We have to look at more critical figures such as circulation (those who buy) and readership (those who read). Then we can calculate the cost-per-thousand buyers or readers. Suppose Journal A has a circulation of 10,000 copies per issue. The cost-per-thousand is £1,000 ÷ 10 which is £100. However, if Journal B has a circulation of only 5,000, its cost-per-thousand is an uneconomical £160 (£800 ÷ 5).

It is a case of getting what you pay for. Although it is often suggested that television advertising is very expensive, it could be very cheap if the rate is divided by millions of viewers. It is only expensive if it is wasteful to convey the sales message to so many people.

There is another way of looking at this issue. What is the *quality* of the readership? While Journal A in the above example may seem a bargain, it could be a waste of money if the journal was read by the wrong social grade(s). Here, it is useful to refer back to Table 3.1 in Chapter 3. For example, a supermarket chain needing to sell to many thousands of customers will find it economic to pay a high rate to reach the millions of readers of the *Sun*, but the maker of a mainframe computer would find the

Sun completely useless and would find it more economic to spend far less to reach the more specialised readership of *The Economist*.

39. Media schedule

Having completed his media study and calculations, the media planner then draws up a *media schedule*. This is a plan or diary of the proposed insertions in the press, or appearances on radio or television, or use of other media, over the period of the advertising campaign, with their costs. This schedule will be included in the presentation made to the client of the whole campaign, or directly to the client if there is no major presentation as can happen if various programmes are being drawn up during the course of a year. When the media schedule has been approved, or amended, it becomes the media buyer's task to make the bookings.

40. Media buyer

The media buyer negotiates with the media for purchase of space and airtime. His skill lies in getting the best positions and times at the best rates. Some media may have to be booked months in advance, and tentative bookings may have to be made before the media schedule is presented for client approval. He will have good relations with the sales representatives of the media who will be contacting him from time to time with offers and proposals which may or may not fit in with the allocations of the media schedule. It should not be thought that space and airtime is simply placed and accepted. The media are eagerly trying to induce the media buyer to use their media. Like any other buyer, the media buyer is constantly being approached by hard-selling sales representatives.

41. Copywriter

The copywriter is responsible for writing the wording of advertisements (*see* also Chapter 11). He or she has to have the ability to convert sales propositions into persuasive selling ideas, creating themes or copy platforms for campaigns and distilling sales arguments into the fewest number of necessary words. His or her writing style is unlike any other. Complete grammatical sentences are not always appropriate. Words and punctuation and their typographical presentation are written like a painter uses colours and shapes. The copywriter can write a one-sentence paragraph that grips the reader's interest and desire and leads to action. The English language can be virtually used for effect. A thousand words may be written but every word will count. He or she can sell. The copywriter may also write scripts for television and radio commercials, or there may be a *scriptwriter*.

Agencies employ copywriters in different ways. There may be a copy department headed by a copy chief, or there may be creative groups headed by senior copywriters. A creative director may use freelance copywriters. Many of the best and most highly paid copywriters work freelance.

42. Art director

Head of the studio, the art director in a large agency will have a team of visualisers, layout artists and typographers (*see* also Chapter 12). In a small agency the art director will perform all these creative tasks. If there is no separate art buyer, artwork will be bought through artists' agents, or direct from artists. Photography will be commissioned and models engaged, usually through a model agency.

43. Visualiser

The visualiser is the creative counterpart of the copywriter, a first-class artist who is able to interpret in visual terms the copywriter's ideas. They usually work together as a team, as in the creative team which works on one or more accounts. Using traditional techniques, the visualiser produces roughs or scamps, and may scribble many versions until the ideas are sufficiently well expressed for them to be finished up with dummy pictures and hand lettering. The client is usually shown visuals without final photography, drawings and typesetting, but they will be sufficient to give a good impression of the finished advertisement. When approved, the artwork is commissioned.

Computerisation of agency studios has brought about a revolution in advertising agency creative departments. Everything traditionally done on the drawing-board can be done on the computer screen – faster and more accurately. Headlines, body copy, photographs, illustrations, line-work, coupons and other page elements can be created and manipulated on screen. It is as easy to work in full colour as in black-and-white, and as economical. Illustrations can be held in a computer 'library' and called up by a few simple key-strokes.

Completed work can be saved to disk, including the many changes it may go through. Every version, including the final one, can be handed or sent to the client on disk, for viewing on their own computer. Alternatively, the work can be sent to the client electronically, down a telephone line. Any changes made before the work goes to production are made computer-to-computer. This eliminates such expensive and time-consuming chores as complete re-typing of copy and re-pasting of illustrations, which were common in the past.

44. Layout artist

A layout is an exact plan of the advertisement, converting the visual into a measured representation of the advertisement which can be followed by the printer or made up as camera-ready copy. Traditionally, the layout will be marked up with instructions regarding typefaces and type sizes. For various

69

space sizes, *adaptations* are made of the original layout. The layout artist draws the layout and adaptations of it.

As with agency creative work, computerisation has revolutionised layout work and typography in agency studios. Everything can now be done electronically. The two main advantages are accuracy and speed. Layouts are perfected just as accurately as on the conventional drawing-board. Type mark-ups have been superseded by scalable type. Modifications and adaptations can be made – and approved – at high speed.

For production, layouts can be delivered digitally to their destinations, both inside and outside the agency. Colour values are maintained throughout the process; what the art director and the client see is what they get when the campaign is eventually run.

45. Typographer

Sometimes the layout artist and typographer will be the same person. A typographer is a master of type, knowing the hundreds of display and text typefaces and how to use them both to create effect and to ensure legibility. The typographer will take the copy and the layout, and select and instruct the typesetter on the faces and sizes required. To do so, the typographer will also cast off the copy, that is calculate the number of words and size of type to fit spaces.

Today's high-tech typographers are equipped with computers and suites of typographical software offering thousands of scalable typefaces. This frees them from the tedium of casting-off. However, it tempts them to use eccentric typography which can damage the legibility of the copywriter's work.

46. Television producer

In the large agencies which handle accounts requiring television campaigns, the producer creates concepts for commercials. These are presented in the form of a storyboard which resembles a series of cartoons in shapes like television screens or rectangles (*see* Chapter 12, Figure 12.5). The TV producer will also be responsible for casting the actors and presenter, hiring music, and appointing a director and production unit. The distinction should be made between the agency producer who creates and assembles the necessary resources, and the outside director and his production unit which actually shoots the film or video.

47. Production manager

The task here is to organise the production of advertising throughout the agency, according to a set timetable, so that advertisements are delivered to the media on time. The production manager acts as a progress chaser, is also responsible for ordering typesettings and supplying finished advertisements as they are required for flexography, photogravure or offset-litho printing (*see* Chapter 13). As offset-litho is now substantially used for printing newspapers and magazines, camera-ready copy has to be supplied. In large agencies, work flow will be maintained by the *traffic controller* who supplies duplicate copies of instructions to all departments which need to be aware of work in progress. As several separate campaigns are likely to be progressing simultaneously, progress has often to be checked several times a day.

ADVERTISING AGENCY JARGON

48. Special terms

A lot of advertising jargon has been used in this chapter. Most of these words with their special meanings have been explained, but a few need further clarification and some others are now introduced. Attention has already been drawn to expressions like recognition and the commission system (**8–10**), à la carte agencies (**19–25**), the advertising manager (**27**), account (**1**), account executive (**30**), circulation and readership (**37–8**), television producer and television director (**46**), and production manager (**47**), which may not be quite what they seem and are frequently misunderstood by examination students.

49. Plans board

In some agencies the plans board system is operated (*see* also Chapter 19). The plans board usually consists of the account executive and the heads of agency departments, generally the marketing manager, copy chief, art director and media planner. When the account executive introduces a new client or product, or an account is renewed, a report is submitted to these departmental heads and a meeting is called. The new proposition is discussed, and the departmental heads disperse to consider ideas and prepare schemes. At the next meeting these ideas and schemes are discussed, and the campaign begins to take shape. After this the campaign is prepared for presentation to the client.

In some advertising agencies there is an overall *account planner* who integrates the work of departments and personnel. Working closely with the account executive, the account planner prepares the creative brief, and is associated with all the research, marketing, promotional strategy and day-to-day internal control of the campaign.

50. Review board

A refinement may be to have a review board comprising executives not involved in the campaign, who review the proposed campaign critically before it is presented to the client.

51. Presentation

This word has two meanings:

(a) the presentation of the campaign to the client with copy and visual ideas and the recommended media schedule;

(b) the presentation or appearance of the advertisement or brochure itself.

52. Copy

There are four meanings to the word 'copy' which are relevant here:

(a) the wording of an advertisement;

(b) the whole advertisement or any material for printing; that is, all the words and illustrations;

(c) a single copy of a newspaper or magazine;

(d) a duplicate, e.g. photocopy.

53. Billings

Strictly speaking, this means the value of space and airtime bookings, but it is more often taken to mean the total financial turnover of an agency.

54. Voucher

A voucher copy is a copy of the publication in which the advertisement has appeared, supplied by the publisher as proof of insertion. The person in charge of vouchers is called the voucher clerk. Sometimes only the advertisement and not the whole publication is sent to the client (or even by the publisher to the agency) and this is called a 'tear sheet'.

55. Media

It should be remembered that the word media is the plural of the word medium. The press is a medium, but radio and television are media. We refer to 'the media' and 'a medium'.

Progress test 4

1. Explain the legal precedent that 'the agency acts as principal'. (6)

2. What is the role of an advertising agency? (6–7)

3. What does 'recognition' mean, and how has this changed since 1979? (8–10)

4. Name the bodies representing different media owners which recognise advertising agencies. **(8)**

5. What is a media independent? **(14)**

6. How does an à la carte advertising agency differ from a full-service agency? **(19)**

7. Identify the different kinds of creative agencies. **(20–25)**

8. What service does a sponsorship agency provide for clients? **(25)**

9. Describe the responsibilities of the account executive. **(30)**

10. What is the importance of the contact report? **(31)**

11. Distinguish between the duties of the media planner and the media buyer. **(36, 40)**

12. What do the initials ABC, NRS, BARB and RAJAR stand for? **(37)**

13. What information is contained in the media schedule? **(39)**

14. How does the copywriter contribute to the creativity of an advertising campaign? **(41)**

15. Describe the work of the visualiser. **(43)**

16. How has computerisation revolutionised the work of advertising agency creative departments? **(43–45)**

17. Distinguish between the roles of the television producer and the television director. **(46)**

18. Explain how the plans board operates. **(49)**

19. Give the two meanings of 'presentation'. **(51)**

20. Give the four meanings of 'copy'. **(52)**

21. What is a voucher copy? **(54)**

5

Advertising media: above-the-line

INTRODUCTION AND DEFINITIONS

1. Variety of media and changing media scene

Advertising media consist of any means by which sales messages can be conveyed to potential buyers. The variety of media is immense in the 'North' (i.e. industrialised countries), but may be very limited in the 'South' (i.e. developing countries). In Britain, for instance, *Benn's Media Directory* lists over 12,000 publications. Almost anything can and has been used as an advertising medium – the sky, bus tickets, matchboxes, street litter bins, taxi cabs, parking meters, shopping bags and ball-point pens. Moreover, there are people who will try to exploit almost anything as an advertising medium, and it is necessary to consider the advertising value very carefully. All too easily, much money can be wasted on weak media, let alone rackets to do with spurious media of no advertising value. Media buying is therefore a skilled business, the object being to get the most effective advertising at the lowest cost.

Alvin Toffler, in his futurist books such as *Future Shock* and *The Third Wave*, had predicted in the 1980s the demassification of the media. The BBC could attract only 28 per cent and the ITV only 47 per cent of the viewing audience in 1993. Now there was competition with UK Gold, satellite and cable TV plus other uses of domestic TV sets. Cable also competed with BT as a supplier of telephone services. ITV advertisement revenue fell, and the inadequacy of licence fees even affected the BBC. Their funding problems were revealed by the hours and hours of repeats which encouraged viewers to subscribe to cable or buy a dish aerial.

The drift in popular newspaper readership was becoming so serious in mid-1993 that Rupert Murdoch spent £900,000 a week throughout the summer by cutting the cover price of the *Sun* from 25 pence to 20 pence. The monster circulations tumbled during the 1990s. Even the economic figure of half a million was lost by *The Times* and only the *Independent on Sunday* showed any significant rise, although the *Daily Mail* and *Mail On Sunday* did well in the mid-market. But the days of four to five million sales were gone. There was a 10 per cent fall in national newspaper circulations between 1986 and 1993, according to the editorial in *Marketing Week*, July 30 1993.

Magazines were experiencing some ups and downs. The famous three, *Woman*, *Woman's Own* and *Woman's Weekly*, launched sixty or more years ago, had met the onslaught of many journals with niche readerships as different as *She*, *Nova*, *Take a Break*, and *Hello*. The German owned *Bella* overtook *Woman's Own* in 1993 with sales of 1.1 million and a readership of 3.5 million. Deregulation of broadcasting programmes (listings) has halved the circulations of *Radio Times* and *TV Times* while permitting the entry of competitors such as *What's On TV* and *TV Quick*. The invasion of foreign women's magazines has eaten into the circulation of the traditional British ones, and new types of challenge by picture story journals about celebrities have made newsagents' shelves look very different. In addition specialist magazines covering classical music, pop music, computers, wildlife, gardening and travel have arrived. The BBC has become a leading publisher, with magazines about topics seen on TV.

Meanwhile, independent local radio has been extended to independent national radio with a third INR station launched in 1994. Classic FM has made serious inroads into BBC classical music audiences.

In London and the surrounding areas there are, at the time of writing, 66 independent commercial local radio stations. Many of the outlying ones can easily be heard in central London. By the time the next edition of this book appears, there will almost certainly be more stations on air, including those using the new digital technology.

The advertiser is thus confronted by diminishing popular media, many changes and new opportunities. Many of these developments occurred with the expansion of direct response marketing which exploits well targeted off-the-page advertisements, inserts of catalogues, and offers of catalogues on TV (e.g. British Gas). This uses many socio-demographic and life style means of targeting which encourage the growth of direct mail and catalogue selling.

2. Above-the-line and below-the-line

With the change in the recognition and commission system brought about by the Restrictive Trade Practices Act 1976 and the Office of Fair Trading ruling of 1979 (*see* 4: **8–10**) the terms 'above-the-line' and 'below-the-line' have lost much of their original significance. While the media independents continue to concentrate on above-the-line media, the creative agencies do not. Moreover, the early 1990s saw a recession in the use of above-the-line media, and a tremendous growth in the use of below-the-line media such as direct mail.

Originally, above-the-line meant the five media which paid commission to advertising agencies, namely *press, radio, television, outdoor* and *cinema*, and it is these which will be discussed in this chapter. The rest (which usually paid no commission and incurred on-cost percentages) were direct mail, exhibitions, point-of-sale display aids, print and sales literature and all kinds of miscellaneous media, referred to as below-the-line media (*see* Chapter 6). The bulk of service agency income is still derived from above-the-line media, and no doubt the two terms will remain a convenient means of distinguishing the different groups of media.

The terms above-the-line and below-the-line, although usually applied to agency and non-agency work, were actually created by Procter & Gamble to separate their different kinds of advertising.

3. Primary and secondary media

Sometimes confused with above-the-line and below-the-line, primary media are those which spearhead a campaign, and secondary are those which provide support. The choice of these media will depend on what is being advertised. Television could be a primary medium for a food product, outdoor supersites for a cigarette, direct mail for magazine subscriptions, a catalogue for a direct response or mail order house and posters on the London Underground for a London shoe shop. Sometimes, a primary medium may be chosen because it is not being used by a rival. One brewer may advertise on television and another may use posters. Secondary media will be those which back up the main thrust of the campaign. The media mix combines the fewest number of media necessary to gain the greatest impact and response.

THE PRESS

4. Importance of the press

As shown in 1: **11**, the press takes up 60 per cent of the total expenditure on above-the-line advertising in Britain. The press predominates in literate, industrial countries. It may be arguable that television has greater impact and realism, and it is true that the biggest spenders on advertising spend most of their money on TV, but the number of TV advertisers is relatively small and the amount of time available for television advertising is limited. The number of advertisers in the press runs into millions and the number of publications exceeds 12,000. It is not really a matter of saying which is best since there is no comparison in their users, usage or volume.

5. Press outside Britain

This situation may differ outside Britain for the following reasons.

(a) Size of country. Local or regional papers based on cities (as in Australia, Canada, Germany and the USA) may replace the national newspapers of Britain, largely for geographical or historical reasons. Britain is a compact country with good road, rail and air communications, and London has always been the capital. For these reasons a London-based national press developed in the nineteenth century.

However, changes have been taking place in the USA with the failure or merger of many famous city newspapers and bids for national circulation by the *Wall Street Journal* followed by the *New York Times* and the space-satellite-supported Garnett company with its *USA Today*.

(b) Extent of literacy. The circulation figures of journals, and the number of titles, is related to educational and literacy standards. A further problem will be multi-ethnic and multi-language situations which require publications either addressed to different ethnic groups or in different languages. Vernacular newspapers, since they appeal to sections of the community, inevitably have smaller circulations than those addressed to a nation as a whole. In Nigeria, for instance, where English-language newspapers have existed since colonial times, there are now newspapers in Hausa and Yoruba. There has also been an increase in the number of Nigerian newspapers.

(c) Purchasing power. In poorer countries, not even the educated and literate may be able to afford to buy newspapers and magazines. The volume of advertising may be small, newsprint will be costly to import, and the cover price will be high.

Note: It is interesting that in countries where newspapers are not widely used, e.g. Arab countries, television is regarded as the superior medium. This is less so in the West Indies where English is standard, and even less so in Hong Kong where some 100 Chinese dailies are published.

6. Characteristics of the press

The power and dominance of the press is explained by some of the following special characteristics.

(a) In-depth coverage and permanence. Both radio and television are ephemeral and usually brief, but newspapers and magazines can provide detailed reports which can be read, re-read and retained if required. This is true even though the life of a city newspaper may be only a few hours, but many publications survive for some time, and items can be cut out and kept. Magazines have a large pass-on readership, and are read in waiting rooms.

(b) Variety of subjects covered. Not only do newspapers represent class, political, religious, ethnic and language groups, but magazines represent every sort of special interest. This is perhaps where the press best demonstrates its strength because by selecting the right journals it is possible to reach particular and well-defined sections of the reading public. This cannot be done with mass media like radio, TV and posters.

(c) Mobility. Newspapers and magazines can be carried about and read almost anywhere, for example in the house, while travelling, at the place of work, in a waiting room or library.

(d) Results assessable. By using coupons, and by the additional use of 'keys' or codes which identify from which publication the coupon was clipped, it is possible to measure the pulling power and cost-effectiveness of different journals. Evaluation is possible by dividing the cost of space by the number of replies received. If a space cost £1,000 and produced 1,000 replies, each would cost £1. If the space cost only £500 but produced only 250 replies, the cost-per-reply would be £2 or double. Thus, the response or hit rate is most important. In the above example the lower cost is the more expensive, and the higher cost is the more economical.

(e) Statistics available. In industrialised countries, and increasingly in others, net sales are audited and readerships are researched so that a wealth of statistical information exists about a large number of newspapers and magazines. The media planner can confront the media salesman with computer calculations to justify his media schedule of recommended space and airtime bookings. (*See* 4: **36–9**.)

(f) Improved printing. The majority of newspapers and magazines are printed offset-litho (*see* Chapter 13). Picture quality, even in black and white, is nowadays very good since the dot screen used for offset-litho is usually nearly twice as fine as that formerly used for letterpress printing. Magazines printed by offset-litho are usually better printed than those produced by photogravure, halftones being produced more sharply and the paper being better finished.

The flexography process was adopted in 1989 by the *Daily Mail* group at their new plant in South East London, this being superior to offset-litho. One advantage of this process is that the printing ink does not dirty one's fingers.

7. Categories of press

There are so many different kinds of newspapers, magazines and other publications that a detailed analysis is necessary in order to appreciate their range and variety and to understand the different terms used.

In Britain we not only speak of advertising in the 'national press' but in which national newspapers. The British press is unique in appealing to particular social grades, whereas in other countries newspapers may appeal to particular religious or political interests or be printed in different languages and be addressed to different ethnic groups.

(a) National newspapers. Published daily in the morning or on Sundays, these are nowadays published in a major city (e.g. London) and distributed throughout the country. However, they are no longer printed in Fleet Street. New plants have been built in the Docklands area of East and South East London, while some newspapers are printed at strategically located plants in, say, Portsmouth.

There are now more national newspapers in Britain than there were a few years ago, largely because modern newspapers printed by web offset-litho and using computerised editorial techniques have replaced the labour-intensive letterpress process, making smaller-circulation newspapers economically viable and even profitable. The *Independent* and the *Independent on Sunday* have joined the national titles. These new newspapers are able to survive with circulations of around 400,000–600,000, whereas the minimum circulation for a newspaper printed by letterpress had to be two million if it was to be profitable. However, some of the quality dailies have been experiencing difficulty in maintaining the magic 400,000 and *The Independent* slipped badly in 1993. Greater competition, and higher cover prices, may be partly responsible, but the 1990s have seen dramatically falling circulations.

The Times may be Britain's best-known newspaper outside Britain, but its circulation is only about twice that of Nigeria's most popular daily, the *Daily Times* of Lagos, that is around 750,000.

Table 5.1 shows approximate circulations of Britain's 25 national dailies and Sundays, based on rounding off their Audit Bureau of Circulation figures.

Recent years have seen the growth of colour supplements or weekend magazines which compete with women's magazines for advertising. These include the *Independent Magazine*, the *Observer Magazine*, the *Sunday Times Magazine*, the *Telegraph Weekend*, *News/World* (*News of the World*), *Sunday Express Magazine*, *Sunday Mirror Magazine*, and *You* (*Mail on Sunday*). This has the effect of increasing the sale of Saturday editions which carry magazines.

Retailers, especially do-it-yourself suppliers, predominate in the top ten users of newspapers.

A significant change in national newspapers from the point of view of advertisers has been the availability of on-the-run (rather than pre-printed) colour which has deprived the big popular women's magazines (e.g. *Woman*, *Woman's Own*, *Woman's Weekly* and *Woman's Realm*) of a third of their advertising revenue.

Table 5.1 ABC circulation data, national newspapers – average circulations, 1998

Daily newspapers		Sunday newspapers	
Quality:		**Quality:**	
Daily Telegraph	1,067,984	Independent on Sunday	255,811
Financial Times	356,549	The Observer	402,314
The Guardian	394,614	Scotland on Sunday	122,926
The Independent	220,853	The Sunday Telegraph	836,232
The Scotsman	80,284	The Sunday Times	1,339,640
The Times	759,290		
Mid-market:		**Mid-market:**	
The Express	1,142,063	Express on Sunday	1,051,432
Daily Mail	2,325,523	The Mail on Sunday	2,242,651
Popular:		**Popular:**	
The Mirror	2,347,058	News of the World	4,232,935
Daily Record	674,854	Sunday Mirror	2,010,474
Daily Star	569,873	Sunday People	1,742,922
The Sun	3,694,565	Sunday Sport	248,467
Sporting:			
Racing Post	71,485		
London evening:			
Evening Standard	439,568		

Source: publishers' ABC declarations

(b) Regional newspapers. Outside London, about a hundred newspapers – mostly evenings – are published daily. In Northern Ireland, Scotland and Wales such regional dailies are virtually the national press for those parts of the UK. There are also a few regional Sunday newspapers. In addition, there are weekly papers covering one or more counties and often published in series with localised titles (e.g. the *Kent Messenger* series with 17 localised titles, the *Surrey Advertiser* series with 19 titles, or the *Packet* newspapers of Cornwall with 10 titles); town weeklies; and – in parts of London, for instance – suburban weeklies.

The regional (or provincial) press was nearly eclipsed after the Second World War by the cost of replacing its old letterpress printing machines. It had been built up by largely political newspapers of historical significance such as the famous Liberal *Mercuries* (e.g. *Leicester Mercury*) while the *Yorkshire Post's* owners used to be called Yorkshire Conservative Newspapers. The arrival of television helped some of the regional evenings which began to publish features about television and other home interests so that these papers became family reading and were able to attract retail and other consumer advertising. Mostly bought on the way home from work, they were taken into the home and read by other members of the household.

However, many regional weeklies were rescued by Woodrow Wyatt's initiative in introducing large American web-offset-litho presses which could be installed strategically to print a number of newspapers over a wide area. This led to colour printing a long time before Fleet Street succumbed to modern printing, followed by computerised photo-typesetting and the paperless newsroom.

In the late 1980s this was extended to the printing of some national news-papers at a number of outside London presses since newspapers such as the *Independent* had no presses of their own. For example, the News Centre at Portsmouth has huge Metroliner presses which run seven days a week, printing regional weeklies, free newspapers, magazines and the six editions a day of its own *News* series with editions for different parts of southern England.

However, there has been a falling off of newspaper sales. Fewer morning newspapers are home-delivered, and fewer people buy an evening as well as a morning newspaper. London, which used to have three evening papers, now has only one, the *Evening Standard*. The *Evening News*, which once sold one and a half million copies, has vanished.

(c) **Free newspapers.** The number of local newspapers delivered free of charge door-to-door trebled between 1980 and 1991, and weekly circulations vary between 30,000 and 300,000. The leading publishers are Thomson Regional Newspapers (81 titles), Northcliffe Newspapers (28 titles), United News-papers (50 titles), Reed International Newspapers (67 titles) and Westminster Press (38 titles). It is interesting that the publishers of free newspapers are (and mostly were originally) publishers of paid-for newspapers. It may be asked why give away a newspaper when it could be sold at a newsagents shop? The answer is rather like that of the controlled circulation magazines (*see* **8c**). A free newspaper attracts greater advertising support than a paid-for one because of its saturation door-to-door distribution through-out an urban area. In particular it attracts domestic advertising such as that for retailers, estate agents, and car dealers which is usually regular advertising. This is a phenomenon of British publishing and one of the reasons why the press is the leading advertising medium. In some large towns two or three free newspapers are delivered to every house every week.

(d) **Consumer magazines.** This term is somewhat loosely applied to popular magazines sold by newsagents. Among them are the numerous women's magazines, many with multi-million circulations. Women's magazines range from long-established ones which have been published for up to 60 years and which loyal readers tend to read for a lifetime, to ones with more sophisticated or special age-group readerships. American, Canadian, French, German and

Table 5.2 NRS readership of selected consumer magazines

Chat	1,731,000
Cosmopolitan	1,763,000
GQ	798,000
House & Garden	1,323,000
Radio Times	4,613,000
TV Times	4,198,000
What's on TV	3,904,000
Woman's Own	3,321,000

Note: These are *readership* figures. Those in Tables 5.1 and 5.3 are circulation figures

Spanish publishers have entered the British market with English versions of foreign or continental magazines often referred to as 'clones'. Other consumer magazines include the very big circulation *Radio Times* and *TV Times*. With the deregulation of programme listings, the *Radio Times* and *TV Times* (while retaining copyright) lost their monopoly so that newspapers and other magazines are now permitted to publish radio and TV programme information in advance. This has also led to rival listings magazines such as the German-published *TV Quick* and *What's on TV*. These weekly full-colour magazines print BBC and ITV television programmes, satellite TV programmes, and BBC, ILR and INR radio programmes.

The January–May 1993 figures of the National Readership Survey resulted from the introduction of a new interviewing technique and the increase of the sample from 28,000 to 35,000. Over the previous year face-to-face interviews were phased out in favour of the Computer Assisted Personal Interview (CAPI). This gave a more accurate measurement of the lesser titles included in the survey, and cut the time lag between collection of data and its publication. The figures showed that 61.8 per cent of adults (28 million) read a national daily newspaper, and that this rose to 69.3 per cent for Sundays. The 1997 circulation figures for magazines were as shown in Table 5.2.

Consumer magazines continue to prosper, particularly the up-market titles, as shown by the figures for January to June 1997 in Table 5.3.

Titles come and go. Most of the leaders have existed for up to 60 years or so. Newer ones like *Elle, Marie Claire, Bella* and *Hello* are now big-selling well-established British versions of foreign magazines.

The one category of magazine which has never succeeded in Britain is the news magazine, unlike the American *Time*. The topic which has spawned the largest number of new magazines in recent years has been the computer, and these range over consumer special interest, trade, technical and professional journals.

(e) Special interest magazines. These journals are also to be seen in news-agents shops and on news-stands, but they cover special interests such as

Table 5.3 ABC circulation data, consumer magazines – average circulations, 1997

Bella	767,698	House Beautiful	297,586
Chat	497,044	Marie Claire	435,006
Company	277,825	Prima	501,154
Cosmopolitan	441,563	Radio Times	1,400,270
Country Life	46,464	Reader's Digest	1,492,549
Country Living	173,783	She	236,093
Elle	210,067	Take a Break	1,447,950
Esquire	92,907	TV Quick	819,056
Good Housekeeping	440,655	TV Times	892,760
GQ	135,563	What's on TV	1,702,184
Harpers & Queen	92,492	Woman's Own	712,494
Hello	574,585	Woman's Weekly	663,384
House & Garden	167,884		

gardening, photography, philately, Hi-fi, computers, motoring, house-buying, health and beauty, and many sports, pastimes and hobbies.

(f) Trade journals. Mainly addressed to trades such as butchers, bakers, chemists and other retailers, they are also published for the larger retailers such as department stores, supermarkets and large mixed retailers.

(g) Technical journals. Sometimes confused with the 'trade press', technical journals are produced for the technical specialists in various industries.

(h) Professional journals. Here we have another group of journals specially edited for professionals such as doctors, teachers, lawyers or architects.

(i) Directories and yearbooks. These annual or periodical volumes can be valuable advertising media, and *Yellow Pages* business telephone directories are familiar world-wide. Some directories are indispensable and because constant reference is made to them they can be useful advertising media. A typical example is *Advertisers Annual*.

8. Methods of distribution

Newspapers and magazines reach their readers by different methods, and the value of a journal as an advertising medium may be influenced by the method of distribution and the effect this may have. The main methods are as follows.

(a) Retail distribution by home delivery, newsagent or street vendor, or in certain other shops, e.g. women's magazines on sale in supermarkets or philately magazines in stamp dealers. Vending machines are also used to sell newspapers.

This form of distribution has become less popular for two reasons: high cover prices and large weekly bills, and the imposition of delivery charges.

(b) Subscription, the journal being subscribed to and delivered by post. This is popular with business magazines.

(c) Controlled circulation. Many trade and technical journals are mailed free of charge to a combination of selected readers and ones who have requested copies. By this method it is possible to obtain better penetration of a market than by journals which rely on subscriptions.

Sometimes a new trade or technical journal will be launched as a controlled circulation journal, but once established it may be sold on a subscription and retail basis with a limited number of free copies. This has happened with *Direct Response*, *Marketing Week* and *PR Week*.

(d) Free circulation. Whether distributed in the street like magazines addressed to office workers and carrying advertisements for office jobs, or newspapers of domestic interest delivered door-to-door, free magazines and newspapers have become numerous in Britain. One successful form of free newspaper is the kind which concentrates on property news and advertisements.

9. Advantages of the press

Certain advantages of the press as an advertising medium are evident from what has been discussed already and from other characteristics. They may be summarised as follows.

(a) The press is one of the cheapest means of reaching a large number of unknown or unidentified prospective buyers, whether in town, region, county or even overseas.

(b) Advertisements can be inserted quickly, compared with the time required for making commercials for television or designing and printing posters. An advertisement could be inserted in a newspaper virtually overnight. Classified (small linage advertisements) are often sold by telephone.

(c) Response can be achieved by means of coupons, or the giving of telephone and fax numbers, email and website addresses. This can be further encouraged by Freepost and Freefone plus credit card facilities.

(d) Press advertising can be targeted at certain people by using the newspapers or magazines read by them.

(e) Newspapers and magazines have the capacity to accept a large number of advertisements compared with the limited time available on television or radio.

(f) Press advertisements can be re-read and retained, and some publications such as magazines have very long lives, being kept, filed or passed on to other readers.

(g) A number of offset-litho printed nationals and regionals offer colour, while the *Observer, Sunday Times, Sunday Telegraph, Mail on Sunday* and *News of the World* and other Saturday and Sunday newspapers have their colour supplements or magazines.

(h) Some publishers encourage enquiries by use of reader-service coupons or cards which make it unnecessary to clip advertisements and write to advertisers individually.

(i) Advertisements for particular products or services are often grouped together so that it is economical for each advertiser to buy only a small space.

10. Disadvantages of the press

All media have their merits and demerits, and while the press dominates in literate countries, it does have its weaknesses, as summarised below.

(a) Short life. A daily or Sunday newspaper is unlikely to survive for more than a day, and in some cases the reading life of a newspaper may be exhausted in a few hours, as when newspapers are read on the way to and from work.

(b) Poorly printed. Web-offset and flexography printing have brought about better printing standards in world media, especially of photographs because of the finer dot halftone screen used.

Nevertheless, two problems remain: the poor quality of newsprint, and the speed with which multi-million circulation newspapers such as the *Sun* have to be printed.

(c) Passive medium. An effort has to be made to read press advertisements, unlike cinema, radio and TV advertisements which have captive audiences. Advertisements in the press have to compete with the editorial for attention and interest, whereas cinema and broadcast advertising does not occur at the same time as the programme.

(d) Static medium. The press advertisement lacks the realism of sound, movement and often the colour of TV or cinema commercials, and the sound of radio advertising.

(e) Badly presented. Advertisements may be massed together so that they may be overlooked, unless an effort is made to find them. With most other media each advertisement is presented individually and can be absorbed one at a time.

(f) The mistake is sometimes made – perhaps because it suits the economics of agency media buying – of taking whole page spaces. In broadsheet newspapers they resemble posters and are too unwieldy for the reader to cope with and absorb. A smaller space can often be more effective. Meanwhile, the tabloid format is replacing the broadsheets of many newspapers, and a whole page ad in a tabloid is more readable. But full pages are often a bad aspect of media buying since it is obviously more economic (for the agency!) to buy full pages, although wasteful for the advertiser who does not understand the agency's more profitable tactic. The advertising manager has to remember his responsibility as buyer.

(g) Unemployment and the recession have affected traditional ways of buying newspapers. With fewer people travelling to work, and buying their morning paper at the station, fewer people buy a paper at all or the same paper regularly. They may buy only occasionally or because they are attracted by a particular editorial feature. Newspapers may thus rely on 'whim' purchases which can make ABC and NRS figures less reliable.

(h) There is all-day news coverage on TV and radio which is more up-to-date than printed news can be.

(i) Cover prices are high and it is a long time since the chief source of revenue was advertising; the cover price was not only negligible but was subsidised by the advertising. Even so, the attempt to compete by cutting the cover price was not very successful when the *Sun* reduced its summer 1993 price from 25p to 20p and the price of *The Times* was experimentally cut from 45p to 30p in parts of Kent. The Henley Centre's *Media Futures* study showed that readers who have their papers home delivered are ignorant of the price.

The *Daily Telegraph* suffered only a temporary fall in circulation, and *The Times* put on 90,000 extra sales so that its October 1993 figure rose to 444,503. In spite of the *Independent*'s relaunch in two sections with colour and a price increase from 45p to 50p in October 1993 it held its circulation at 332,435.

(j) Aliteracy (which has spread to Britain from the USA) is affecting newspaper sales since younger people, although literate, find reading an arduous activity. For them reading is not a pleasure, and this applies particularly to the reading of AB broadsheets.

(k) The sheer volume of reading provided by the Sundays with their extra sections and magazines eats into Monday reading, which has become the lowest selling day for newspapers, especially the quality dailies.

RADIO

11. Development of radio advertising in Britain

In many parts of the world radio advertising accompanied the introduction of radio, and has been a long-established medium, but this was not so in

Britain where it is comparatively new. Before the Second World War, the only commercial radio listened to in Britain were English-language programmes transmitted from continental stations in France, Holland and Luxembourg, of which only Radio Luxembourg returned after the war until it finally closed down in early 1993. In the 1960s there were some off-shore pirate radio stations, but they were made illegal under the Marine Broadcasting Offences Act 1967. Their popularity, and the success of commercial television since the 1950s, encouraged the setting up of Independent Local Radio (ILR), and with the Sound Broadcasting Act 1972 the Independent Television Authority (the commercial counterpart to the BBC) became the Independent Broadcasting Authority (IBA). By the end of 1984, about 50 ILR stations were operating. Today there is a great variety of commercial and non-commercial radio stations, and there are ones aimed at special interest audiences. Under the Radio Authority, commercial radio promise considerable development in the future. Two important developments are the sponsorship of programmes and the setting up of three national commercial radio stations.

The Radio Authority (RA) began its regulatory and licensing role on 1 January 1991, when the Broadcasting Act 1990 came into force. It is one of the three bodies which replaced the IBA.

The chairman, deputy chairman and other members are appointed by the Secretary of State for Culture, Media and Sport. They are supported by full-time and part-time staff.

The RA licenses and regulates independent radio services, otherwise known as commercial radio. These comprise national, local, cable and satellite services, and the national FM subcarrier. They also license restricted services; for example, 'special event' radio and highly localised permanent services such as hospital and student radio.

The RA is responsible for monitoring the obligations of its licensees as required by the Broadcasting Acts 1990 and 1996. It has three main tasks:

(a) plan frequencies;

(b) appoint licensees with a view to broadening listener choice and enforcing ownership rules;

(c) regulate programming and advertising.

It is required, after consultation, to publish codes to which its licensees must adhere. These cover engineering, programmes, advertising and sponsorship. The RA can apply sanctions to licensees who break the rules. Sanctions include broadcast apologies and corrections, fines and the shortening or revocation of licences. The RA plays an active role in the discussion and formulation of policies affecting the commercial radio industry and its listeners.

Licensees pay annual fees to the RA, and fees are charged to those applying for licences. This is the RA's only source of income, and covers all its operating costs.

Table 5.4 RAJAR quarterly listening summary

	Survey period ending 28 March 1999		
	Weekly reach %	Average hours per listener	Share of listening listening %
All radio	89	22.4	100
All commercial radio	66	14.4	47.5
All BBC radio	64	15.8	50.3
All ILR	56	13.8	38.6
Classic FM	13	6.8	4.3
Atlantic 252	7	4.3	1.5
BBC Radio 1	23	8.7	9.8

Weekly reach: Percentage of UK adults (15+) population listening for at least five minutes in an average week. Average hours: Total hours of listening in a week, averaged across all listeners. Share of listening: Percentage of total listening time accounted for in the UK.

Source: RAJAR/Ipsos-RSL

A feature of commercial radio in Britain has been the growth of *split frequency* broadcasting, where one station appeals to two types of audience on different frequencies. This has attracted larger radio audiences, and enabled advertisers to target audiences more precisely, both geographically and demographically. Examples are the two London stations LBC 1152 (AM) and News Direct 97.3 (FM); Southern Sound Classic Hits (FM) and South Coast Radio (AM), and Invicta (FM) and Invicta Supergold (AM).

Not surprisingly, radio advertising had not until recently attained in Britain the importance it enjoys elsewhere in the world, one reason being its newness, and another its localised character. In addition, local commercial radio has to compete with national and local BBC stations which do not carry advertisements.

With the successful launch of Classic FM in 1992, Branson's Virgin 1215 pop radio in 1993, and Talk Radio in 1994, national commercial radio attracts national advertisers far more effectively than Radio Luxembourg was ever able to do, even in its heyday when the BBC did not broadcast popular programmes.

Audience surveys are published quarterly by Radio Joint Audience Research and those published in March 1999 showed that independent local radio (ILR) had increased its weekly reach to 56 per cent of the total listening audience (see Table 5.4). The research is based on the percentage of adults listening for at least five minutes in a week. Audience figures for the first of the new national commercial radio stations reached 4.5 million listeners a week, representing more than 10 per cent of the whole UK population. In London, Jazz FM was the capital's fastest growing radio station, its adult audience growing by 26 per cent. These figures are encouraging for advertisers who are apt to be sceptical about radio advertising yet have to comply with tighter budgets.

12. Importance of radio advertising outside Britain

The importance of radio as an advertising medium is best looked at from an international standpoint, where its impact is greatest, before returning to the British scene. In such world-wide terms, the nature and value of the medium can be summarised as follows.

(a) Cheapness. It costs little to own and run a radio set, especially with the introduction of the battery-operated transistorised portable radio, even if batteries are sometimes expensive in poorer developing countries. Clockwork-driven radios are increasingly popular in countries where mains electricity is not universally available. However, the purchase price is usually higher than mains radios. Radios are often placed in public places, and in some countries rediffusion services at low rentals are popular. In addition, it is cheaper to produce a radio commercial than a TV commercial – in fact, the former can merely be read out as a spot announcement.

(b) Penetration. Provided the signal is sufficiently powerful, radio can reach large audiences over great distances, and is a means of reaching people who may have access to no other media. Moreover, where there are multi-language and multi-ethnic societies, radio messages can be broadcast in different languages as in Belgium, Israel, Kenya and Zambia. In Britain, commercial stations such as Sunrise (Asian), London Greek and London Turkish broadcast both in English and their respective languages. This applies to advertising commercials, as well as news and entertainment content. Radio can also reach illiterates who cannot read the newspapers, while battery-operated and clockwork receivers and car radios overcome lack of electricity. These are all advantages which help to make radio popular in developing countries.

(c) Transmission times. Radio programmes are usually broadcast for many hours of the day, often round the clock.

(d) Human voice and music. The use of sound, whether vocal or musical, makes it a live medium compared with passive and static media such as the press, outdoor, print, direct mail and point-of-sale displays. Sound effects can also be used.

(e) Does not require sole attention. Unlike reading a newspaper or watching television, radio does not demand the listener's sole attention. He or she can do other things at the same time, from working to driving a car, and radio can be listened to in numerous locations or situations.

(f) Companionship. Radio is often listened to as a form of companionship.

The above are general characteristics, but there are more specific ones which apply to radio advertising in Britain.

13. Characteristics of British radio

These relate to a situation where radio has to be compared with existing, and often much longer established, media, in a country where the conditions are usually the opposite to those in developing countries. People are literate, the press is widely read, and most people have electricity. In these very different circumstances, radio advertising has to be seen as an important medium for quite different reasons.

(a) **It can be local**. Although there are large advertisers who place radio commercials on a large number of stations, networking as they do on television, and there are now INR stations, it is also an excellent medium for local advertisers, competing with the regional press.

(b) **It can be addressed to different audiences**. People of different kinds listen to radio at different times of the day, and commercials can be broadcast accordingly. There are those who like to listen to radio at breakfast time for a time-check, others who listen to their car radios when driving to and from work, housewives who listen while doing their housework, factory workers who listen while they work, and young people who listen to pop music at night when their parents are watching television. The medium thus becomes attractive to advertisers who wish to reach certain audiences, and such audiences are more distinct than occurs with television. There is also split-frequency radio with the same local station broadcasting to different classes of listener.

(c) **In addition to television**. Moreover, for many people radio can be listened to when they cannot watch television. Its mobility, whether about the house, out-of-doors or in the car, makes radio more accessible than most other media. Radios go almost everywhere – on building sites, on the milk float, in the car park attendant's kiosk, on the beach, and on foot when people wear headphones and a Walkman set.

14. Resistance to radio advertising

There has been a certain amount of reluctance by some British advertisers to use radio largely because it cannot be seen and physically evaluated like other media. This could be a foolhardy prejudice because the versatility of radio is remarkable. It is perhaps less easy to measure than other media, but as shown in Table 5.4 RAJAR quarterly figures are impressive. The CRCA represents all the RA-appointed stations. Although radio advertising (ILR) has been available in Britain for 20 years it is probably Britain's most underrated medium.

15. UK independent radio stations

At the time of writing, stations licensed by the RA are as listed in Table 5.5.

16. Digital radio

This is the latest and most sophisticated development in radio technology. It is a new transmission system which provides the listener with bundles of audio services called multiplexes. The main advantage, and benefit to the listener is that it gives unparalleled clear reception. Being digital, it can also

Table 5.5 Stations licensed by the Radio Authority

NATIONAL		
Classic FM		
Talk Radio		
Virgin 1215		

SCOTLAND

Radio Borders	The Borders
Central FM	Stirling
Clyde 1 FM	Glasgow
Clyde 2	Glasgow
Forth AM	Edinburgh
Forth FM	Edinburgh
Heartland FM	Pitlochry & Aberfeldy
Isles FM	Western Isles
Kingdom FM	Fife
Lochbroom FM	Ullapool
Moray Firth Radio	Inverness
NECR	Inverurie
Nevis Radio	Fort William
Northsound One	Aberdeen
Northsound Two	Aberdeen
Oban FM	Oban
96.3 QFM	Paisley
Scot FM	Central Scotland. Regional
SIBC	Shetland
South West Sound	Stranraer, Dumfries & Galloway
Radio Tay AM	Dundee/Perth
Tay FM	Dundee/Perth
Waves Radio Peterhead	Peterhead
West FM	Ayr
West Sound AM	Ayr

NORTHERN IRELAND

City Beat 96.7	Belfast
Cool FM	Northern Ireland
Downtown Radio	Northern Ireland
Gold Beat 828	Cookstown
Heart Beat 1521	Craigavon
Q102.9 FM	Londonderry

WALES

Radio Ceredigion	Ceredigion
Champion FM	Caernarfon
Coast FM	North Wales Coast
Radio Maldwyn	Montgomeryshire
Red Dragon FM	Cardiff/Newport
Swansea Sound	Swansea
Touch Radio	Cardiff & Newport
Valleys Radio	Heads of South Wales Valleys
The Wave 96.4 FM	Swansea

ENGLAND

Active 107.5 FM	Havering
96.3 Aire FM	Leeds
Alpha 103.2	Darlington
107.8 Arrow FM	Hastings
Asian Sound Radio	East Lancashire
B97 Chiltern FM	Bedford
The Bay	Morecambe Bay
103.4 The Beach	Great Yarmouth & Lowestoft
Beacon FM	Wolverhampton, Shrewsbury & Telford
FM 102 – The Bear	Stratford-upon-Avon
The Breeze	Southend & Chelmsford

Table 5.5 (*continued*)

96.4 FM BRMB	Birmingham	936/1161 AM Classic Gold	Wiltshire
Broadland 102	Great Yarmouth & Norwich	954/1530 Classic Gold	Hereford & Worcester
Cambridge Café Radio	Cambridge	Classic Gold 1260	Bristol & Bath
95.8 Capital FM	Greater London	Classic Gold 1278/1530	Bradford & Huddersfield
Capital Gold (1152)	Birmingham	Classic Gold 1332 AM	Peterborough
Capital Gold (1170 & 1557)	South Hampshire	Classic Gold 1359	Coventry
Capital Gold (1242 & 603)	Maidstone, Medway & East Kent	Classic Gold 1431/1485	Reading, Basingstoke & Andover
Capital Gold (1323 & 945)	Sussex	Classic Gold 1557	Northampton
Capital Gold (1548)	Greater London	Connect FM	Wellingborough
107.5 Cat FM	Cheltenham	County Sound 1476 AM	Guildford
Centre fm	South-East Staffordshire	RTL Country 1035 AM	Greater London
Century 105	North West England. Regional	Crash FM	Merseyside
Century 106	East Midlands. Regional	106 CTFM Radio	Canterbury
Century Radio	North East. Regional	Delta Radio 97.1 FM	Haslemere
CFM	Carlisle	Dune FM	Southport
CFM	West Cumbria	96.4 The Eagle	Guildford
Channel 103 FM	Jersey	Eleven Seventy	High Wycombe
Channel Travel Radio	M20 & Kent Channel Ports	Essex FM	Southend & Chelmsford
Chelmer FM	Chelmsford	Fame 1521	Reigate & Crawley
Cheltenham Radio	Cheltenham	5 Valleys Radio	Stroud
Chiltern FM	Luton	FLR 107.3	Lewisham
Choice FM	Birmingham	Freeway Radio	Hinckley & South West Leicestershire
Choice FM	Brixton	Fox FM	Oxford & Banbury
Radio City 96.7	Liverpool	Galaxy 101	Severn Estuary. Regional
Classic Gold Amber	Great Yarmouth & Norwich	Galaxy 102	Manchester
Classic Gold Amber	Suffolk	Galaxy 105	Yorkshire. Regional
Classic Gold GEM	Nottingham/Derby	Gemini AM	Exeter/Torbay
Classic Gold WABC	Wolverhampton, Shrewsbury & Telford	Gemini FM	Exeter/Torbay
		97.4 Gold Radio	Shaftesbury
Classic Gold 774	Gloucester/ Cheltenham	GWR FM	Bristol & Bath
		GWR FM	Swindon & West Wiltshire
Classic Gold 792/828	Luton/Bedford	Hallam FM	South Yorkshire
		100.7 Heart FM	West Midlands. Regional
Classic Gold 828	Bournemouth		
Classic Gold	Swindon & West	Heart 106.2	Greater London

Table 5.5 (continued)

102.7 Hereward FM	Peterborough	Minster FM	York
FM 103 Horizon	Milton Keynes	Mix 96	Aylesbury
Huddersfield FM	Huddersfield	Neptune Radio	Dover & Folkestone
Invicta FM	Maidstone, Medway & East Kent	News Direct 97.3 FM	Greater London
Island FM	Guernsey	Northants 96	Northampton
Isle of Wight Radio	Isle of Wight	Oak FM	Loughborough
Jazz FM 100.4	North West England. Regional	96.6 Oasis FM	St Albans & Watford
		Ocean FM	South Hampshire
Jazz FM 102.2	Greater London	Orchard FM	Yeovil & Taunton
KCBC	Kettering	Oxygen 107.9 FM	Oxford
107.6 Kestrel FM	Basingstoke	Peak 107 FM	Chesterfield
Key 103	Manchester	Piccadilly Radio 1152 AM	Manchester
KFM	Tunbridge Wells & Sevenoaks	Pirate FM102	Cornwall
Kiss 100 FM	Greater London	Plymouth Sound AM	Plymouth
Kix 96	Coventry		
KL.FM 96.7	King's Lynn	Plymouth Sound FM	Plymouth
Lantern FGM	Barnstaple	Power FM	South Hampshire
LBC 1152	Greater London	Premier Radio	Greater London
Leicester Sound	Leicester	The Pulse	Bradford & Huddersfield
963/972 AM	Greater London		
Liberty Radio		Q103 FM	Cambridge & Newmarket
Lincs FM	Lincoln		
1458 Lite AM	Manchester	Quay West Radio	West Somerset
London Greek Radio	North London	RAM FM	Derby
London Turkish Radio	North London	Red Rose 999	Preston & Blackpool
		Rock FM	Preston & Blackpool
Magic 828	Leeds	Rutland Radio	Rutland & Stamford
Magic 1152	Newcastle	Sabras	Leicester
Magic 1161 AM	Humberside	Severn Sound	Gloucester/
Magic (1170)	Teesside		Cheltenham
Magic 1548	Liverpool	SGR Colchester	Colchester
Magic AM	South Yorkshire	SGR FM	Ipswich & Bury St
Radio Mansfield	Mansfield & Ashfield		Edmunds
Marcher Gold	Wrexham & Chester	Signal FM	Stockport
Medway FM	Medway Towns	Signal One	Stoke-on-Trent
Mellow 1557	Tendring	Signal Two	Stoke-on-Trent
Melody/Magic 105.4 FM	Greater London	Silk FM	Macclesfield
		Southern FM	East Sussex
Mercia FM	Coventry	Sovereign Radio	Eastbourne
Mercury FM	Reigate & Crawley	Spectrum	Greater London
Metro FM	Tyne & Wear	International	
MFM 97.1	Wirral	Spire FM	Salisbury
MFM 103.4	Wrexham & Chester	Spirit FM	Chichester, Bognor
Millennium Radio	Thamesmead		Regis & Littlehampton

Table 5.5 (*continued*)

Star FM	Slough, Windsor & Maidenhead	Independent Radio News
		Lucas Media
97.2 Stray FM	Harrogate	Metro Networks (UK) Ltd
Sun FM	Sunderland	Sportsmedia Broadcasting
Sunrise FM	Bradford	

SATELLITE SERVICES

Sunrise Radio	Greater London	Asda FM	National in-store radio
Sunshine 855	Ludlow	
Surf 107	Brighton	Radio Asia Canada International
Ten 17	Harlow	Asian Sound Radio (Satellite) Ltd
TFM	Teesside	Channel 7 Europe
107.8 FM Thames Radio	Kingston-upon-Thames	CMR – Country Music Radio for Europe
Thanet Local Radio	Thanet	Costcutter Satellite Radio
Trax FM	Bassetlaw	EKR – European Klassik Rock
96 Trent FM	Nottingham/Derby	EKR – Night Tracks
2CR FM	Bournemouth	FEM FM/BHS Radio
2-TEN FM	Reading, Basingstoke & Andover	Gfm
		Homebase FM
Vibe FM	South of England. Regional	MBC FM Ltd
		The Network
96.9 Viking FM	Humberside	Trans World Radio – Europe (TWR)
Virgin 105.8	Greater London	United Christian Broadcasters (UCR)
The Wave 96.5	Blackpool	World Radio Network (WRN)
Wave 105 FM	Solent Area. Regional	

CABLE SERVICES

Wessex FM	Weymouth & Dorchester	BCB	Community radio, Bradford
Wey Valley Radio	Alton	Birmingham BHBN
107.2 Wire FM	Warrington	Castle fm
102.4 Wish FM	Wigan	CRMK	Community radio, Milton Keynes
107.7 The Wolf	Wolverhampton	Cruise FM	Salisbury, Andover & Romsey
Wyvern FM	Hereford & Worcester	Gemini AM	33–35-year-olds
Xfm	Greater London	Gemini FM	33–35-year-olds
Radio XL 1296 AM	Birmingham	Lite FM
Yorkshire Coast Radio	Scarborough	Max FM	Southampton, Eastleigh & Winchester
Yorkshire Dales Radio	Yorkshire Dales with Skipton	Music Choice Europe

NEWS SERVICES

AA Roadwatch		Radio Phoenix	Hospital, Neath
Bloomberg Information Radio		Town FM	North London
Bloomberg Radio Network		Radio Verulam	Community, West Herts
Unique Business News		Radio Victory Ltd
Unique Entertainment News		

broadcast data services, such as electronic publishing, road traffic and Internet-type information.

In 1998 only one organisation submitted an application for the first national commercial digital multiplex licence. The applicant, Digital One Ltd, was awarded the licence in October 1998. The company is owned by GWR Digital Radio Ltd, NTL Digital Radio Ltd and Talk Radio UK Ltd.

Digital radio has been described by technology experts as equivalent to the invention of television. RA chairman Sir Peter Gibbings, commenting on the award of the licence, described the technology as being capable of transforming radio listening.

With an air date of October 1999, Digital One is a 24-hours a day station, with a total of ten broadcasting streams. These are shown in Table 5.6.

The RA's allocation of digital licences took into account its plans to establish local digital multiplexes in the main population centres of most regions in the UK. A further tier of region-wide digital services in six regions was planned, taking the licence award schedule to the year 2001.

Table 5.6 Digital One broadcasting streams

Classic FM	Classical music
Virgin Radio	Contemporary rock-oriented music
Talk Radio	Listener-led debate, discussions and interviews
Classic Gold Rock	Hits and most popular classic rock
Soft AC	Female-biased service
Teen & Chart Hits	Mainstream chart hits
Club Dance	Dance and classic genres
Plays, books, productions, comedy	
Rolling News	World, national and regional
Sports Channel	Commentary, comment and coverage

17. Airtime buying

A number of specialist agencies buy airtime for clients, but so do many media independents and general advertising agencies which have AIRC recognition. A typical specialist marketing company is the Radio Advertising Bureau which provides a planning service through Sound Planning.

TELEVISION

18. Television advertising in Britain

Since the 1950s television has been a major advertising medium in Britain, but from 1991 all forms of broadcasting were revolutionised by the Broadcasting Act 1990. This was not the only change in broadcasting because cable television had been gaining a foothold in previous years, Sky satellite television (both by dish and cable) was stealing audiences from the BBC in 1990, taking over the ill-fated British Satellite Broadcasting.

The Broadcasting Bill was debated in Parliament in 1990, and was based on the White Paper, *Broadcasting in the 90s: Competition, Choice and Quality*, published on 8 November 1988. Its controversial proposals were the replacement of ITV (the commercial stations) by regional Channel 3 with reduced public service obligations, no requirements to produce networked programmes, and station contracts (subject to suitability tests) to be auctioned instead of being appointed. A fifth channel was proposed which would be funded by advertising, sponsorship and subscription. The BBC licence fee was to be replaced by subscriptions. The IBA and the Cable Authority were to be combined in a new Independent Television Commission and regulated by 'light touch'. Commercial radio was to have its own Radio Authority. There were many other proposals which were debated before the bill received the Royal Assent at the end of 1990 with effect in 1991. However, the industry still refers to 'ITV'. The fifth channel eventually went on air in 1997.

The result of the new Act was chaotic in some respects, and as a result of bidding competitively for licences some good TV companies such as Thames and TV-am lost. But there were innovations such as the sponsorship of programmes, which helped TV contractors who needed extra revenue. Modern TV has become very expensive to run, and many programmes are now made by outside producers. Carlton Television won the licence for Channel 3; Thames survived as a company, and now creates and produces television programmes in great variety.

CAM and LCCI students are recommended to obtain copies of the codes of practice and programme sponsorship rules from the Independent Television Commission and the Radio Authority, whose addresses are given in Appendix 1.

Some examples of sponsored TV programmes and their sponsors have been PowerGen and Legal & General Insurance (weather forecasts), Soccer World Cup (National Power), Rugby World Cup (Sony), *Rumpole* (Croft port), *Inspector Morse* (Beamish stout), *Maigret* (Kronenbourg lager), *Wish You Were Here* (Barclaycard), *Darling Buds of May* (Tetley Tea), *Hercule Poirot* (AEG) and *Taggart* (Strathmore spring water). Radio has seen the sponsorship of Virgin 1215's chart show being sponsored by the Canadian brewer Labatt.

Some interesting surveys revealed changing attitudes towards television. In a report published by the IBA in 1990, 80 per cent of viewers (in a sample of 1,170 adults) wanted to see more recently released films (which was shown by the popularity of Sky Movies in a later survey). Two-thirds of viewers wanted more nature and wildlife programmes, and half thought there should be more adult education, plays, drama and comedy. Only a

Table 5.7 Milestones in UK television

March 1930	The first transmission of 30-line TV with synchronised audio
November 1936	The BBC launches the first high-definition television service
May 1937	BBC television's first outside broadcast: the coronation of King George VI
June 1946	The BBC resumes television broadcasts, following its close-down during the Second World War
September 1955	The launch of ITV, Independent Television
June 1962	Telstar provides the first satellite transmission from the USA
April 1964	The BBC launches BBC2, the first 625-line television service
June 1966	Television pictures transmitted live from the moon
July 1967	The BBC launches its first regular colour transmissions on BBC2
November 1969	BBC1 and ITV begin colour transmissions
November 1982	Channel 4 launched
February 1989	Sky satellite television launched
March 1997	Channel 5 launched
July 1998	The launch of ONdigital television
December 1998	Digital terrestrial television launched in the UK

third wanted more international news, only a quarter more national news. Half of those interviewed wanted fewer soap operas (in line with the diminished popularity of soaps like *Dynasty* and *Dallas* in the USA), while two-fifths were opposed to chat, game and quiz shows.

On the same day the Institute of Practitioners in Advertising reported in *Attitudes to Television in 1989* that viewing figures were decreasing, and that advertisers were alarmed because ITV attracted down-market and older viewers while BBC 1 attracted younger, more upmarket people. Significantly, a report on Sky satellite television showed that it attracted down-market viewers. Trends seem to suggest that television is mostly watched by those with the least spending power, which is bad news for advertisers, but also for commercial television companies which are funded by advertising revenue. Against this has been the complaint in recent years that the Government has bought so much airtime (e.g. to promote privatisation share issues) that commercial advertisers have been deprived of airtime. In the current reality, this state of affairs has not materialised. Advertisers seem to be doing as well out of television as ever.

The nature of advertisers on TV has changed over the years. While many FMCGs such as detergents, drinks, pet foods, toiletries and confectionery are still advertised on television they no longer dominate as was the case, for instance, with the 'whiter than white' detergent wars. In spite of the reports mentioned above, leading TV advertisers in the 1990s have included British Telecom, Transco Gas, building societies, insurance companies, banks, fast food restaurants, cars, airlines, holiday venues such as Cyprus and Jamaica, rail travel, mobile phones, supermarkets such as Sainsbury and Tesco, paints and DIY stores.

For a national advertiser of a FMCG it is economic to pay the apparently high cost of television advertising, although increases in media rates are criticised for being far in excess of the rate of inflation.

19. What is advertised on television?

Few homes are without a television set, and some have more than one. For popular goods to be found in any High Street throughout the country, it is an impactive medium since it takes the advertisement right into the home where it will be seen by the prospective buyer including others in the household who influence purchase. Consequently, commercials generally advertise popular goods and also consumer durables such as domestic appliances and lawnmowers. In recent years, more expensive products and services have appeared on television as shown above.

Motor-cars are advertised and launched on TV. In 1999 BMW, Ford, Renault, Rover, Toyota, Vauxhall and Volvo were all advertising on TV. The Vauxhall Corsa commercial (which was part of a £10m television, press and poster campaign) in 1993 employed six fashion models who were each believed to have cost £500,000, and was criticised for featuring the black model Naomi Campbell in 'bondage gear'. Anti-pornography protesters picketed the offices of Lowe Howard-Spink, the advertising agency responsible for the commercials, and the ITC received 40 letters of protest which it rejected. The commercial was supposed to be an ironic commentary on the traditionally sexist use of women in car advertising. However, it was agreed to withhold showing commercials which included the offending costume until after 9pm. It might have been better to have given the new car a more easily remembered name, as Ford had done with their Mondeo and Renault had also done with their Clio.

TV advertising has created its own characters and run its own soap operas, and these add the power of repetition and continuity to this form of advertising. Yellow Pages created J.R. Hartley, the man who uses Yellow Pages to find a copy of one of his books in a Charing Cross Road bookshop. It was almost a reality to the extent that a book on fly fishing was actually published in the name of the imaginary author. It sold 80,000 copies and a sequel followed in 1992.

In 1990 Nescafé Gold Blend began its sequence of 30-second commercials about a yuppie couple played by Sharon Maughan and Tony Head. It was rated the worst TV commercial of the year in 1990, but it sold more Gold Blend, and the series continued year after year. The commercials were converted into a 312-page paperback novel *Love Over Gold*, and published by Transworld. They printed 100,000 copies, significant since 50,000 sales mean a best-selling paperback.

Sometimes a TV commercial can sell the wrong thing. Another Yellow Pages commercial showed a cricket umpire buying a new panama hat in Cheltenham before being seen leaving the pavilion in his crisp white hat. The commercial was repeated many times on prime time TV. There was a remarkable increase in the sale of panama hats.

20. Advantages of television

These apply worldwide, although a few are specifically British. An exception is Japanese television, the commercials providing entertainment followed by a bold name display. The attributes of the product are not featured. Instead, the commercial aims to create a pleasant feeling towards the advertiser.

(a) Realism. Because of the combination of colour, sound and action, television has assets no other medium can offer (with the exception of the cinema which no longer has the big audiences which existed prior to television). With these advantages the advertiser can show and demonstrate the product. If it is a packaged food, pack recognition is established so that the buyer knows what he or she is looking for in the shop, or there is quick recognition even if the advertisement has been temporarily forgotten. Ingenious effects can be achieved by computer graphics.

(b) Receptive audiences. Being received in the home in an entertainment atmosphere, commercials are well received, especially as they are produced to high technical standards and the presenter is often a well-known personality or at least a good actor or actress who presents the product authentically. In fact the quality of British commercials is so high that its creators are the ones who also produce some of the best cinema films.

(c) Repetition. The advertisement can be repeated to the point when a sufficient number of viewers have seen it enough times for the advertisement to have impact. Nowadays, advertisers do not indulge in saturation advertising, which is not only expensive but offensive. A good advertisement should be capable of being shown again after a rest without boring its audience.

The classic example of this is the chimp series which has been shown for some 30 years, advertising Brooke Bond PG Tips tea. The series that was launched in 1984 actually had flashbacks to sequences in old chimp commercials. One of this series, 'Mr Piano Shifter', has been shown so many times on television it has won a place in the *Guinness Book of Records*. The series continued to develop into the late 1990s. Advertising agents, using the ratings supplied weekly by the Broadcasters' Audience Research Board (BARB, *see* 17: **19**), are able to calculate when sufficient audience volume has been attained so that the commercial can be taken off.

(d) Zoning and networking. In Britain, there are currently 16 ITV area contractors licensed by the Independent Television Commission (ITC), two being in London. A full list of the ITV companies currently licensed under the new requirements of the Broadcasting Act 1990 is given in Table 5.8 (*see* p. 103). An advertiser can use one or any combination of stations, or network them all if he or she wishes.

(e) Appeal to retailers. Television advertising can reach retailers as well as consumers, both because retailers watch television just like anyone else, and because commercials can be addressed solely to them. Retailers know that if something is advertised on television there will be demand and it will sell. It can sometimes be very difficult for sales representatives to sell products to retailers unless they can promise the back-up of television advertising, and this can be imperative when dealing with supermarket chains with hundreds of outlets. These are fast-moving goods, and nothing moves goods faster than television advertising.

(f) Linked with other media. The TV commercial may be fleeting, but if fuller information, or a means of returning an enquiry coupon is required, this can be done by advertising in the weekly listings magazines *Radio Times, TV Quick, TV Times,* or *What's On TV* or in newspapers carrying supportive advertisements can be named in the commercials. Press ads may refer to 'as on TV'. The television companies also offer telephone enquiry services, and computerised ordering facilities, the number being given in the commercial. Many advertisers are now adding a website as a response element in their commercials.

It is interesting that there has been no confusion between KitKat the chocolate biscuit which runs TV campaigns (*see* 6: **17**) and Kit-e-Kat the catfood. This pet food market is another huge one like that of the chocolate countlines, for which TV is an apt medium. Nevertheless, it is difficult sometimes for the viewer to differentiate between brands unless the advertising is original and distinctive. Kit-e-Kat has made much of friendly kittens, with good pack displays and almost as many varieties as the Heinz famous '57'. Felix has used a black and white cartoon with a cheeky cat (*see* Figure 5.1). Spillers once had the advantage of its original famous performing cat Arthur which pawed meat out of a can, but his successor lacks the old appeal.

Among dog goods, Pedigree Chum feeds the Crufts winner, and one of its commercials of a breeder and her romping, healthy dogs has been repeated for years, showing the value of familiarity with the presenter, the audience and the scene. There is plenty of competition in the stores from

Figure 5.1 Label of Felix cat food can which links with black and white cat in TV commercial

own labels. A problem for pet food manufacturers is that, no matter what blandishments the advertisements offer, the pets themselves are very choosy. They cannot read what's good for them.

21. Weakness of commercial television

If commercial television was the last word in effective advertising media one would be entitled to ask how have all the other media survived, and how is it that the press continues to dominate? Of course, realistic and powerful as it may be, television does have its limitations.

(a) It tends to reach mass audiences, whereas one can be much more select-ive with the press.

(b) If a lot of detail is required by prospective buyers, the press wins again.

(c) Little else can be done while watching television, compared with radio, although 'zapping' is possible when irritated viewers (using their remote control) eliminate the commercials or at least the sound, or switch channels.

If they are playing recorded programmes they can jump the commercials by 'zipping', that is using the fast forwarding button on their remote control.

(d) Because of the audience size it is costly, and there are thousands of advertisers who appeal to smaller markets and cannot justify the cost of television.

(e) It does not lend itself to urgent advertisements as it takes time to produce a commercial.

(f) In countries where there are either many TV stations, or small audiences, airtime rates may be low enough to permit long or many commercials which bore viewers with too much advertising.

(g) A serious mistake made by producers of TV commercials, according to Virginia Matthews writing about the subject in *Marketing Week,* is to use the same presenter as a number of other advertisers, which is both boring and confusing. Who is advertising what? One of the worst over exposures of the same personality is that of Joanna Lumley, who became known as the 'Lumley disease'. Maybe she made a change from the 11-year stint by Nanette Newman in Fairy Liquid commercials. She also does voice-overs.

But as Virginia Matthews wrote, 'While the current crop of Lumleys are traceable to a recent Bafta award, this otherwise blameless personage of whom I complain has in fact a long history of appearing in too many ads'. She has appeared in ads for Asda, British Telecom, Birds Coffee, Hitachi, British Gas, Fairy Liquid, Muller and *Today* newspaper (which serialised her life story).

John Cleese disease occurred in the 1980s, and continued in the late 1990s. At least he was funny but he had to retire abroad to a tax haven. The earnings from TV commercials are enormous. Felicity Kendall also appeared in a spate of commercials.

Nevertheless, in the Leeds and National & Provincial building societies' merger, George Cole's performance in the Leeds commercials helped to make it the dominant partner in the discussions, and it was intended to retain him for future advertising for the new society.

There are pros and cons regarding each medium discussed in this book, and the media planner has to choose the medium which is likely to be both effective and economical in achieving the objectives of the campaign.

22. Regional TV companies

The Independent Television Commission (ITC) currently licences over 250 analogue terrestrial, cable and satellite television services. As digital television makes gains in the market, this figure will increase substantially. The licensing of television services involves the detailed application of UK broadcasting legislation. Increasingly, with the growth of international satellite

Table 5.8 National and regional TV licensees

Licensees	Region
Anglia Television Ltd	East of England
Border Television plc	Borders and the Isle of Man
Carlton Television Limited	London weekday (Monday to Friday)
Central Independent Television plc	East, West and South Midlands
Channel Television Limited	Channel Islands
GMTV Limited	National breakfast-time (6.00 to 9.25 am)
Grampian Television Limited	North of Scotland
Granada Television Limited	North West England
HTV Group Limited	Wales and the West of England
LWT Television Limited	London weekend (Friday 5.15 pm to Sunday)
Meridian Broadcasting Limited	South and South East England
Scottish Television Limited	Central Scotland
Tyne Tees Television Limited	North East England
Ulster Television plc	Northern Ireland
Westcountry Television Limited	South West England
Yorkshire Television Limited	Yorkshire

National broadcasting licensees
Channel Four Television Corporation
Channel 5 Broadcasting Limited

Digital terrestrial television licensees
British Digital Broadcasting plc (Multiplex B, C and D)
Digital 3 and 4 Limited (Channel 3 and Channel 4 Multiplex)

Public Teletext Service licensee
Teletext Limited

services, there will be greater consideration of relevant European Community legislation.

Terrestrial television broadcasting licences are issued for the 15 regional ITV companies and GMTV, which together comprise Channel 3. Channel 4 is also subject to an ITC licence. Terrestrial licences are also issued for the Public Teletext Service on Channels 3 and 4. Channel 5 was granted a licence in April 1996, and commenced broadcasting on Easter Sunday 1997.

At the time this edition was updated, digital television was beginning to gain ground, and should continue to do so. In 1997 digital broadcasting licences were awarded to British Digital Broadcasting plc (BDB), enabling them to operate multiplexes B, C and D. Digital 3 and 4 Ltd was awarded a licence to run programme services on behalf of the Channel 3 companies; Channel 4 was also granted a multiplex licence. Both BDB and Digital 3 and 4 announced their intention to commence broadcasting digital terrestrial services towards the end of 1998.

Table 5.8 shows the regional television companies responsible for providing the ITV programme service, and for selling airtime in the commercial breaks in ITV programmes in their own areas. GMTV is a separate ITV company providing a nation-wide breakfast-time television service.

However, while the Broadcasting Act 1990 had its innovations such as sponsored programmes, and the decision to set up separate Authorities for television and radio, the government's idea of auctioning TV companies to the highest bidder instead of according to their merits as programme broadcasters, led to chaos and financial disasters.

Since out-bidding TV-am, GMTV has suffered huge losses. Yorkshire Tyne-Tees Television went through a series of financial programmes until in November 1993 both the chairman and chief executive were obliged to resign because £15m of advertising airtime could not be delivered. YTTV simply could not meet the targets set by its excessive bids.

ALTERNATIVE TELEVISION

23. Introduction

Now we come to the bogey of mass audience commercial television, and what Alvin Toffler in his book *The Third Wave* (Pan Books, London, 1981) has described as the de-massification of the media. It is a change which is happening fast. An early example of de-massification was the community newspaper circulated to the residents of a small area in competition with both local newspapers and free newspapers. In television, however, the revolution is likely to be as decisive as the death of the 3,000-seater Odeon cinemas. Before television became popular there were big cinemas which attracted large audiences, but television stole these audiences and the cinemas were closed, altered to provide two or three small cinemas in the same building, or converted into bingo halls. A recent development has been the multiplex cinema, a purpose-built entertainment centre comprising a number of small cinemas plus cafés and shops.

Alternative television presents a similar threat to the type of mass audience television offered by the 16 regional contractors in Britain. The effect of alternative television is to dissipate the mass audiences for BBC and commercial programmes because viewers will be able to use their television sets to view a wide choice of other channels, or even turn to totally different uses of their sets.

24. Effect on advertising

At present television advertising appears only on commercial stations, airtime being sold by the contractors to appear in commercial breaks in their programmes. There may be two effects of alternative television.

(a) The commercial television audience may diminish so that it becomes increasingly less possible for advertisers to reach large audiences, and the rates for airtime might need to fall to compensate for smaller audiences.

(b) The television audience could be demassified by the proliferation of channels, to mention only UK Gold, BSkyB, TV Asia and the home-shopping QVC channel.

Thus, the whole concept of television is likely to be revolutionised, although this process will take a number of years to complete. Nevertheless, the changes are already evident in many homes, to mention only the popularity of the video cassette recorder (*see* **28**). In fact the VCR is popular in countries like Malawi which do not yet have television (*see* **35**), or Botswana where viewers can normally watch only programmes from South Africa.

25. Cable television

In the USA cable television was welcomed because it offered programmes superior to those put out by the large number of small local TV stations. However, the situation was different in Britain where a rent (on top of the BBC annual licence fee) had to be paid when a few large television companies were transmitting good quality programmes. The arrival of satellite television, with even greater choice of programme, gave cable television a much needed boost in 1990. Miles of streets throughout urban Britain were dug up and cabled in the 1980s and 1990s, but for a long time the take up was slow and disappointing, although 14.5 million homes could be reached.

By 1993 between five and eight million households became capable of receiving cable services, with well over half the population of Britain able to receive cable services. This could dramatically affect the way in which people could choose their entertainment, make their telephone calls, and receive cabled information.

Cable and satellite TV has resulted in multichannel TV. Zenith Media Worldwide has predicted that Europe's total advertising expenditure would increase by 58.9 per cent by 2003. By then 75 million European homes would have multichannel TV.

However, Zenith's optimism was not shared by the survey *Media Futures* conducted by Research International and published by the Henley Centre. The report drew a negative image of television by saying it was mostly watched by the poor who watch 11 hours a week of TV while 60 per cent of the sample of 1500 said they preferred being out and about rather than at home watching TV. Twenty-two per cent of viewers regarded TV programmes as dull. It anticipated no more than 4.5m dishes by the year 2000, reaching only 12 per cent of the viewing audiences.

There was greater regard for newspapers which still had considerable advantages over electronic media. Press advertising was considered less obtrusive, while TV commercials were found irritating and to be avoided. The report referred to the 'clutter effect' of too much advertising, and an interesting comment from respondents that they were more interested in local than international news. Perhaps TV has devoted too much news bulletin time to foreign wars and catastrophes, topics which hardly appear in the popular press. There are many contradictions in all this and the fall in TV audiences may be more to do with the quality of programmes than the proliferation of channels. The Henley Centre report does point out that the press remains the predominant advertising medium in spite of the impact of TV's vision, colour, sound and movement.

The Cable Authority was set up in December 1984 as a licensing body but not as a regulatory body like the IBA. However, the Cable Authority was absorbed into the Independent Television Commission, successor to the Independent Broadcasting Authority under the Broadcasting Act 1990.

Cable television became more popular when it competed with British Telecom, Cable & Wireless and Mercury to offer domestic telephone services. Most of the cable companies in Britain are American-owned and they exploited cheap telephone services in Britain in order to win their acceptance in the USA. These services, which are permitted to provide television, telecommunication and interactive facilities, are known as *broad band cable*. They can carry 30 to 45 television channels, if not more. Narrowband cable refers to some 50 older systems limited to television programmes. In 1993 cable television took off, partly because of its variety of competitive services, but also because of the publicity given its programmes by the listing magazines.

The channels available on cable television are shown in Table 5.9, and Figure 5.2 shows how cable gets to the home.

To receive satellite television it is necessary to fix a dish to the premises, but to receive terrestrial channels (BBC/ITV), and satellite plus cable only, and telephone services, it is necessary to rent a cable service.

26. Digital television

Digital terrestrial television (DTT) is an all-digital system. It differs from the PAL transmission system, which is analogue. The main advantage of digital TV is that studio-quality pictures can be viewed by consumers at home. At the time this book was being updated, two digital service companies were competing for consumer business: ONdigital and Digital TV.

Both systems claimed to need only the consumer's existing TV aerial for reception. Neither additional dish nor cable installation is required. However, a set-top decoder box did need to be bought, usually from a high street retailer. At the launch in early 1999, the cost of this equipment was expensive, about £200. On the other hand, it was about the same cost as a combined satellite dish receiver and decoder, and some retailers were including free installation in the package. In both cases, a subscription charge

Table 5.9 Terrestrial, digital, cable and satellite channels available in the UK

BBC1
BBC2
Channel 3 (ITV)
Channel 4
Channel 5

Non-subscripition digital channels:
BBC Choice Available via Sky Digital and On Digital
ITV 2

Satellite channels:
Sky 1 (entertainment)
Sky Sports 1
Sky Sports 2
Sky Sports 3
Eurosport
UK Gold

Animal Planet
Bravo (Classic movies)
Carlton Network
Challenge TV
Discovery
Disney
Granada Plus
History
Living
MTV
National Graphic
Nickelodeon
Paramount Comedy
Performance
Sci-Fi
UK Arena
UK Horizons
UK Style
VH-1

Movie channels:
Sky Premier
Moviemax
Cinema
Box Office
Film Four

107

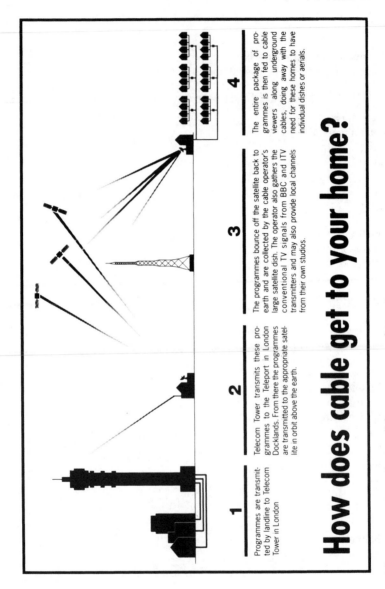

How does cable get to your home?

1 Programmes are transmitted by landline to Telecom Tower in London

2 Telecom Tower transmits these programmes to the Teleport in London Docklands. From there the programmes are transmitted to the appropriate satellite in orbit above the earth.

3 The programmes bounce off the satellite back to earth and are collected by the cable operator's large satellite dish. The operator also gathers the conventional TV signals from BBC and ITV transmitters and may also provide local channels from their own studios.

4 The entire package of programmes is then fed to cable viewers along underground cables, doing away with the need for these homes to have individual dishes or aerials.

Figure 5.2 How does cable get to your home?

was made for connection to the service. Where the service was interactive, there was also the cost of telephone calls to the service provider.

ONdigital receives its channels at a multiplex centre in London, by digital fibre cable from a number of play-out centres. The video material is compressed and combined with sound, subtitling and data services into groups of programme services. These can be transmitted to viewers' homes more efficiently than with analogue systems. An electronic programme guide is added, and the digital signals are encrypted to prevent unauthorised access.

The groups of services are then distributed by fibre cable to 81 transmission sites throughout the UK. From there they are transmitted to customers on UHF channels alongside existing analogue PAL transmissions. This is how ordinary television aerials are able to receive digital television. These transmissions are more robust than PAL, ensuring interference-free reception.

The customer's set-top decoder box tunes to the digital channels. With the use of a valid 'smart' card, the decoder de-encrypts the signals, uncompresses the pictures and delivers the output to the customer's television receiver. A 'smart' card becomes smart only when the appropriate subscription has been paid. At the present time, digital decoder boxes need to be sited between the aerial socket and the television set. In due course, integrated digital television sets will be capable of plugging direct into customers' aerial sockets.

DTT provides a wide range of worthwhile benefits to viewers. There is the promise of more high-quality channels, better sound, better-quality pictures and a new range of services. For example, many of the services offered will be interactive, so that the viewer will be able to communicate with banks and shops, surf the net and send and receive Emails.

There are other benefits to take into account. As the broadcasting spectrum becomes seriously crowded, the allocation of additional frequencies becomes more difficult. DTT uses the broadcasting spectrum more economically than its analogue counterpart.

The government has undertaken to abolish analogue transmissions within 15 years, with all broadcasters switching to digital. Parts of the frequency spectrum may be auctioned, raising billions of pounds. In theory this should strengthen the economy of the UK, provide new business opportunities and increase the number of jobs in the television industry. At the moment television supports nearly half a million jobs, and better multi-channel use of the frequency spectrum could expand this substantially.

27. Satellite television

The extent of satellite television is shown in the previous section on cable television, pioneered by Sky Channel which was founded in 1981 as Satellite Television plc with first transmission on 26 April 1982. In June 1983 News International plc (headed by Rupert Murdoch) acquired 65 per cent of Satellite Television's capital. The name Sky Channel was adopted in 1984.

In 1990 the British-based British Satellite Broadcasting satellite channel was launched. Both Sky and BSB were suffering huge financial losses. On 2 November 1990, the shock decision was announced that the two satellite channels were to merge, Sky taking over BSB and the combined channel being called BSkyB.

Rupert Murdoch made another appearance on the satellite scene when, in July 1993, he bought a controlling stake worth £350m in the Hong Kong Star Television group. Star TV has a multi-national footprint stretching from the Far East to Turkey and capturing the largest TV audience in India.

In August 1993 seven new satellite channels went on air in Europe, adding to the superfluity of channels available to British viewers who were offered a Sky Multi-Channels subscription package. To the original Sky group of programmes were added Bravo and Discovery (already on UK cable), the Family Channel (owned by the American company which bought TVS), Living and Country Music Television, and Nickelodeon, the American children's channel. A totally new concept in commercial TV arrived in October 1993 with the homeshopping QVC channel which consisted entirely of shopping offers.

28. Videocassette recorders

The first competitor to regular TV programmes is the VCR and such viewing is now surveyed by BARB (*see* also 17: **19**). Time-switching occurs when viewers record programmes and play them back at some future time, probably to the elimination of another regular programme and the advertising during its commercial break. In fact, advertisers on both programmes may suffer. That is not all, however: the viewer may use normal programme time to play back video films he has bought, borrowed or hired, and may have a video camera and play back personal videos like home movies. With a VCR, now common in thousands of homes, the viewer can show what he or she likes and either ignore off-air programmes or be very selective about what programmes are switched on. This form of alternative television, and this degree of de-massification, has existed for some time, receiving a big boost with the Royal Wedding in 1981 when more VCRs had been sold in Britain by July than had been forecast for the whole year! Britain has more VCRs per household than any other country.

29. Video games

Although these may have been over-sold, video games remain an important aspect of the video scene, and some of the more ingenious and popular software such as chess will doubtless survive as usurpers of regular screen time. Japanese video games such as Nintendo and Sega also compete with viewing time although they have their own viewing systems.

In addition there are the new interactive systems such as Philips CDi, some of entertainment and others of educational value.

30. Home computers

Ownership of personal computers per capita in the UK is higher than in most of Europe. It is comparable to that of the USA. The time spent at a PC screen, viewing videos on CD-ROM, surfing the Internet, at educational pursuits or computer games, keeps the user from viewing television. Even radio stations which put their transmissions on the Internet can be accessed from a home computer anywhere in the world. In early 1999, the London station LBC was called by a listener in Illinois who was sitting at his computer. A long conversation ensued with the presenter in London, presumably at the cost of a local call in Illinois.

A dynamic volume of new computer educational and recreational software is constantly streaming on to the market. It follows that a lot of time can be taken up operating a home PC – at the expense of regular TV viewing.

31. Videotext

This form of alternative television has been with us for some time. While British Telecom's Prestel Viewdata, introduced in 1979, has not been widely taken up by domestic viewers, an increasing number of sets equipped to receive the BBC's Ceefax and commercial television's Teletext systems have entered British homes. With these systems pages of information can be called up and viewed, and while they are being watched the regular programme is eliminated. When the commercials are on it is very convenient to transfer to Teletext or Ceefax to check on the latest news, the weather forecast, sporting results or even one's horoscope. The sound can be left on so that one knows when the programme is resumed after the commercials. Again, the advertiser has been penalised.

Teletext can be used for advertising purposes, but only in computer-held text form and not with film-like commercials.

32. Advertisements on video

There are advertisers who offer videos about their products or services, and obviously they can only be viewed to the exclusion of the regular programme. This means that a small advertiser who would never use television can virtually absorb television time on domestic sets at no airtime cost to himself. A number of advertisers have offered videos in their press advertisements. Tourist organisations often supply videos through travel agencies which may be borrowed by potential holiday-makers.

33. Public relations videos

There are also numerous public relations videos ranging from house journals which employees can enjoy watching at home to those issued by voluntary bodies as diverse as the Royal Society for the Protection of Birds to the British Diabetic Association. These can absorb a considerable amount of normal viewing time.

34. Learning programmes

There are also video versions of distance learning courses which can be watched via VCR and TV receiver.

35. Developing countries

Video has its special uses in developing countries, and a clever use of video has been made in Malawi where there is no television. The Lonrho textile company David Whitehead & Sons (Malawi) Ltd has created its own video studio to make tapes of fashion shows which it takes round the country to show villagers the range of materials available for dressmaking. The company has a special demonstration vehicle, and one side drops down to make a stage on which models display dresses made from Whitehead materials.

CINEMA

36. Introduction

In Britain, the size of the cinema audience and the number of cinemas fell dramatically with the arrival of television in the 1950s, and the make-up of audiences became a predominantly young one which made the cinema a special medium for advertisers wishing to reach young people.

However, there has been a steady rise in monthly cinema admissions, and CAA/Gallup/Marplan figures show that in 1991 there were 92,527,574 compared with 88,702,531 in the previous year.

The number of cinema screens has also increased mainly due to the opening of multiplex cinemas. First introduced in the USA by AMC, multiplex cinemas came to Britain with the Point at Milton Keynes in 1985, and consist of purpose-built cinema sites with from six to 14 cinemas with seating of around 150–250, supported by adjacent facilities such as shops and cafés. By 1991 there were over 500 multiplex screens in the UK.

By the end of 1989 the number of UK cinema screens taking advertising had risen to 1,424 and 1,530 by June 1990. Currently there are more than 1,600 cinema screens recording more than 95 million admissions annually.

37. Advantages of the cinema

There are certain characteristics which distinguish the cinema from other media, although it shares many of the advantages enjoyed by television such as its realism through the combination of sound, colour and action.

(a) **Captive audience**. There is truly a captive audience since the cinema is purpose built and there are none of the distractions surrounding the home viewing of television.

(b) **Longer video**. The cinema commercial can be longer than the TV commercial, and so is less abrupt and kaleidoscopic.

(c) **Larger screen**. Being shown on a larger and wider screen than that of the TV set, the picture is more dramatic, realistic and impactive.

(d) **No interruption of programme**. There are no commercial breaks, the commercials being shown as a complete segment before or after films, and since they are shown the same number of times as the films, they are seen by each audience.

(e) **Zoning**. While TV commercials can be shown in selected regions, cinema commercials can be shown in selected towns.

(f) **Entertainment atmosphere**. Cinema advertising is seen in a pleasant, receptive entertainment atmosphere, whether this be in a public cinema, in the shipboard cinemas as found on cruise ships, on aeroplanes with in-flight movies, in Forces cinemas, or on mobile cinema circuits.

38. Weaknesses

Like broadcast media, it is a *transient* medium and it relies on remembering the message, and this may depend on how often the commercial is seen. However, research has shown that the recall rate can be as high as 50 per cent of cinema-goers interviewed being able to recall correctly a cinema commercial seen seven days earlier.

39. Characteristics of cinema audiences

Limited audiences. There are two principal characteristics which limit screen advertising compared with any other medium. The audience is young, mostly between 7 and 34-year-olds, the largest group being the 15–24-year-olds. With the unemployment and few job opportunities of the recession years, these age groups represent the lowest spenders. The highest spenders have become the over 50s and those form the smallest group of cinema-goers. The second poor characteristic is that more than half the audience is in the lower social grades.

40. A special cinema service

Pearl and Dean and Rank Screen Advertising offer to advertisers their Audience Delivery Plan (ADP) whereby a specified audience is delivered at a fixed cost. The contractors monitor weekly cinema attendances and control the duration of a cinema screen advertising campaign so that the specified audience volume is achieved. This is rather like showing a TV commercial until sufficient audience ratings have been obtained, after which it is withdrawn.

General instructions on the length of the commercial, campaign areas, campaign period and number of cinema-goers to be reached are supplied by the advertiser. A minimum of one million cinema admissions nationally, or on an equivalent scale in ITV areas, must be booked and the campaign should be run for six to eight weeks. Weekly estimates of admissions are provided by Gallup, who are appointed by the Cinema Advertising Association for this purpose. The sample is made up of ten main circuits and 40 independent cinema owners who are checked every month.

OUTDOOR AND TRANSPORTATION

41. Introduction

Outdoor advertising is the oldest established form of advertising, and evidence of its use has been found on Greek and Roman remains. This is not surprising because even in those days public announcements had to be made, and a wall was as good a place as any on which to carve a message. One of the earliest forms of outdoor advertising was the inn sign which has remained in use to the present day. It is believed that the spread of the Great Fire of London in 1666 was assisted by the wooden signs which reached across the narrow streets of the City from one building to another.

In the 1930s the well-designed posters on the hoardings were nicknamed the 'poor man's art gallery'.

Among the wonderful 'art gallery' posters of the 1930s were those for Pears Soap, especially the one of a filthy tramp writing a letter, the opening words being 'Since using your soap I have used no other'. There was the one of a man in blue pyjamas astride a large jar of Bovril which was floating on the sea, and the message was 'Bovril prevents that sinking feeling'. Then there was the one of the man packing for his holidays who could not find his tin of Andrews liver salts which was projecting from his back trouser pocket. Cigarette posters often had beautiful sunset scenes, while there was the two-headed figure saying 'that was Shell, that was'. Humour and artistry were characteristic of posters sixty years ago. Today they seem to depend on clever word play and the oblique attempts by one advertiser to avoid encouraging people to smoke!

Today, outdoor advertising has seen innovations such as the illuminated bus-shelter poster (Adshel); the moving, illuminated newscaster, spelling out its message high up on a building; or the spangled flutter signs, common in Asiatic cities, which are now to be seen in London. There are also novel sites on which a number of different advertisements are produced on slats which revolve to show a succession of advertisements (e.g. Ultravision sites). Thus movement is introduced into an otherwise static poster site. *See* **47**. According to the *Media Register*, the breakdown of outdoor advertisers is:

- tobacco 14 per cent;

- soft and alcoholic drinks 22 per cent;

- food/confectionery 11 per cent;

- finance 8 per cent;

- motor-car 14 per cent;

- entertainment/leisure 4 per cent;

- travel 6 per cent;

- retail 5 per cent;

- others 10 per cent.

When commercial TV arrived in 1955 it lured many advertisers to the new medium, and outdoor advertising suffered a decline. For a long time it became known as the 'booze and baccy' medium, especially since cigarette advertising was banned on TV. But posters have recovered their popularity.

Together with transportation advertising, this medium has shown great resilience and ingenuity as times, fortunes and regulations have had their impact on it. In developing countries it has proved to be an excellent means of advertising to multi-language, multi-ethnic or illiterate people. Even in countries like China, where commercial advertising might be least expected, there are illuminated signs and large posters. The streets of Hong Kong are overhung with scores of advertising signs erected on bamboo frames, and lit up at night. It is a universal medium.

42. Outdoor and transportation distinguished

The two are often put together and described collectively as 'outdoor' but a distinction is necessary. Outdoor advertising consists of posters of various sizes, and painted, metal and illuminated signs displayed on outdoor sites. Transportation advertising consists of similar advertising on the outside and inside of vehicles (which are moving sites), and on transportation property and premises which can include *indoor* sites such as within bus and railway stations, airports and seaports. The advertisements inside public

Table 5.10 48-sheet poster distribution by TV region

TV Region	Outdoor Advertising Association	Maiden Outdoor	Adult population profile
London	26.5	22.3	19.7
Midlands	16.0	20.5	16.1
Lancashire	16.1	17.8	12.6
Yorkshire	10.5	10.5	9.9
North East	4.0	3.8	5.3
Central Scotland	7.4	8.8	6.6
Wales & West	6.0	6.8	7.9
Southern	6.5	5.5	9.0
East of England	3.9	1.8	6.7
South West	1.2	0.3	2.9
Border	0.4	0.2	1.1
Northern Scotland	1.5	1.7	2.2
	100.0	100.0	100.0

Note: 96-sheet panels are concentrated in the London TV region with over 50 per cent of all 96-sheet panels in that region (68 per cent of Maiden Outdoor 96 sheets).

Source: OSCAR

transport vehicles and trains, and inside buildings where people are waiting, allow for more detailed messages or copy than is possible on posters and signs seen by passers-by.

43. Importance of outdoor advertising

This medium has special qualities different again from other media described in this book, and like all the others it has changed with the times, especially regarding its users. Its main use is for reminder advertisements, as with brands of FMCGs, or as secondary media to support press or TV campaigns on highways leading to the point-of-sale and so reiterating the main media campaign. Outdoor advertisements used to remain in position for weeks, months or even years, posters generally being pasted for periods of 13 weeks, while many painted or illuminated signs are more or less permanent fixtures. This long life in prominent positions gives the advertisements repetitive value.

However, the current trend is to run heavier, shorter campaigns, such as 1500–2000 48-sheets nationwide for two weeks.

The 6-sheet poster in a variety of forms has also brought new life to posters, and this size (sometimes with rear lighting) is to be seen on pavement, in shopping precincts and on bus shelter sites and, as Table 5.10 shows, it is an increasingly popular size. It is used by many beverage advertisers such as Nescafé. Yet another new outdoor site is the 'pepperpot'-shaped pavement site.

An excellent report, *Posters in Perspective*, is published by the poster contractors Maiden Outdoor. It provides a comprehensive review of the poster market, with particular reference to the dominance of the 48-sheet poster, to attract an even broader range of advertisers, and to provide a guide to Maiden Outdoor's services. The company has operated since 1925.

44. Characteristics of outdoor advertising

There are many sizes of poster ranging from the small double crown bills to the large ones on hoardings or bulletin boards which are also known as supersites (*see* **46**). The characteristics of the medium may be summarised as follows.

(a) Size and dominance. Because of its size the poster dominates the view.

(b) Colour. Most posters are in full colour, with realistic scenes and pictures of products.

(c) Brief copy. Since the appeal is to people on the move, and the posters may be seen from a distance, the copy is usually confined to a slogan and a name printed in large letters.

(d) Zoning. Campaigns can be organised in selected regions or towns, but national campaigns can be planned using a minimum number of posters per town to secure maximum opportunities to see. Strategically sited posters can provide a very economical advertising campaign. To coincide with multi-media planning, standard TV regions are used to plan regional or network campaigns.

(e) Probably the most important characteristic of posters is their ability to create, through boldness, colour, size and repetition, brand awareness.

They can also be a feature of pan-European advertising, using the services of a pan-European poster agency, and this can be less complicated and more effective than using a very large number of newspapers.

Poster sites are rented, and posters are pasted by contractors. The three largest account for about 70 per cent of revenue. There are agencies which specialise in booking outdoor and transportation advertising.

Computer mapping is a method of selecting sites. Key roads can be plotted and sites can be chosen to coincide with retail outlets, or linked to geo-demographic systems such as Acorn and Mosaic, or to suit particular campaign objectives.

The audience research system for the roadside poster-industry is POSTAR (Poster Advertising Research), formerly OSCAR (Outdoor Site Classification and Audience Research) which calculates audience scores for any campaign configuration, and also estimates cover and frequency for a target audience. At one time most campaigns ran for 13 weeks but monthly campaigns are

Table 5.11

All adults (index)	Cover 100	Frequency 100
Men	114	109
Up market adults (ABC1)	112	109
Young adults (15–24 year olds)	116	118
Light TV viewers	112	130
Financial Times readers	142	173
Up market Sunday readers	109	120

Source: OSCAR. An average OSCAR score of 95.5 (on average 95,500 opportunities to see (OTC) per panel per week is scored by Maiden Outdoor 48 sheets)

now common. Coverage and frequency can also be maximised by rotating sites half-monthly or by changing sizes. Heavier weight shorter campaigns have become more popular than the larger traditional campaigns. This fits in better with the length of campaigns using other media.

Posters reach all sectors of the population, and its audience is unfragmented unlike that of other media, but is especially effective in reaching young and upmarket adults. The OSCAR figures in Table 5.11 indicate how a poster audience may be constituted.

45. Weaknesses

Chiefly, the weaknesses of outdoor advertising are the inability to use much copy, possible damage by vandals or the weather, the lack of concentration on the message by passers-by, and the time it takes to design, print and exhibit posters.

46. Poster sizes and sites

The following are the standard poster sizes and kinds of site.

(a) *Double crown*: 762 mm × 508 mm (30 in. × 20 in.). This is the unit size for larger sizes, e.g. 16-sheet is the equivalent of 16 double crowns. Double crowns are used on billboards (e.g. newsbills outside newsagents shops) and on public information panels located on pavements and in shopping precincts. Note that in Britain 'billboard' refers to a small poster, whereas the Americans refer to large posters as billboards. It is also the size of the typical travel and airline poster displayed on travel agency premises.

(b) *Quad crown*: 762 mm × 1,016 mm (30 in. × 40 in.). This is a size often used to advertise entertainments.

(c) *4-sheet*: 1,016 mm × 1,524 mm (40 in. × 60 in.). Often printed on vandal-proof vinyl and nicknamed the 'pedestrian housewife poster' because of its use in shopping precincts.

(d) *16-sheet*: 3,048 mm × 2,032 mm (10 ft × 6 ft 8 in.). The standard upright poster seen on the hoardings.

(e) *32-sheet*: 3,048 mm × 4,064 mm (10 ft × 13 ft 4 in.).

(f) *48-sheet*: 3,048 mm × 6,096 mm (10 ft × 20 ft).

(g) *64-sheet*: 3,048 mm × 8,128 mm (10 ft × 26 ft 8 in.).

(h) For *bulletin boards* or *supersites* (which are specially built on large sites, often set out in gardens and sometimes floodlit at night) the measurements are slightly different from 64-sheet, being 9 ft 6 in. deep by 27 ft (2,897 × 8,230 mm), with even larger ones measuring 36 ft (10,973 mm) or 45 ft (13,716 mm) wide.

Although poster measurements are defined by number of sheets this does not mean that a large poster is made up of 16, 34 or 64 separate sheets of paper. Large posters consist of a few separate pieces of paper.

There are four chief size formats for roadside posters, these being the 4 sheet, 6 sheet, 48 sheet and 96 sheet which account for more than 90 per cent of all panels and over 95% of all roadside poster revenue. Of those, the 6 sheet (usually seen on bus shelters), the 48 sheet and the 96 sheet are now predominating. This concentration and rationalisation is a key factor in contractors' strategies.

47. Ultravision

This is a trade name for panels with slats which rotate to form three differ-ent faces, thus giving movement to a static medium. They are usually placed on dominant sites, often high up on buildings, as at the Elephant and Castle, London. For instance, Maiden have fifteen 48 sheet Ultravisions in the London area. They have the advantages of 100 per cent illumination, high-impact audience-catching locations and eye-catching movement.

48. Importance of transportation advertising

This medium is seen by the travelling public who have the time while waiting at terminals or stations or while travelling on public transport to absorb messages. In fact, reading advertisements may help pass the time. Consequently, transportation advertisements, unless perhaps where they are on the exteriors of vehicles (e.g. buses, trams, delivery vans or taxi-cabs), can be much more detailed.

In Britain, a very important part of transportation advertising is the ex-tensive *London Underground railway system* which carries millions of passen-gers daily, and lesser systems in Liverpool, Newcastle and Glasgow. On the Underground there is a great variety of sites in the vestibules, corridors and lifts, on the escalators and on the platforms. On the wall across the tracks

119

and facing the platforms are 16-sheet posters, but most wall posters are quad crown, with framed cards on the walls of the escalator tunnel. In the trains there are cards above the windows. Since many travellers are women going to and from work, this is a popular medium for women's goods, while the entertainment industry makes intensive use of quad crown wall posters.

The travelling public has changed, and is less confined to 'rush hour' commuter traffic. Daytime travellers have increased, partly due to unemployment, partly due to an increase in pensioners and the holding of travel passes. This means that transportation advertising on buses and trains is seen by a very large audience.

A number of countries like Hong Kong and Singapore also have underground railway systems. An innovation on the Hong Kong Mass Transit Railway (MTR) is the *recycled plastic ticket*, on which advertisement space is sold. MTR station walls also carry large illuminated photographic posters which are very attractive.

A special feature, found less in London today than in other parts of the world, is the *painted bus or tram* monopolised by a single advertiser as in Hong Kong. British Transport Advertising Ltd now calls the painted bus the ColourBus, and these buses are restricted to one trade in any one bus depot area. A second kind of bus available to a single advertiser is the UniBus on which the advertiser may have a single continuous advertisement band, 80 ft in length (24.4 m), which encircles the bus, whether double deck or single deck.

Taxi-cab advertising, with plates on the nearside front door, is a popular medium in London and regional cities although a drawback is that such vehicles must not drive on roads through the Royal Parks.

Taxi Media Ltd of London paints taxis in exactly the colour clients want, such as the house colour which forms part of their corporate identity scheme. For example, Carlton TV had taxis painted in Pantone 2326 pink. They have a Quantel Paint Box computer facility which allows clients to compare proposed designs in advance.

49. Characteristics of transportation advertising

Some have been mentioned already, but ones special to the medium are as follows.

(a) **Variety of sites and sizes**. Throughout the road, rail, sea and air passenger and goods transportation system there is a great variety of sites and sizes so that the medium lends itself to the campaigns of many advertisers, local, metropolitan, national and – in some cases such as airlines – international.

(b) **Selectivity**. Because the medium has so many sites at different locations or routes it is possible to select the ones most suitable for a campaign. Like the special positions in the press, or the time-of-day segments on radio and TV, the costs of sites will relate to the volume of traffic. For example, it costs more to advertise at Piccadilly Circus Underground station than at a station on the outskirts of London. This facility also makes zoning possible if the advertiser wishes to concentrate a campaign on a certain area of London or of the country.

(c) Short-term campaigns. Short-term advertising is more possible with transportation than with outdoor advertising, as when exhibitions are advertised for only a week or two. Transportation is useful for local traders, auctioneers, cinemas and theatres who may change their posters every week.

(d) A mobile medium. A special feature of buses, trams, taxis and trains is that as passengers change there is a cumulative audience who see the interior advertising, while exterior advertising is seen by yet another cumulative audience as the vehicle travels along its route. This is very different from the regular readership of various publications. While there is no control over who might see transportation advertising, it is likely to reach a large number of people repeatedly over a period. In a highly urbanised country like Britain, where 80 per cent of the population live in towns and either use or are aware of public transport, this medium offers penetration and coverage of the mass market. Yet it also offers opportunity for specialists as already shown regarding the London Underground.

50. Weaknesses

On above ground and underground railway stations it is necessary to display sufficient posters for people to notice them, and the same applies to roof cards since they appear in separate compartments of the train. On some routes it is possible that there are irregular volumes of passenger traffic, and that at peak times when most people are travelling it is less easy to see advertisements in crowded compartments.

An advertisement rate may appear to be modest, but it will be expensive if the advertisement appears in empty compartments or on deserted platforms. The same production costs apply whatever the size of the audience or the attention paid to the advertisement. However, in central London the Underground has become increasingly busy throughout the day, and is less affected by the fluctuations of commuter traffic than above ground trains.

Progress test 5

1. What classes of media may be called (a) above-the-line and (b) below-the-line? **(2)**

2. What are primary and secondary media? **(3)**

3. Name the British national newspapers, and give an approximation of their individual circulations. **(7)**

4. What are the main advantages of the press as an advertising medium? **(9)**

5. What are the main disadvantages of the press as an advertising medium? **(10)**

6. Explain the expression 'Independent Local Radio'. **(11)**

7. What are the advantages of television advertising? **(20)**

8. Describe some of the forms of alternative television. **(25–34)**

9. What is the predominant characteristic of the British cinema audience? **(36, 39)**

10. Distingush between *outdoor* and *transportation* advertising **(42)**

11. Which poster size has become the most commonly used? **(46)**

12. Describe the special characteristics of underground railway advertising. **(48)**

6

Advertising media: below-the-line

INTRODUCTION

1. Definition

Traditionally, 'below-the-line' is the term used to describe all the other advertising media which exist in addition to the five described in Chapter 5. The difference between above-the-line media (sometimes called media advertising) and below-the-line media is explained in 5: **2**. Separate chapters are given to *sales promotion, sponsorship, direct mail* (with direct response marketing), and *exhibitions*. This still leaves us with a great many other media to discuss in this chapter. They range from essential media such as catalogues to those which exploit special opportunities and some which may be considered as fringe media.

The mistake is sometimes made – even in the trade press – of including public relations under below-the-line. Since public relations is not a form of advertising, has its own budget, and is usually conducted by separate personnel (either in-house or consultancy) it has no place in below-the-line advertising media.

Similarly, it is wrong to refer to public relations as 'below-the-line', as some marketing people do, as if distinguishing between two kinds of advertising. Public relations campaigns often have their own objectives which have nothing to do with advertising or sales promotion.

Packaging is very much a part of point-of-sale. Today it is not only a case of getting products on the shelves but of fighting de-listing by the big supermarket chains, that is keeping products on the shelves. The Kellogg Corn Flakes packet says 'We don't make cereals for anybody else'. KP Nuts redesigned its nine packs in 1993 and ran a £2m TV campaign on GMTV to relaunch the brand, and to introduce a new resealable pocket-sized tube for snacking on the move. KP held 57 per cent of the £138m market, with Smiths holding second place with a market share of 52.9 per cent. The real threat was from own label nuts which had moved up from 26.7 per cent to 31.2 per cent of the market.

Another strategy has been for Nescafé to place advertisements containing cash vouchers in popular newspapers and magazines. The promotion ran for a certain number of weeks on one supermarket chain, such as Sainsbury's, where the vouchers would be redeemed against purchase of the coffee. Nescafé have always proclaimed that they do not pack own label brands. This is known as a third party promotion.

Fifty per cent of the food products stocked by supermarkets are now own label. This means that national brands have to fight hard to retain their outlets, using media advertising, sales promotion schemes, favourable trade terms and so on in a situation where space forbids the use of very much traditional point-of-sale display material. The ability of the package to pull sales has never been so essential, as will be seen by studying the packaging designs on supermarket shelves. Many have had face lifts in recent years to sharpen their appeal.

2. Importance

The reader is reminded that below-the-line are not necessarily inferior or minor media; for some advertisers they may be more effective than above-the-line media. It is up to the advertiser to decide whether a medium is value for money and fits the campaign, and not simply be persuaded by a salesperson.

TYPES OF MEDIA AND THEIR APPLICATIONS

3. Sales literature

Many goods and services are more easily sold if the customer can be given explanatory literature. This may be offered in an advertisement, accompany a mailing shot, be supplied with a product, or be available at the point of sale. There are many forms of sales print, including the following.

(a) **Leaflet**. This is a single sheet of unfolded paper.

(b) **Folder**. As the name implies, this is a sheet of print – which may be quite large – reduced to a convenient size by means of folds, or which may be folded concertina fashion to form a number of separate pages without need for binding. A good reason for folding may be so that the item fits into an envelope for mailing, or is easy to carry in the pocket.

(c) **Brochures and booklets**. If multiples of four pages are used they can be bound by some form of stitching. Single sheets can be bound by the process of 'perfect binding' when the left-hand edges are glued and the whole bound in a cover.

(d) Broadsheet. This is really another kind of folder which unfolds to a size similar to a large newspaper page. Maps, charts and small posters may be produced in this style. Note that this term also refers to a large page newspaper as distinct from a tabloid.

(e) Catalogues. These are brochures which describe and usually illustrate the range of products available and give their prices. They can be of any size from pocket-size to something resembling a telephone directory according to the nature of the business.

(f) Timetables. These are generally brochures, and may be of handy size like airline timetables, or even small folders like those for bus and railway services, while those embracing all rail or air services are large, bound books.

(g) Picture postcards. Useful publicity can be gained by supplying customers with postcards as with hotels, airlines and shipping lines. People often collect them.

(h) Hotel stationery. Letterheadings and printed envelopes placed in hotel rooms are not only a service but a useful form of advertising.

(i) Stuffers. These are leaflets inserted (or 'stuffed') in the package. They contain instructions on how to use a product, and can also be used to advertise the product or sister products.

(j) Diaries. Whether desk or pocket, they are of long-lasting advertising value since they are referred to throughout the year, and refills or new diaries can be supplied every year as Christmas gifts.

(k) Telephone number reminders. These can be supplied as hanging cards, or message pads, and can occupy a permanent place by the telephone.

(l) Swing tags. Attached by card to products of many kinds, they identify the product and may give advice on how to use or take care of it.

(m) Guarantee cards. In addition to requiring the customer to register ownership for guarantee purposes, these cards can be used to request purchasing details for research. It can be very useful when planning advertising to know *who* buys the product, for whom, and whether it is the first or a succeeding purchase of the company's products.

(n) Price lists and order forms. These may be combined or separate items. Order forms need to be designed so that they are easy to complete and produce accurate information such as the correct total amount of the order or payment, and the full address of the sender. Orders cannot be fulfilled if the information given is incomplete. For use with computers, it is necessary to request information clearly so that the customer is not confused. The computer then gets data which are accurate and useful, and serve a marketing purpose. If credit or charge card facilities are offered, it must be simple for customers to state their card numbers, and it may be necessary to illustrate the cards which are accepted.

(o) Competition entry forms. These are important pieces of sales literature requiring very careful writing and design so that they are easy to complete. (*See also* 7: **5**.)

4. Point-of-sale (POS) display material

Some of the sales literature described in **3** may be distributed as give-away material at point-of-sale (point-of-purchase), but in this section we refer to material which is designed specifically to attract attention and encourage sales. It may also identify the premises as a source of supply.

Display space is scarce in shops, and some goods or services are seasonal so that the possible period of display is also limited. The supplier has to budget carefully and avoid waste. It is best if material is supplied against requests, or displays are arranged by the sales representative. Some suppliers produce broadsheets illustrating available display material, together with an order form. It can be very costly and often wasteful to distribute display material speculatively.

Again, many examples can be given, some being more suitable for certain advertisers than others.

(a) Mobiles. Not to be confused with travelling exhibitions and demonstrations (as occur in developing countries, including mobile cinemas), mobiles at POS consist of ingenious cut-out displays suspended from the shop ceiling so that they move with the air currents. They are useful in supermarkets where there is limited display space.

(b) Posters. Crown and double crown posters are a familiar feature of shop displays, decorating walls, doors and windows. In addition to colourful pictorial posters, there are those screen printed in bright colours which stores use to announce special offers. Some firms (e.g. insurance companies) supply stock posters bearing their names with blank space which can be overprinted to advertise local events such as sports days, amateur theatricals or flower shows.

(c) Pelmets. One of the oldest forms of display material which can have a very long life, pelmets are paper strips which can be pasted along the top edge of a window.

(d) Dummy packs. Empty display cases, packets and bottles are useful for window displays, especially when real products would deteriorate if left in a window for any period, or too much stock would otherwise be tied up in this way.

(e) Dumpers and dump bins. Decorated with the name of the product, they are filled with the branded product and placed near check-outs in supermarkets to induce impulse-buying.

(f) Wire stands. Either self-standing or small enough to stand on the counter or hang near the cash register, these contain a stock of the product and encourage self-service. They must carry the manufacturer's name-plate to encourage refilling with the same brand, otherwise there is a danger of the retailer finding them convenient for the display of other or rival goods.

(g) Showcards. Strutted or hanging, and printed on board or metal, these are portable displays which a retailer can move about the shop or use from time to time, and they can often have a very long life, especially if strongly made. Some, such as those advertising credit card and other services, may remain permanent displays on, say, a hotel reception desk.

(h) Dispenser boxes. Rather like showcards, they are portable and may remain in position permanently if they contain leaflets which satisfy a regular demand. A typical use is for the display of insurance prospectuses, tourist leaflets and official forms. There are also very attractive free-standing or wall-mounted ones made of clear acrylic which reveal contents, unlike cardboard or wooden ones which reveal only the top of the literature. They are supplied by The Showcard Group of Letchworth.

(i) Clocks. Again, this is a popular and permanent form of POS display, every glance at the time disclosing the advertiser's name.

(j) Trade figures. Johnnie Walker, the Michelin Man and the Sandeman figure have been used in displays for decades. They appear as moulded figures and cardboard cut-outs, with various versions of the Michelin rubber man. Some figures are static, others are animated or articulated models.

(k) Models. Very realistic because of their three-dimensional form are scale models, especially when the real subject is too large or impossible to display. Good examples are ships and aircraft.

(l) Working models. These always fascinate, for few people can resist stopping and staring at a model which is active. One which was very amusing was a model baby elephant which bounced up and down in an armchair to demonstrate how well the chair was sprung. They can be very useful for the windows of, say, building societies, where normal displays are inevitably static.

(m) Illuminated displays. In a similar way, as when the lights go on and off or change colour, the lighted sign in a window attracts attention, particularly of window-shoppers and passers-by after dark when the shop is closed.

(n) Display stands. According to the trade these may be standard or custom-built, and may be enclosed, perhaps velvet-lined for expensive products. They give exclusiveness to goods. They can also be simple stands to hold small items like paperback books or confectionery. A problem, however, is to limit their use to the supplier's products, and it is essential to fix the supplier's name to the stand. The refrigerated stand is a good example, the equipment being intended for the supplier's ice cream products, but the retailer misuses it by storing rival brands in it.

(o) Dispenser cards/packs. These may be complete in themselves for hanging on the wall like cards from which packets of nuts are detached, or they may be individual self-display dispenser bubble packs, bags or sachets hanging on hooks for items like toys, razor blades, music cassettes, ironmongery, confectionery, or ball-point pens. The hooks may be on the retailer's wall or on a special stand or fitting supplied by the manufacturer who thus provides permanent POS material that permits self-service.

(p) Display outers. Very useful for small items like confectionery sold in units, packets of soup, or other compact single items, display outers consist of containers holding a quantity of items, the lid folding back to produce a display. The carton can then be placed on the counter or shelf and goods sold from it. This is very economical and effective since the original container becomes its own display piece.

(q) Crowners. When bottled goods are displayed, collars or crowners can be slipped over the necks, to state the price, display a slogan or promotional message. They are used mainly for soft and alcoholic drinks.

(r) Stickers and transfers. Often these are carried by the sales representative who positions them on various surfaces such as walls, doors, windows and even cash registers. They are supplied in a self-adhesive pull-off form.

(s) Cash mats. Because of their utility – preventing coins from rolling off the counter – they are likely to be welcomed by retailers and kept in a regular position.

(t) Samples. Sampling will be referred to again under sales promotion (*see* 7: **20**), but it may be point-of-sale strategy for the manufacturer to supply free samples, perhaps in special packs like sachets of coffee or miniature bottles of wine.

(u) Drip mats/coasters. Whether made of cork, aluminium or paper, these can be used in bars, cafés and other catering situations such as on board airliners, placing prominent advertising in a very convenient form.

Most drip mats found on bar tables are circular, but Britvic fruit juice has one with a cut-out of a bottle and the words:

its
BIGGER
its
BETTER
its
BRITVIC

The word 'its' lacks the necessary apostrophe.

The drip mat, like the advertising matchbox, is a popular collector's item, thus perpetuating its advertising value. Drip mats, or coasters, are usually made of absorbent material, but Malaysia Airlines have a set of Selangor pewter ones bearing their Kelantan Kite symbol, which passengers may buy.

Some brewers, such as Bass and Lanot pils, provide rectangular cotton drip mats on which glasses can be placed on a bar counter.

(v) Ashtrays. These are much used by drinks and tobacco manufacturers, and are freely distributed to bars and restaurants where customers drink and smoke. The advertisements are usually screen printed on to the various shaped trays made from a variety of materials.

(w) Tickets. Advertisers such as Coca-Cola take space on transportation tickets including airline boarding passes, which is very appropriate when the product is immediately available.

(x) Shelf edging. This is a very popular POS display on the edges of shelves facing customers across the counter or bar.

(y) In-store advertising. Using videos and TV screens, public address systems, electronic newscasters with colourful LED letters, trolley ads and other devices, products and special offers can be announced to shoppers in the store. Video ads may also be introduced into juke boxes when these are played.

(z) Menu cards. The supply of menu cards printed with the advertiser's name, logo and slogan is a method of advertising long used in the catering, food and drinks trades. Some are more elaborate with magazine material which is changed from time to time to maintain the interest of regular customers. Menu cards provide a service both to caterer and customer.

5. Aerial advertising

While this may be regarded as 'outdoor' advertising, it is not usually classed as above-the-line. It is a medium which exploits elements of drama and surprise, involving curiosity. The forms of aerial advertising available in different countries depend on the laws which apply, especially to low flying over urban areas, on the ingenuity of promoters, and sometimes on what is peculiar to or possible in certain countries. For instance, if there is a coastline it is possible to carry aerial advertisements low over the sea in view of holidaymakers on the beach. The following are examples of this medium.

(a) Sky writing. Emitting a trail of smoke, an aircraft writes a word or words in the sky. This does, of course, require a clear sky and is limited by the weather.

129

(b) Sky shouting. In the aftermath of Rhodesian UDI, when the army used helicopters and loud-hailers to address villagers, this technique of shouting messages from the sky has been converted into an advertising medium in Zimbabwe.

(c) Sky banners. One of the oldest forms of aerial advertising is the use of slow aircraft to trail an advertising banner. A spectacular form seen in Holland is to have three aircraft tied together, each trailing a banner.

(d) Lighted aircraft, airships, balloons. At night aircraft can carry illuminated messages on the undersides of wings, while the Goodyear airships are a familiar sight in the USA and in Europe. Normally, Goodyear airships do not carry advertising over Britain but on the eve of the Royal Wedding in 1981 London read 'Loyal Greetings' in lights on the side of the Goodyear *Europa*.

Smaller airships have become popular in recent years, and have been used for semi-advertising semi-public relations purposes. The German-built Fuji airship often visits Britain, making passenger flights and appearing on TV programmes. Large and often colourful, they attract considerable attention as when the Fuji airship is painted in the characteristic red and green colours, or Coca-Cola displays its well-known house colour.

These airships are colourful eye catchers and are seen by thousands of people on the ground, but locations and routes should be chosen with discretion. It was surely foolish to fly the Coca-Cola airship above the motionless motorists held up during the construction of the extra lanes to the M25 motorway near Heathrow.

Figure 6.1 The Fujifilm airship on a visit to Britain. It is painted in the same characteristic red and green colours of the Fujifilm pack

Hot air balloons are not only painted in the colours of sponsors, but are often produced in the remarkable shapes of the products they advertise. These balloons may feature at outdoor events, or compete in races organised by the Balloon Club of Great Britain.

Tethered inflatables, often in the shape of packages or products, and small airships can be tethered as an eye-catching advertisement, or to promote something on the ground below such as a supermarket or car showroom. Spherical balloons can be tethered to marker buoys in the sea off holiday beaches.

(e) Projected advertisements. A few attempts have been made to project advertisements on the night sky with laser beams, or with a searchlight effect on low cloud. The effects can be weird and startling, but make a strong and lasting impact.

6. Calendars

Here we have a very old medium, one that is popular all over the world and has produced some famous calendars which have become collectors' items with collections like Pirelli's reaching the auction rooms. It is significant that Pirelli gave up using the famous calendars a few years ago only to return with a new series. They must have been missed! Calendars have a mixture of public relations goodwill and advertising reminder value, and so may be used for either or both purposes. They last a year, are displayed prominently, and consulted repeatedly.

Some advertisers may reproduce individual calendars, while others take advantage of stock calendars on which they can have their name and business details overprinted. Firms like Bemrose, Evershed and K. & J. Lockwood offer excellent designs which they change each year. Evershed have won international awards with their designs. Calendars take the following forms.

(a) Pictorial. Probably the most popular, the pictorial calendar can be of one, six or twelve sheets with a similar number of pictures. For some trades, the glamour girl calendar may be appropriate, for others, landscapes, paintings or cartoons may be preferred. For international use, months can be printed in more than one language.

(b) Block. This kind of calendar consists of a block of tear-off dates.

(c) Digital. Possibly combined with a clock and usually electric or electronic, the digital calendar can look modern and efficient.

(d) Scroll. Hanging vertically like a scroll, this type displays all the dates of the year.

(e) Quarterly. Here we have a clever idea because the quarterly calendar can be issued during the year at the right time, and avoids competition with the conventional calendars distributed at Christmas.

Bemrose report that the 1990s have seen wildlife calendars more popular than girlie calendars, which have slumped by 20 per cent. Ones with 'green' or charity messages are also popular.

7. CDs, CD-ROMs, audio and video cassettes

Increasing use is made of these devices, especially with the widespread availability of CD players, computers, tape and video recorders. They can be used for sampling purposes as *Reader's Digest* and Linguaphone do, or as Record Tokens have done with the offer of an audio tape on promotion tapes. Audio and video cassettes and CDs can be offered in press advertisements.

8. Adbags and carrier bags

Both can carry advertising messages, adbags being the more durable type of in-flight or sports bag, the carrier bag being a plastic one supplied by a retailer to carry shopping and having a shorter life. Both convey the advertiser's name to countless people who see the bag being carried about. This advertising can be well-placed if a sportsman carries his gear to a match.

9. Body media

This is perhaps an astonishing medium. People, especially teenagers, are willing to buy and wear clothing advertising radio stations, drinks and other commercial interests. Guinness have advertised their named shirts in the weekend colour magazines.

Specialist firms provide a comprehensive range of promotional leisure clothing such as:

- T-shirts,
- sweatshirts,
- caps,
- hats,
- headbands,
- visors,
- pullovers,
- jogging suits,
- bodywarmers,
- anoraks,
- scarves,
- umbrellas,

- rain-suits,

- ties,

- squares,

- aprons,

- rally jackets,

- sportshirts,

- light-weight jackets,

- tracksuits,

- ski wear,

- sashes,

- towels.

Staff and members' ties are another popular form of body media which are mainly a way of creating and promoting corporate identity. They may have emblems screen printed on polyester, woven into fabrics such as silk or embroidered.

10. Flags

This is a medium which is particularly popular in certain countries like Germany where premises such as car showrooms fronting a main highway attract attention with a long row of masts with large flags run up. On a lesser scale are the smaller flags projected from shops and kiosks advertising, say, ice-cream. There are also company flags which adorn and identify factories and other company premises. Not only are they colourful but they flap in the breeze, and therefore have attention-getting movement.

11. Playing cards

Another old medium, with Carta Mundi and Waddington well-known suppliers, is packs of playing cards bearing advertisements on the backs.

12. Bookmatches

In a similar way to menu cards, bookmatches provide a service to the customer, as well as advertising the proprietor such as a hotelier or restaurateur. They are a very practical form of point-of-sale material. Designs can be clever and of different size and shape container with various kinds of matches. However, since fewer people smoke today this medium has its limitations. Bookmatches are highly collectable.

13. Give-aways

Under this heading come numerous gifts and novelties, some of which may have genuine usefulness and therefore long promotional life. Probably the most popular are pens and key-rings, but there are many more, including pencils, rulers, paper-knives, penknives, bottle openers, wallets, card-holders, calculators, drinking mugs and acrylic paperweights containing souvenirs. CDs and CD-ROMs are popular give-aways.

14. Paper-clips

Perhaps one of the best ideas in recent years is the plastic ad-clip, a large, colourful advertising paper-clip which can convey an advertising message with correspondence and become reusable since the modest paper-clip is rarely thrown away. Produced by Westfield of Birmingham, they are supplied in tubs containing 100 Super Ad-Clips. There are also larger Midi Ad-Clips, and even bigger Giant and Giant Heart Ad-Clips.

15. Video media

Video has become a most versatile medium, emerging as an alternative mode of domestic television, and appearing in various ways at the point-of-sale to demonstrate, for example, new cars or give 'film' presentations of holiday attractions. When the new version of the Alfa-Romeo 164 was introduced, buyers of the original model were sent a video which demonstrated the new one.

The Post Office videoservice is an ingenious example of the use of video in retail outlets. In large post offices where there is a single queue leading up to the counter clerks, a large TV-like monitor gives a continuous presentation of video ads. Some are for Post Office services but other advertisers have included Servowarm central heating, Pentel pens, Canon cameras, Stork margarine, CreditPlan loans, Pilot pens, Ordnance Survey maps, Thomas Cook, Truprint and Bonusprint film processing. The video commercial usually refers to leaflets displayed in dispensers on the premises.

16. Book advertising

Advertisements were common in novels many years ago, and when Penguins were first introduced by Alan Lane in the 1930s, advertisements were included in the paperbacks. Now *Burke's Peerage* have reintroduced advertising into popular books and, by so doing, have helped to subsidise the prices of the books. Another form of book advertising is the insertion of a loose card, used by some insurance companies, readers often retaining this as a bookmark. Promotional bookmarks are used in advertising, PR and marketing directories and annuals, and similar publications in other fields.

17. Badges

The badge bearing a logo has many promotional uses; for example, establishing personal, corporate and product identity. The badge of identity on the bonnet of a car is almost always used in its advertising, PR and sales promotion. Probably the best known producers of badges of every type are Fattorini of Birmingham.

18. Stickers

Again, these have a variety of uses such as on shop windows, car windows or for application to stationery. A variation on this is the transfer.

19. An overview of future trends

Media are constantly changing, often reflecting economic, social, ethnic and political changes. The press, while losing some circulation among the more sensational tabloids and the politically boring heavies, predominates chiefly because of its long life, portability, and ability to reach any required target audience. Radio, both local and national, has acquired a new importance in the UK, and suits tight budgets. Posters, because of the rationalisation of sites and sizes and the offering of strategically planned campaigns, has resumed its former position. Direct mail continues to boom in spite of the occasional inefficiency of the Post Office but thanks to the growth of direct response marketing. Cinema has shown a marked increase in audience figures. Transportation advertising does not seem to appeal to advertisers judging by the number of buses one sees naked of posters.

Exhibitions have had mixed fortunes according to the location and extent, if any, of government support. Exhibitions and trade fairs are popular but many exhibitors are seeking export markets which has meant showing in Asia, Europe and the Gulf rather than in Britain. New exhibition centres have been built in Hong Kong, Jakarta, Kuala Lumpur and Singapore, representing the growing prosperity of the 'dragon countries' of Asia, with their inter-country trade (some of it barter), and Indonesia's economic expansion since its switch to non-oil industries. Despite the downturn in some Asian and Far Eastern national economies, there is no reason to assume that the trend towards bigger and better international exhibitions will slow down. Their popularity demonstrates that everybody needs them as much as ever for profitable trade.

But the medium which is really losing favour is television. This is partly because some of its audiences have low spending power and partly because of the proliferation of channels plus the temptation to zap from one channel to another when the commercials come on. Moreover, some commercials are so obtuse it is difficult to know what they are offering; while the detergent ads of the 1990s have been the dullest ever imposed on TV audiences already bored by endless repeats. There is now such a clutter of commercials scattered over numerous channels that the audience has become fractured. The rising medium for advertising is the Internet. Although it can be highly interactive, it is treated by some advertisers as a below-the-line medium, or disregarded altogether. The push-pull potential of advertising on the Web is still not properly appreciated. When advertisers devote as much of their budgets to the Internet as to other forms of sales promotion, it might be possible to claim that it has truly 'arrived'. That day may be some way off.

Progress test 6

1. List the main classes of below-the-line media. **(3–18)**

2. What are (a) mobiles; (b) dumpers and dump bins; (c) display outers; (d) crowners; (e) shelf edgings? **(4)**

3. Describe the various kinds of aerial advertising. **(5)**

4. What is the advertising value of the calendar? **(6)**

5. How can audio cassettes be used as advertising media? Give an example. **(7)**

6. What are body media? **(9)**

7. How can flags be used for advertising purposes? **(10)**

8. Describe some uses of videotapes as advertising media. **(15)**

9. How have media changed in recent years? **(19)**

7

Sales promotion

GROWING IMPORTANCE OF SALES PROMOTION

1. Definitions

The term 'sales promotion' has become widely accepted as covering special promotional schemes, usually of limited duration, at the point-of-sale or point-of-purchase. Such schemes were formerly referred to as 'merchandising', and the old term is still used in some quarters, for example by the sales departments of television companies. However, with the growing influence of the Institute of Sales Promotion, the existence of the British Codes of Advertising and Sales Promotion (*see* 18: **35**), and the appearance of sales promotion features in the trade press, the old expression 'merchandising' in the promotional sense is falling into disuse. Sales promotion has also acquired two other names, scene advertising and tactical advertising.

The advent of the single European market, in which countries some forms of give-away or premium offer sales promotion are illegal, led in 1990 to the creation of a European Code of Conduct under the European Federation of Sales Promotion.

Sales promotion can also be linked with direct response marketing. Various games and gimmicks can accompany mailshots. Gifts such as small cameras and carriage clocks may be offered to those who buy bonds or insurance policies by mail from firms like Norwich Union and Sun Alliance. Horticultural suppliers offer gifts to those who place orders of a certain value.

2. Reasons for growth

Sales promotion has grown enormously in recent years, and sales promotion consultancies have reported record business. The chief reasons for this are outlined below.

(a) The desire of advertisers, often worried by the high cost of media advertising (e.g. TV), which has increased faster than the rate of inflation, to find more cost-effective forms of promotion.

(b) The growth of huge supermarket chains and out-of-town superstores and the need for aggressive on-the-shelf competitive promotions, both to sell in and to sell out.

(c) The opportunities provided by supermarkets, hypermarkets and large-scale mixed retailing to promote on the premises.

(d) The need to propel sales, both to satisfy the cash flow of retailers and to maintain output from high volume production plants.

(e) The availability of greater expertise in creating sales promotion schemes, as demonstrated by the emergence and growth of successful sales promotion consultancies. They have filled the gap left by traditional advertising agencies which were reluctant to indulge in other than commission-paying above-the-line media advertising.

(f) The goodwill aspect of sales promotion which tends to bring the manufacturer closer to the retailer. Media advertising tends to be remote whereas sales promotion is more personal, linking the manufacturer with the customer at the place of sale wherever this may be.

(g) The introduction of a certain fun and excitement into promotions which customers can enjoy as participants. This, again, is quite different from media advertising with its strident clamour to buy.

(h) The ability, with small unit FMCGs, to encourage impulse buying and attract first-time buyers.

(i) The extension of sales promotion into new areas such as financial institutions promotion (e.g. banking and charge cards), and to the promotion of consumer durables from cameras to cars, plus many services such as holidays, travel, hotels and restaurants. It is by no means limited to the supermarkets and High Street stores (*see* **3**). It has also been extended to multinational and international marketing of products such as beer.

(j) The growth of direct response marketing which often uses sales promotion devices and gimmicks as inserts in mailings, or as rewards and bonuses to buyers.

3. Sales promotion consultancy clients

The importance today of sales promotion is borne out by the fact that the clients of British sales promotion consultancies include names as diverse as Allied Breweries Overseas Trading, American Express, Bass, Birds Eye, Booker Health Foods, Boots, British Airways, Citicorp Travellers Cheques, Dunhill, Duracell, Guinness Overseas, Hertz, The Jamaica Tourist Board, Lloyds Bank, LRC Products, L'Oreal, Pan Books, Peugeot, Royal Worcester, Sterling Health, Seiko, Smirnoff (Europe), Times Newspapers and Hiram Walker.

TYPES OF SALES PROMOTION SCHEME

4. Variety of choice

A remarkable variety of sales promotion techniques is available, and a walk around a supermarket will reveal the large number of very different schemes which are operating simultaneously. Equally, at one's bank, travel agency, building society, filling station, hotel or corner shop all manner of schemes will be apparent. Often, they work on the principle that few people can resist a free gift, price reduction or special offer. The appeal is basically to greed!

In recent years there have been changes in the popularity of certain types of offer, while some older kinds have returned. There are still premium offers which require the sending in of cash and proof of purchase, but competitive prices in High Street shops have made some of the offers of household articles less attractive (*see* 4: **24**). Moreover, offers with immediate take-up while shopping have become more popular than those requiring the effort of mailing in. There has also been the innovation of charity promotions (*see* **16**), while free draws have been introduced by Woolworths and some petrol companies such as BP, Esso, Mobil and Shell (*see* 18: **22**). The matching halves of coupons idea has been revived with original versions such as Mobil's Scrabble and Shell's Mastermind.

While sales promotion schemes may induce habit buying or the buying of quantities to the exclusion of other brands, they can also induce frenetic brand switching and the loss of brand loyalty. The 'cherry picker' is the person who goes round a store selecting the special offers, probably irrespective of brand. On the other hand, sales promotion encourages greater competitiveness at the point-of-sale which can, of course, widen consumer choice and encourage people to make experimental first-time buys. All these implications have to be considered carefully by the promoter of any of the sales promotion schemes discussed below.

5. Competitions and free prize draws

Prize contests depend for success on the value or originality of the prize, and perhaps on the additional chances of winning offered by consolation prizes. The entry requirement can be proof of purchase such as a token or entry coupon detached from the pack, extra entries requiring extra purchases. To be legal, contests require an element of skill (*see* 18: **22**), there should be sufficient permutations of, say, answers to avoid division of the prize. A secondary part of the contest (such as 'why I wish to win' statement) may be adopted as a tie-breaker in the event of the main contest producing more than one winner. Contests should be organised with adequate time for proper adjudication, and there should be publicised announcement of results.

Competitions should not be inhibited by the nature of the prize. For example, a cash prize or a car may be more attractive than something like a holiday which may not suit the winner's personal affairs and may be an embarrassment. With some prizes such as holidays, cash alternatives are seldom possible. However, it depends where the contest is being held; in a developing country a car might be inappropriate whereas a holiday abroad could be very attractive. Money prizes are usually universally acceptable, as evident by the international success of football pools, sweepstakes and public lotteries.

There is a distinction between a prize *competition* which requires an element of skill, and a *free draw* which depends on chance. To avoid the illegality of a lottery, no proof of purchase or in fact any purchase is required, and the promoter offers prizes to lucky entrants. One football pool promoter, for instance, has offered free flights on Concorde whether or not the entrant invests in the pools. Mailings, such as those of *Reader's Digest*, may combine sales promotion and direct response. They often contain YES or NO reply options. Improbable though it may seem, it was reported in *Direct Response* that the majority of winners are NOs! Is this because more NOs are received than YESes?

Unfortunately some of these free draws lie in a grey area between a legal and an illegal lottery. A legal lottery is one conducted by a non-commercial sponsor such as a charity. To say 'no purchase necessary' is hardly credible since there is no point in spending money on a prize unless the object is to promote sales. Commercial firms are not public benefactors. The prize must be an inducement to achieve something if only an increase in store traffic.

Weetabix have repeated their children's bike competition and offer. It was quite a complicated promotion. One side panel of the Weetabix carton pictured the Raleigh bike which was suitable for 7–10 year olds, and 100 bikes were to be won, ten each month for nine months, with the last ten to be won by the closing date. To enter, three questions had to be answered plus a 12-word statement on why Raleigh and Weetabix made a winning combination. Also on the side panel were on-pack offers of accessories for cash and tokens.

6. Self-liquidating premium offers

The meaning of the expression 'self-liquidating' is not that slow selling goods or old stock are sold off cheaply, but that special lines are bought by the promoter and offered at a premium (i.e. less than normal retail price) which will liquidate the cost. Many such lines are, however, made up specially and are not available in the shops, and care has to be taken not to make a false reference to retail value. Premium offers have the irresistible appeal of the bargain that must not be forsaken.

7. Mail-in free offers

Here, no payment is required, only proof of purchase or perhaps a token payment to cover postage and packing. Care is necessary to control demand and supply, and it is best to limit the offer in some way. John Player & Sons met disaster with their King Size cigarette offer of a free lighter. They were obliged to distribute 2,250,000 lighters, each costing the company £1! (*See* also **32.**)

8. Free gifts with goods

The gift is usually attached to the product, as with a toothbrush attached to a carton of toothpaste. Toys (carefully packed separately) may be inserted in packets of breakfast cereals. Alternatively, the customer may have to request the gift from the retailer, e.g. wine glasses or Air Miles tokens with petrol purchases.

9. Picture cards

Originating with cigarette cards of years ago, these require collecting and so encourage repeat buying in order to obtain the set. They may be inserted in packs, or printed as cut-outs on cartons. Such cards are sometimes contained in boxes of tea bags.

10. Gift coupons

Again, these have to be collected in order to qualify for gifts, and so require repeat purchasing. A catalogue of gifts must be made available. This has been a favourite with cigarette companies.

11. Cash dividends

Cash refunds against the collection of tokens with a cash value also induce repeat purchase. Tea firms have used this method.

12. Matching halves

Popular with the petrol companies, coupon halves are given with the purchases, and certain matching halves have claimable cash values.

13. Cash premium vouchers or coupons

These can be redeemed at the retailers as a price reduction. They may be printed in press advertisements, delivered door-to-door, or printed on packs as money off the next purchase.

An example of door-to-door delivery of coupons is the very successful *The Coupon Book* in which advertisers such as Brooke Bond, Colgate Palmolive, Colmans, Johnson Wax, Procter & Gamble, Lever Brothers and Dulux have taken space for coupon offers. This method is claimed to be very economical, production costs being 50 per cent less than for door-to-door leaflet distribution, while the cost of redeeming a coupon is 7.5p compared with 40p from the national press.

14. Cross-couponing offers and other schemes

This is a popular co-operation scheme whereby an on-pack coupon or token enables the customer to buy another product (not necessarily made by the same manufacturer) at a reduced price. A great variety of offers have been made such as free railway tickets, reductions on package holidays, or reductions on products associated with the one making the offer. The reference to another brand on a pack, whether as an advertisement or as a premium offer, is also known as 'cross-branding'.

Shredded Wheat have run a number of schemes which have required the collecting of tokens for offers at a premium price. One such offer was for a rose bush for 10 tokens and a payment of £1.50. Another Shredded Wheat offer required 10 tokens to participate in a half-fare scheme with P & O Ferries.

Bisto are constant users of sales promotion schemes, usually of the money-off next purchase kind, but an attractive one for a family product was the Bisto Kids Tea Towel offer. The on-pack wording was very simple to follow even though three choices were available. The towels had caricature pictures of the Bisto Kids. Two tokens had to be collected for each towel, choice of towel had to be identified in boxes on the coupon, and sent to RHM Foods Ltd together with £1.40 per towel (95p for Tea Towel plus 45p towards postage and packing). A 16oz pack carried two tokens, an 8oz pack one token. The customer was asked to indicate first choice in case an alternative had to be supplied. There was a closing date.

An attractive on-pack offer which combined a simple purchase or a special offer for tokens plus a 20p coin was that on Kelloggs Corn Flakes packs for models of the land speed record cars Bluebird, Railton Mobil Special, Spirit of America – Sonic 1, and Thrust 2. Each car was offered for 9 tokens (3 tokens to a large 750g box) plus a 20p coin. The instructions were specific that a coin and not stamps should accompany the token, a point missed by some other offers. Or all four models could be bought for a cheque or postal order for £7.99. The closing date unusually extended to six months after the launch, encouraging repeat buying. Some closing dates are so soon that the customer has to buy and store a stock of the product in order to participate in the offer while the right packs are still in the shops.

The Checkout Saver is one way of encouraging the co-operation of dealers, and this was first introduced into 5,000 stores in the USA by Catalina

Electronic Marketing, and adopted in the UK by Asda supermarkets. The idea is to avoid wasted coupons, as can occur in mail-drops and more expensively in press advertisements, by targeting them at likely users. These people can be identified by an electronic device at the check-out which matches purchases against offers, even to the extent of providing a sales promotion offer to the buyer of a rival brand, or a similar product. Thus coupons are targeted according to purchases, and a scheme for a sugar-free product is not given to the purchaser of cereal covered in sugar. It also obviates misredemptions, and if the system is widely accepted by large supermarket chains it could make coupons one of the most heavily used forms of sales promotion.

15. High Street redemption schemes

This is a fairly recent on-pack idea, whereby a product carries a premium coupon entitling the customer to a discount at a named store. This is liked by the store because the discount can lead to other purchases.

An interesting scheme which combined the schemes outlined in **14** and **15** was that which offered a free 250ml trial size of Crown Solo paint on packs of Kellogg's Bran Flakes. Eight tokens and 40p to cover postage had to be sent to the fulfilment house (one in the UK, one in Ireland), and the large 750g carton carried three tokens. The association of paint and cereals may seem strange, but actually some serious thinking went into the promotion. Steve Duncan, Marketing Manager Retail Paint for Crown Berger, recognised that Bran Flakes has an adult target market as does painting, especially gloss painting. Both products were brand leaders and the promotion offered both parties a benefit. In the case of Kellogg's there was a high perceived value offer, the free sample being worth £1.89. Crown Berger liked the scheme because the distribution channels were not common, the daily traffic of consumers through grocery multiples far exceeding that of a DIY superstore. Thus the profile of the new paint was raised more significantly than by relying on promoting it within the retail paint market. See illustration of pack in Figure 7.1. This is a form of 'third party' dealing.

16. Charity promotions

Cash value tokens are printed on packs, and if these are sent to the charity it can redeem them with the promoter of the scheme. However, the redeemable amount must be worthwhile. One food manufacturer ran a scheme which offered to help finance school sports funds, customers giving their children the tokens to take to school. The value of the tokens was so trivial, and so many tokens had to be collected to redeem cash, that there were protests from schools. It is also vital to avoid political overtones as has happened with some promotions linked to controversial Olympic Games.

143

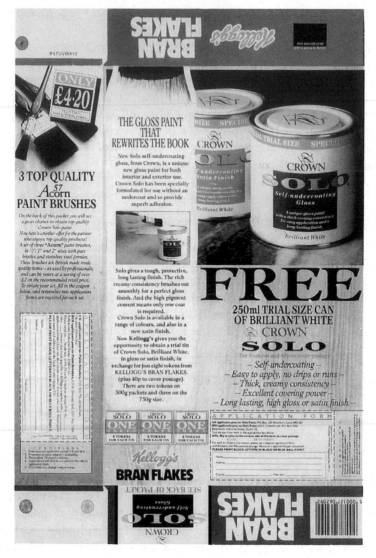

Figure 7.1 The Kellogg's Bran Flakes pack, as printed flat before folding, and described in section 15

There is an integral public relations element in charity promotions which could have a good or bad effect on the company image, depending on how the scheme is devised and managed.

A charity scheme was linked with Lucozade's sponsorship of athletics when packs of the new product aimed at the youth market carried tokens which schools could collect to raise funds.

W.H. Smith's Free Books For Schools ran a summer scheme which offered £5m worth of books to schools. With every purchase of £2 the customer received a voucher. Schools had to collect a minimum of 500 vouchers in order to claim £50 worth of free books, a maximum of 5,000 vouchers being redeemable for £500 worth of books. The scheme was supported by a £500,000 national press and poster campaign.

17. Jumbo or multiple packs

This means that a number of items are packed together or the container is extra large, and offered at a special price. It is an economical way of both packing and buying such items, and ensures that the customer is well stocked with the product and may thus become a habit buyer. Special holiday and Christmas packs are typical examples.

KitKat (see Figure 7.2), Britain's best selling countline, combined a jumbo pack with a price cut (eight bars for the price of seven) for a Woolworths promotion. It incorporated a sharper typeface for the name with its big capital Ks, created by Nestlé's in-house designers. First launched in 1935 as chocolate crisp, it became KitKat in 1937. It has a £200m market share and an advertising budget of £4.6m. Its nearest rival is Mars Bar.

18. Banded packs

Similarly, a number of items are banded together and sold at a bulk price, e.g. bars of soap, bars of chocolate.

19. Flash packs

Special offers, or money-off offers, are 'flashed', that is, printed on the wrapper or carton, a sure way of inducing impulse buying. The Trade Descriptions Act 1968 must be observed by stating the normal recommended price when a price cut is 'flashed'. This is one of the most popular sales promotion schemes, and very easy to operate, having immediate appeal to the impulse buyer.

20. In-store demonstrations

Here, a demonstrator will have a booth in the store and demonstrate the product (e.g. an ironing board) or offer samples (e.g. drinks), and either sell the product direct or pass sales to the regular shop assistant.

21. Promotional games

These have become popular in recent years, and include scratch cards revealing a possible cash claim which the promoter will redeem. Some resemble football pools or bingo.

Figure 7.2 KitKat special offer combined with jumbo pack

22. Advertorials

Advertorials are also termed 'advertisement promotions'. An old favourite when a new product is launched is to supply it to a newspaper or magazine which provides an editorial feature and makes readers a special introductory offer. This has been used to launch lipsticks and shampoos through mass-circulation women's magazines, and it has been developed in many other joint ventures with publishers offering a wide variety of products and services from camera lenses to holidays. For some publishers it has become an additional business activity while providing a reader service.

However, advertorials have acquired a dubious reputation when sponsored features have been dressed up to look like legitimate public relations features, that is instead of being genuine editorials the space has been paid for at a special rate.

The Sales Promotion Code lays down that advertisers, publishers and owners of other media should ensure that advertisements are designed and presented in such a way that they can be easily distinguished from editorial. This usually means that the advertiser's name and address are shown, and that the word 'Advertisement' appears at the top of the insertion (Clauses 23.1 and 41.1).

23. On-pack direct marketing

A number of product packs, such as Swan Vestas matches and Tate & Lyle sugar bags, carry offers which are perhaps more than premium offers, and are really an extra form of trading. McDougall's famous cookery book has been advertised with a mail order coupon on flour bags.

TERMINOLOGY

24. Bolt-on promotion

This is a ready-made promotion, often specially produced and offered to manufacturers, such as scratch-card games.

25. Fulfilment house

This is a specialist firm which warehouses sales promotion gifts or premium offers, and despatches them to applicants. The address of the fulfilment house usually appears on the offer. It should not be confused with a sales promotion agency which organises the scheme. Fulfilment houses also handle requests for catalogues and brochures which have been advertised.

Fulfilment houses have to be capable of handling response very quickly, and this is not always the case, leading to irritated customers. For instance, a very successful user of direct response catalogues, Racing Green, depended on quick delivery of its fashion wear. Two fulfilment houses failed to despatch promptly and the company had to set up its own in-house despatch department.

26. Contract packer

A firm which not only packs normal retail packs (e.g. aerosols, blister packs, sachets) for manufacturers, but produces special promotional packs.

27. Redemption

The payment of cash in response to cash premium offers, or the acceptance of premium vouchers.

28. Misredemption and malredemption

Acceptance of premium vouchers or coupons as part payment for goods other than that of the product being promoted is referred to as misredemption (*see* **35**). Malredemption means criminal misuse of premium vouchers such as by theft. The terms mis- and malredemption are loosely used to mean the same thing, but strictly speaking malredemption refers to a malpractice.

29. Extrinsic

Additional in value to that of the basic product, e.g. garden bulbs or Christmas cards offered free to purchasers of, say, a brand of tea. This is often called 'value added'.

PROBLEMS AND RISKS

30. Disappointed customers

An important public relations aspect of sales promotion is that while money-off offers can be welcome, and premium offers can be enjoyed, and it may be entertaining to enter for a prize contest, promotions have a magnetic appeal which in itself poses risks of damage to company goodwill and product images. If, for some reason, customers are offended or disappointed, the promotion can turn sour, or if the fulfilment house is slow to deliver, this is bad public relations.

There have been many examples of stocks being exhausted by unpredicted demand, long delays in the delivery of merchandise, arrival of damaged goods owing to poor packing, or in the case of contests inefficient announcement of results.

In an article in *Campaign*, 'Special Offers Out of Control', Brian Oliver described the experience of Smiths Foods who ran a James Bond watch offer for £6.99 plus proof of purchase of Monster Munch. Demand was so incredible that initial stocks and repeat orders of the watch were exhausted, and it became impossible to obtain further stocks. Refunds had to be sent to disappointed youngsters. Fisher-Price dolls were offered in a promotion for Sterling Health's Baby Wet Ones, but supplies ran out and apologies had to be mailed to disappointed applicants.

More recently, Hoover Offered purchasers of vacuum cleaners free flights to the USA. The demand was so overwhelming that the scheme had to be abandoned. The company suffered not only financial loss, but also the threat of legal action from irate, disappointed customers.

A primary skill in operating sales promotion schemes is the ability to estimate demand. This is not always easy and some suggestions are made below. If an offer is made in a press advertisement it is necessary to appreciate the pulling power of the medium.

31. How to avoid disappointing customers

While this may not be easy with FMCGs which have rapid sales to the mass market, certain precautions can be taken, such as the following.

(a) Make sure that the supplier of the offer can supply on time and in repeat quantities if necessary. This may not be possible with imported items.

(b) Limit the offer to a given number of applicants.

(c) Put a time limit on the offer.

(d) If possible, include in the offer an acceptable substitute if stocks run out. A cash voucher is seldom satisfactory.

(e) Warn applicants not to expect delivery until, say, 28 days after sending in the application.

(f) Employ a reliable fulfilment house (*see* **25**) to handle despatches.

(g) Demonstrate thoughtfulness by including in the package a note offering to replace any item damaged in the post. Thank you notes, hoping applicants will enjoy a premium product, are always good public relations. While sales promotion in itself is not public relations, there are important public relations aspects in the extent to which goodwill is gained or lost.

32. Retailer attitudes

It is important that the retailer likes a sales promotion scheme and is prepared to co-operate with it. As Brian Oliver said in an article 'Offers They Cannot Refuse' in *Marketing*: 'If retailers see the premium as a competing product, they might not give the promotion the display space you're after. They might even refuse to stock the product.'

33. Sales force enthusiasm

A sales promotion scheme can fail if it is not fully supported by the company's own salespeople. In another article in *Marketing* Peter Hood stated: 'The communication begins at home: if the promotion is not sold to the company's own management and sales force there can be little chance of them selling it to anyone else.'

34. Too-enthusiastic consumers

It is also necessary to ensure that the enthusiasm of consumers for a promotion does not create problems which both harm the promotion and embarrass the company. Some ideas can be too clever, as occurred with the Cadbury's chocolate cream Easter egg treasure hunt scheme. There was a treasure hunt for 12 'gold' eggs worth £10,000 each. One hundred thousand people wrote in for the storybook containing the treasure hunt clues. One of the 'golden eggs' was hidden in a field, and when some participants started digging up an archaeological site in Cornwall, Cadbury had to cancel the hunt for this particular egg.

35. Misredemptions

A serious problem with cash premium vouchers which can be redeemed at the shop when purchasing the promoted product is that the response can be misleading if retailers accept them as part payment for other goods. Some manufacturers print warnings on the vouchers that they may be redeemed only for the specific product (*see* **37**), but this is ineffective when leading supermarket chains openly announce that they will accept any premium vouchers against any purchase provided the promoted product is stocked. Consequently, when the retailer seeks payment from the manufacturer the latter may have no idea of the effect of the scheme upon sales other than perhaps the level of reordering. Thus, the vouchers could have been redeemed for rival brands, and the level of reordering could have been static so that the effect of the promotion had been either nullified or less than forecast.

One method of discovering the extent of misredemption is discussed in **36** below.

36. Coupon redemption analysis

An interesting example of the application of marketing research to sales promotion is the RETAL service which has been developed by Nielsen

Clearing House (NCH) of Corby. The company acts as a clearing house for premium coupon redemptions, and handles more than one million redemptions a day. It enables clients to see a summary of coupon redemptions by individual retailers. The analysis offers subscribers three benefits. First, it identifies major sources of coupon redemption. Second, it enables comparisons to be made between products sold into outlet and coupons redeemed. Third, it enables comparisons to be made between individual retailer contribution to coupon promotions.

The RETAL report shows the total number of coupons contained in all claims processed by NCH during the selected period for the named retailer. It gives the value of coupons paid for all claims processed by NCH in the selected period for the named retailer. There is an analysis of the individual coupons or group totals for the named retailer and an individual analysis of the number of coupons redeemed within each code or group by retailer within the given period. This includes a percentage of all coupons within each code or group within the period.

Thus promoters of premium coupons can see how their sales promotion scheme performed in respect of different retailers and also in relation to stocks supplied to these retailers. This can also reveal the extent, if any, of misredemption, as when coupon redemptions exceed supplies to a retailer.

37. Example of redemption

On packs of Birds trifle there was an on-pack offer of a triple pack of Cadburys chocolate buttons. This was a slightly complicated scheme, the customer being required to cut two tokens from the special Birds pack. This entitled the customer to affix the tokens to a cut-out coupon and redeem it from the retailer. The tokens, as affixed, were worth either a triple pack of Cadburys buttons or 68 pence towards any Cadburys buttons. The promoters were Kraft General Foods Ltd. The offer was worded as follows to avoid mis-redemption:

> TO THE CONSUMER. This voucher, when completed with 2 Buttons tokens, entitles you to a FREE Cadburys Buttons Triple Pack or 68p towards any Cadburys Button purchase. This voucher may not be used towards the purchase of any other item and may only be used at participating retailers. Offer subject to availability. No change will be given. Voucher not redeemable for cash (UK only). Valid until 30.9.93.
>
> TO THE RETAILER. Valid only for the purchase of a Cadburys Button Triple pack or 68p towards any Cadburys Buttons purchase. Kraft General Foods Ltd reserve the right to refuse redemption of vouchers which, in their opinion, are damaged, defaced or invalidly redeemed. Voucher only valid with 2 Buttons tokens affixed. Kraft General Foods Ltd will repay the face value of this voucher for each voucher received. For reimbursement send voucher via your Head Office to NCH, Dept 944, Corby, Northants, NN17 1NN. VOUCHER VALUE 68p.

151

One wonders whether anyone reads this sort of small print, and the above example is hedged about with a remarkable set of restrictions. The address is the Nielsen Clearing House at Corby.

Progress test 7

1. Define sales promotion. **(1)**

2. Why has sales promotion become so important? **(2)**

3. What changes have occurred in sales promotion practice? **(4)**

4. Why is the nature of the prize so important when running a competition? **(5)**

5. Explain the terms: (a) self-liquidating premium offer; and (b) mail-in free offer. **(6, 7)**

6. What is a cross-couponing offer? **(14)**

7. What is a High Street redemption scheme? **(15)**

8. How are charity promotions conducted? **(16)**

9. Explain the use of flash packs. **(19)**

10. Distinguish between misredemption and malredemption. **(28)**

11. How can the sales promotion organiser avoid disappointing customers? **(31)**

12. Describe the essentials of the RETAL system of researching sales promotion. **(36)**

8

Sponsorship

DEFINITION AND EXAMPLES

1. Definitions

Sponsorship consists of the giving of monetary or other support to a beneficiary in order to make its activites financially viable, sometimes for altruistic reasons, but usually to gain some advertising, public relations or marketing advantage (see **7–10**).

The support could consist of money, as in the case of prizes, but may comprise trophies or other gifts in kind. The beneficiary could be an organisation or an individual. While some sponsors may simply wish to be philanthropic this is seldom so today when the object is more often deliberately commercial.

In Britain a new type of sponsorship was introduced by the Broadcasting Act 1990 which permitted the commercial sponsorship of both radio (ILR and INR) and television (ITV) programmes. The sponsor may use copylines in sponsored radio programmes, and is allowed brief credits in trailers, intros, and bumper breaks during ITV programmes, and at the close. But the sponsor is not allowed to contribute to the making of the programme, nor may its products be used during the programme. This form of sponsorship may be defined as the commercial sponsorship of an ILR, INR or ITV programme for a fee.

2. Growth of sponsorship

There has been a 12 per cent increase in sponsorships over the past 10 years. In the UK, expenditure totals about £322m. Worldwide, the breakdown is about 3.2m North America; 8.5m USA; 1.5m Japan; and 2.8m Europe (in dollars).

Arts sponsorship has become increasingly popular in recent years with more than 1,000 businesses sponsoring arts interests. It is popular worldwide with large and small advertisers. Historically, its origins go back to the sponsorship or patronage of artists and musicians by royalty and other wealthy benefactors. We still see this today with the commercial sponsorship of symphony orchestras, art exhibitions and the theatre. However, the bulk of sponsorship money is spent on sport, and while this support is given mainly to the major sports of athletics, football, rugby, motor-racing, horse-racing, show-jumping, cricket, tennis and golf, a number of other sports have become popular through sponsorship and television coverage, to mention only bowls, snooker, netball, and darts.

In recent years major sports and sporting events have become sponsored when this would have been unheard of in the past. Cornhill Insurance, for example, have sponsored test cricket: Carling, the FA Premiership; Nationwide, the English Football League and England football team. The Derby has been sponsored by Vodaphone (*see* 14: **22–30**). The Colt Car Co. Ltd, the *Sun*, Seagram and Martell brandy have financed the Grand National, and Gillette, Mars and Nutra-Sweet have backed the London Marathon. International events such as yacht races, car rallies and safaris also have their sponsors. Sometimes there are multiple sponsorships embracing the event itself, section prizes, and the individual competitors or their vehicles, horses or boats.

Canon were the original sponsors of the Football League, and at the end of their three-year sponsorship costing £3 million they were able to boast that there was hardly an office in Britain which did not have a Canon machine. The strength of this sponsorship was that British football is played for many months of the year by 92 teams, thus producing constant media coverage.

Athletics is another sport with the continuing interest in various championships. Lucozade, in its isotonic, non-fizzy style, sponsors athletics, and winners of events receive a bottle of the drink.

The best sports to sponsor are ones which occur repeatedly, rather than a single event such as a golf sponsorship. The two most popular sports are athletics and football, both of which achieve regular TV coverage.

Sponsorships are rarely continuous and usually last two or three years when sponsors may or may not renew the arrangement. Camel cigarettes (RJR Tobacco International) first sponsored the Williams and Benetton Formula One racing teams in 1987, but ended their £27m support in 1993. Rothmans took over the Williams team with an £11m two-year deal, extending it in 1996 for a further two years in a deal worth £20m.

3. What can be sponsored?

While the biggest, costliest and probably most cost-effective sponsorships are those which make popular news, and are mainly in the realms of sport, there are many categories of sponsorship, and some may suit particular sponsors better than others. It is not necessary to spend a fortune, and support for a local event in the vicinity of the company's headquarters may be of minimal cost but have maximum effect on, say, staff relations or recruitment. The main categories of sponsorship are as follows.

(a) Books and other publications such as maps. Some of these may be sold as legitimate publications.

(b) Exhibitions which may be sponsored by trade associations and professional societies, or by newspapers and magazines, or company-sponsored private exhibitions.

(c) Education, in the form of grants, bursaries, scholarships and fellowships. Grants may be made for research for a book. Heinz sponsored the first UK chair in brand management at Bradford University.

(d) Expeditions, explorations, mountaineering, round-the-world voyages and other adventures.

(e) Sport, as already described and spreading to many of the minor sports.

(f) The arts such as music, painting, literature and the theatre.

(g) Causes and charities, especially by helping them to promote their activities. For instance, pharmaceutical companies produce videos to explain the causes, nature and treatment of illnesses. The National Trust has numerous sponsors, while organisations such as the Automobile Association sponsor NT publications.

(h) Local events can be supported with prizes, as with horse shows, gymkhanas, sports meetings and flower shows.

(i) Professional awards for people associated with the sponsor's industry such as photographers, journalists, architects and others. Canon, for instance, in conjunction with *UK Press Gazette,* sponsor a Press Pictures of the Year competition which is very appropriate for a *camera manufacturer.* Nikon also have a contest for press photographers.

The year 1993 saw brewers sponsoring summer pop music festivals with their huge outdoor audiences. Murphy's (which has been competing mercilessly with Guinness) supported the Fleadh in Finsbury Park, London; Greene King backed the Cambridge Folk Festival; and Courage sponsored the Great British Rhythm and Blues Festival at Colne in Lancashire. These were events where the sponsor was able to enjoy huge on-the-spot sales.

4. Examples of sponsorship

Table 8.1 lists examples of sponsorship.

Table 8.2 shows which companies or brands were associated with particular sports. It is significant that they all received considerable media and especially TV coverage.

155

Table 8.1 Sponsored events

Activity	Sponsor or supporter
NSPCC anti-child-abuse campaign	Microsoft
Countdown (quiz show), Channel 4	Seven Seas
Movie Premiere (ITV)	Stella Artois
1999 Oxford and Cambridge boat race	Aberdeen Asset Management
Tyrrell F1 racing team	Brother (business equipment)
Williams F1 racing team 1999	Brother (business equipment)
Drama Premiere (Channel 4)	HSBC (Midland Bank)
Bournemouth Symphony Orchestra	Southern Electric
British Tiger, Round Britain and Ireland Yacht Race	Barclays Life
Round The World Yacht Race	Whitbread
National Basketball Association World tour	Converse sports shoes
Football League	Endsleigh Insurance
Vauxhall Invitation athletics	Vauxhall Motors
British Library (computer systems)	Digital Equipment Company
Gilbeys Ulster Oaks, The Bailies Ladies Flat, Smirnoff Sprint Handicap, and Budweiser Handicap Hurdle, Down Royal, N. Ireland	Gilbeys
London Marathon	Nutra Sweet
Young Athletics League	McDonald's
Women's European Nations U21 Hockey Cup	Edinburgh Airport
Rugby World Cup Sevens	Famous Grouse whisky
Amateur Swimming Association awards	Kia-Ora
Professional Tour of Britain Cycle Race	Kelloggs
Scottish Badminton Championships	Hydro Electric
International Junior Swimming Match for physically disabled and blind swimmers	Rotary International
Dance Umbrella dance festival	Prudential Insurance
European Football Championship	Sega
Everest Expedition 1993	DHL
Arts America season, Institute of Contemporary Arts	American Airlines
Citizens Advice Bureau	Nationwide Building Society

5. Sponsorship agencies

The planning and conducting of sponsorships, including the preliminary liaison between interests seeking sponsors and likely sponsors, and between potential sponsors and the bodies representing things which might be sponsored, is a very complicated and skilled business. Consequently, a number of specialist consultancies exist (*see* also 4: **25**). Two which are responsible for many of the major sponsorships are Alan Pascoe Associates and CSS

Table 8.2 Top ten sports sponsorships

1st	Embassy/snooker
2nd	Marlboro/motorsports
3rd	Benson & Hedges/snooker
4th=	Benson & Hedges/cricket
4th=	Mars/road running
6th	Rothmans/motorsports
7th	Nike/athletics
8th	Benson & Hedges/motorsports
9th	Adidas/athletics
10th=	Robinsons/tennis
10th=	Carling/football

Source: Sponsortest, October to December 1997. Sponsortest is a unique weekly tracking survey interviewing 1,600 people each month. It records spontaneous association of companies or brands with specific sports and sporting events.

Promotions. Alan Pascoe Associates handled the athletics sponsorship by Lucozade, the Cadbury sponsorship of pantomime in 41 theatres, and the Persil Funfit scheme for children. CSS Promotions were responsible for the very complicated Canon Football League sponsorship. On the other hand, leading Japanese advertising agencies such as Dentsu and Hakuhodo have sponsorship divisions.

The creation of a sponsorship scheme calls for research at the preparatory stage, and not merely on a company's decision to spend a certain sum on it. Alan Pascoe goes through the following nine initial stages:

(1) Audit of existing policy. Has the client engaged in sponsorship before? Does it donate to charities? The two are quite different and should be dealt with separately but in some companies the two may be regarded as the same thing. This is quite wrong. A donation to charity is a gift, a form of do-gooding, and it has no practical objective or expectation of a reward. Sponsorship should aim to achieve something specific. So it is necessary to know what the company has funded in the past.

(2) Objectives. What is the marketing communications policy? (These are discussed in 7, 9 and 10 below.)

(3) Strategy. What kind of and what purpose? This links with *objectives*. What methods shall be adopted to satisfy what intentions?

(4) Third party negotiations. This involves dealing with, say, the association which controls the subject of the sponsorship, e.g. the Amateur Athletics Association and an athletics event. Such associations usually own special rights which need to be interpreted in the sponsorship.

(5) Press conference. As early as possible a press conference should be called to announce the sponsorship.

(6) Contact with city services. If the event takes place on the public highway, such as a cycle race or a marathon, arrangements have to be made with all appropriate city services such as the police, ambulance service, fire brigade; other services such as the AA or RAC may be required to supply and fix route signs.

(7) Implementation of the scheme. This entails putting the plan on paper such as by producing an instruction manual or rules governing the award of prizes.

(8) Management of event on the site. Expert marshals will be required to control the event, guiding participants and managing spectators.

(9) Analysis. Finally, there should be a method of analysing the event and deciding how it might be done better next time. A video record of the event may be an excellent way of re-running it to check how it was conducted.

For fuller information about subjects sponsored, sponsors and sponsorship agencies the reader is recommended to study the comprehensive information in *Hollis Sponsorship and Donations Annual.*

OBJECTIVES

6. An investment

As stated at the end of the definitions in **1**, the aim of a sponsorship is to gain results associated with the advertising, public relations or marketing strategy. It is an investment to gain a desired positive result. Before becoming committed to any sort of expenditure, large or small, the prospective sponsor needs to check that these results are attainable.

It is not uncommon for a sponsorship to have a blend of advertising, public relations and marketing objectives and benefits, which could be quite different. Although this book is concerned mainly with advertising, all three aspects of sponsorship are analysed in **7–10** below. This analysis will show both the scope of this activity, and distinguish between the three aspects. It would be wrong to think that all the benefits of sponsorship were in terms of advertising.

7. Advertising objectives

There are many possible advertising objectives for sponsorship:

(a) When media advertising is banned. The product may be banned by certain media, e.g. cigarettes cannot be advertised on British TV, although this may not apply in other countries. This is a controversial question, but cigarette manufacturers have succeeded in gaining considerable TV programme coverage by sponsoring cricket, golf and motor-racing, the John Player Special being a well-known racing car.

(b) Associated advertising. In association with sponsorship, arena advertising in the form of boards and bunting can be displayed at racecourses, sports stadiums, motor-racing circuits and other venues so that they are inevitably picked up by the TV cameras covering the event, apart from being seen by spectators on the spot. The Marlboro cigarette displays are familiar at grand prix motor races, and the Coral boards at horse-races sponsored by the bookmakers.

(c) To promote products. When Yamaha sponsored snooker they used the main display to establish that it was Yamaha Keyboards and not Yamaha Motor-cycles which was responsible for the event. Canon have used perimeter boards at football stadiums to show that they are makers of office equipment and not only cameras.

(d) To introduce a new product. When Coors beer came to Britain in 1993 it was not only advertised on TV, but Coors sponsored a TV series based on Robbie Coltrane's drive across the USA in an old Cadillac. The Oaks, previously sponsored by Ever Ready's sister product, was re-named the Energiser Oaks following the American company's acquisition of Ever Ready. We have already mentioned the use of athletics sponsorship to re-position the newly constituted Lucozade as a young people's rather than a sickbed drink.

(e) To exploit other advertising opportunities. These may not always be available. They include free programme advertising, or facilities for product displays and demonstrations at the venue.

Daihatsu launched a new golf cart simply by supplying them to players in a golf tournament.

The opportunity may also be taken to incorporate references to a sponsorship in press and poster advertising, for instance. This involves giving the dates of sponsored events and encouraging customers to take an interest by, say, watching on TV the grand prix motor race in which the company is involved in sponsorship.

8. Controversy

Confusion and controversy have raged regarding the permissible extent of visible publicity, and a muddle of acceptance and limitation has existed over the years, especially concerning displays (and mentions) during broadcast programmes. Names have been allowed on athletes', footballers' and cricketers' clothing, yet not on boxers' shorts, although permitted on the dressing gowns they wear to the ring. Some athletes have objected to wearing shirts bearing the name of brewers. There have not been objections to the naming of sponsored events, and in motor-racing, yacht racing and motor-boat racing each entrant has been clearly identified with its sponsor's or sponsors' names.

The media, the authorities (government, BBC, ITC) and pressure groups representing anti-smoking, teetotal, health and religious interests may regard all the publicity generated by sponsorship as *advertising*, but as will now be explained, the sponsor's aims may be defined differently. The purpose of advertising is to make known, promote and sell, but a sponsorship may have other purposes besides selling.

9. Public relations objectives

These objectives do not seek to advertise (even by reminder advertising) in order to persuade and sell, but aim to develop knowledge and understanding of the organisation or the product. This in turn may *contribute* to advertising so that it becomes easier or more economical to advertise and sell. The principle is applied that people like what they know, that 'familiarity breeds content', to reword the phrase in an advertising sense.

(a) **Goodwill**. An important public relations objective may be to create goodwill towards the company, locally, nationally or internationally. A large corporation, making big profits, may adopt a social conscience by donating funds or gifts to society. It might give financial aid to a library, college, theatre, hospital or medical research fund. This sort of funding goes back to the sponsorship of libraries, art galleries and museums which to this day bear the name of an original sponsor such as Carnegie, Horniman and Tate.

By sponsoring sports or arts it may be seen to be acting in the public interest, or in its customers' interests. When a foreign company enters export markets, where it may be unknown or possibly greeted with prejudice or suspicion, sponsorship can help create a friendly attitude without which it would be impossible to sell. Goodyear has done this by using its airships to make public announcements at night with illuminated messages.

Japanese firms the world over have used sponsorship in this way. There was a time when Japanese cars were burned in the streets of Asiatic countries which had been victims of wartime occupation. Today a British car is a rare sight in Bangkok, Hong Kong, Jakarta, Kuala Lumpur or Singapore.

In Hong Kong, where the Chinese love gambling, but it is regarded as unethical, the Royal Hong Kong Jockey Club (with its two race courses and scores of betting shops) has sponsored many amenities such as parks and swimming pools. It was originally responsible for funding the creation of

Ocean Park with its remarkable aquarium where fish can be viewed at three below-water levels.

(b) Corporate image. Allied to what has been said above about goodwill, there may be a need to create understanding of the character of the company. A name may just be a name, but what does it represent and what does it do? Until a few years ago, 80 per cent of the British male population had a poor image, if any at all, of Cornhill Insurance. Sponsoring test cricket has changed that.

(c) Corporate identity. Sponsorship can help to identify a company by making its logo and colour scheme familiar to people. This has been well achieved by firms such as Coca-Cola which sponsor sports, athletics and swimming world-wide.

(d) Familiarising the name. This, of course, is implicit in (**b**) and (**c**) above, but sponsorships usually involve continuous repetition of the name, especially in media coverage when reports and commentators describe the event (or the prize or competitor) by the sponsor's name. When calculating the results of a sponsorship, these references can be monitored and assessments made. For instance, during the football season there are references almost every night to the various sponsors when match results are announced. Snooker championships occupy several days' play, and the sponsor's name is given with every report in the press and on the radio and television in addition to the actual televising of the action. This is a typical press or media relations aspect of sponsorship and it is public relations not advertising, although in addition the TV cameras will pick up advertising signs.

(e) Hospitality. While not to be disregarded when considering the costs of a sponsorship, hospitality can provide numerous opportunities for socialising. The managing director can invite a party of business friends or important customers to the sponsored event, whether it be a cricket or football match, golf tournament, show-jumping event or athletics meeting. In fact, the *ability* to offer such hospitality may be a major reason for sponsoring. It is also usual for the sponsor to provide media commentators with lunches and refreshments.

(f) Encouraging interests of journalists. Very popular is the presenting of awards to journalists for their skill and knowledge when writing about the sponsor's subject or industry. These awards are announced and reported in journals such as the *UK Press Gazette*, and a number have become annual events. Some examples are Nikon Press Photographer of the Month Award and the Nikon Awards for the Provincial Press Photographer of the Year, the Bank of Scotland's Press Awards, and the Blue Circle Awards for Industrial Journalism.

161

10. Marketing objectives

Here we have aims which are different again from advertising and public relations objectives, although the three may be blended together in a single sponsorship. The important thing is to understand the differences between the three, and their distinct purposes. The following are examples of marketing objectives.

(a) **Positioning a product**. The company may seek to identify the product with a certain segment of the market such as sex, age group, or income group. To do this it could sponsor a male or female interest; youth, young executive or mature person's interest; or a working-class, middle-class or upper-middle-class interest. Not every sponsor is interested in the whole audience. It is therefore clear that Coca-Cola and Haig whisky, the *Sun* and the *Financial Times,* and the Midland Bank (e.g. farmers) and Woolwich Equitable Building Society (e.g. young home builders) are aiming their sponsorships at very different market segments.

In 1990, seeking to position itself with younger borrowers and investors, Abbey National Building Society (now a bank) sponsored a Madonna concert televised by Sky. Because of the American singer's behaviour at a Wembley pop concert controversy arose, and some Abbey National shareholders (the building society had 'gone public') threatened to sell their shares. These shareholders were, on the whole, older people.

In the case of Lucozade, sponsorship was used to re-position a well-known product, exploiting the preference of young people for soft drinks while still maintaining the product image of a healthy drink. In this case the product went through two phases to satisfy the athletic authorities. First Lucozade Sport was launched in 1990, with sponsorship of the 221 Premier League football clubs. Then came Lucozade Still in a new pack and support for Elite Athletics.

(b) **Supporting dealers**. A successful participation, as when a car wins a motor rally (or the winning car uses certain equipment such as tyres), provides excellent back-up for retailers with opportunities for topical displays coinciding with topical advertising placed by the manufacturer. Dealers are more likely to stock, display prominently and sell products whose performance is proven.

(c) **Establishing a change in marketing policy**. If a company is well established in a particular product field it can be very difficult, even through advertising, to obtain quick and widespread acceptance that the company has diversified into other product or service areas. A company which makes women's products like perfume may decide to make men's toiletries, as with Yardley some years ago, when for a time they sponsored the young men's sport of motor-racing. Or a firm well-known for cameras may produce office machinery (like Canon), or keyboard instruments as well as motor-cycles (like Yamaha). Again, it may wish to further the interests of different divisions as Dunlop has done with tyres and tennis racquets (although there have now been changes in the structure of that company). These are all marketing policy decisions which have used sponsorship for the purpose.

(d) Launching a new product. As part of the strategy of launching a new product, sponsorship may be an excellent vehicle, and also a kind of public test for its performance. This has been applied to many new products such as tyres, tennis racquets, golf carts, cars and sports wear.

(e) Opening of branches. One of the spin-offs of the Canon Football League sponsorship, which involved 92 football clubs, was that when the company opened new premises it was able to call on the local football clubs to provide star players to perform opening ceremonies, often with follow-on local media coverage.

The strong point about the Canon sponsorship of the Football League, and also the *Sun* sponsorship of the Grand National, was that they worked at it and exploited every opportunity. Barclays Bank did not throw itself so wholeheartedly into its sponsorship of the Football League.

(f) International marketing. Mention has been made already of using sponsorship for public relations purposes in overseas markets. Sponsorship can also be part of the marketing strategy to establish the product in these markets, to attract dealers and agents, and to prove the suitability of the imported product in a market with special conditions. For example, it may be good marketing strategy to sponsor local or national events in which the product can be seen to perform as well as or better than indigenous products with which the market is familiar. Foreign goods are not necessarily accepted because they come from a country with a good reputation for such things.

The Japanese are said to be 'golf mad', and some Japanese firms have sponsored British golf tournaments because the British television coverage of the events would also be shown on Japanese television! This sort of thing has increased with satellite TV.

(g) Encouraging product use. Activities can be sponsored to develop the market, as when London brewers Truman have sponsored darts championships, with TV coverage, to popularise the pub.

Again, a well-established foreign importer may find sponsorship a good way of fending off competition from a new importer. The Japanese have been quick to use sponsorship to win their way into foreign markets (including the British), and it may be a good idea for British firms to defend their overseas markets by adopting sponsorship as a tactic which earns recognition, praise and respect in markets under attack.

COST-EFFECTIVENESS

11. Justification for sponsorship

The attractions of sponsorship, and maybe the temptations, are great, but is it worthwhile? In this chapter many examples and reasons are given. It is not good enough to indulge in sponsorship merely to show off or to copy other people and to be in the fashion. However great or small the cost, it has to be justified as a trading cost.

12. Testing results

It is possible to assess the success or otherwise of a sponsorship. The following are typical methods.

(a) Monitoring media coverage to record not only the extent of column centimetres and airtime, but also the quality of this coverage, by analysing in which publications or programmes sponsorships are reported or commentated upon, in what tone, and by whom. It would be valueless to have great coverage in media irrelevant to the market, yet very valuable to have even modest coverage in media which reached the particular market segment.

(b) By using market research techniques which can record the situation before, during and after sponsorship to show whether the objective had been achieved. This could range from opinion polls to dealer audit according to the purpose of the sponsorship. For instance, has name familiarity been improved, is there a better understanding of the corporate image, has there been acceptance in a new or foreign market, has a greater brand share of the market been achieved?

For example, Audits of Great Britain were commissioned by Lloyds Bank to evaluate their sponsorship of the BBC Young Musician of the Year competition which appeared week by week on BBC2. One result was that 53 per cent of informants strongly agreed that it was a suitable and worthwhile event for Lloyds Bank to sponsor.

13. A new trend

Among the reasons for spending money on sponsorship is a new and interesting one, which may also in some cases explain the phenomenal increase in expenditure on public relations. The cost of advertising media has risen out of all proportion to the rate of inflation, and at the point when, for some companies, media advertising ceases to be cost-effective, public relations techniques, of which sponsorship can be one, have been found more cost-effective.

This does not mean that public relations is a substitute for advertising but that whereas public relations was mostly applied as a pre-advertising preparation of the market it is now being used for post-advertising consolidation of the market. In other words, there can be a point when advertising can do no more to sell the product but sponsorship can continue to maintain goodwill, reputation, understanding of the corporate image, reiteration of the corporate identity and name familiarity, thus strengthening the advertising which is conducted.

14. The perils of sponsorship

Sponsorship provides great exposure, and usually the sponsor is anxious to obtain plenty of media coverage, especially on TV. When Canon sponsored the Football League it enjoyed the publicity resulting from 92 football clubs playing for nine months of the year, with the Canon League football results on TV practically every night of the week. This continuity and volume of coverage made it one of the most desirable of sponsorships. But it nearly became a disaster when hooliganism made football unpopular, there were two football stand tragedies, and at one stage ITV threatened not to cover matches.

A real disaster hit Britain's premier horse race, the Grand National, in April 1993 when there were two false starts and the race became a fiasco. Nine horses did not even start. Some completed one circuit. Others ran and there was a shattered winner of a race that never was. Bookmakers had to refund all bets. This sponsorship is worth £4m over seven years, and in 1993 the sponsor was Martell brandy. It not only put up the sponsorship money but spent £750,000 on entertaining 600 guests at the Aintree racecourse.

What a contrast with a previous occasion when Martell's parent company Seagram sponsored the race which was won by a horse called Seagram!

15. Sponsored ITV and ILR/INR programmes

An interesting result of the Broadcasting Act 1990 has not only been the division of ITV and ILR/INR under separate authorities, the Independent Television Commission and the Radio Authority (with cable television being supervised by the ITC instead of having its own body) but the commercial sponsorship of whole programmes. This, to some extent, takes British broadcasting back to the original American radio soap operas of over sixty years ago when soap and other companies sponsored whole radio shows.

The British development is partly due to the need for independent broadcasting to find fresh sources of income. ITV companies can afford to produce few programmes themselves and buy most programmes from independent producers. ITV news and current affairs programmes welcome video news releases because they cannot afford to cover outside events.

Much of this is to do with the recession, and the ITV companies are caught between high production costs, cut-backs in advertising expenditure, and competition from satellite TV with a plethora of rival channels. The take-up of sponsored TV was slow during the initial period of 1991–93, and fees rarely exceeded £600,000 for drama series, unless the programme was shown frequently as with weather forecasts.

There are restrictions in that the sponsor's name may appear only in trailers, credits and bumper breaks, i.e. in commercial breaks. The sponsor's product may not be featured in the programme. This is different from the sponsored TV in, say, Nigeria where Guinness or Coca-Cola may be mentioned or drunk during the programme itself.

The British type of sponsorship, with its brevity, seems to require a characteristic touch to make it effective. A beer and a beer drinking detective, a multi-coloured umbrella or sunshade and a weather forecast, and a jolly cartoon tea party with *The Darling Buds of May*, went together very well. The sponsors were Beamish stout, Kronenbourg lager, Legal and General Insurance and Tetley tea.

But it is hard to understand PowerGen's long-running sponsorship of the national ITV weather forecast (except at the time of privatisation), or Diet Coke's £3m funding of movie premieres to which ITV has terrestrial rights. More appropriate was Unilever subsidising Elida Gibbs' £500,000 deal for a 5-week package of peak Saturday night movies. But was Agatha Christie's Hercule Poirot a suitable vehicle for AEG appliances?

In collaboration with ITV, Worthington exploited its sponsorship of a seven-a-side rugby international with weeks of advance build-up publicity. This joint effort sought to attract audiences which would justify the cost of the sponsorship.

Sony did well with its ingenious support for an ITV Rugby International, bumper breaks featuring trivial pursuit style questions, and discs being made of the accompanying music including Dame Kiri Te Kanawa's singing of the theme song. Research conducted by ITV showed that this five-week event did much to popularise rugby. It is doubtful whether the earlier sponsorship of the Soccer World Cup by National Power justified the expenditure. Viewers were said to be puzzled by this funding whereas they responded well to Sony's imaginative support for the Rugby International.

Sony's sponsorship was timed well to encourage stocking up for Christmas, and for Christmas sales. This was also true of the pre-Christmas support for *Rumpole of the Bailey* by Croft Port. It was also very econonomical. For a similar cost, Croft could have bought airtime in the London area only, but the *Rumpole* series was networked.

However, this new kind of funding, with original credits and bumper breaks from agencies such as Media Dimensions, has produced criticisms. These claim that together with normal commercials, arena and other advertising at stadiums, race courses and sports circuits, sponsors' exploitation of events or subjects which they are sponsoring (e.g. saddle cloths of horses, sportswear, and decorated racing cars), plus all the additional channels, there is a new form of advertising 'clutter'.

ILR programmes may be sponsored by firms which are permitted to take credit by means of a copy line read by the presenter, and since programme items are short these commercial references can be frequent and so add to the clutter of broadcast advertising.

INR's first station, Classic FM, went on the air in 1992 and its classical music programmes were sponsored by advertisers such as Black Magic and W.H. Smith, the latter's Saturday morning programme being appropriate for the promotion of classical discs. The second national commercial radio station, Richard Branson's Virgin 1215, began broadcasting pop music on 30 April 1993 with the promise of four million listeners in the 24–44 year old age group. Its first advertisers were Carling Black Label, McDonald's and Express Newspapers. Labatt, the Canadian brewer, sponsored Virgin 1215's album chart show at a fee of £750,000. The Labatt deal included credits, trailers and advertising slots. The data was collected until late on Saturday by Gallup for the three-hour album chart countdown hosted by Russ Williams.

However, both forms of programme sponsorship are covered by Codes of Practice published by the two authorities, and copies of the ITC and Radio Authority Codes may be obtained from the ITC at 33 Foley Street, London, W1P 7LB, and the Radio Authority at 14B Great Queen Street, London WC2 5DG.

The two kinds of sponsorship need to be clearly understood. An event, such as the Derby or the Grand National, may be sponsored, and it may be televised by either or both the BBC and ITV. Equally, no one may decide to televise it. The new kind of TV sponsorship means that the advertiser pays the broadcaster a fee towards the cost of independently producing the programme, and is credited for doing so. The credits are not obtrusive, and often attractive.

16. Pan-European arts sponsorship

According to a report based on a survey of 200 companies in 10 countries by Arthur Andersen for CEREC, the European sponsorship committee, sponsorship of pan-European events was expected to grow twice as fast as single-country events in two years. The advantage of such cross-frontier sponsorships is that they can unify a single European company image. Take up of such sponsorships depends on likely media coverage and the location of event.

Progress test 8

1. Define sponsorship. (1)

2. What is the total value of sponsorship in Britain? (2)

3. What can be sponsored? (3)

4. Name some of the biggest sports sponsorships. (4)

5. What is the role of a sponsorship agency? (5)

6. What advertising objectives can be achieved through sponsorship? (7)

7. What controversies have occurred concerning sponsorship? (8, 10)

8. Explain the public relations aspects of sponsorship. (9)

9. What marketing objectives can be achieved through sponsorship? (10)

10. How can sponsorship assist international marketing? (10)

11. How can the effectiveness of sponsorship be measured? (12)

12. What changes regarding sponsorship resulted from the Broadcasting Act 1990? (15)

13. What limitations are imposed on those who sponsor British radio or television programmes? (15)

14. What is a bumper break? (15)

9

Direct mail and direct response

INTRODUCTION

1. Growth in importance

Shopping without shops or direct marketing has become very big business, aided by direct mail, TV commercials and teletext, off-the-page selling, the telephone, the computer, and the credit card. Mail order is nowadays better known as direct or direct-response marketing. Direct mail is so involved in all this that the British Direct Mail Advertising Association changed its name to the British Direct Marketing Association (BDMA). The BDMA then became the Direct Marketing Association (DMA). The DMA Code of Practice came into force on 31 March 1993 and it has since introduced another code on telemarketing (*see* **31**). In Britain, direct mail takes third place to press and television and takes up 10 per cent of the total advertising expenditure.

According to Royal Mail figures, of 2,246 million items mailed recently, 51 per cent were received by AB households. The top ten users were direct response firms, insurance, banks, retailers, magazines, credit card firms, manufacturers, charities, book clubs and building societies in that order. The *Advertising Statistics Yearbook* for 1992 gives the total cost of postage as £342m, production £603m. These figures rise annually, of course, with inflation and other influences such as the cost of labour and materials.

Royal Mail has vigorously promoted the medium and the annual Direct Marketing Awards are made by the DMA and Royal Mail. The value of direct mail is seen in a small country like Botswana where the press is negligible and broadcast media is mostly South African. It is also an excellent medium for international advertising when it is more economical to airmail selected prospects than to advertise in the press which may be very limited.

Alternative mailing services, such as TNT, can be used very economically, especially for overseas mailings.

2. Definitions

Confusion of terms can be avoided by remembering that direct mail is an *advertising medium* but mail order (or direct response) is a *form of distribution*, that is, trading by mail whatever medium is used for advertising sales offers. Consequently, direct mail is not limited to direct marketing: a retailer can use direct mail to attract shoppers to his or her store.

CHARACTERISTICS OF DIRECT MAIL

3. Controlled

It is not aimed at unknown readers, listeners, viewers, audiences or passers-by or travellers like all the above-the-line media described in Chapter 5. Instead it is addressed to selected, named recipients or at least to chosen people at selected addresses whether they be householders or managing directors. The quantity can be controlled, the message can be varied to suit different groups of people, and the timing can be controlled or at any rate estimated within postal limits.

4. Economical

Because of the controls mentioned in **3**, it is economical in the sense that even the selected lists can be culled of unwanted addresses. De-duplication can be applied when a number of lists are being used in which certain names are repeated. It is also economical because in a mail shot more copy and illustrations can be used than would fill a whole page broadsheet newspaper, and at a fraction of the cost.

5. Personal

Unlike any other medium, except possibly the telephone, it is a one-to-one personal medium, like a conversation on paper. Generally, people like receiving mail, and if the recipient is well-chosen the mail shot will be welcomed.

This medium is also personal in the sense that sales letters and envelopes can be addressed by name (personalised). Using special techniques like laser printing, dramatic and colourful effects can be achieved with the recipient's name inserted at various points in the body of the letter itself. This should not be overdone otherwise the letter will sound insincere, but neither should letters be addressed 'Dear Sir/Madam' which looks careless and indifferent. If a formal salutation is necessary it is better to have letters addressed separately, 'Dear Sir' and 'Dear Madam'. However, this rule is not set in concrete. Some organisations using large, impersonal consumer mailing lists have no choice but 'Dear Sir or Madam', and nevertheless receive a worthwhile response.

6. Speed

A direct mail campaign can be mounted very quickly, in a few hours if necessary given the facilities to write and reproduce a sales letter, and pack and post it with or without an enclosure. It is therefore a very flexible medium which can be used in an emergency. Such an emergency might be to clear stocks, announce a special offer, out-do a competitor, or take advantage of a topical opportunity.

7. A primary medium

For those advertisers who (a) have or can hire a reliable mailing list and (b) need to supply considerable information, direct mail can be their first line or primary advertising medium. In fact, they may use no other, except perhaps sales literature as enclosures. Others may use press advertising to produce enquiries or initial orders which provide a mailing list for future use.

For instance, press advertising could be useless for some advertisers because the cost of adequate space to include all the necessary information would be prohibitive. If this detailed information cannot be given, the response could be negligible. All the affordable press advertisement can do is attract enquiries, but that is introducing another time-wasting and inconvenient stage in the marketing strategy. The direct mail shot which eliminates this stage and attracts immediate *orders*, not enquiries, is more productive and cost-effective.

8. Testing and evaluating

It is possible to pre-test mailings by sending out test mailings of either offers of different merchandise, or offers of the same merchandise at different prices to a sample of prospective customers, and then to record the response. For example, the price may be around 100 (pence, cents, etc.) but some variation on this price may prove to be more psychologically attractive. The product may draw more sales at, say 98 or 102. People judge by price and 98 may seem inexpensive while 102 may suggest quality, and 100 could have an indecisive effect.

Direct mail shots are easily evaluated by the response they produce, and this can be calculated on a cost-per-reply basis (the cost of the shot divided by the number of replies), and cost-per-sales (which can be either the cost of selling a given volume of stock, or the cost of selling one unit). Experience can then guide the planning and budgeting of the marketing strategy – what merchandise will sell to whom and at what price, what form the mailing should take, and how much should be spent on a mailing to achieve the sales target.

It is sometimes claimed that direct response produces only a two per cent response, but Graeme McCorkell asked what this really meant in an article in *Direct Response* and the following extract is interesting in the contrasts which can be made with other media, most of which may produce no *direct* response at all.

> The first step towards straight thinking is to rid your mind of response rates as a valid measure. Cost-per-response may be a valid measure. Cost-per-order is often a valid measure. Cost-per-sale is certainly a valid measure.
>
> If you think in terms of these unit costs, you are now able to make inter-media comparisons, comparing direct mail with inserts, door drops, space ads, or broadcast media advertising. This is a prerequisite for the sensible allocation of a direct response budget.
>
> Thinking in these terms, you can also see the absurdity of pundits wringing their hands about two per cent response or any other given response rate. Do they imagine that every time George Cole appears on the box we all leap out of our armchairs and race down to deposit money in the Leeds cash machine?
>
> Do they realise it takes a heavyweight TV campaign to achieve 60 per cent unaided recall in tracking studies a month later? And that you can achieve the same level easily with just one solus mailing?
>
> The response rate from any given mailing is primarily determined by what the recipient is asked to do. If you ask recipients to enter a prize draw to win £200,000 you will get a high response rate. If you ask them to buy a set of books for £1,000 you will get a low response rate. This does not mean that all mailings in the first category are successful and that all mailings in the second category are unsuccessful. It does not even mean that all mailings in the first category are necessarily more interesting or well liked by recipients. It just means they allow more recipients to participate.
>
> The next most important variable is targeting, the main distinction being between mailings to customers, enquirers or former customers and mailings that are not targeted to any of these groups. Mailings that are targeted to customers, as we all know pull better than cold mailings. . . .
>
> Cold mailings justify a slice of the new business budget to the extent that they outperform other media in terms of their efficiency at pulling in business.

THE SALES LETTER AND ENCLOSURES

9. Writing the sales letter

A sales letter is not just a business letter. It is a special form of copywriting with its own techniques. The length of the letter will depend on the extent to which the reader's interest can be sustained. There are some excellent sales letters which extend to as many as four pages, perhaps in a four-page folder style rather than two or four separate sheets, but generally there is a psychological value in a single-page letter when the signature is visible at the foot of the page.

This is a controversial topic, with 'experts' expressing different views, but when there is a lot of direct mail and it competes for attention, the short letter uncluttered by too many inserts, is likely to command the most attention. The length of a letter really depends on its interest to the recipient. Some 'begging letters' from charities are remarkably long and long-winded which seems psychologically perverse. Those who are inundated with charity appeals may regard them as the worst form of junk mail.

The letter may present a complete selling proposition, or it can be a covering letter referring the reader to an enclosure. In the latter case the letter should not laboriously repeat the contents of the enclosure but highlight special features of it. Not all sales letters include a salutation, and this may be a way of avoiding uncertainty over the identity or sex of the recipient. Other letters may be personalised as already described in 5. Either way, with or without a salutation, a sales letter can benefit from a strong, motivating, attention-grabbing headline.

Another controversial part of direct mail is whether or not to use a postscript. It seems to be a naïve device, but does this somewhat amateur approach attract readers? Research has shown that a postscript increases response. There are even people who claim they read only postscripts!

10. A pattern to follow

If the sales letter presents a self-contained proposition a useful pattern is as follows.

(a) **Opening paragraph**. This needs to hold the reader's attention, but it need not disclose the selling proposition. Various intriguing devices are used such as posing a question or even telling an anecdote. This should induce the recipient to read on. It is the sugar on the pill, or the bait.

(b) **The proposition**. The heart of the letter should now set out your proposition.

(c) **Convincing the reader**. The next stage is to convince the reader. There may be a price concession if the offer is taken up quickly, or the offer may have a time limit.

(d) **Final paragraph**. The letter should close with instructions on how to respond or order. This may refer to an enclosed order form or card, and there may be an unstamped envelope, or reply-paid or Freepost envelope or card. Faxback forms are popular. Email addresses are used to solicit orders and enquiries, and websites to take orders and money.

Adopting the above four-point formula, Figure 9.1 is an example of how a sales letter might be written.

Mr A Browne
14 Riverside
Newtown
Hampshire NT5 3LG

12 April 2001

Dear Mr Browne,

"Darling, when are you going to mow the lawn?"

What do you do when you hear the dreaded call? Turn over a new leaf – in the book you're reading? Switch TV channels? Take the dog for a walk? Or just pray for rain?

When you have an old backbreaker of a lawnmower that's agony to push up and down on a hot day, you probably do all of them.

You should be getting your hands on the new **Smith & Jones Electric LawnBoy**. You don't have to push it – you simply steer. The machine does all the work, and the pleasure is all yours!

Your wife will be surprised how quickly you take your LawnBoy out of the garden shed and get cracking. She may even have a drink waiting for you afterwards – not that you'll need it, though. And it will be good to sit with her and admire your neat, trim lawn. Nice work, Mr Browne.

This weekend, you can see the whole range of new LawnBoys at the Newtown Garden Centre. It's open all weekend, so you can call in whenever it suits you, and get expert advice too. The LawnBoy comes in a pack you can put in your car boot and take home right away.

Why not bring your wife along too? I'm sure she'll approve.

Yours sincerely,

John Donaldson
Manager

PS: Bring this letter with you, and I'll give you 10% off the cost of your new LawnBoy.

'LawnBoy does the job – beautifully!'

SMITH & JONES GARDEN PRODUCTS   POBox 108, High Wycombe, HW1 2WH, Bucks

Figure 9.1 Example of a sales letter

Strange as it may seem, the postscript is said to be the second most read part of a direct mail letter. Perhaps it is because it makes the letter look more like private than business correspondence. A natural gimmick!

11. Appropriate language

When writing a sales letter it is necessary to use language which is appropriate to the medium, the product and the reader. The *Financial Times Industrial Companies Year Book* is no doubt an excellent reference work, but in a letter to potential advertisers it was rather silly of the advertising sales executive to write: 'We thought it would be a good idea for you to advertise your services in this exciting new book.' It was not exactly a holiday in Bali, and advertising clichés like 'exciting' need to be used with discrimination. When every offer is 'exciting' the credibility tends to pall.

12. Enclosures

The contents of the envelope should be kept to a minimum. Some mailings consist of so many items of different shapes and sizes that the recipient is bewildered and may well discard the whole lot! Good enclosures are those which supplement the sales letter.

Some of the best examples of well-planned shots are the *one-piece mailers* which contain all the necessary information and the order form, making an accompanying sales letter unnecessary. One-piece mailers are usually in folder form, either folding out to make a flat sheet, consisting of a series of panes in concertina fashion, or following some other ingenious design which contains everything in a single piece of print. There are thus no untidy, loose bits and pieces, and the information and ordering facility is neatly and conveniently limited to one item of print. They are also easily inserted into envelopes.

Some mailshots benefit from the opposite treatment. One mail-order catalogue company discovered, by direct experiment, that eight enclosed items were needed in each mailing to ensure the highest response. Fewer enclosures, or more, produced a lower response. What's more, they found that the number of colours used for some of the enclosures was critical. Six of the enclosures had to be in full colour; anything less produced a lower response. The lesson to be learnt here is: put your current method on trial, and adapt to the solution that works for *you*, and is proven.

13. Printed envelopes

Whether or not printed envelopes should be used is a decision which may depend on where and by whom the shot will be received. If the recipient is never likely to see the envelope because the letter will be opened by a secretary, or in a post room, a printed envelope can be a costly irrelevancy, unless it is likely to influence a secretary. If the recipient, such as a private individual or shopkeeper, opens his or her own mail, then the sales message can begin with the envelope. Good examples of this are holiday brochures and mail order catalogues. *Reader's Digest* have exploited the printed and the window envelope to command immediate attention and interest. But, of course, it could operate adversely if identification of the sender invites instant rejection and the mail is not even opened! Elderly people receiving charity appeals from Help The Aged will certainly be put off by a printed envelope.

A Direct Mail Information Service survey of 500 people showed that overprinting on the envelope, and especially use of words like 'urgent' identified junk mail. The ASA has condemned the deceitful overprinting of direct mail envelopes with the words 'private and confidential'.

In a sense, a printed envelope can be an advertisement just like the packaging of a retail product. It is the first thing people see. It can attract attention and invite curiosity about the contents, and if sufficiently interesting to the recipient the printed envelope could achieve priority over other correspondence received at the same time.

14. Postage

While direct mail is in many respects an economical medium, there are certain special costs which must be considered and carefully controlled. A primary cost is postage, and while the Post Office does offer special rates for bulk mailings, the postage will depend on the weight of the shot. This weight problem can be controlled by the size of enclosures, and also by the weight of paper used for printed literature.

Mailsort has replaced earlier Post Office discount and rebate schemes. The discount is based on the proportion of the mailing that can be pre-sorted and according to the quantity mailed. The minimum quantity is 4,000 letters or 1,000 packets of which 85 per cent must be fully postcoded. There are three options:

(a) Mailsort 1 – 1st class, target delivery next working day. Maximum discount 15 per cent

(b) Mailsort 2 – 2nd class, target delivery within 3 working days. Maximum discount 13 per cent

(c) Mailsort 3 – economy class, target delivery within 7 working days. Maximum discount 32 per cent

Unfortunately Mailsort encourages mass (and often ill selected) mailings; the Mailsort special printed stamp is a give-away and the mailing may be regarded as junk mail; and when used for legitimate business purposes envelopes bearing the Mailsort stamp may be unwittingly discarded. It can be a false economy.

15. Using suitable envelopes

Another cost is that of envelopes, the size of which can be controlled by the format of printed enclosures. Large leaflets in large envelopes can arrive in a very battered state whereas smaller leaflets in smaller envelopes are more likely to arrive in the same condition as when packed. Senders of direct mail seldom seem to realise the rigours of the mail. Heavy catalogues need to be protected by tough manilla envelopes, yet they are often put in large thin envelopes which get torn round the edges so that the contents arrive in a very dog-eared condition. Mail is manhandled many times in bags which are flung in and out of vans and trains.

An economical form of envelope is the heat-sealed or self-seal see through polythene type which are commonly used for mailing magazines and catalogues. The address can be on a separate insert, printed on the exterior, or labels may be affixed.

Another psychological factor occurs here. Most people will tend to open small or DL envelopes first, even putting aside large envelopes for the time being, unless a large envelope obviously contains something they are waiting for.

MAILING LISTS

16. Setting up mailing lists

The following are some of the ways in which mailing lists can be created or obtained.

(a) From invoices bearing the names and addresses of purchasers.

(b) From the response to advertisements which either invite requests for literature and catalogues, or sell off-the-page, customers paying by cheque or credit card or being invoiced on delivery. A database can thus be built up.

(c) From yearbooks, annuals, directories and membership lists. In the latter case some organisations sell addresses in the form of addressed envelopes or labels. Care has to be taken in using a recent edition of a directory, remembering that it probably took months to compile and could be partially out-of-date on publication. However, there are excellent directories which list the names of senior personnel so that mailings can be addressed personally. It is better to address people by name and not merely by job description such as Managing Director or Marketing Manager.

(d) By using a direct mail house, either to create and manage the whole mailing, selecting lists from their catalogue, or to address and post a mailing produced in-house.

Table 9.1 CACI Acorn Profile of Great Britain

ACORN stands for 'A Classification of Residential Neighbourhoods'. The system was developed by CACI. The table below shows ACORN's 38 neighbourhood types, the 11 groups they form, and their share of the GB population of 54,680,920 in 1991. ACORN is based on the Government's Census of Great Britain conducted in 1981. The 1991 populations of the 1981 census neighbourhoods are derived from CACI's proprietary demographic model of Great Britain.

ACORN types		% of 1991 population	ACORN groups	
A	1 Agricultural villages	2.6		A
A	2 Areas of farms and smallholdings	0.7	Agricultural areas	
B	3 Post-war functional private housing	4.4		
B	4 Modern private housing, young families	3.7		
B	5 Established private family housing	6.0	Modern family housing, higher incomes	B
B	6 New detached houses, young families	2.9		
B	7 Military bases	0.7		
C	8 Mixed owner-occ'd & council estates	3.5		
C	9 Small town centres & flats above shops	4.1		
C	10 Villages with non-farm employment	4.9	Older housing of intermediate status	C
C	11 Older private housing, skilled workers	5.5		
D	12 Unmodernised terraces, older people	2.4		
D	13 Older terraces, lower income families	1.4	Older terraced housing	D
D	14 Tenement flats lacking amenities	0.4		
E	15 Council estates, well-off older workers	3.4		
E	16 Recent council estates	2.8		
E	17 Better council estates, younger workers	5.0	Council estates – category I	E
E	18 Small council houses, often Scottish	1.9		

Table 9.1 (*continued*)

		ACORN types	*% of 1991 population*		*ACORN groups*	
F	19	Low rise estates in industrial towns	4.6			
F	20	Inter-war council estates, older people	2.8	8.8	Council estates – category II	F
F	21	Council housing, elderly people	1.4			
G	22	New council estates in inner cities	2.0			
G	23	Overspill estates, higher unemployment	3.0	7.0	Council estates – category III	G
G	24	Council estates with some overcrowding	1.5			
G	25	Council estates with greatest hardship	0.6			
H	26	Multi-occupied older housing	0.4			
H	27	Cosmopolitan owner-occupied terraces	1.0	3.8	Mixed inner metropolitan areas	H
H	28	Multi-let housing in cosmopolitan areas	0.7			
H	29	Better-off cosmopolitan areas	1.7			
I	30	High status non-family areas	2.1			
I	31	Multi-let big old houses and flats	1.5	4.1	High status non-family areas	I
I	32	Furnished flats, mostly single people	0.5			
J	33	Inter-war semis, white collar workers	5.7			
J	34	Spacious inter-war semis, big gardens	5.0	15.8	Affluent suburban housing	J
J	35	Villages with wealthy older commuters	2.9			
J	36	Detached houses, exclusive suburbs	2.3			
K	37	Private houses, well-off older residents	2.3	3.8	Better-off retirement areas	K
K	38	Private flats, older single people	1.5			
U	39	Unclassified	0.5	0.5	Unclassified	U
			100.0			

(e) By hiring a list from list-brokers who specialise in this service. There are also firms which specialise in client's lists on computerised databases, adding and deleting names as requested, and so managing and maintaining a client's own list.

A problem with using other people's lists is that the user has no control over their compilation, and they can include irrelevant addresses. It is not so much the obvious waste of money that is involved in mis-mailings, but recipients are easily annoyed at receiving pointless mailings. They are encouraged to regard direct mail as junk mail and they gain a poor opinion of the sender, whom they consider incompetent.

(f) By using the ACORN (A Classification Of Residential Neighbourhoods) marketing segmentation system to select people by residential classifications. This system, based on census figures, was evolved by CACI Market Analysis Division. (*See* Table 9.1, pages 178–9.)

In addition to ACORN there are rival systems based on similar geo-demographic principles. MOSAIC defines 58 lifestyle categories, and differs from other systems by analysing Britain at postcode level rather than census enumeration district level. Super Profiles links postal geography with 10 lifestyles and 37 target markets. Monica (*see* **20**) is a CACI database which predicts age group of prospects by their first name, and claims this is true of 75 per cent of cases.

17. Updating, culling and some faults discussed

It is important to have an up-to-date mailing list, and it is bad policy to build a continuous mailing list which is never checked or revised. People do move, change their names or die. A mailing list of customers can be out-of-date after two years and in some cases in six months. Culling is important. Check mailings are sent out by some firms, enclosing request cards for their latest catalogue. It costs a lot of money to print catalogues so they should not be wasted.

Lists should not be added to indiscriminately, and sometimes it is better to compile a new list for each mailing if they are carried out at long intervals. Computerised lists can be attractive if they are used regularly, but if errors are entered wrong addresses will continue to be used because no complaints may be forthcoming. If the same address is entered in varying styles it can be very difficult to trace all the alternative duplicates and eliminate them. Recipients can be irritated by repeat mailings of the same shot. This is a medium where it is easy to please or displease the recipient.

Because direct mail can annoy people it is sometimes, and often unfairly, denigrated as *junk mail*. True, it is unsolicited and people may object to receiving commercial offers, but it all depends on whether the mailing has been well targeted to those likely to respond to offers and propositions.

Much of the criticism of junk mail has arisen because so many people's names and addresses have become available. One of the biggest users of direct mail are financial firms which exploit the availability of huge share registers of privatised companies. They mail shareholders with offers of other investments such as unit trusts, insurance schemes and pension schemes. Inevitably, there can be repetition.

A common mistake which occurs with database marketing is that a customer's name and address is entered into the computer file every time they make a purchase so that they receive as many mailings as the purchases they make. This is not always because the person's name is entered differently, such as initials or spelt out first names. There are systems of de-duplication but unfortunately even big users of direct mail do not bother to apply them. The recipient of six identical mailings is apt to take a poor view of the sender.

There is also the carelessness which causes irritation when a charity addresses a prospect as 'Dear Contributor' or 'Dear Donor' when they have never previously made a donation.

This does seem to be a medium where carelessness and indifference prevails, and yet no one would be so irresponsible with press, poster, cinema, radio or TV advertising. The worst examples usually emanate from direct mail houses which are supposed to be experts. The only beneficiaries of bad direct response marketing are these houses, list brokers, printers and the Post Office.

The Direct Mail Information Service survey referred to in 13 claimed that only one per cent of respondents said their chief reason for responding to direct mail was to make a donation. This is disturbing news since charities spend fortunes on direct mail, but is it misspent? True, one has to spend money to make money but many charity mailings are packed with inserts, have four-page sales letters, and generally appear to be a waste of funds given by generous people. Help The Aged spend £2 million on above- and below-the-line advertising. Why does it repeatedly mail old age pensioners for funds? Is this good targeting? Moreover, charity mailings are repetitive. Once a donation is made another begging letter arrives. Charities do not seem to follow the golden rule of advertising which is *spend the least to gain the most*.

How can recipients be encouraged to open your mailshot, and having done so how can their attention and interest be won so that there is a reasonable chance of securing a response? The simple answer is that the mailer should resemble a personal letter, and the offer should be relevant to the recipient. Many of those produced by direct mail houses (and often win awards!) do not. They are too clever by half. Maybe direct mail should be confined to in-house production.

Here are some guidelines for the successful direct mail campaign, remembering that direct mail can be immensely successful and economical if used properly. Some people may scoff at these simple but practical proposals, but a number of money-making businesses have adopted them for many years.

(a) Use a postage stamp, not a franking or Mailsort symbol.

(b) Use a white DL size envelope with end flap for easy filling.

(c) Do not use labels, especially ones bearing code numbers or letters. Personal letters have typed addresses.

(d) Do not print anything on the envelope. Return addresses invite just that.

(e) If a sales letter is to be used, confine it to one page.

(f) Do not be over-familiar by laser printing the recipient's name in the body of the letter.

(g) If an enclosure is used make sure it is necessary and ideally limit it to one item such as a descriptive folder, order form or reply envelope. A one-piece mailer is even better.

(h) If lists are bought or hired go through them and delete irrelevant addresses. Never mail every name in a membership list or directory. Remember that people may be members of more than one organisation, and could be repeated in a mailing. Mailing irrelevant addresses is both wasteful and annoying. For instance, a publisher of children's books may mail schools with a catalogue, but a mailing list of 'schools' will not discriminate between different kinds of school. There is no point in sending a catalogue of children's books to the Henley Centre, Ashridge, a catering college or perhaps one for the blind. But it happens all the time.

18. The Mailing Preference Service

Not everyone wishes to receive promotional material at home, while some are willing to accept more. A practical development in the resolution of this situation in the UK is the Mailing Preference Service (MPS).

The service is sponsored by the DMA, the Mail Order Traders' Association and the Royal Mail. It acts as a safety valve for those who object to receiving mailshots, and helps to maintain the good name of the medium. It also has a great deal of power, because it is also supported by the Data Protection Registrar, the Office of Fair Trading, the ASA, the DTI and the Home Office.

The MPS is funded by the industry itself, which pays a levy whenever it uses Mailsort, the Royal Mail service for volume mailings.

The MPS exists to:

- allay fears and misapprehensions about direct mail;
- promote good practice within the industry;
- help consumers have their names removed from or added to mailing lists.

Many consumers are concerned that private information about them is being kept on file by organisations they have never dealt with. In fact, the only data normally held are name and address; possibly also information that they have bought a certain type of product is held. The MPS respects consumers' right to choose whether they want this information to remain on mailing lists.

As responsible professionals, direct mailers are keen to ensure that their messages reach the people who will respond to it. The last thing advertisers want is to waste money by mailing people who are not interested in receiving it. Targeting helps to achieve advertising cost-effectiveness, and the MPS also makes a substantial contribution to it.

Receiving information by post has many advantages. For example, it offers consumers the chance to make unpressured decisions in their own homes. This is particularly helpful when they are considering financial services. Shopping from home is convenient, and can often bring better value. Direct mail presents opportunities to take advantage of special value offers and gain details of new products. Many charities could not hope to remain as active as they are without donations raised via direct mail.

For consumers, on the other hand, removing their names from lists may prevent them from receiving information they may find of interest in the future. As a member of the Committee of Advertising Practice, the MPS, with the backing of the Data Protection Registrar, can give consumers the opportunity to make the choices they want.

Members of the public have direct access to the MPS, and can apply to have their names removed from mailing lists. On the application form, there is a section enabling householders to have names of deceased persons removed from mailing lists, while themselves continuing to receive direct mail.

Aspects of the service include:

(a) A name removed by the MPS from a list remains on the 'removed' file for five years. If consumers want to continue receiving the service beyond this date, they need to apply again.

(b) If consumers receive mailings with incorrect versions of their names and addresses, they need to contact the mailer direct to correct the errors.

(c) Consumers will still receive mailings from companies with whom they have done business in the past, as well as from some small local companies. If consumers wish to stop these mailings, they need to contact the companies direct.

(d) Three months should be allowed before mail starts to decrease.

(e) Unaddressed mail is not covered by the MPS.

19. Telephone and Fax Preference Services

In addition to the MPS, described in **18**, there are also services designed to protect consumers and businesses from unsolicited material being delivered by telephone and fax.

(a) Fax Preference Service (FPS). This free service applies to communications from organisations with which the recipient has no on-going or contractual relationship.

On the one hand, the FPS does some good in preventing unsolicited faxes from being sent to individuals and businesses who have no interest in the products and services being promoted. On the other, excluding unwanted material could prevent consumers receiving information that they may like to have or that would be of benefit to them. Businesses could cut themselves off from information of value, and from worthwhile business opportunities.

Of course, if the advertiser is doing their job, targeting prospective customers accurately, unsolicited faxes would always be information useful, interesting and of value to recipients.

In February 1999, the Office of Telecommunications (OFTEL) issued an invitation to tender for the management of new telephone and fax opt-out schemes. The Direct Marketing Association (DMA) won the contract, and now runs both the new Fax Preference Service (FPS) and the Telephone Preference Service (TPS).

Under the new regulations, it is unlawful to fax to individuals unless the advertiser has their prior consent. The term 'individual' in UK law includes consumers, sole traders and (except in Scotland) partnerships. The new regulations also enable businesses to register their objection to receiving direct marketing faxes. They stipulate that an advertiser should not send faxes to a business which has previously notified that such faxes are unwelcome.

(b) Telephone Preference Service (TPS). The TPS is regulated by the Telecommunications (Data Protection and Privacy) (Direct Marketing) Regulations 1998. They are intended to protect consumers, and in some cases businesses, against receiving unwanted direct marketing telephone calls and faxes.

The regulations came into effect in May 1999. It is now unlawful for a business (including charities or other voluntary organisations) to make such calls to individuals, where those individuals have advised that business or organisation that they do not want to receive such calls. The same applies where individuals have registered with the Telephone Preference Service that they do not wish to receive such calls from *any* business or organisation. Individuals are defined as consumers, sole traders and (except in Scotland) partnerships.

There are two ways in which consumers can make sure that their telephone numbers are unavailable to organisations who may telephone with unwanted offers and information. One is to contact companies direct, asking them not to telephone. The other is to register with the central TPS to stop all such calls.

Registering with the TPS will not stop calls from market research organisations. Consumers wishing to stop these calls, or any other non-direct-marketing calls, should contact each company direct.

It usually takes up to 28 days for a TPS registration to take effect.

20. Monica

As mentioned in **16**, Monica is a CACI system which helps to identify age groups by their Christian or first names. In spite of some criticism it has been found useful for both direct response and electioneering purposes. The Monica database resulted from a survey of 43 million adults on the Acorn list, and identified the age profiles by linking the neighbourhoods in which names were found with the age profiles of certain CACI small-area neighbourhoods. CACI concluded that 75 per cent of the British adult population have a first name which implies age. Some New Testament names occur in all age groups while others are often associated with royalty, film stars and celebrities at the time of birth.

21. People*UK

At the time this 4th edition is being prepared, a sophisticated consumer targeting tool recently launched by CACI is People*UK. Unlike previous systems that work at postcode level, People*UK assigns different people within the same household to different types. Using such a tool therefore enables advertisers to target prospective customers in greater detail than with conventional postcode techniques. This brings a high precision to consumer targeting at individual level. The system is extremely accurate, because it can differentiate between two people sharing the same house.

People*UK is described by its creators as the first all-purpose, non-sector-specific, individual segmentation system, working across all market sectors, particularly where life-stage is a key driver.

It is a mix of geo-demographics, life-stage and lifestyle data, condensed in an easy-to-use format. The data are pre-organised, summarising all the different individual characteristics into 46 types. They are grouped into eight life-stages, as shown in Table 9.2.

The main advantage to advertisers is in its classification of individuals rather than postcodes. There are a number of distinctive practical market area applications, including retail, leisure and direct marketing. Its main user areas include advertisers wanting:

185

- an easy-to-use, individual level targeting tool for the whole of their database;

- to take postcode or household level targeting to a finer level of detail;

- a highly targeted, individually selectable prospect pool for new customer acquisition;

- to calculate market potential at customer level;

- a network planning tool for organisations with very tightly defined catchment areas.

Contact information for CACI is given in Appendix 1.

Table 9.2 Life-stages as defined for People*UK

Life-stage	Description	Number of types
1	Starting out	4
2	Young with toddlers	3
3	Young families	7
4	Singles/couples, no kids	4
5	Middle-aged families	9
6	Empty nesters	6
7	Retired couples	6
8	Older singles	7

MAIL DROPS

22. Door-to-door distribution

Not all direct advertising, or distribution of materials, is sent by post. A large volume is delivered door-to-door to houses, shops or offices. This can provide saturation coverage of chosen areas, although it need not be as haphazard or wasteful as might be thought. Computers can once again be of considerable use in advertising to provide selectivity by enumerating districts from computer tapes based on the statistics of the national census.

There are three types of mail-drop service:

(a) by specialist door-to-door distributors;

(b) by the Post Office;

(c) in conjunction with the delivery of free newspapers. Areas for campaigns can be based on the ACORN system (*see* **16 (f)**).

23. Typical mail-drop material

In the case of door-to-door distributors, teams, usually part-timers, are used to hand-deliver samples, leaflets and special promotional items such as money-off premium vouchers which can be redeemed at local shops. Envelopes for posting films to film processors are often hand-delivered, as are shopping magazines containing advertisers' offers which again contain cash vouchers. Bonusprint advertise on television and tell viewers an envelope will be delivered at their homes for sending films for processing. They also refer to their mail drops in their ads on the Post Office video service screens (*see* 6: **15**). This kind of direct advertising can be a sales promotion aid. Trade advertising can also be conducted in this way, mail drops being made to selected retailers.

Research has shown that the maildrops which produce the greatest response are redeemable cash vouchers, which can be taken to a local shop and used to claim money off the price of the promoted product.

24. Advantages and disadvantages

Mail drops are obviously cheaper than direct mail, requiring no envelopes, addressing or postage. Saturation coverage is possible, which is desirable with products and services used by the mass market. If it is desired to support retailers, or to boost sales in certain areas, it is a valuable medium. However, if a number of items are distributed simultaneously, as often happens, householders may resent a litter of leaflets, and perhaps pay less attention to them than they would if a single item was delivered with its solus or monopoly effect.

The Post Office offers advertisers a mail-drop service as part of its routine door-to-door deliveries.

DIRECT RESPONSE MARKETING

25. Reasons for growth

It is no accident that direct response marketing has had such a remarkable success in recent years. The history of distribution has come full circle for direct response rejects the impersonal nature of mass media advertising and supermarket-style shopping and has brought the manufacturer and the buyer closer together, resembling the original face-to-face situation of seller and buyer in the marketplace or small shop. The reasons for the growth and success of direct marketing are as follows:

(a) Lack of personal services in self-service stores, supermarkets and hypermarkets.

(b) Problems of car-parking and road congestion near shopping centres.

(c) Popularity of credit, debit and charge cards.

(d) High cost of using sales representatives, whether in consumer or business-to-business marketing.

(e) Arrival of new media such as magazines with weekend newspapers and encouragement to use the telephone instead of the post in order to buy – even if the offer came by post.

(f) Arrival of new products or services which are sold direct. A good example of this is the Midland Bank's 24-hour 365 days a year telephone banking service, First Direct. This new look at banking was the Midland's answer to its problems. But customers seldom switch banks. Wolff Olins was brought in on the positioning and naming of the bank, and First Direct summed up its nature. Using TV commercials to launch the bank it aimed to win 100,000 customers in its first 15 months. The final phase was a direct response campaign, once the name was established. Press advertising has been used since. Most of the campaigns were quite extraordinary and did not explain banking at all. Nevertheless 350,000 customers were achieved by January 1993, and First Direct was conducting its services by telephone instead of over the counter.

The industry has its own monthly magazine, *Direct Response*.

26. Range of methods

Today the variety of means by which 'armchair' shopping can be conducted are only limited by the ability of modern mail order traders to conceive yet another technique of what is now called direct response marketing. We have moved a long way from the mail-order bargains of the popular press or the mail order club catalogues, although both still exist. It is now a sophisticated business extending rapidly into most media. At the same time, traditional media continue to be used, but this does now include commercial television, as with recorded music producers. The largest single user of direct response is insurance, and offers of catalogues in TV commercials.

Some large firms combine television advertising with direct response, using the commercial to produce demand for a catalogue. This is called direct response TV (DRTV). Littlewoods have used this technique for a number of years, promoting its Janet Frazer Catalogue (part of Littlewood's £1bn catalogue business). A telemarketing agency is used to receive requests. The commercials appear in breaks in 'soaps' such as *Brookside*, and the cost is less than for press ads with premium gifts.

A newer use of this combined media technique was British Gas with actress Joanna Lumley presenting the catalogue in the commercial. The campaign was aimed at ABC social grades who probably never visited a British gas showroom, satisfied buyers, and the disabled and elderly. As British Gas operates through regions the catalogue had a wraparound section giving local information. Over £3m was invested in the first catalogue.

27. Direct marketing agencies

Reference was made to direct response agencies in 4: **22 (c)**, and this has become a very substantial area of agency business, conducted either by specialist agencies, or by specialist advertising agencies. A major reason for the expansion of direct response marketing has been the demand from clients for 'accountable advertising' where they can measure the response in enquiries, sales leads or sales.

28. Off-the-page

From small black and white ads in the popular press to full-colour, full-page ads in the weekend colour supplements, a huge variety of goods and services are sold off-the-page. Most hobby and enthusiasts magazines carry ads offering goods by post, from foreign stamps to computer software. The business pages offer unit trusts, and even the popular papers offer life insurance, vehicle and private hospital insurance. Correspondence courses have long been sold this way. Even the sale of shares is conducted by prospectuses published in the press, and privatisation has involved the spectacular issues of public shares in British Aerospace, British Gas, British Telecom, BP, Cable & Wireless and Jaguar. One can buy anything from cases of wine to Isle of Man platinum Nobles by post.

In addition to off-the-page press advertisements there has been a boom in *inserts* tipped into publications. Some readers find them a nuisance and put them in the bin before reading the magazine, but it depends on their interest value to readers, that is, how well they are targeted. A good way to avoid having inserts thrown away is to print them the same size or nearly the same size as the magazine page. This has become big business and large publishers have special machines for tipping in inserts. A number of catalogues such as *Innovations*, and holiday brochures are inserted in magazines.

29. Catalogue selling

Club catalogues will be dealt with separately in **30**. A number of commercial and non-commercial organisations sell from catalogues which may be advertised in the press and on TV (perhaps with a press ad tie-up in, say, *TV Times*), or sent to regular customers, members or donors, or direct mailed against selected mailing lists. Such catalogues are usually distributed annually or seasonally, but some are issued more frequently. They may be for specific products or services such as garden seeds, bulbs or roses; foreign stamps or coins; fashion goods; wines; pipes; or perhaps tour holidays. One of the biggest in this field is the Automobile Association. Another is the Royal Mint. Many charities raise funds by distributing catalogues of Christmas cards, calendars and gifts, and occasionally they may issue gift catalogues at other times of the year.

Five major groups continue to dominate the catalogue industry and their 80 per cent share of the market is divided among them as follows:

Great Universal Stores	39%
Littlewoods	22%
Freemans	16%
Grattan	13%
Empire Stores	10%

Among them nearly 100 catalogues are published. They used to employ large staffs but they have been more than halved by the introduction of modern technology. They all run a variety of subsidiary companies. Freemans was taken over by the American Sears organisation in 1988, one of the pioneers of mail order in the mid-19th century. Retail interests are now linked with catalogue selling, and the Freemans catalogue features sections from high street chains such as Miss Selfridge, Dolcis, Adams and Olympus. Other catalogues are targeted at particular market segments and age groups such as a specialogue offering Wallis retail merchandise.

The research group Verdict reported in August 1993 that Great Universal Stores had increased its share of the home shopping market by taking one per cent from Littlewoods, Freemans and Empire.

There was a time when mail order catalogues were free. Today the press advertisement for *Next Directory* offers a 350-page pictorial catalogue for £3. This tactic may be adopted to deter unlikely customers, but selling the catalogue first contrasts with the free gifts which are offered to induce applications. Presumably one could run quite a remunerative business selling catalogues, and armchair buyers could buy them for the pleasure of dreaming over things they cannot afford to buy.

30. Clubs

There are two kinds, those for club agents who enrol a circle of members, with the agents earning commission on the sales; and clubs for individual members who usually undertake to buy a minimum number of books, videos or CDs a year. Some of the first kind are run by the big firms mentioned in **29**. The Royal Mint operates a coin club, notifying regular customers of new issues but not requiring minimum purchases. Some airlines operate mail order clubs for passengers.

The first group enrol agents by means of ads in the women's press and in listing magazines like *TV Times* and *Radio Times*. The reader should note the special wording of the application coupons in these ads. Particular information is requested such as whether the applicant has a telephone, and there is generally an age limit and perhaps geographical limits.

31. Television

With certain advertisers such as CD and video distribution companies (e.g. Tellydisc), TV has become a prime medium. The viewer telephones the order to a TV service number where it is entered on a computer, and the advertiser receives a print-out of orders within 24 hours.

32. Telephone selling

The telephone has become a medium in itself, and according to Lester Wunderman of Wunderman International, the two biggest media in the USA are the two direct media of direct mail and the telephone. The more compact urbanised conditions in Britain probably preclude this happening on the American scale, but there have been big developments in what is called telemarketing. In fact some advertising agencies now have a sub-sidiary engaged in telephone marketing.

However, like junk mail, telephone selling has its merits and demerits. It is an excellent way of selling advertisement space including classifieds, and for business-to-business promotions. But a number of home improvement firms often annoy householders by ringing them in the evening, perhaps interrupting their favourite television programme.

It is also the medium used by time share racketeers, who ring up to announce that a fabulous holiday has been won in a competition the receiver had never entered, this being a con to attend a sales presentation of a time share project in some apparently exotic place. Another con is for the caller to pretend to be conducting a market research survey, known as 'sugging'.

The Direct Marketing Association has introduced a Code of Practice to combat abuses of telemarketing such as by time share operators and the system of 'sugging'.

Telephone selling can be inward or outward. Other media may produce orders which are telephoned in, or telephone sales staff can telephone existing customers or 'cold call' prospects. It has been adopted by a surprising variety of enterprises, from those selling theatre tickets to home-delivered meals.

Anyone contemplating this method of selling needs to consider the neces-sary organisation. If handled internally special staff and probably a compu-terised order-taking system will be required. This may extend to all hours. Consequently, it may pay to engage an outside telemarketing service which can make or receive calls. These outside specialists need to be well briefed in order to talk knowledgeably to customers.

33. Card decks

This method consists of packs of individual cards packed in a plastic film wrapper which may be plain or custom designed. Each card advertises a different product on one side, the reverse side being an order form and return address, usually postage-paid.

Marketing Week mails its readers with Card packs promoting marketing services and accessories. Book publishers promote books with a different card for each title. Scottish Widows have advertised insurance this way and so have Saga holidays. Several firms specialise in designing and mailing card decks.

34. Direct marketing organisation

As stated in the first paragraph of this chapter, the Direct Marketing Association is the trade association of the industry. It holds forums, conferences and exhibitions, and publishes a membership directory.

The Institute of Direct Marketing is the professional body, and it holds its Diploma in Direct Marketing examination for which courses are held at Kingston, London, Manchester, Bristol and Bradford universities.

CONSUMER PROTECTION

35. Mail Order Protection Scheme

Direct marketing relies on trust. Customers have to send money in advance and do not see the goods until they arrive. That is why this form of trading is less common in developing countries.

In Britain, the Mail Order Protection Scheme means that customers are protected by the publishers who do not wish to receive complaints from readers (*see* Figure 9.2).

36. Direct mail standards

Established with Royal Mail support, the Direct Mail Services Standards Board promotes improvements in the ethical and professional standards of the industry.

37. Legal and voluntary protection

It is important to understand the difference between the self-regulatory requirements of voluntary codes, plus the house rules of the media owners, and the statutes which make certain practices illegal and liable to prosecution. The British Codes of Advertising and Sales Promotion (*see* 18: **36**), among other things, stipulate what may be said about the investment value of collectables (coins, medals, plates, etc.). One of the problems which media owners seek to prevent is the advertising of products which are not stocked until orders are received. By that time the supplier's price may have risen, possibly leading to bankruptcy if the advertiser honours the orders at the

THE NATIONAL NEWSPAPER

MAIL ORDER PROTECTION SCHEME

ORDER WITH CONFIDENCE

Mail order advertisements within this newspaper requiring payment to be sent in direct response are approved under the terms of the Mail Order Protection Scheme (MOPS).

This means that you are fully protected from financial loss should the advertiser default and cease to trade.

The scheme does not cover certain types of advertisements including classified announcements and purchases from catalogues and brochures.

Should you have an enquiry or need advice about mail order advertisements write to the MOPS office in London giving the following details: –

i) date of the advertisement;
ii) name and address of the advertiser;
iii) nature of product and method of payment.

REMEMBER MOPS exists for your benefit.

Full details of the scheme and the excluded categories of advertising can be obtained by sending a S.A.E. to **The National Newspaper Mail Order Protection Scheme (MOPS)**, 16 Tooks Court, London EC4A 1LB.

Figure 9.2 Typical MOPS advertisement

quoted price. The law, on the other hand, may be concerned with the correct description of goods. For example, a one-time racket was to describe textiles as 'art. silk'. In small type, the full point between art and silk could be deceptive, and it was easy for readers to assume mistakenly that the garment was made of silk when in fact the words meant artificial silk, i.e. rayon.

There are over 250 Acts of Parliament affecting the direct response marketer, and some may be of general application wherever the goods are sold. Relevant statutes are explained in Chapter 18. To these may be added the common law of contract. Most of these laws apply to off-the-page direct response, some apply to all forms of direct response marketing, and the Radio Authority and ITC Codes apply solely to commercial radio and television.

The question of legal versus voluntary control is discussed more fully in Chapter 18.

Progress test 9

1. Distinguish between *direct mail* and *mail order*. (2)

2. What are the special characteristics of direct mail? (3–8)

3. When can direct mail be a primary advertising medium? (7)

4. Describe the pattern of an effective sales letter. (10)

5. What is a one-piece mailer? (12)

6. When is a printed envelope important to a direct mail campaign? (13)

7. How may mailing lists be compiled? (16)

8. What do the letters ACORN stand for, and how can it be applied to direct mail? (16)

9. Describe the Mailing Preference, Fax Preference and Telephone Preference Services. (18)

10. How does a mail drop differ from direct mail? (22)

11. What is the Direct Marketing Association? (1, 34)

12. What is direct response marketing? (25, 26)

13. Explain the meaning of 'off-the-page'. (28)

14. Explain the direct response methods of catalogue selling and mail order clubs. (29, 30)

15. What are the latest techniques in direct response marketing? (31–33)

16. How do the media protect consumers from abuses of mail-order trading or direct response marketing? (35)

17. How are consumers given legal protection from abuses of mail order trading or direct response marketing? (37)

10

Exhibitions

IMPORTANCE OF EXHIBITIONS

1. History

Exhibitions are popular throughout the world and have a long history, originating with old trading markets such as the 'marts' in what are today Belgium and the Netherlands, where British merchants sold their wool and woollens in the fourteenth century. The exhibition developed into the show attended by either the trade or the general public. London for many years became a major exhibition centre, to mention only the Great Exhibition of 1851, the Wembley Exhibition of 1924, and the Festival of Britain in 1951. In recent years the National Exhibition Centre in Birmingham has rivalled London although many events are held at Olympia, Earls Court, the Horticultural Halls and the Barbican Centre in the City, together with the G-Mex Centre at Manchester and the SECC in Glasgow. The NEC at Birmingham is the 10th largest exhibition centre in Europe, which is not a flattering position, largely due to the lack of Government support in Britain.

Exhibitions are the only advertising medium which appeal to all five senses of sight, hearing, smell, taste and touch. Total expenditure on exhibitions in Britain is about £525 million.

Germany, with its big shows in Hanover, Frankfurt, Munich, Berlin, Cologne and Leipzig, and others in Hamburg, Stuttgart and Dusseldorf, has good reason for its dominance. They are often referred to as 'Messe', which relates to the medieval trade fairs which were founded on the continental trade routes.

2. International exhibitions

Throughout the world there are major exhibition centres, often government supported (unlike Britain!), the chief ones in Europe being Basle, Frankfurt, Geneva and Milan. Many foreign centres have the advantage of being close to airports. Many exhibitions are nowadays held in the Gulf states, an indication of the need to develop their emergent economies. Permanent trade exhibition centres exist in developing countries such as Indonesia, Malaysia and Singapore. The Department of Trade and Industry supports exhibitors interested in exports by organising British exhibitions abroad, taking British pavilions at Expos and arranging Joint Venture schemes with subsidies for British participants. The DTI lists exhibition dates in its monthly journal, *Overseas Trade*, free to applicants. The DTI also funds local Chambers of Commerce for members to attend trade fairs.

Foreign exhibitions, and international ones, tend to predominate. Perhaps the main weakness of British exhibitions is their remote location compared with those held in Europe which are easily visited by people from neighbouring countries, or American ones which draw visitors from a larger area, or Asiatic ones in centres such as Kuala Lumpur, Jakarta and Singapore which attract visitors from nearby Asian and Far East countries.

Although there has been an overall increase in the costs of participation since 1983, there has been a rise in expenditure by British exhibitors in overseas shows but a fall in expenditure on shows held in the UK.

TYPES OF EXHIBITION

3. Introduction

This is a versatile medium, and its many forms are described in **4–14** below.

4. Public indoor

Usually held in specially built halls, the public show is based on a theme of public interest such as food, the home, do-it-yourself, gardening or holidays and travel. The most famous is the *Daily Mail* Ideal Home Exhibition which has been held for more than 50 years.

5. Trade or business indoor

A more specialised type of exhibition, this will probably have a smaller attendance consisting of *bona fide* visitors who are invited, given tickets in their trade journal or admitted on presentation of their business card.

6. Joint trade and public indoor

Some events, such as motor shows, may have days allocated to trade or public visitors.

7. Private indoor

These are usually confined to one sponsor, but occasionally consist of a few sponsors with associated but not rival interests. Venues are usually hotels, local halls, libraries, building centres or company premises if suitable.

8. Outdoor

Certain subjects lend themselves to outdoor exhibitions, for instance aviation, farm equipment (at agricultural shows), camping and large construction equipment. Exhibition stands may also be available at outdoor or tented events like flower shows, gymkhanas and horse shows. In hotter countries, exhibitions normally held indoors in the northern hemisphere will be held out-of-doors.

9. Travelling

Mobile exhibitions can be transported by caravan, specially built exhibition vehicles, converted double-decker buses, trains, aircraft and ships. British Rail had its special Ambassador exhibition train which could be used by a single client and taken to a choice of railway stations throughout the country where visitors could be received. Such mobile venues can also be taken to European countries. Mobile van shows are common in developing countries, travelling from town to town and village to village.

10. Portable

This is the kind of knock-down exhibition which can be carried in an estate car or small van, and put up in hotels, shops, public halls and libraries. It can be supported by sales staff, demonstrations, seminars and slide or video shows. Some can be left unattended in public places if they are self-explanatory, like a book exhibition in a public library.

11. In-store

These are popular with foreign sponsors who organise weeks in different towns to display foods, wines, fabrics, pottery, glassware or tourist attractions. Similarly, British Weeks are organised in foreign cities. The displays are usually in appropriate stores, but a special entertainment evening may be organised for the public in a theatre or hall, when singers, dancers and videos may constitute the programme. In-store demonstrations and fashion shows may also be organised such as those for sewing machines, while Marks & Spencer have organised public fashion shows during the evening at their stores.

12. Permanent exhibitions

Some large organisations may hold exhibitions within their premises or in special halls or parks. A particularly attractive one is Legoland, at Windsor, and there is a children's park at Billund, Denmark, which demonstrates Lego toys.

The following are well worth visiting, combining as they do well mounted exhibits with video shows:

The Thames Barrier Exhibition, near Woolwich.
The *Mary Rose* Exhibition, Portsmouth Dockyard.
The Eurotunnel Exhibition, Folkestone.

13. Conferences

In association with annual conferences there is often an exhibition supported by suppliers which delegates may visit between and after conference sessions. Some of them are quite small, perhaps arranged in an ante-room or in the foyer of the hotel, but others are as big as the conference itself. The larger exhibitions are usually held at venues like Brighton or Harrogate where there are combined conference and exhibition facilities.

14. Window

Here we have a special use of the portable exhibition, when the window of a business can be made more attractive by accepting the loan of a ready-made exhibit. This idea has been taken up by a great many building societies. Some exhibits, like those of Rentokil, may be relevant to property owners, but an astonishing array of subjects are shown in this way. They are certainly more attractive than the usual displays of interest rates which do not differ much from one building society to another whatever names they may give to similar investment schemes. Thus, both the exhibitor and the building society benefit from the attention gained.

CHARACTERISTICS OF EXHIBITIONS

15. Introduction

Exhibitions are unlike any other forms of advertising and can include selling direct off-the-stand to visitors. The special characteristics of exhibitions are summarised in **16–21**.

16. Focal point and magnet

The chief value of an exhibition is that it draws attention to its subject and so attracts people, often from great distances. Thus the exhibitor has the opportunity of meeting people he would never meet nor have time to contact. The message of the exhibition, and often that of individual exhibitors, spreads far beyond the event itself, and coverage is possible throughout the appropriate media at home and abroad. Air and motor shows at venues such as Farnborough and Paris will be seen on British TV shows and news bulletins. However, this last point depends on how far the exhibitor exploits the public relations opportunities, which often means collaborating with the exhibition press officer months in advance. One public relations opportunity is to *invite* the official opener to visit the stand since he or she usually has an itinerary arranged in advance for a short tour of the exhibition.

17. Time-consuming

An exhibition requires a lot of time for its preparation, and for manning the stand. It is essential that the stand is manned by knowledgeable people capable of answering visitors' questions. It may be necessary to employ linguists. For an international or overseas show sales literature will be needed in the languages of visiting nationalities.

18. Prototypes

Exhibitions provide opportunities to display prototypes of new products, and to receive visitors' comments and criticisms.

19. Face-to-face confrontation

Confidence, credibility and goodwill can be established by meeting potential customers face-to-face. This applies to both distributors and consumers.

The American International Exhibitors Association claims that while it may cost £250 for a sales representative to make a sales call, an exhibition lead is likely to cost only £38. The total cost of making a sale may cost £600, whereas sales generated at trade exhibitions can cost as little as £130. The exhibition brings the buyer to the salesperson, quickly and at one venue so that far more potential buyers can be reached in a short time compared with the travel time involved in meeting these buyers. In fact, the salesperson on the stand may well meet buyers he or she did not know existed.

20. Demonstration and sampling

There are ideal opportunities actually to show the product which is more authentic than describing and illustrating it in advertisements, catalogues and sales literature. Similarly, sampling provides a good sales promotion opportunity. Prototypes can be demonstrated on a stand and comments made by visitors may lead to useful modifications.

21. Atmosphere

The atmosphere of an exhibition is very congenial, even though a long visit may be hard on the feet. For many people it is an outing to be enjoyed and there is an atmosphere of entertainment like going to the circus or the theatre. An exhibitor will make himself very agreeable if he has a reception room where visitors may sit down.

USING EXHIBITIONS

22. Information about exhibitions

There are many trade papers which give forward dates of exhibitions, the most complete details appearing in *Exhibition Bulletin*. Other publications which announce exhibition details are *British Rate and Data*, *Conferences and Exhibitions International*, *Sales and Marketing Management* and *Overseas Trade*.

23. A checklist for potential exhibitions

The following points should be borne in mind before booking space in an exhibition.

(a) Organisers. Is the event organised by a responsible firm? Are they members of the Association of Exhibition Organisers? Have they run this or other shows before?

(b) Date. What is the date, is it convenient and does it clash with any other event?

(c) Venue. Is it a good venue, that is one likely to attract a good attendance? 'A good attendance' could mean attendance by the right people. An event for financial firms would be better staged at the Barbican in the City of London than at the NEC in Birmingham. Is it a convenient one for transporting exhibits to and from? Some foreign venues may impose transportation and customs problems. Does it have good transport links? Is there adequate car-parking? Are there nearby hotels?

(d) Cost of sites. What is the charge per square metre and are, perhaps, modestly priced shell schemes available?

(e) Facilities. Are all the necessary facilities available such as telephone, water, gas or electricity, if they are required?

(f) Publicity. How will visitors be attracted?

(g) Build-up and knock-down. Is there adequate time allowed before and after the show for erection and dismantling of stands?

(h) Public relations. What press office and press visit facilities will there be?
   This is an aspect of exhibitions which is overlooked by many exhibitors. It pays to co-operate with the exhibition press officer months before the event. Valuable press, radio and television coverage can be gained from exhibitions, and this is a valuable bonus. Hundreds of journalists visit shows,

looking for good stories and pictures. They do not carry suitcases and will shun clumsy press kits packed with irrelevant material.

For the press room simple news releases containing newsworthy information, and preferably not exceeding one page, should be supplied for display. Photographs must be captioned. Sales literature should not be supplied to the exhibition press room unless requested.

Press receptions can also be held on stands, but usually there is a press day when journalists have a preview tour of the exhibition.

(i) Associated events. Are there any associated events like a conference or video shows?

(j) Is it justified? Is the cost of designing and constructing a stand, renting space, printing sales literature, providing hospitality (especially at a trade show) and taking staff away from their regular work justified? Has the company something new to show, does it need to meet distributors and/or customers, must it compete with rival exhibitors? What value may be anticipated for the money spent – in goodwill or sales, including perhaps the finding and appointing of new agents or distributors?

In his very useful book, *Exhibitions and Conferences from A to Z* (Modina Press), Sam Black makes the following comment:

> Exhibitions are visited by people expecting to see actual objects. Photographs, diagrams and illustrations play an important part in conveying technical or general information but they should be subsidiary to the three-dimensional exhibits. People will read quite detailed explanatory copy on an exhibition stand if it explains an exhibit which has attracted their curiosity, but isolated panels of text will rarely be read.

To help choose an exhibition in which to participate there is the annual analysis of UK shows, *Which Exhibition*, published by Conference and Travel Publications of Forest Row.

24. Auditing attendances

Estimating the volume and value of attendance at exhibitions is not easy, and much depends on the kind of exhibition. For example, an entire family attending a leisure or home interest exhibition could be valuable, whereas while a business exhibition is limited to business people their seniority and buying power would be important.

Some years ago an attendance audit scheme was introduced, but it required too much information which some exhibitors were unwilling to release. The Exhibitions Audience Profile was launched but proved to be an oversimplification. In 1993 the Audit Bureau of Circulations brought out a newsingle standard method for auditing exhibition attendance data, and awards the

Certificate of Attendance (COA). This is the result of two years' work with representatives of all sides of the industry.

The Exhibition Industry Federation recognises three audit systems, the Certificate of Attendance, the Exhibition Audience Audit and the Open Audit Specification. The EAA audit is expensive but goes into details such as how many people passing through exhibitions are students or exhibitors themselves, plus details about the characteristics such as who visitors work for and what newspapers they read.

The COA is less comprehensive, and is becoming the more generally adopted. Currently (1999), a COA for consumer exhibitions costs £1,030 to £2,500, depending on attendance figures and audit time. For trade shows a standard COA costs £547 to £671. The important thing is that there should be reliable media data about exhibitors just as there is about press, radio, TV, cinema and outdoor.

Progress test 10

1. Describe the main types of public, trade and private exhibitions. **(4–14)**

2. What are the main characteristics of the exhibition as an advertising medium? **(16–21)**

3. Where would you find information about dates and venues of forthcoming exhibitions? **(22)**

4. If you were considering participation in an exhibition what points would you check before signing a contract for space? **(23)**

5. Why are press kits a waste of money? **(23h)**

6. How can media coverage be obtained by co-operating with the press officer? **(23h)**

7. What is the COA? **(24)**

11

Copywriting

WRITING COPY THAT SELLS

1. The creative team

As the IPA definition states, advertising must present 'the most persuasive selling message'. Copywriting is the art of writing selling messages. It is salesmanship in print. If it fails to provoke the desired attention, interest, desire, conviction and action it has failed (*see* 12: **2**). Of course, it is likely to be assisted by other forms of creativity such as pictures, typography and perhaps colour, but the copywriter should think *visually* and direct these other elements to achieve his or her purpose.

The copywriter should work closely with the visualiser and typographer to obtain artistic and typographical interpretation of his or her copy. The copywriter cannot successfully work in isolation, merely writing the words, with artists working in similar isolation to create the physical appearance of the advertisement. Ideally, and for practical reasons, the complete advertisement should be a team effort. The design or layout should give effective presentation of the words, the illustrations should give emphasis and support, and the typography (choice of typefaces, and their size and weight) should make the copy legible and give emphasis where necessary. The copywriter should always try to write with the final appearance of the advertisement in mind.

2. Special literary style

The writing of advertisement copy is a specially skilled kind of writing, and has a *raison d'être* and style utterly different from that of a book, poem, article, short story or news report. Advertising and public relations writing require two very distinct literary techniques. Even the copy for a press advertisement, a sales letter and a piece of sales literature each require their own special treatment, although all three aim to sell.

3. Basic rules

The essential characteristics of copywriting are as follows.

(a) It must sell, even if it only reminds.

(b) The secret of successful advertising is repetition, whether by continuously advertising or by the use of repetition in the advertisement.

(c) People do not necessarily want to read the advertisement. Therefore the message must not waste words, and must convey its message quickly and with impact.

(d) If the reader hesitates at an unknown word, attention is lost. Therefore every word must be easily understood and there must be no ambiguity.

(e) Short words, short sentences, short paragraphs help to demonstrate the message and make it easy and quick to read and absorb.

(f) While taking care to write clearly and accurately when *using* language, copywriters must also develop skills for *abusing* language to achieve the results demanded by the brief.

COPY DEVICES

4. Introduction

To achieve its special literary style, and its persuasiveness, the devices described in **6, 11** can be used.

5. Clichés

There are certain simple, well-used and sometimes seemingly banal words which are actually highly successful in advertising. They are sometimes called *buzz words*. The most powerful word in advertising is 'free'. It can be applied in many ways, even in the address if Freepost or Freephone facilities can be offered. Even when there is not really a free gift or sample, it is more compelling to offer a free leaflet or a free catalogue. Few people can resist something for nothing!

Other effective advertising clichés are 'Now', 'New', 'Here', 'At Last' and 'Today'.

But meaningless clichés like those so often used by politicians, e.g. this point in time, and like a turkey praying for Christmas, should be avoided.

6. Action words

Verbs can be used to give the copy a sense of urgency and to help the copy to move along. These are almost all short words. They give the copy pace. Typical examples are:

Buy	Write	Taste	Look
Try	Phone	Watch	Take
Ask	Call	Smell	Drink
Get	Send	Hear	Let
See	Cut	Listen	Do
Ring	Post	Drive	Start
Come	Fill	Eat	Enjoy

Here are some examples of how these words can be used, together with the clichés mentioned earlier.

(a) 'Send today for your free sample, and try the new flavour.'

(b) 'Fill in and cut the coupon, and post it today.'

(c) 'Hear the surf, smell the flowers, taste the wine and enjoy yourself.'

(d) 'Call in and buy one now.'

While the action words above are all short there are, of course, longer ones which can have their positive effect too, such as:

Discover	Remember	Protect
Explore	Examine	Replace
Restore	Complete	Renovate
Repair	Donate	Present
Consider	Decide	Apply

Obviously, there are scores of verbs which can be used in copy but, by isolating the examples given, attention is drawn to the kind of words which help to enliven the sales message. As will be shown, however, there are many other devices which the copywriter can exploit.

7. Emotive or exciting words

These are adjectives, words which are descriptive and enhance the facts. For example, the caption to a picture in a tourist advertisement or brochure could read:

'View from bedroom window.'

However, that does not say very much. It is not very exciting. If the reader looks closely at the picture, the picture may seem to be very nice. The reader has to make an effort to arrive at this conclusion. Why should he bother? The copywriter can do it for him by saying:

'The magnificent view from the bedroom window.'

Even this is not very personal. It does not relate to the potential tourist who has not yet been convinced that the advertised holiday is for him or her. So why not say:

'You can enjoy this magnificent view from your bedroom window.'

Now we are getting somewhere, but what is the view *of*? The picture cannot speak for itself, so why not be explicit and say, using another descriptive word:

'You can enjoy this magnificent view of the mighty Matterhorn from your bedroom window.'

Now the reader is truly 'put in the picture', and we have added yet another device with the alliterative use of three 'Ms', magnificent, mighty and Matterhorn (*see* 8).

Some of the adjectives which can be used in copy include:

Splendid	Delightful	Wonderful
Amazing	Gorgeous	Beautiful

We can also use more practical emotive generalities such as:

Economical	Money saving	Time saving
Labour saving	Mouth watering	Inexpensive
Value for money	Satisfying	Rewarding

They give no details, yet these words help to create a mental image of the product or service, and to *create desire* and *inspire confidence*. The car is economical because it uses less petrol, the holiday is inexpensive and value for money because the price includes so much, and the conference will prove to be a rewarding experience.

8. Alliteration

Alliteration results from repeating sounds, and is thus a form of repetition (*see* example in 7). This repetition of sounds should be pleasing to the ear, not overdone and so obvious that it is irritating. All the devices suggested in this chapter should be accepted by the reader as the natural words to use, even though the effect is specially contrived. Copy may be cleverly written, but it should never appear to be clever, otherwise it will sound false and the reader will feel cheated. Nevertheless, if readers are considering holidays they expect them to be something exciting which can be looked forward to. They do not want them to sound like jail sentences. Below are some famous uses of alliteration and rhyme in advertisements which have appeared over the years.

> Players please
> Mars are marvellous
> Let the train take the strain
> Three Nuns, none nicer
> Don't be vague, ask for Haig
> Go well, go Shell
> If anyone can Canon can
> Land Rover, The Best 4 × 4 × Far

Alliteration lends itself very well to slogans, making them memorable, but it can be used discreetly and pleasantly in sentences in the text like this:

> 'Take a ride round the town in the new Crown roadster.'

9. Colloquialisms

Once upon a time the prestige ads in *The Times* and the serious ones in the technical and professional journals used impeccable English. Some of the prestige ads were even written by famous authors, just to give them literary flow. Not so today. They have short, sharp copy just like the ones for FMCGs.

They, like so many consumer ads today, use chatty, conversational colloquialisms such as 'don't', 'couldn't', 'wouldn't', 'won't', 'you'd', 'what's', 'that's', and other abbreviations. We also have snappy expressions like 'Pick'n'Choose', 'Fish'n'Chips'.

10. Punctuation and grammar

The modern copywriter would probably fail an English examination, if only for abuse of punctuation to achieve effect. One-word sentences that cannot possibly be parsed may be used. Prepositions and conjunctions will be omitted and nouns, verbs, adverbs and adjectives will be linked with dashes or dots. The ellipsis is used freely. Sentences like this will be written:

> 'Now – special offer! – only 50p if you rush today
> – biggest value you've ever seen.'

or:

> 'Now. Special offer! Only 50p if you rush today.
> Biggest value you've ever seen.'

Much use may be made of the *screamer*, as the exclamation mark is called. In contrast and in contradiction, apparently pedantic use is made of the full point or full stop at the end of some headlines. This is deliberate, giving impact to the headline, and it is known as the *emphatic full point*. Here is an example:

> 'Write his name in gold.' (Remy Martin)

And here is one which made a charity appeal ad extra compelling:

> 'Save the children. Now.'

11. Repetition

Finally, there is the use of repetition, which may occur in the following ways.

(a) Using the same word to open each paragraph of the text.

(b) Promoting the company or brand name throughout the text.

(c) Repeating the name throughout the headline, pictures, captions, sub-headings, text, signature slogan and logo.

(d) Repetition of the ad itself or repeating the same style in a series, or maintaining the same style of layout and typography whenever ads appear. Use of the same position in a publication is also a useful form of repetition, although that is a matter for the media buyer.

COPY ELEMENTS

12. Seven elements

Now that we have considered the various literary devices which the copy-writer can use, let us look at the whole advertisement by analysing the seven elements which may constitute a hard-selling advertisement. In addition to these copy elements there will be the visual creative elements of layout, shape, illustrations, typography and perhaps colour, but in this chapter we are concerned only with the wording.

The seven copy elements are:

- headline,
- subheadings,
- body copy,
- price,
- name and address,
- coupon (if there is one),
- signature slogan or strapline.

13. Headline

In the past headlines were usually short, and they were often slogans. Today they are more often statements extending to one or two sentences, and displayed so boldly that they are virtually seen rather than read. This visual change in headline writing is probably a result of television with its emphasis on looking. There are also many different kinds of headline so that the copywriter can choose the most original and attention-getting kind of headline for the purpose, and also so that one can be used which is different from that used to advertise rival products. Here are 25 kinds of headline, with an invented example of each.

(a) Declarative. The world's toughest tyre.

(b) Interrogative. Do you want more interest?

(c) Commanding. Buy your books at Brown's.

(d) Challenging. Why put up with higher prices?

(e) Testimonial. 'I always use Washo', says Millicent Day.

(f) Association of ideas. Even Roger Bacon liked eggs.

(g) News. The new Royal cooker.

(h) Emotional. No one knows she's crying.

(i) Incongruous. The fat to make you thin.

(j) Identification. Bullman's Brown Ale.

(k) Curiosity. Ever heard of a pig cleaning a pipe?

(l) Bargain. Now only 99p.

(m) Humorous. Josephine's Restaurant is open every night!

(n) Picture and caption. She's enjoying an indoor tan (below picture of girl with sun lamp).

(o) Topical. The sherry to cheer your Christmas guests.

(p) Slogan. Crookes the cleanest cleaners.

(q) Play on words. Who's for Denis?

(r) Alliterative. The wonderful watches by Waterman.

(s) Gimmick. z-z-z-z-Buzz-z-z-z-z-Bar.

(t) Negative. Don't spend it, bank it.

(u) Displayed copy.

> This is the lawnmower
> which takes you for a ride
> -round your lawn.

(v) TV tie-up. Perfect picture control (repeating TV commercial jingle).

(w) Quotation. 'My kingdom for a horse' – play it safe with Bronco Brakes.

(x) Split. An armchair in the sky (picture of passenger on airline) with Pacific Airlines.

(y) Intriguing. What's square about a round hole?

14. Subheadings

It is in the writing of subheadings that the copywriter is encouraged to write visually for they contribute very much to the design and typography of the advertisement. They introduce contrast and emphasis since subheadings can be printed in a different typeface, or in larger and bolder type, or possibly in a different colour. The purpose of subheadings can be to:

(a) maintain a sense of movement so that the eye is carried progressively through the copy;

(b) provide typographical contrast as stated above;

(c) emphasise selling points;

(d) divide the ad into sections if there are different ideas or items;

(e) absorb the interest of glancers who take in only the display lines;

(f) make the ad more interesting, more readable, more legible and not a mass of dull, grey type.

15. The body copy

The text consists of the body matter or the main wording of the advertisement which is printed in smaller type than the display lines. The display lines consist of the headline, subheadings, prices, name and address and the strapline or signature slogan. Thus, when writing the main copy for an advertisement the copywriter should use his imagination to think how he can use display or bold lines of type to highlight the text and encourage people to read it. He may also write briefly in order to allow the use of larger type or the use of white space.

Indented paragraph starts lead the reader's eye into the body copy, and from the end of one paragraph to the start of the next.

Just as there are many kinds of headline to choose from so there are different ways in which the text can be written. Twelve kinds of body copy are described below.

(a) **Emotive**. Within this kind of copy the emotions can be appealed to. The principal emotional needs are self-assertion, sex and love, companionship, self-preservation, acquisitiveness, curiosity, comfort and security.

A fine example of this technique is used by Kodak, who put most of its consumer advertising effort not into selling film, but into encouraging consumers to take better pictures and preserve precious memories.

An insurance ad may appeal to the emotional need for security from the hazards of fire, burglary, injury or family responsibilities. A gift advertisement may appeal to the emotion of love, and one for collectables such as stamps, coins or antiques to the emotion of acquisitiveness. Ads for health products appeal to the emotional need for self-preservation. Many charity ads appeal to the emotions in different ways.

These owe much to the instincts and emotions of the psychologist William McDougall:

Instincts	Emotions
Flight	Fear
Repulsion	Disgust
Curiosity	Wonder
Pugnacity	Anger
Self-abasement (or subjection)	Self-assertion (or self-display)
Parental	Tender

together with the instincts of reproduction, gregariousness, acquisition and construction which can all be applied to motivation in advertising copy.

(b) Factual – hard-selling. This is the typical ad which follows the five-point AIDCA formula (*see* 12: **2**). It is very competitive, persuasive and action promoting. The action may be provoked by a free offer or price cut, and there may be addresses to write to or call at and phone numbers to ring, or response may be sought by means of a coupon.

(c) Factual – educational. This is still a hard-selling ad, but it will be more informative, like the ads for the latest-model car.

(d) Narrative. Here we have a more literary and leisurely written text, but this style is not limited to prestige ads. The copy is more like a story, and it might be used to promote a holiday cruise. Such copy is also used in the business press to tell the story of a bank or insurance company, and it has been used to recruit nurses and police.

(e) Prestige. Again, the copy may be in the narrative style, but being used mainly for public relations purposes the modern corporate ad has taken on a more vigorous character, setting out facts and arguments in no-nonsense terms.

(f) Picture and caption. In this kind of ad there is usually a series of pictures or cartoons with captions, perhaps explaining how to use the product.

(g) Monologue or dialogue. Real or fictitious characters may be used to present the sales message. This could be a testimonial advertisement with well-known personalities expounding the merits of the product or the service.

(h) Gimmick. Difficult to put over effectively because there is usually need for concentrated reading, this style is sometimes used when a very original presentation is required. It is more likely to be used in magazines, which are read less hurriedly than newspapers, and addressed to sophisticated readerships.

(i) Reader. Such advertisements are usually headed by a statement that it is an advertiser's announcement because editors do not like advertisements which pretend to be editorial. However, there are shopping features in which a series of reader ads (usually illustrated) are assembled.

(j) Testimonial. This may be in the form of a monologue, but it could be a testimonial statement linked to normal text copy. Here is an example from an advertisement for Fotopost Express:

> 'I never trust my colour films to anyone else.' Wendy Craig.

Although this was virtually a headline (accompanied by a portrait of the actress) it occupied half the space, the rest of the copy being details of the service, special offers and order coupon.

(k) Quotation. It is possible at times to find a statement in a book, play or speech which is relevant to the subject, such as a famous person's description of a place. The following was used in a tourist ad for Botswana: 'Said Frederick Courtney Selous in 1870, "*I never enjoyed any part of my wanderings so much*".'

(l) Back-selling. This is used to tell readers about a material, ingredient or component which is contained in a finished product, the object being to encourage its continued usage and especially to encourage buyers of the finished product to insist that it includes this item. It could also be applied to equipment in a new house such as the central heating system.

16. Price

People are very price conscious, and can be turned off by an advertisement which does not state at least a minimum price. If one looks through a newspaper or magazine it will be seen that a very large number of ads make a major selling point of price, and that it is often displayed boldly. There can be a psychological appeal to price: it can be a bargain not to be missed, it may be exceptional value for money, while a high price can suggest quality and possibly even greater desirability. There can also be allusions to price ranging from 'hundreds of bargains' to 'It's not the cheapest' according to the class of product or service. Or, as Stella Artois puts it, 'Reassuringly expensive'.

17. Name and address

It may be sufficient merely to identify the name of the product or company, supported by the logo, but other advertisers – in order to identify themselves clearly, and to attract response – feature their name and address boldly. Usually, this is featured at the end of the ad. If there is a coupon it should be included in both the main part of the ad and in the coupon, otherwise the address will disappear with the coupon and the reader will have lost the identity of the advertiser should further reference be necessary.

18. Coupon

The writing of coupons is more serious than may be thought, and it is seldom sufficient to ask for no more than a name and address. It is essential that the coupon makes the offer clear, and sets out very clearly any choice of offers, so that the reader understands what he or she is requesting (or ordering), and so that the advertiser can supply satisfactorily. The name and address must be fully given, and this may require a declaration regarding, 'Mr, Mrs or Miss', or 'First name', and the reader should be asked to clarify the address by stating town, county, country, postcode or zip code. This is very important because the same town names occur in both different parts of a country and different parts of the world. Postcodes help immensely in securing safe delivery. A telephone number may also be desirable.

When readers are asked to send money the instructions regarding payments should be clear and specific. There are requirements under the Advertisements (Hire Purchase) Act that when payment may be made by instalments the number and cost of instalments shall be stated together with the full price so that the consumer is aware of any higher price as a result of paying by instalments.

Advertisers have to be careful, if enquiries are to be used as leads for salespeople, to give the reader the opportunity to refuse a salesperson's call. This requirement is specified in the British Codes of Advertising and Sales Promotion. Readers should not be pestered by uninvited salespeople.

19. Signature slogan or strapline

This is the pay-off line, and it can be used as a device to create a corporate image. It has become a common practice to conclude ads with a signature slogan, and Table 11.1 shows some examples.

Table 11.1 Campaign slogans

Advertiser	Product	Slogan
AEG	Electrical appliances	Advanced engineering from Germany
Alpen	Breakfast cereal	Wake up to Alpen
Asahi Shimbun	Newspaper	We're out to open minds for you
Barclays	Banking	Open for business
BASF	Coatings	The better way to cover things
BBC	Broadcasting	York make it what it is

213

Table 11.1 (*continued*)

Advertiser	Product	Slogan
BMW	Cars	The ultimate driving machine
Boots	Pharmacy	The Right Chemistry
Bosch	Auto, corporate	We bring innovation
Bosch	Domestic appliances	Excellence comes as standard
Bose	Audio	Better sound through research
British Midland	Airline	The Airline for Europe
BT	Telecoms	Why not change the way we work?
C&A	Store	Better value than Ever
Canon	Reprographics	You and Canon Can
Carphone Warehouse	Mobile phones	Simple Impartial Advice
Compaq	Computers	Better answers
CTS Horizons	Travel	Perfecting the art of travel
Cyprus	Tourism	Nobody ever goes just once
DFS	Furniture	Britain's leading upholstery specialist
Daewoo	Cars	That'll be the Daewoo
De Beers	Diamonds	A diamond is forever
DHL	Couriers	We keep your promises
Duxiana	Beds	Advanced technology in sleeping
Fiat	Cars	Driven by passion
Fiat Punto	Car	Spirito di Punto
Great Thorpe Park	Leisure park	Great, whatever the weather
Hasselblad	Cameras	The Image of Perfection
Honda	Cars	First man, then machine
Hong Kong	Tourism	City of Life
HSE Health & Safety Executive		Reducing risks protecting people
IBM	Computers	Solutions for a small planet
Intel	Computer chips	The Computer Inside
Iridium	Comms networks	Calling planet earth
Irish Ferries	Ferry	You'll enjoy our Irish ways
JAL	Airline	A better approach to business
Korean Air	Airline	Beyond your imagination
Magnet	Kitchens	Designed for living. Built for life
Mitsubishi	Cars	Re-inventing the wheel
Mobil	Lubricants	Feel the difference
National Traineeships	Training	Getting school leavers into the right company
Nature's Best	Food supplements	Health for life
Natwest	Banking	More than just a bank
NFU Mutual	Insurance	The best in the country
Nokia	Mobile phones	Connecting people
Novell	Computer networking	21st century solutions

Table 11.1 (*continued*)

Advertiser	Product	Slogan
P&O Scottish Ferries	Ferry	Only P&O know how
Pergo	Flooring	A new way to look at floors
Peugeot	Cars	The drive of your life
Propain	Analgesic	Powerful pain relief
Rado	Watches	Rado. A different world
Railtrack	Tracks, stations	The heart of the railway
Rémy Martin	Brandy	Fine Champagne Cognac
Ricoh	Digital copiers	We lead. Others copy
Sainsbury	Supermarket chain	Fresh food, fresh ideas
		Food costs less at Sainsbury's
		Fresh ideas from Sainsbury's
		Making life taste better
Savlon	Skin cream	Trust Savlon to make it better
Schroders	Investment	The name that stands for long-term performance
Scottish Widows Bank	Mortgages, savings	Looking good for your money
Selective Marketplace	Clothes	Classic good looks
Sheffield Business School		Education for business and the professions
Sitel Corporation	Telecom call centres	We speak your language
South African Airways	Airline	Africa's warmest welcome
Specsavers	Opticians	Now you can believe your eyes
Springers	Footwear	Sandals and shoes for a brighter world
Standard Life Bank	Banking	Saving has never been simpler
Swissair	Airline	The refreshing airline
Tesco	Supermarket chain	Every little helps
The Equitable Life	Pensions	You profit from our principles
Thorntons	Chocolate	Chocolate Heaven Since 1911
Time	Computers	We're on your side
Tivoli	Computer networking	The Power to Manage. Anything. Anywhere.
Toyota	Cars	The car in front is a Toyota
Triton	Electric showers	The power behind the shower
TSC	IT solutions	Delivering Business Benefits Through Technology
United Airlines	Airline	Rising
Vodaphone	Telephone airtime	The Word is Vodaphone
W.H. Smith	Stationers	WHatever you're into, get into WHSmith
Xircom	PC components	Get mobile. Stay connected. Go places.

Progress test 11

1. What is meant by the section of the IPA definition which reads 'the most persuasive selling message'? **(1)**

2. Why should advertisement copy never contain words which potential readers are unlikely to understand? **(3)**

3. Give an example of a 'buzz word'. **(5)**

4. Give five examples of action words. **(6)**

5. What is alliteration? Give an example of a slogan which uses alliteration. **(8)**

6. Name the seven copy elements. **(12)**

7. Invent examples of declarative, curiosity, topical and play on words headlines. **(13)**

8. What are the six purposes of subheadings? **(14)**

9. What is a reader advertisement? **(15)**

10. Why can price be an important part of the copy? **(16)**

11. Write the wording for a coupon so that readers may apply for a free holiday brochure. **(18)**

12. Give six examples of actual signature slogans or strap-lines used in current advertising campaigns. **(19)**

12

Layout and typography

PLANNING THE ADVERTISEMENT

1. Teamwork

Advertisements are often produced separately by the art director, who designs them, and the copywriter, who writes the text and creates the basic idea and theme known as the copy platform. As has already been emphasised in 11: 1 these two creative experts should work as a team. The copywriter should think visually, that is consider *how* the words should be seen as well as read. It is a bad system for the two to work in isolation, and for the visualiser merely to fit words to a design. If there is no teamwork, and no discussion between visualiser and copywriter, the result could be an advertisement crammed with too much copy printed too small to be legible. Similarly, the copywriter could suggest how the advertisements should be illustrated, while the visualiser could suggest how many words are required for the available space.

2. AIDCA (Attention, Interest, Desire, Conviction, Action) formula

This well-used formula helps in the overall planning of an advertisement, and it is particularly applicable to the hard-selling advertisement. It applies not only to the copy, layout and typography but also to the choice of medium, the space size and its position in the publication. An analysis of the five elements of the formula will explain this more precisely.

3. Attention

Unless an advertisement grabs *attention*, diverting the reader from either the editorial or other advertisement, it will not even be noticed. Attention may be achieved by position in the publication (either which page or on which part of a page), or by the size or shape of the advertisement. Even a tiny advertisement will attract attention if it is in the right position (e.g. a house for sale classified or a holiday resort ad in a section on holidays). Generally, a top right-hand position on a right-hand page gains the most attention when the advertisement does not fill the whole or half the page. Creative devices can be used to attract attention, e.g. colour, headline, illustration together with the general layout and choice of typeface. Thus, attention-getting may depend on a blend of factors, not forgetting the subject of the advertisement itself.

4. Interest

There is no point in using these devices to make people look at the advertisement unless it also gains their *interest*. It may do so selectively, and certain readers will be interested in advertisements for, say, cosmetics, foods, clothing, property, cars or computers. Interest may be achieved by the offer, the pictures, or the copy, and these will in turn be strengthened by the impact of the wording and presentation.

5. Desire

Readers must be more than attracted and interested, they must be encouraged to *desire* the product or service. How, creatively, can it be made desirable? What benefits are offered? There is an exchange situation: what will the reader gain by paying the price? Why should the reader sacrifice his or her money?

6. Conviction

It is all very well creating the wish to buy, own or enjoy the product or service, but it is also necessary to inspire *conviction* that it really is worth buying and that it will give satisfaction. This may require convincing facts, proof of added value, performance, testimonials and so on. Readers are likely to lose interest if essential information is missing from an advertisement.

Such information could include the *price*, which can be one way of judging a product or service. Is it good value for money? Some advertisers are very foolish about omitting prices, as if they are afraid this will put people off, or feel that, in the case of a luxury item, it does not matter. Price can be a very convincing factor, whether it be low or high. People do tend to believe that they get what they pay for. Consequently, price is often a major factor in the majority of advertisements, and may even be one of the methods of attracting attention in the first place.

7. Action

How can the advertisement induce response? A press advertisement is static, and it is not easy to provoke the reader into taking some desired action. Of course, there may be an immediate appeal to action in the headline, or it may be implicit in the entire advertisement. However, certain devices may be used, such as a coupon, invitation to sample or test, exhortation to visit a dealer or showroom, or a list of stockists which make it easy to find a supplier. Some advertisements merely remind, others build up interest and desire against some future time when a purchase may be made, but others seek immediate action. This is especially true of direct response advertising which seeks orders by post, email, fax or telephone, and one way of making this easy for the customers is to illustrate acceptable credit cards.

DESIGN AND LAYOUT

8. Stages in design

The design of a press advertisement goes through a number of stages. First, rough scribbles, scamps or *visuals* will be sketched in pencil or marker pen, and numerous experimental versions will be produced by the visualiser, until he or she arrives at either two or three alternatives or the final one. Final ideas will be worked up in a form which is sufficiently intelligible and can be shown to the client for approval. As a provisional layout, it will have no final artwork, photography, lettering, typesetting or type mark-up. Illustrations will be represented by sketches or maybe Polaroid photographs or stock pictures, and the wording will be shown in a 'Greek' jumble of characters. It is also universal nowadays to design with a DTP system.

When this layout is approved, artwork is commissioned, and the layout artist produces finished layouts with typographical mark-ups regarding typefaces and sizes. Studio drawing-board-based layouts, artwork and typesetting are rapidly giving way to the computer-based versions of those techniques. For litho-printed advertisements, camera-ready copy will be produced for photography and platemaking by the printer. This can be produced on an Apple Macintosh computer, although not all agencies are so equipped. However, computer-to-film and computer-to-plate systems are in widespread use, offering savings in time and money to advertisers and publishers. Printing processes are explained in Chapter 13.

9. Example

This is demonstrated in Figure 12.1, the visual for the eventual advertisement in Figure 12.2. This is the traditional way of designing an advertisement.

In the LCCI Advertising examination there is usually a compulsory first question requiring copy and layout which should be produced separately. The copy should be capable of being typed (although handwritten in the

Figure 12.1 Visual of press advertisement

examination). It should contain every word which is to appear in the advertisement – headline, subheadings, text, name and address and the wording of the coupon if one is to be included. The layout should be rather like Figure 12.1, the only wording being the display lines, with body copy 'greeked' in.

Figure 12.2 The finished advertisement as it appeared in the press

10. The eight laws of design

The basic principles of design, which can be applied to advertisements, are:

- law of unity;
- law of variety;

- law of balance;

- law of rhythm;

- law of harmony;

- law of proportion;

- law of scale;

- law of emphasis.

These will now be discussed in detail.

11. Law of unity

All parts of a layout should unite to make a whole. This unity can be disturbed by an irritating border, too many different and conflicting typefaces, badly distributed colour, disproportionate elements, or 'busy' layouts containing a confusion of parts.

12. Law of variety

Nevertheless, there should be change and contrast as with bold and medium weight of type, or good use of white space. The advertisement should not be monotonous, and grey masses of small print need to be enlivened by subheadings. Variety can also be introduced by the use of pictures.

13. Law of balance

It is essential that an advertisement should be well balanced. The *optical* balance is one-third down a space, not half-way. A picture or headline may occupy one-third, and the text copy two-thirds, so achieving an optical balance. The *symmetrical* balance falls mid-way so that a design can be divided into equal halves, quarters and so on, but care should be taken not to divide an advertisement into halves which look like separate advertisements.

14. Law of rhythm

Even though a printed advertisement is static it is still possible to obtain a sense of movement so that the eye is carried down and through the advertisement. A simple device is to indent paragraphs of text (as in a book or newspaper report) so that the eye is led from paragraph to paragraph. But the general flow of the overall design should be pleasantly rhythmic.

15. Law of harmony

There should be no sharp, annoying and jerky contrasts – unless perhaps that is the deliberate intention as in some kinds of store or direct response ads which use bombastic shock tactics. Normally, all the elements should harmonise, helping to create unity.

16. Law of proportion

This applies particularly to the type sizes used for different widths of copy: the wider the column (or *measure*) the larger the type size, and vice versa. A narrow advertisement needs small text type, but a wide advertisement needs larger text type, unless the type is set in columns. Wider columns and larger type also need greater leading (interline spacing).

17. Law of scale

Visibility depends on the scale of tones and colours, some appearing to recede, others appearing to advance. Pale, pastel colours recede while bold, primary colours advance. Black looks closer to the eye than grey, and red is the most dominant colour. Black on either yellow or orange is very bold whereas white on yellow is weak. The law of scale can be used with typographical design when headlines and subheadings are made to contrast with grey areas of text type. Where colours are concerned, this principle can be applied whenever full colour is used in press advertisements, TV commercials, posters and packaging.

18. Law of emphasis

The rule here is that *all emphasis is no emphasis*, which occurs if too much bold type is used, or there are too many capital letters. A sentence in upper and lower case lettering reads more easily than one wholly in capital letters. Yet emphasis is essential, and this links up with the other laws of variety and scale. An advertisement can be made to *look* interesting if there is emphasis such as bold type or if certain words are emphasised in a second colour.

White space – daylight! – can also be an effective way of creating emphasis. Every inch of space does not have to be filled with words just because it has been paid for! One wonders how many people bother to read the pages of small print in the prospectuses for new share issues which appear in the *Financial Times*, or the tedious whole page advertisements crammed with small print which are sometimes placed by foreign governments.

Another form of contrast is to reverse white on black, a method often used with logotypes and name-plates. Reverse colour should not be overdone for it tends to reduce legibility. A bad mistake is to print a lot of text in white on a black or coloured background.

223

19. Other forms of white space

Apart from providing emphasis, white space can also give clarity and legibility to the message. This can be done in two ways: by indenting paragraphs (i.e. book style, unlike the block paragraph of business letters), and by spacing between lines of type. The latter is known as leading (pronounced 'ledding' because with hot metal setting it consists of strips of lead which are not type-high). It can be set by using a type size such as '10 on 11' meaning that a 10 point type has 1 point leading, this separating the lines of type with one point (1/72 in.) of white space.

20. Arrangement of headlines

The headline can be made more legible, meaningful and attention-getting or impactive if care is taken in its layout. To achieve this it may be necessary to select words of suitable length, or the best number of words for effect. A long headline may be broken up or stepped so that it achieves these design effects. This also depends on the shape of the space – is it a wide half page or a narrow column?

Below is an example of a headline set as one line to suit a wide space, and then stepped to suit a narrower or a narrow one.

You may not like hot dogs

You may not
like hot dogs

You may
not like
hot dogs

Sometimes the designer has to make *adaptations* to suit different space sizes and shapes.

21. Illustrations

Pictures used to illustrate advertisements may be tonal photographs and wash drawings, or line drawings. Before deciding on the art medium it is wise to know the printing process and the kind of paper used by the newspapers and magazines in which the advertisement is to appear. A picture may reproduce well on the supercalendered or similar paper used for magazines, but be disappointing on the poor quality newsprint used for newspapers. Now that offset-litho printing has largely replaced photogravure printing, most magazines use special litho papers which have a shiny finish superior to that formerly used for magazine printing.

However, excellent pictures can be printed in newspapers, especially now that so many newspapers are printed by offset-litho or even flexography. Much finer dot screens are used for reproducing photographs.

GOUDY EXTRA BOLD
abcdefghijklmnopqrstuvwxyz
ABCDEFGHIJKLMNOPQRSTUVWXYZ
1234567890 ß &?!£$[.,;:)

HORATIO MEDIUM
abcdefghijklmnopqrstuvwxyz
ABCDEFGHIJKLMNOPQRSTUVWXYZ
1234567890 ß &?!£$(.,;:)

FUTURA DEMI BOLD
abcdefghijklmnopqrstuvwxyz
ABCDEFGHIJKLMNOPQRSTUVWXYZ
1234567890 ß &?!£$(.,;:)

ROCKWELL BOLD
abcdefghijklmnopqrstuvwxyz
ABCDEFGHIJKLMNOPQRSTUVWXYZ
1234567890 æøßÆØ &?!£$(.,;:)

PROTEUS BOLD
abcdefghijklmnopqrstuvwxyz
ABCDEFGHIJKLMNOPQRSTUVWXYZ
1234567890 æøßÆØ &?!£$%(.,;:)

MICROGRAMMA MEDIUM EXTENDED
abcdefghijklmnopqrstuvwxyz
ABCDEFGHIJKLMNOPQRSTU
VWXYZ
1234567890 &?!£$(.,;:)

Figure 12.3 Examples of display faces

TYPOGRAPHY

22. Definitions

Typography is the art of selecting typefaces, of which there are thousands of designs; blending different typefaces; casting off the number of words to fit spaces; and marking up copy for typesetting, using different sizes and weights.

A *fount* of type is a whole alphabet complete with signs and punctuation marks, and a *family* is a set of different weights, widths, sizes and varieties of a particular typeface. There are two main groups of typefaces, *display* (*see* Figure 12.3) and *book* or *text*, although the larger sizes of text types can be

225

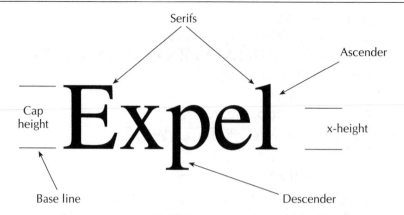

Figure 12.4 The anatomy of a typeface

used for display purposes. A typical mix of display and text faces might be a *sans serif* type for display and a *serif* type for the small print. The serif is the thin line drawn across the ends of stems and arms of letters. A serif face is easier to read in small size type, and especially on shiny paper, than a sans serif type. Books and newspapers are generally set in serif type (*see* Figure 12.4).

Good typography leads to legibility, and attractiveness, and certain designs of type can create style and character or be characteristic of the advertised subject.

Companies with corporate identity schemes often design their own typefaces, or specify a particular typeface for all print including advertisements, thus establishing a house style. However, it is important that the particular typeface is universally available from all printers and publishers, unless this problem can be overcome by providing camera-ready copy. One national estate agent adopted a type-face which was not available from all local newspapers in which the agent's property ads appeared. This problem can exist with modern computerised photo-typesetting when printers may have a limited range of typefaces, compared with the days when printers accumulated magazines holding numerous type faces for hot-metal setting.

23. Typesetting

Originally, type was set by hand. The expressions 'upper case' and 'lower case' for capital letters and small letters respectively were derived from the cases or drawers in the type cabinet in which individual characters were located. Hot metal mechanical setting is still used in some print shops and may consist of Linotype typesetting machines which set slugs of type the width of the column, or Monotype typesetting machines which set individual characters.

24. Photo-typesetting

Today, however, most copy is produced on photo-typesetting machines, and no metal is used. The alphabet is on a disc and the characters are photographed to the required size, the setting being produced on film or paper. Nowadays, such machines are also computerised with visual display unit screens so that corrections can be made by running the original and correcting it. A writer can produce copy on a word-processor and upload it by telephone direct to the computerised typesetting machine at the printers.

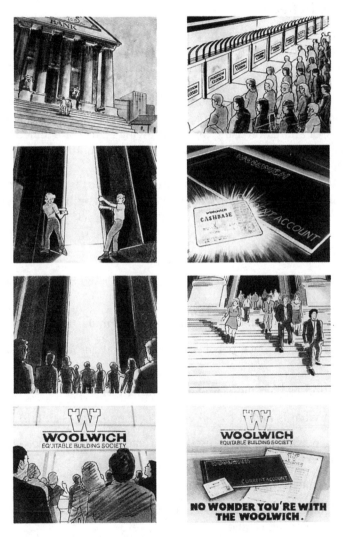

Figure 12.5 Part of the storyboard for a TV commercial produced by Alliance International for Woolwich Equitable Building Society. The theme music was *We've Got To Get Out of This Place* (The Animals)

TELEVISION COMMERCIALS

25. Storyboard

The 'visual' for a TV commercial is a set of drawings set in TV-screen shapes or rectangles which tell the story of the proposed commercial. This is known as the *storyboard* as shown in Figure 12.5. The client approves this, together with the copy, before any shooting is done.

26. Special effects

The agency's TV producer is responsible for the conception of the TV commercial. The actual commercial is then made by an outside director and production unit (*see* 4: **46**). Most commercials are first made on film, but can be transferred to video for post-production treatments such as special effects and computer graphics. Others are videotaped in the first instance. Other special effects can be used such as stop-motion as when packages unwrap themselves, or animation using cartoon drawings which are filmed as movies. Morphing is the name for making things or people on screen distort, bend or stretch.

The married print, combining picture and sound, is usually made after the commercial has been approved by the television authorities. This enables corrections to be made if necessary to the sound track.

Progress test 12

1. Why should the visualiser and the copywriter work together as a team? **(1)**

2. What are the five elements of the AIDCA formula? **(2–7)**

3. Explain the difference between a rough visual and a finished layout. **(8, 9)**

4. Name and explain the eight laws of design. **(10–18)**

5. Explain what is meant by 'all emphasis is no emphasis'. **(18)**

6. How can white space be used as an effective part of the design of an advertisement? **(18, 19)**

7. What is meant by indenting paragraphs and leading? **(19)**

8. Which of these elements need to be taken into account when considering the printing of illustrations:
   (a) Type of illustration to be reproduced, for example:
   – Photographs
   – Line drawings

– Line and wash drawings
– Computer-generated images
(b) The printing process
(c) The paper to be used
(d) The halftone screen
(e) The printing ink
(f) Number of colours to be used? **(21)**

9. Explain the terms 'fount', 'family', 'display typeface' and 'text typeface', 'sans serif' and 'serif'. **(22)**

10. What effects can be achieved by good typography? **(22)**

11. What is a storyboard? **(25)**

12. Explain the terms 'stop-motion' and 'animation'. **(26)**

13. What is the difference between a TV producer and a TV director? **(26)**

13

Printing processes

THE SIX MAIN PROCESSES

1. Introduction

While it is not necessary for the advertising student to understand the technical intricacies of printing processes and machines, it is important to have a general knowledge of printing processes, and especially the particular classes of work which can be produced by them. This chapter discusses the six main processes: letterpress, lithography, photogravure, flexography, silk screen and digital. Of these, letterpress is little used today, and lithography has tended to replace photogravure.

2. Letterpress

This is a relief printing system, which may be likened to a date stamp or a typewriter character in that printing is achieved by pressing an inked raised surface to the paper. The machine may be flat-bed or rotary, and it may use single sheets of paper or, in the case of rotary machines, a continuous reel or web of paper.

For letterpress printing all printing areas must be raised above the surface as dots (halftone), lines or type. The non-raised or non-type high areas will leave white or un-inked space.

This is a very versatile process and one of its advantages is that every kind of paper can be used. Where tonal pictures are required halftone screens from very coarse to very fine can be used to suit the paper. Literally anything from a business card to high quality full-colour catalogues or books can be produced by letterpress, and there are special machines which can print on delicate materials such as foil.

The disadvantages of the letterpress process are usually that rotary machines are big, and they require a large number of operatives, while it is not very economical for very large runs unless plates are stereotyped and perhaps replaced, or several machines are used.

Moreover, the production of metal type and printing plates requires a whole department – literally a foundry floor in the old Fleet Street newspaper plants. This required a large and costly work-force. This whole department has disappeared in the change-over to offset-litho which is not only less labour intensive and cheaper to operate but produces better quality print. Nevertheless, a number of small jobbing printers still use letterpress.

Since the type is cast from hot metal, the process is often referred to as a hot metal system compared with other processes which have cold composition on film or tape. Pictures can be reproduced by means of halftone screens with all processes except photogravure.

3. Lithography

This is a very old process, and very popular with printers worldwide. Originally, lithographic printing required a large slab of porous stone, and litho stone came from the Jura mountains in Germany. The process is a 'planographic' one, in that the printing image is laid flat on the 'stone' or plate. Printing from it works on the principle that grease and water will not mix. Thus, if the image (the printing area) is greasy or greased, and it is inked, the application of water will remove the excess ink and leave ink only on the greasy area. Hence the original porous stone. Today, lithography uses metal plates, and there are rotary as well as flat-bed machines, printing from webs of paper as well as from flat sheets.

Desk top publishing is by no means limited to in-house print shops or for the production of house journals, when the complete made-up pages are transferred to disk and either sent or telephoned on-line to the printer. DTP will be found in book printers and newspapers. Using PageMaker or Quark Express, copy can be written, set and pages laid out. Typography is flexible with scalable or decimal point type sizes while it is possible to position, expand or condense display lines on screen.

4. Offset-lithography

The expression *offset* is commonly used for lithography. It means that there are in effect three cylinders in the offset-litho machine. The image-carrying plate, curved round the *plate cylinder* with the image in positive form, first prints on to a second *blanket cylinder* so that the image becomes negative or reversed. The blanket cylinder then offsets the image on to the paper which is conveyed through the machine by a third *impression* cylinder. Figure 13.1 shows the process.

5. Advantages of lithography

The process has become universally adopted in many forms including small office machines. It has the following advantages.

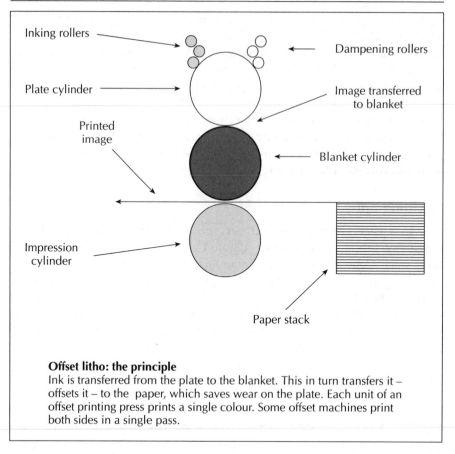

Offset litho: the principle
Ink is transferred from the plate to the blanket. This in turn transfers it – offsets it – to the paper, which saves wear on the plate. Each unit of an offset printing press prints a single colour. Some offset machines print both sides in a single pass.

Figure 13.1 Offset-lithography

(a) Machines are compact.

(b) Special papers have been produced for the process, both in sheet and web form.

(c) A fine screen can be used for halftones (even for newspaper printing).

(d) Illustrations are less expensive to reproduce because separate halftone plates are unnecessary.

(e) Photo-typesetting can be used, or desk top publishing systems such as Apple-Macintosh.

(f) High quality inks with extra pigment and glossy effects can be used. The combination of finished papers and glossy inks mean a greatly improved appearance for popular magazines.

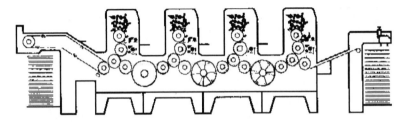

Figure 13.2 Four-colour litho machine. Courtesy, Heidelberg

(g) The preparation of the printing plate is cleaner and simpler since there is no hot metal. The print shop resembles a hospital rather than the hot, noisy and dirty letterpress print-shop.

(h) Copy is pasted down and photographed for plate-making. Customers can supply computer disks or camera-ready artwork instead of the metal blocks, typesettings or stereos used for letterpress printing.

(i) Litho machines are very suitable for multi-colour work. Figure 13.2 is an outline drawing of a typical four-colour litho machine.

(j) The process is so quick that in a computerised newsroom and offset litho presses it can take only minutes from writing the copy to printing the paper.

6. Photogravure

The chief merit of photogravure is the long life of the printing cylinder or *sleeve*, and its ability to print on comparatively cheap and apparently good quality shiny supercalendered paper as once used by women's magazines. In a better quality version, photogravure is used for printing postage stamps and reproductions of works of art. The system was introduced into the UK to print long runs of popular magazines, and was subsequently used to print weekend colour magazines. However, the newer women's magazines and the listings magazines have turned to web-offset litho as this process has been able to use webs of superior paper.

Originally, photogravure was the opposite to letterpress and lithography in being an 'intaglio' process with the printing surface recessed in tiny square cells of different depths to accept quantities of ink to produce depths of colour. The ink is literally sucked out of the cells on to the paper. This resembles the copper etching in which the design is etched or cut into the surface. Today, photogravure is also used for printing labels and packaging materials. (*See also* Figure 13.3.)

7. Hard-dot system

A newer version of photogravure, which produces print comparable in quality to offset-litho, is the German electronic Klischograph hard-dot cylinder

233

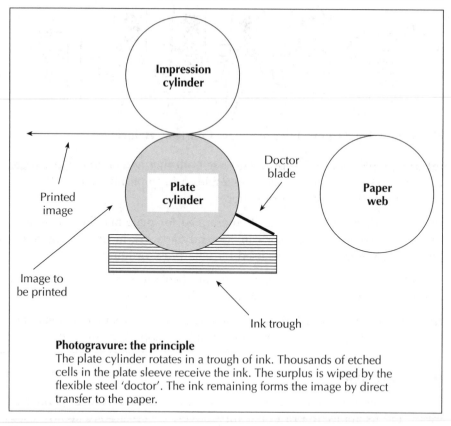

Photogravure: the principle
The plate cylinder rotates in a trough of ink. Thousands of etched cells in the plate sleeve receive the ink. The surplus is wiped by the flexible steel 'doctor'. The ink remaining forms the image by direct transfer to the paper.

Figure 13.3 Photogravure

gravure system which is a surface instead of a recessed process. It has surface areas of various sizes according to the lightness or darkness of tone, instead of having recessed cells of different depths according to the depth of tone.

8. Flexography

Originally used in Britain for printing on delicate materials, such as foil for confectionery wrappings, flexography was developed in the USA for newspaper production. The process is now used by the *Daily Mail* and its sister publications at its new plant in SE London.

It is a rotary web letterpress process but one which uses flexible rubber plates, and rapid drying solvent or water-based inks. By applying improved photopolymer plates and special inks flexography has been adapted for newspaper production, rivalling offset-litho. Flexo inks are brighter than offset inks and, as the *Daily Mail* has advertised, they do not rub off on the reader's fingers. There is also very good picture and colour reproduction.

9. Screen printing

This was originally an ancient Chinese printing process using a screen or mesh made of human hair. The basic principle is the stencil, ink being pushed or rolled through a cut-out design placed over a screen of silk, nylon, organdie or metal mesh. From very simple cut-out designs to photographic ones, screen presses are capable of printing on both a variety of materials and on non-flat surfaces such as bottles. It is therefore a very versatile process which can print on paper, board, plastic, glass, wood, textiles, rubber and so on. Typical examples are posters (e.g. those seen on shop windows) but also large ones such as bus sides; book jackets; clock faces and instrument panels; ashtrays; advertising pens; milk, soft drink and beer bottles; T-shirts; balloons; and ties. (*See also* Figure 13.4.)

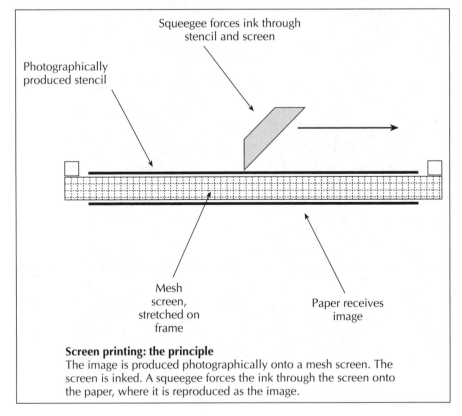

Screen printing: the principle
The image is produced photographically onto a mesh screen. The screen is inked. A squeegee forces the ink through the screen onto the paper, where it is reproduced as the image.

Figure 13.4 Screen printing

Figure 13.5 Webs of newsprint being loaded on to a Metroliner offset-litho press at the News Centre, Portsmouth

10. Digital printing

Digital printing is becoming the main contender for short-run and on-demand printing of high quality. It is a technology which allows printed material to be produced without printing plates, imagesetting, film, stripping, halftone screening or scanning. The colour quality is as good as, and often better than, high-quality conventional litho printing.

Unusually among printing technologies, it allows marketers and advertisers to create promotional material targeted to small groups of recipients, or even specified individuals. It can be used cost-effectively for quantities as low as ten copies. This unique feature differentiates digital printing from conventional methods: every single page can be different. Even parts of a page can be personalised, so that no two news releases, sales letters, house journals, leaflets, booklets and posters, for example, need be the same. The variable data are imported from a database, and merged with the elements of the page which do not need changing.

There are no limitations on the type of data to be merged, so that text, line illustrations and halftone images can be varied on each copy printed. This, of course, is ideal for personalised advertising communications. It opens up a vast range of new opportunities for marketers, advertising departments and agencies.

One international organisation specialising in office supplies produces both a main, full-length catalogue and seven mini-catalogues aimed at sub-groups of its target audience. The sub-targets are classified by their loyalty to the supplier, their level of spending and volume of purchases, and the type of product they order. The products featured in each of the mini-catalogues vary accordingly; the more the customer has purchased in the past, the bigger the discount they are offered.

In theory, using digital print, each individual customer could be offered an individual catalogue. Obviously this would not be cost-effective, but the company gets as close as it can to this ideal. At the time of writing, the company is considering individual front covers to their mini-catalogues, each carrying discount offers matched to the recipient's previous purchases.

Typically, a digital colour press can produce over 2,000 double-sided colour pages an hour. Make-ready is limited to loading the press with the paper or other material to be printed. This gives the printer or in-house print manager the opportunity to complete a job 60 per cent faster than conventional offset litho. One printer using this technology reports that on 4-colour runs, it can also be more economical.

One of the most important features of digital printing is its ability to accept computer-generated data. It converts computer-generated data into printed images. The origination is produced on a PC or Mac in any PostScript application. After everything has been finalised, the job is saved and sent for printing, on disk, by modem or ISDN line (Integrated Systems Digital

237

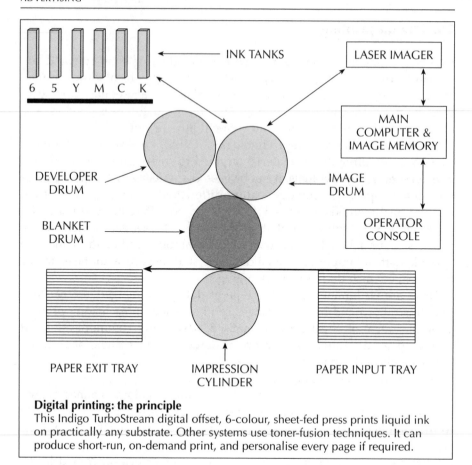

INK TANKS

LASER IMAGER

6   5   Y   M   C   K

MAIN
COMPUTER &
IMAGE MEMORY

DEVELOPER
DRUM

IMAGE
DRUM

BLANKET
DRUM

OPERATOR
CONSOLE

PAPER EXIT TRAY

IMPRESSION
CYLINDER

PAPER INPUT TRAY

Digital printing: the principle
This Indigo TurboStream digital offset, 6-colour, sheet-fed press prints liquid ink on practically any substrate. Other systems use toner-fusion techniques. It can produce short-run, on-demand print, and personalise every page if required.

Figure 13.6 Digital printing

Network, a high-quality data transmission system). After being set up for the job, the files go from the printer's computer direct to the press.

Instant reprinting is a further major option of digital printing. It enables past print jobs to be retrieved from the computerised archive and reprinted on demand. This completely eliminates the printing and storage of quantities of print for future distribution.

Technically, the system accepts data in PostScript form, either direct from a disk or via ISDN. It converts the data into a bitmap image via a Raster Image Processor (RIP), then reproduces the image direct onto the material to be printed.

Note: the term *substrate* is used to describe materials subjected to printing processes. In former times, paper, board and fabrics were the only material used. Today, virtually any material can be printed with an image; with screen printing, you can even 'print' on water.

There are several technologies now available marketed as digital print. These range from colour photocopiers from Canon, Océ and others to the Heidelberg DI press using Computer to Plate (CTP) technology. However, it is generally recognised that digital printing allows for every page printed to be different. There are two systems offering this, manufactured by Indigo and Xeikon.

Xeikon-based systems are reel-fed and use the xerographic (toner) process. The system is also sold by Xerox, Agfa and IBM. Research programmes by Mitsubishi, Man Roland and Océ, using their own technologies, could be under way during the life of this edition.

Indigo presses use proprietary liquid ink (ElectroInk) to produce 'digital offset colour' printing. These presses can either be sheet-fed or reel-fed, and are self-contained units capable of 6-colour, high-quality print output.

Xeikon and Indigo systems are capable of short run, on-demand printing as well as personalisation and Variable Information Printing (VIP). Both can print duplex (both sides) while the Indigo sheet-fed presses also feature electronic collation.

The main differences between Xeikon and Indigo lie in:

- the greater substrate range that can be printed on the Indigo presses;

- the method of delivering the image to the substrate;

- the greater ability to match colours by the Indigo presses;

- the wider format available with the Xeikon press.

With Indigo's TurboStream press, short runs are viable and jobs can be grouped together. This means that the press runs continuously on successive jobs without the need to stop and restart the press each time a new job is introduced. A printer using TurboStream can therefore save time and money producing a print job, and presumably can pass on the benefits to customers in the form of lower prices.

The Indigo Omnius, another press in the range, was designed for printing labels and packaging materials. It is web-fed and can handle a variety of materials (substrates), from paper and plastic film to metal foil.

CHOICE OF PROCESS

11. Availability of processes

The print-buyer should be aware of both the processes available, and the process which is most suitable for the job. All six main processes are used in Britain and western Europe, but this is not true of every country in the world. In fact, in many developing countries where new newspapers were launched, offset-litho machines were installed many years before Britain's national newspapers adopted the process. The various kinds of lithography are most universally available.

12. Print spec checklist

It makes sense to take into account all stages of a print job before asking printers to quote. You need to give a printer all the information needed for this purpose. The main elements of a print specification are shown in Figure 13.7.

- Job no.:
- Client or department:
- Project title:
- Date of this spec:
1. Critical dates:
2. Delivery date:
3. Delivery details:
4. No. of pages:
5. Process:
6. Size & format:
7. Print run:
8. Stock: Cover

         Inside pages
         Other

9. Colours: Cover

         Inside pages
         Other

10. Pre-press: Cover

         Inside pages
         Other
         Layout
         Illustrations
         Diagrams/charts
         Bleeds
         Paste-ups
         Separations

11. Proofs: Deliver . . . copies to:
12. Finishing: Binding

         Lamination
         Inserts
         Other

Printers' quotes:

1	Name	Quote, £	Per 1,000 run on, £
2	Name	Quote, £	Per 1,000 run on, £
3	Name	Quote, £	Per 1,000 run on, £

Figure 13.7 Main elements of a print specification

13. Consulting the printer

It is wise to discuss print jobs with different printers, in order to understand the process being used and the quality of work that can be undertaken. Quotations should be requested, and if the reasons for different prices are not readily understood printers should be asked why the quotation is either so high or so low. One simple explanation may be the speed of the printer's machine. Price may depend on the paper sheet size which a machine can accept. This can affect either the number of copies which can be cut from a sheet, or the extent of waste if trimming is necessary. It is always best to discuss print work with printers rather than simply present them with a design and copy. A print job involves technicalities such as typefaces, paper, use of colours, size of the finished job, binding and especially folding. Given the opportunity, the printer can give advice which can result in a better-looking, more practical and perhaps more economical job.

Progress test 13

1. What is the principle of the letterpress printing process? **(2)**

2. What is the principle of the lithographic printing process? **(3)**

3. Explain the term 'offset'. **(4)**

4. What is the principle of the photogravure printing process? **(6)**

5. How does the Klischograph system differ from traditional photogravure? **(7)**

6. What is flexography? **(8)**

7. What is the principle of the silk screen process? **(9)**

8. What is digital printing? What are its main characteristics and advantages? **(10)**

9. In what ways does silk screen differ regarding items which can be printed by this process? **(9)**

10. What are the main elements needed when preparing a print specification? **(12)**

11. Why is it important to obtain quotations from different printers, and to question why prices for the same job may differ considerably? **(13)**

14

Public relations

DIFFERENCES BETWEEN PUBLIC RELATIONS AND ADVERTISING

1. Introduction

Public relations is often confused with advertising, and sometimes wrongly termed 'publicity' and placed in the promotional mix as in the fourth P of the Four Ps concept of the marketing mix. Worse still, public relations is wrongly regarded as a form of advertising, even as 'free advertising'. Public relations is even confused with sales promotion. It is therefore essential, especially in books on advertising, to understand the nature of public relations and how it differs from advertising. The two are very different forms of communication, but advertising is likely to be more effective if public relations is well carried out.

Briefly, public relations aims to create understanding through knowledge (see 13) and, if it is to be successful in educating the market, it must be factual, credible and impartial. Advertising, as already demonstrated in previous chapters, has to be *persuasive* in order to sell and it may be emotional, dramatic and certainly partial. Thus, a basic difference is that in order to succeed public relations must be unbiased while advertising has to be biased.

However, it is a lot easier to advertise something people know and understand, so advertising can be made more effective and economic if there is a public relations back up. For instance, potential holidaymakers will feel more confident about booking a holiday in Barbados or Mauritius if they know where these islands are, what sort of climate they have and other special characteristics. This may be learned from travel articles or TV programmes like *Wish You Were Here*.

Public relations may be thought to consist only of press relations, or rather media relations since radio and television are also involved. Modern public relations extends into all the functions of commercial and non-commercial, public and private organisations. It deals with matters far removed from marketing and advertising, to mention only community, employee, shareholder and political relations. This is demonstrated by the

British Gas study at the end of this chapter. A major area of public relations in recent years has been the handling of crisis situations such as strikes, disasters and take-over bids. Another has been political public relations and the lobbying of politicians, not forgetting EC politicians in Strasbourg, Luxembourg and Brussels. Some of this has to do with legislation and directives on advertising. For a fuller account of public relations the reader is advised to read the author's companion handbook *Public Relations*.

2. Definitions of public relations

Here are two well-known definitions, the first being that of the (British) Institute of Public Relations, and the second resulting from an international conference of public relations institutions held in Mexico City.

(a) IPR definition. 'Public relations practice is the planned and sustained effort to establish and maintain goodwill and mutual understanding between an organisation and its publics.'

The importance of this definition lies in its emphasis on *planning* public relations – just like an advertising campaign – and on *mutual* (or two-way) communication. Inflow of information and feedback is just as valuable in public relations as outflow of information. Public relations can be likened to the eyes and ears as well as the voice of an organisation. It is a kind of intelligence system. But unlike advertising, the communication process is two-way.

(b) The Mexican statement. 'Public relations practice is the art and social science of analysing trends, predicting their consequences, counselling organisation leaders, and implementing planned programmes of action which will serve both the organisation and the public interest.'

This very interesting definition emphasises three aspects of public relations: the need to carry out research in order to appreciate the situation before planning a public relations programme; the giving of advice to management; and the need for public relations to be in the public interest. The latter also implies the need for public relations messages to be authentic, truthful and credible.

3. Differences

The principal differences between public relations and advertising are outlined below.

(a) Public relations writing (and other creative communications such as house journals and video) must be factual and informative, and free of 'puffery' (*see* **20**). To achieve credibility it needs to be educational rather than persuasive, giving factual information rather than making emotional or dramatic claims (unlike copywriting) and should avoid self-praise. Totally different writing skills are required.

(b) Public relations applies to many organisations which may not engage in advertising. A fire brigade does not advertise for fires.

(c) Public relations deals with the editors and producers of the media, but advertising with the sellers of advertisement space or airtime.

(d) Whereas advertising is usually addressed to particular market segments and certain social grades, public relations may be addressed to the numerous publics or groups of people with whom an organisation has to communicate. They may not be buyers of the company's goods or services, e.g. investors or employees. (*See* also **4**.)

(e) The costs of public relations are different. In advertising, major costs are creative, space, airtime and production. In public relations they are time, since public relations is labour-intensive; plus production costs such as printing house journals or making videos.

(f) In each case the media are different. Advertising will mostly use existing commercial media such as press, radio and TV, plus direct mail and exhibitions. Public relations will use a much bigger variety of commercial media, plus the created media of house journals, slides, video, audio tapes, private exhibitions, educational print, seminars and sponsorship. The latter has become an increasingly important public relations tool. (*See* also **16**.)

(g) Advertising agencies and public relations consultancies may be remunerated differently, the former receiving commissions from the media and discounts on supplies (or charging percentages), although some charge fees. The latter depend mainly on fees based on time, and do not usually receive commission or discounts.

(h) While the majority of advertising personnel work in agencies, the majority of public relations personnel do not work in consultancies but in companies and other organisations. A survey conducted by Cranfield School of Management on behalf of the Institute of Public Relations showed that 60 per cent of public relations staff worked in-house. It is therefore a fallacy that the public relations world is dominated by consultancies, however glamorous they may seem to the outsider.

(i) Advertising aims to persuade people to take some desired action such as visit a shop, respond by post or telephone, or simply remember, in order to buy. Public relations aims to create mutual understanding, which may be of the organisation itself (the corporate image), or of products or services. However, it may extend to other things as will be seen when *publics* are discussed in **4**.

From the above comparisons it will be seen that public relations and advertising are entirely different worlds, and that even in a business organisation public relations may enter into many more facets than advertising. Many in-house public relations managers have nothing to do with advertising, report direct to top management, and service the total organisation and not merely marketing. Advertising should not be regarded as the more important simply because it costs more. Forms of communication which result from training, such as behaviour towards customers, are expressions of public relations, since they may affect goodwill, confidence and reputation.

Some dictionaries have misleading definitions of public relations of which one of the silliest is the following from *The New Collins Concise Dictionary of the English Language*: 'The practice of creating, promoting, or maintaining goodwill and a favourable image among the public towards an institution, public body, etc.'

First, public relations is not concerned with 'the public' (or the 'general public') but with numerous groups or publics. *See* **4** below.

Second, public relations does not seek to create a favourable image. An image cannot be created: it can be only what it is. It may be necessary to establish a *correct image* but it may not be a favourable one. How does one create a *favourable* image for the prison service, HM Customs and Excise, the Inland Revenue or even, sometimes, the police, the Post Office or Railtrack? But unpleasant or bad things can be explained so that they are understood. The word 'favourable' is best forgotten in public relations for the world is a mixture of good and bad.

4. Who are the publics?

The plural word 'publics' is generally used in public relations. The basic publics are as follows.

(a) The community. In the vicinity of the company premises or location there are usually people who are its neighbours. Good relations with the community can be very important to the success of an organisation. This is well explained in the British Gas case study at the end of the chapter.

(b) Potential employees. They may exist in the community, schools, colleges, universities, other companies or even overseas.

(c) Employees. Every category of employee is included here, from gate-keeper to CEO.

(d) Suppliers. They will range from public services to suppliers of business services, components and raw materials.

(e) The money market. The local bank manager, shareholders, investment analysts, the financial institutions and the Stock Exchange make up the money market. Public relations can be involved in avoiding a take-over bid by keeping the City well informed, and the share price maintained.

(f) Distributors. Everyone concerned with transferring the product or service to the customers or users are distributors. They may be wholesalers, brokers, retailers, importers or exporters.

(g) Customers and users. The current buyers, actual or potential, form this important public which may embrace many groups (e.g. children) who are not necessarily addressed by advertising.

(h) Opinion formers or leaders. These are people who express opinions which may help or harm an organisation according to the extent or correctness of their knowledge. They could be parents, teachers, politicians, newspaper columnists or TV personalities. They can have a good or bad effect on advertised products and the reputations of companies.

PUBLIC RELATIONS CONSULTANCY SERVICES

5. Consultancies in the UK

There are some 1,200 public relations consultancies in the UK, and about 100 of those handling the major volume of consultancy business are members of the Public Relations Consultants Association. After an upsurge in consultancy business in the mid to late 1980s, consultancies lost clients as the result of the recession, but the in-house public relations department retained its long-established importance.

6. Types of consultancy

Consultancies range from very big ones of which Two-Ten Communications, Shandwick, Hill & Knowlton, Burson-Marsteller, and Daniel J. Edelman are among the biggest, often with international networks, down to one-person businesses. In addition, there are those which specialise in certain areas of public relations such as corporate and financial (mostly located in the City), sponsorship, parliamentary liaison (giving advice on parliamentary matters and procedures affecting clients) and house journal production. Others offer special knowledge of certain industries like food, fashion, cars or travel.

The financial consultancies grew with the need to service privatisation share offers although most of the 'crown jewels' have now been sold off, and to deal with take-over bids and rights issues. There has also been demand to train clients in crisis situations, it being recognised nowadays that any organisation can suffer any kind of crisis.

A form of crisis which has become prevalent in recent years has been the contamination of food products in supermarkets, although fortunately most of them have proved to be hoaxes. Nevertheless, firms like Heinz and Mars have suffered the double handicap of loss of public faith in their products, and removal of their products from supermarket shelves to protect the good name of retailers. Such events, perpetrated by activist groups, gain maximum media cover which has to be counteracted. A scare may last only three days but it may take three months to regain lost sales.

7. Use of consultancies

There are at least five special uses of consultancies.

(a) When there is no in-house public relations department a public relations consultancy may be employed to conduct a public relations programme.

(b) When the public relations department is exceptionally busy, an outside unit can augment its activities.

(c) When an outside advisory service is required.

(d) When a special *ad hoc* service is required like those mentioned above in 6, a consultancy may be employed because, for instance, there is to be a new share issue, sponsorship is contemplated, or legislation is passing through the House of Commons which concerns a company and it is necessary to know what is going on.

(e) When a company is located at a distance from media centres like London, a consultancy may be employed because it is better located to deal with the media. However, this has become less vital and consultancies are located throughout the UK.

8. Cost

A consultancy is paid for the volume of work it performs, and it is essential that the fee is adequate to cover the amount of work involved. Consultancy services are carefully budgeted, but whereas many advertising agency services cost the client nothing if media purchases provide sufficient commission income, the consultancy client does have to pay for everything including the time of the account executive. This is perfectly fair and professional, and it is not necessarily true that consultancies are expensive and that it is cheaper to have one's own staff public relations officer. Sometimes consultancy fees and public relations officer salaries are falsely compared: the in-house public relations officer costs more than just his salary for he or she has operational and resource expenses beginning with an office and secretary. The in-house public relations job is usually a full-time one, thus costing more than part-time or *ad hoc* consultancy services. As with use of an advertising agency, a share of a consultancy's facilities may be bought.

9. Advantages of consultancies

The special merits of consultancies (which may be compared with those of the company public relations department, *see* **11** below) are as follows.

(a) Experience based on handling a variety of accounts.

(b) Knowledge of and contact with a great variety of media of all kinds.

(c) An independent outside point-of-view which is valuable when performing the important advisory role of public relations. This service is more common than in the case of an advertising agency.

(d) Buying ability and knowledge of sources of supply such as printers, photographers, video producers and so on.

(e) Well-trained professional staff, especially when holding CAM qualifications and IPR membership.

(f) Special skills which can be shared with other clients, and which would be uneconomic to employ full-time.

(g) International contacts such as overseas associates or offices in other countries, which can be useful if the company exports or operates internationally.

IN-HOUSE PUBLIC RELATIONS DEPARTMENTS

10. Position in company

Ideally, the public relations department should be independent, servicing production, finance and marketing, but directly answerable to the chief executive (*see* Figure 14.1). In many large companies the public relations officer (whatever his or her title and there are many variations) is a board director. This ideal situation does not always occur, and the public relations officer may be positioned in the marketing department which suggests limited public relations duties and status. In other companies the responsibility

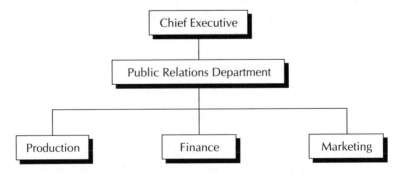

Figure 14.1 Structure of the public relations department in a small company

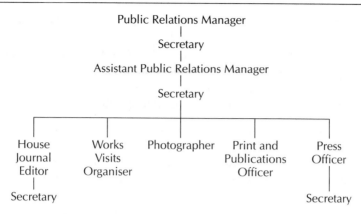

Figure 14.2 Possible staffing of a public relations department in a large manufacturing company

for public relations may fall on the shoulders of various executives such as marketing, advertising, product or sales promotion managers; again this suggests a very limited use of public relations.

In some developing countries where management has not yet accepted the importance to them of public relations, the in-house public relations officer may occupy a less senior or well-defined position, perhaps being concerned more with personnel and protocol matters.

Figure 14.2 illustrates how a public relations department might be staffed.

11. Advantages of in-house public relations officer

The advantages of an in-house public relations officer as compared with a public relations consultancy, are as follows.

(a) The staff public relations officer works full-time for the company, unlike the consultant whose time is controlled by the size of the fee. This is an important point to remember. Fees are based on time being charged on an hourly or daily rate. If the consultant gives the client more time than he or she is paid for, one of two things must occur. Either, the value of the fee is reduced or the time must be taken from another client. Either way, the consultant could go bankrupt which is why it is necessary to maintain strict time-sheet control of the work.

(b) Working inside the company, the staff public relations officer has the opportunity to be familiar with the whole business. Indeed, the public relations officer should know more about the company than anyone else in it if he or she is really to advise the chief executive. This demands good internal lines of communication, which is often helped if the public relations officer edits the staff newspaper and so has to meet and interview people throughout the organisation.

249

(c) The public relations officer may be a product of the company or industry and have technical knowledge, although this is not absolutely vital. A good public relations officer, if well trained, qualified and experienced, should be able to apply expertise to any communication problem. For instance, it used to be the case that banking public relations officers were bankers first, but many outsiders have now come into banking public relations.

(d) Because of the public relations officer's close links within the organisation, he or she could have ready access to information, and especially the ability to check the accuracy of information; the consultant may be more remote from such sources. The consultant is liable to deal with only one person representing the client.

PUBLIC RELATIONS AND ADVERTISING

12. Value of public relations to advertising

From what has been described so far it will be seen that public relations concerns the total communications of the total organisation. It is not confined to marketing, nor is it a form of advertising. Public relations is not a 'soft sell'. Nevertheless, advertising can benefit from public relations activity. In fact, advertising may well fail because of lack of public relations. This does not mean that public relations is superior to advertising, but that it is different and because of its own communication techniques it can contribute to the success of advertising just as it can contribute to good management–employee relations or good financial relations. The chief benefit lies in the creation of understanding.

13. Public relations transfer process

The creation of understanding is best explained by reference to the 'public relations transfer process', demonstrated by the model in Figure 14.3.

A company, product or service may be subject to one or more of the four negative states in the left-hand box of the public relations transfer process model. Here are some examples.

(a) **Hostility**. There may be hostility towards a company because company behaviour has been criticised, a product has performed badly, a company personality has received bad publicity, the company is of foreign origin, or simply because it is very big! There may also be hostility towards the industry because it is believed to be hazardous, or endangers the environment. Hostility may be undeserved or quite irrational. There are people who dislike nationalised industries, multinationals, chemical companies and those which create noise, smell or other inconveniences. Hostility can last a long time and be difficult to eradicate. It is many years since a fire in a Sandoz

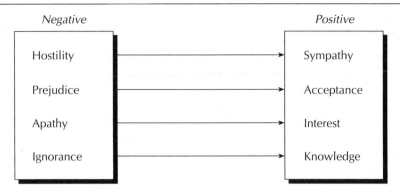

Figure 14.3 The public relations transfer process: knowledge leads to understanding

warehouse near Geneva polluted the Rhine with deadly chemicals, washed there by the water used to put out the fire. Although there are now fish swimming in the Rhine hostility towards Sandoz remains.

(b) Prejudice. This is a more difficult obstacle to overcome, and is usually long-standing and derived from family, educational, ethnic or even geographical influences. Many people are still prejudiced about flying, holidays abroad, foreign foods, computers or advertising and public relations. Travel firms had to fight prejudice about holidays in Russia, but this was broken down by taking travel writers to Russia, who afterwards wrote about unusual holidays there.

(c) Apathy. Disinterest is very hard to overcome. People tend to be conservative, set in their ways and unwilling to try new things. They may be so satisfied with their closest interests – family, home, job, hobbies – that they do not wish to extend their interests further. They may be apathetic about things that could benefit them such as banking, insurance, savings, diet, holidays or different kinds of clothes.

(d) Ignorance. In a complex world everyone is ignorant about many things. It is inevitable. There was a time when most people were ignorant about detergents, television, central heating or air conditioning, woodworm, convenience foods, videocassettes, show-jumping or hovercraft, all of which are taken for granted today. For example, when householders saw holes in wood in their homes they thought woodworm insects had bored their way in, whereas the insects had actually escaped.

These are all negative attitudes with which advertisers have to contend, and which public relations is concerned with changing into positive attitudes. Much of public relations is about effecting change. It is no use advertising a product if sales will be impossible because of sales resistance based on hostility, prejudice, apathy or ignorance. Vast expenditures on advertising will not demolish that sales resistance. At best, unnecessarily heavy expenditures on advertising may be necessary because public relations methods have not been used to create a receptive marketing situation in which advertising can work economically and effectively.

14. Pre-advertising public relations

In some cases, especially with new inventions and technical products, or new services, an advertising campaign is more likely to succeed if people understand what is being advertised. In other words, the market has to be educated or developed. Depending on the kind of product or service, this could take a few months or two to three years. The market has to be familiarised with the new idea.

A good example is Eurotunnel. The Eurotunnel project, one of the world's all-time technical marvels, is also a classic example of public relations having to battle with the four negative states of hostility, prejudice, apathy and ignorance. Instead of being regarded as a national triumph, it is a victim of unprecedented misunderstanding and abuse. This is not so in France where the French have eagerly bought up Eurotunnel shares. The scaremonger British media have exploited fears of rabies, water leakage, fire hazard and terrorist attack on the basis that bad news is good news and that is what sells newspapers. You do not sell newspapers by lauding the feats of tunnel engineers. Only the death of one makes news.

All this was helped by the indifference of a private enterprise oriented government, the indecisiveness of British Rail, the unpredictable fate of Kent property owners, and the introduction of a giant catamaran Channel ferry. There were squabbles between the tunnel owners and the contractors over escalating costs, the need for new bank loans and a further public share issue, with the likely date of profits receding further into the future.

It was a public relations nightmare. The one objective media treatment was the excellent TV programme, *Tomorrow's World*, which did portray the tunnel as an admirable technical achievement. At Folkestone there is the splendid purpose-built Eurotunnel exhibition, packed with visitors, which is a practical proactive effort to present the facts and enlighten the public.

Sixty years ago people scoffed at the idea of flying passengers across the Atlantic, although the German airship *Graf Zeppelin* was doing so weekly, until the Americans flew their bombers to Britain during the Second World War. They thought Thomas Cook was mad when he launched holidays in Switzerland, but now you can have a package tour to Beijing. In the 1930s they laughed at Baird's television, and now we have instant world television news by satellite. London was always depicted as 'foggy London town', until coal fires were banned. Video cameras were clumsy pieces of twin equipment, but Sony has produced one you can palm in the hand. Nine million people now own shares, but it took privatisations to educate the

British people about the merits of owning shares. Things change, and public relations is very much to do with helping to effect change by spreading knowledge and creating understanding.

Over the years, non-drip paint, central heating, double-glazing, woodworm treatment, holidays in Russia, colour television, videocassette recorders, home computers, and various investment and savings schemes have benefited from public relations to prepare the market. A product which failed and cost the advertisers a fortune because of the lack of public relations build-up was New Smoking Mixture cigarettes made of a substitute for tobacco.

15. Coincidental public relations

For security reasons, it may not be possible or sensible to give prior an-nouncement of a new product or service because of the intensity of com-petition. This applies to many FMCGs such as foods and confectionery, and also new models of cars. The public relations has to coincide with the launch, and coverage will be sought in the mass media.

16. Post-advertising public relations

A new development has been that for some products, especially those using commercial TV, a point may be reached when media advertising becomes decreasingly cost-effective. The alternative may be public relations, sponsor-ship being a typical example. While sponsorship may be used for advertis-ing or marketing purposes, it is becoming increasingly popular as a public relations technique when it is necessary to familiarise the market and to establish a corporate image (*see* 8: 9). Canon's £3m sponsorship of the Foot-ball League was an effort to do what advertising could not do economically in creating market awareness (the company was shocked to find how it had been eclipsed by Olympus in the British market). Canon estimate that to have used advertising would have cost five times more than the sponsorship.

17. Continuous public relations

Now let us consider another contrast between advertising and public rela-tions. Most advertising campaigns are seasonal or of short duration, except those that remind us repeatedly of well-known products, mail-order clubs which are constantly seeking members, and direct response firms which promote a regular series of offers. There are two reasons for this. Certain goods sell only or mostly at certain times of the year. For example, summer holidays are promoted at the beginning of the year, clocks at Easter and Christmas, sherry and toys at Christmas, central heating in the autumn, garden aids in the spring and early summer, and clothes to suit the seasons. Advertising money is spent when sales are heaviest, or at least the heaviest expenditure is at such times.

Public relations, however, is a continuous process, and it occurs irrespective of advertising and quite often in entirely different media. It is wrong to assume, or even to expect, that because certain media are used for advertising purposes public relations coverage should be gained, or will be automatically provided, in the same media. There is no relationship between the two. Advertisements may be placed in publications which do not use, or rarely use, public relations material and vice versa, e.g. Sunday newspaper colour supplements and the *Radio Times*. A food firm may advertise mostly in national newspapers and on TV, but public relations coverage may be largely in women's magazines which do not appear on the advertising media schedule.

The continuity of public relations activity, and its independence from advertising, results in the company or its products being in the news throughout the year. A holiday resort can be newsworthy at any time, but holiday advertising has to be pitched when people are planning holidays and perhaps have Christmas bonuses with which to pay for a deposit on a package tour.

Whereas advertising uses the advertisement columns and commercial airtime, public relations material contributes to the editorial and programme content. But it is not confined to the mass media, and there are also created private public relations media such as videos, private exhibitions, educational print and house journals.

House journals are the oldest form of organised public relations, and there are records of house journals being published 150 years ago, and a number appeared in the mid-19th century. In spite of recession house journals are better produced, more widely used, and more strongly supported than ever before. More than 1,000 are published in Britain.

An example is *Barclays News* which is distributed every two months to 118,000 employees and pensioners of the various Barclays financial companies world-wide. Under the editorship of Kevin O'Neill, it won eight awards, among them Best Magazine award of the British Association of Industrial Editors and the Grand Prix de L'Europe of the Federation of European Industrial Editors Association.

There are both internal and external publications – magazines and tabloid newspapers for employees and external journals, often of a very high and authoritative technical standard. These are distributed to clients, customers, retailers, specifiers and formulators according to the nature of the product which penetrate specific readerships and are yet another way in which public relations can complement advertising.

The external has a long history. Singer used a customer magazine on how to use a sewing machine, in the mid-19th century, and the Travelers Insurance Company informed brokers about new insurance policies by means of a house journal, and this has continued publication for a century.

The video has become a major public relations medium, replacing the prestigious 16mm documentary film with its heavy cans of film and whirring projector with projectionist. Videos can be quite short – 8 to 10 minutes but seldom longer than 20 minutes. They can be made for special purposes and for selected audiences. They can be used for induction, training, safety or relocation purposes; for use on exhibition stands or in permanent exhibitions; to accompany talks, seminars, conferences and press receptions; and for various market education purposes as when loaned by travel agents to view holiday venues on the home VCR; and similarly they can be offered in press advertisements.

When Alfa-Romeo launched their new version of the 164 sports saloon, the company adopted the public relations tactic of sending a video to buyers of the first version. This could have been excellent but the message and the medium were muddled. The commentary was a sales pitch in the flowery language of a glossy sales brochure, destroying the credibility of the medium. If the video had stuck to facts instead of fancy it would have achieved the objective of educating the market. It was an example of how ignorant advertising people can be of public relations techniques.

PRESS RELATIONS

18. Definition

Press relations aims to achieve maximum publication or broadcasting of public relations information in order to create knowledge and understanding. While the old expression 'press release' has given way to 'news release', the terms 'press relations' and 'press officer' have tended to remain although 'media relations' would be more accurate and 'media manager' is a job title sometimes used. Whatever the terms used, press relations means servicing the media with news, pictures and feature articles, arranging interviews and organising news events.

19. News and advertising compared

There is a very big distinction between the nature of news and advertising. The only reasons why an editor will print public relations material is because it is of interest and value to readers. If he or she published material which failed to meet this criterion readers would be lost, the paper would fold and the editor would be fired. The public relations officer therefore has to make sure that everything supplied to the media is newsworthy and publishable, although there is no guarantee that it will be published since space is limited and the inflow of competing materials may be enormous.

The situation is different with advertising. Once the space has been bought in whatever quantity permitted by the appropriation, the advertiser can say anything within the limits of the law and the British Codes of Advertising and Sales Promotion. The actual appearance can be controlled by booking dates, and the position and size of the space by booking accordingly.

With public relations material, no such control exists for the editor will decide if, when, where, and how to use the information or pictures supplied. In fact, the editor could rewrite a news release, add good or bad comments, or put it in the waste-paper basket. About 70 per cent of news releases are rejected because they are unpublishable. A news release should resemble a report published in the news columns of a newspaper. Releases rarely do. They are usually what someone wants printed, not what readers are likely to want to read. A primary reason for rejection is that they are really 'puffs' or advertisements.

There are three simple rules about writing publishable news releases:

(a) The subject should be in the first three words.

(b) The opening paragraph should summarise the whole story, and be capable of telling the story in a nutshell if only the first paragraph is printed.

(c) There should be no superlatives or self-praise.

20. What is a puff?

A puff is a piece of writing which proclaims the virtues of a company, product or service, praising it and urging readers to favour it, e.g. by making a purchase. In other words, it is an advertisement masquerading as editorial. It is a piece of copywriting, not journalism. It is a good description of 80 per cent of the news releases which infuriate editors.

Unfortunately, many people engaged in advertising, marketing or sales do not understand the difference between the writing of news and the writing of advertisements. They insist on clever headlines, and try to make the story lively by inserting adjectives. They turn it into an advertisement and kill it. But public relations is not about advertising or selling anything: its job is to provide the media with information of *interest and value* to readers, viewers or listeners. If it is used, valuable publicity will result – but only if it satisfies the editor and pleases the editor's audience. Put bluntly, it has to help sell newspapers, not products.

21. Conclusion

In this chapter some comparisons have been made between public relations and advertising techniques. This is deliberate. Much misunderstanding occurs between those engaged in advertising, marketing, public relations and journalism because these differences are not realised let alone understood or practised. On the one hand advertising and marketing people tend to expect public relations material to be a kind of advertising while editors complain about receiving public relations material which is really advertising. The simple distinction has to be remembered: public relations educates and informs and is impartial, but advertising persuades and sells and is partial.

CASE STUDY 1: THE EVER READY DERBY

22. Introduction

The Derby, a horse-race for three-year-olds and run over one-and-a-half miles at Epsom in June, is Britain's premier classic horse-racing event. Its bi-centenary was celebrated in 1979. Until 1984, it had never been sponsored. On 6 June 1984 the Derby was sponsored by Ever Ready Ltd, and in an exciting finish the odds-on favourite El San Greco was beaten by Secreto.

In succeeding years Ever Ready have continued to sponsor this famous horse-race which attracts punters who may never place a bet on any other race. Millions of people watch the Derby on TV, but it is preceded by some two hours of Derby Day programmes which usually includes the arrival of the Royal Family.

23. Background

The company was emerging from a difficult five-year period, which can be analysed in six stages. The growth of the Alkaline Long Life Sector was slow but steady, but Ever Ready Ltd had a poor market share of only 5.7 per cent in 1982–83. Before this period the management had considered a product name change from Ever Ready, a famous name in batteries, to Berec (representing British Ever Ready Electrical Company) in order to further development of a world brand name. In December 1981 the company was taken over by the Hanson Trust, resulting in reorganisation. The Ever Ready image, which had been a strong one, had deteriorated by 1982. The new management set up in 1982 was determined to re-establish pre-eminence of the name and by the end of that year there was a large increase in the advertising spend. In October 1983 there was a very heavy spend on the launch of Cold Seal, the new Alkaline Long Life range of batteries.

24. Hanson Trust

The new owners of Ever Ready were a very successful industrial management company with important holdings in the UK (Ever Ready, Allders, London Brick, Crabtree) and are of a similar size in the USA.

25. United Racecourses Ltd

This company owns the racecourses at Epsom, Sandown and Kempton Park. The Derby is a costly event needing significant funds to remain competitive in world terms. The winner of the Derby usually goes on eventually to earn substantial stud fees. However, the economics of racing demand that there is an increasing need for supplementary funds for the Derby. A new stand has been built in recent years.

26. Timing/the deal

Sponsorship has not been favoured for the main classics, but in 1983 this opposition was dropped and United Racecourses, for economic reasons, actively sought sponsors for the Derby and also for the Oaks, the fillies classic which follows the Derby three days later. Modern sports sponsorships often come about in this way, sports promoters seeking sponsors and potential sponsors seeking events to support. Several companies expressed interest, but these were mainly foreign. This was the year when Japanese companies came to dominate sports sponsorship, not only in Britain but in many parts of the world.

An approach was made to Hanson Trust, specifically to Sir Gordon White, chairman of the US end of the business. This was in December 1983. Rapid negotiations were concluded and a deal was struck on 13 January 1984. The base cost of the sponsorship is £600,000 a year with a three-year contract totalling £1.8 million which has since been renewed. To this must be added the extra costs of the press conference Derby Luncheon, and hospitality for company guests on the day. Ever Ready also ran trade promotions, sales incentives and advertising relating to the Ever Ready Derby in the months running up to the event.

27. Special rights

The sponsorship fee entitles the company to the following privileges with their consequent advertising or publicity value.

(a) Rights to the names *Ever Ready Derby* and *Gold Seal Oaks*.

(b) Rights to all racecourse advertising.

(c) Special privileged places and positions for the company's trade guests.

(d) Rights to advertising in the racecard.

(e) Free advertising for TV monitors round the course.

(f) The Ever Ready name on the winning post.

28. Organisation

The specialist consultancy responsible for organising the sponsorship was British Equestrian Promotions whose managing director was the well-known show-jumping commentator, the late Raymond Brooks-Ward.

29. Development of the event

This was conducted in 1984 by a committee consisting of P.J. Bonner, marketing director, D. Westwood, advertising and promotions manager, and

A.J. Maskens, senior product manager (for Ever Ready Ltd); Raymond Brooks-Ward and Neil Fairley (for British Equestrian Promotions); Tim Neligan, managing director, and Robert Browse (for United Racecourses Ltd); Andy Bryant (for Allen Brady and Marsh, advertising agents); and Stuart Rose (for Jones-Rose (PR), public relations consultants).

30. Main functions

There were four main functions, the press conference for press and TV journalists at the Grosvenor House Hotel on 13 January 1984 when the sponsorship was announced; the Derby Luncheon for all trainers, owners, jockeys and the media; the Ever Ready Derby at Epsom on 6 June 1984 and the Gold Seal Oaks at Epsom on 9 June 1984.

31. Coverage

The Derby is the biggest event in the British racing calendar and consequently during the spring and early summer there are constant references to the Ever Ready Derby. There is a bonus even in the fact that there are many earlier races when Derby hopefuls are on trial, and speculation occurs about both horses and riders, culminating in the actual event. The race is not only televised and broadcast, but there are repeats during the evening. There is usually a magnificent TV shot when the saddle cloth boldly named Ever Ready is placed on the winning horse in the winner's enclosure. The story persists after the event with interviews and commentaries.

In 1993 Ever Ready was taken over by the American Energizer Company. It retained the sponsorship of the Derby in the Ever Ready name, but the Oaks sponsorship was changed from Gold Seal Oaks to Energizer Oaks.

CASE STUDY 2: BRITISH GAS NORTH THAMES

The mistake is often made, as was stated at the beginning of this chapter, of confusing public relations with advertising, even of regarding it as free advertising, a notion subscribed to by leading marketing writers like Philip Kotler which has had the unfortunate effect of making marketing people misunderstand public relations. But we are really concerned with all forms of communication at all levels of an organisation, commercial or non-commercial. Ultimately, of course, it may help to make advertising operate better if only because people like the organisation.

An example of this rather oblique approach is the following case study. British Gas North Thames, one of the 12 regional divisions of British Gas, (now called 'BG'), was involved in a very sensitive undertaking, the laying

259

of a new gas main across Hampstead Heath without arousing the antagonism of residents and lovers of the Heath. Its achievement was a fine example of the maintaining of community relations, essential to the sale of gas and gas appliances to several million customers, mostly in North London. The public relations story was submitted for the Community Relations category of the Institute of Public Relations 1993 Sword of Excellence awards. Called *Making the Connection*, it not only won the category award but the Sword of Excellence for the overall winner. By permission of British Gas North Thames the original submission is reproduced here.

THE INSTITUTE OF PUBLIC RELATIONS 1993 SWORD OF EXCELLENCE AWARDS

Submission from British Gas North Thames for the Community Relations category

Making the Connection

Introduction

Soaring demand for gas in London increased the pressure on British Gas North Thames (one of 12 regions of British Gas) to boost supplies to the Capital. Company engineers planned a £12 million three-year programme, the Region's biggest engineering operation for more than two decades, to meet predicted peak loads for the mid-nineties and into the next century.

The Public Relations department of North Thames recommended a planned and sustained effort to explain the reasons for the essential work, to overcome potential criticism about the inconvenience it would cause. The main task was to build a seven-kilometre link from Temple Fortune in Barnet down to Gospel Oak in Camden.

Many possible routes were examined. One by one, they were all discarded – mainly because of the dirt, noise and long-term inconvenience to which they would have subjected residents and road users. In some cases, engineers found the ground beneath the London streets was already too full of pipework and cables. That left one highly controversial route for the lower part of the link – across Hampstead Heath.

The engineers first turned pale and then turned for help to regional head of public relations Derek Dutton and his in-house team. Thus began the most sensitive and challenging public relations exercise British Gas North Thames has undertaken in the past 20 years.

The problem

Hampstead is home to some of the most influential and articulate opinion-formers in the country. They see the Heath, 800 acres of outstanding natural beauty, as sacrosanct. Commonsense suggested that the Region could face a major protest from local MPs (and other MPs who live there), residents' associations, ecology groups and the public, as well as the City of London Corporation which was just taking over management of the Heath. In all, there were 39 interested organisations.

People had to be kept fully informed at all stages so they understood the need for the work. They had to be reassured that inconvenience would be kept to a minimum and, above all, that there would be no lasting scars.

The solution

Much of the success of this project is attributed to the way Public Relations worked hand in glove with the engineers. The team produced a campaign timetable covering the period from before work started in autumn 1990 until after it finished in October 1992. The primary requirement was painstaking research to discover individuals and groups affected along the route through Hampstead and over the Heath. Presentations would be needed to be certain of the more influential groups. These had to be identified.

A thorough examination of the route was carried out to spot likely hazards, requiring Public Relations help. First came a specialised planning submission document – *The case for a new gas main under Hampstead Heath'*, produced by the public relations team. This document was designed to brief the two local authorities and the City of London Corporation. It formed part of the case for permission. If that had failed, the story would have ended here. A booklet was needed for distribution around Hampstead to give people the background to the project. This full-colour publication, *Engineering work around Hampstead* included facts about the Heath's ecology and history as well as about the gas supply work. An updated version, *The Hampstead Heath Connection* followed later. (This booklet was translated into other languages and sent abroad, demonstrating to potential customers how British Gas handles environmentally sensitive assignments.)

Local school teachers had expressed interest in the major engineering project and were identified as a valuable way of spreading the message. Educational consultants were called in to prepare an exercise for children invited to visit the site.

Plans were drawn up also for a competition to be run with the local weekly newspaper, the *Ham and High*. Journalists were briefed and letters prepared for all residents on the route and for the community interest groups. (Letters of thanks went to everyone as the project moved on.)

An information centre was built as a source of information for all Heath users. A video was commissioned for release after the project to local organisations and City financial audiences. In addition, it will be used for internal training.

Experts on flora and fauna were consulted to identify any rare specimens on the route of the main and to ensure no long-term damage was done. The route across the Heath was adjusted to go round some shrubs and trees. An aboriculturist was commissioned to advise on transplanting a 30-year-old hornbeam tree.

Following discussion with public relations, the engineers made it a condition that the contractors kept inconvenience to a minimum, working only during weekdays on the street sections, and keeping the area safe and tidy by removing spoil from the site each day. Work near schools was undertaken during school holidays only. There were other restrictions for when the work moved on to the Heath.

Running alongside the external campaign would be an exercise to keep employees informed, especially those working in the Hampstead area. They were the company's ambassadors and needed to grasp the importance of the campaign.

Implementing the strategy

The strategy in place, the plans could be announced. It was now early 1991 and display advertisements started appearing in the local newspapers. Maps were given personally to local MPs Sir Geoffrey Finsberg (Conservative, Hampstead and Highgate) and John Marshall (Conservative, Hendon South). The information centre was opened in April at one of the main pedestrian entrances to the Heath, and was manned during normal office hours. Thousands of letters were hand delivered to residents affected, carrying the name, address and telephone number of the top engineer so people knew exactly whom to contact.

The first issue of the booklet, written by North Thames public relations manager Mike Purdie, was then distributed to residents, schools and local organisations. It won praise from Ramblers' Association secretary Betty Franks for being the 'best potted history of the Heath' she had seen.

The pipeline reached the Heath in 1991. The second colour booklet was published and included extracts from some of the many complimentary letters the engineers had received. Forty thousand copies were distributed with the influential *Ham and High* local newspaper. The joint competition, the paper's most successful ever, was run in that edition.

Attractive prizes, not least video equipment and televisions, brought in 350 entries. (All entrants received a specially designed pen.) Local ornithologist and television comedian Bill Oddie presented the prizes.

Many hundreds of children were bussed in to see the work in operation, 400 in one week alone. They were each given a soil-testing exercise, a pen, a calculator and a four-page worksheet – commended by teachers – echoing the style of the Region's education magazine, *Classwork*.

A press day was arranged for a visit by MPs John Marshall and Glenda Jackson (who had by then replaced Sir Geoffrey Finsberg) and City and local dignitaries. The media – national and local newspapers and television – were sent a series of releases keeping them up to date with the project.

During the work, the engineers discussed with Public Relations any complaints received. The decision was taken to respond quickly to complainants, ensuring that, if anything was wrong, it was put right without delay; complaints were given no time to fester. Throughout the project employees were kept up to date by means of briefing notes and, in particular, coverage in *Thames Gas*, the Region's employee newspaper.

Evaluating the results

Making the Connection was judged a great success for a range of positive reasons. The communications strategy had gone precisely as planned. Objections did not materialise; indeed, it was quite the reverse. From where protest had been feared came only praise. There were fewer than 30 letters of complaint from individuals – and many of these were found to refer to work undertaken by other utilities. Public relations wrote to each of the 39 local groups asking if they had any comments or complaints. These would be borne in mind for any similar operation in the future. There were some helpful comments but no complaints.

Press comment was largely favourable: the potential for a bad press nationally – and internationally – on a very public project such as this was enormous.

Careful targeting at the outset of MPs, other opinion-formers and the 39 interested organisations – plus the application of the North Thames public relations planning principle of 'check and check again' – had prepared the ground for this most environmentally and politically sensitive of tasks. It could have been a nightmare, if badly handled. It might even have had to be abandoned.

The comments from VIPs underline the success. Glenda Jackson praised the speed and tidiness of the excavation and the high level of information. 'What I think is so good is that they informed everyone before they started,' she said. A number of journalists and diarists gently poked fun at residents who complained that their habitual daily dog-walking route or favourite sunbathing spot was temporarily unavailable to them.

A correspondent in the *Evening Standard* in May 1992 wrote: 'I am in no doubt that by this time next year there will be no sign that any work has taken place.' That correspondent is right. Nature now is completing the work.

The total Public Relations budget for *Making the Connection* during the two and a half year project, including all print costs, video production, education items for schools and children's competition prizes was £60,500.

Progress test 14

1. Define public relations. **(2)**

2. Describe some of the main differences between public relations and advertising. **(3)**

3. Name the eight basic publics. **(4)**

4. What is parliamentary liaison? **(6)**

5. Name five special uses of public relations consultancies. **(7)**

6. How does a public relations consultancy obtain payment from its clients, and how does this differ from the advertising agency commission system? **(8)**

7. How should the in-house public relations officer be positioned in the management structure of an organisation? **(10)**

8. What are the special advantages of employing an in-house public relations officer? **(11)**

9. Draw a chart to demonstrate the public relations transfer process. **(13)**

10. What is meant by pre-advertising, coincidental and post-advertising public relations? **(14, 15, 16)**

11. For what reasons would an editor print a news release? **(19)**

12. What is 'puffery', and why should it be avoided when writing public relations material? **(20)**

15

Corporate advertising

INTRODUCTION

1. Definition

In this chapter we are not concerned with advertising which is addressed to consumers to buy goods or services, or to distributors to buy stock for resale or with business-to-business advertising. Instead, we shall now consider some uses of advertising on the company's own behalf. The broad expression 'corporate advertising' refers to special advertising to promote the business or financial interests of a company. It includes prestige (or institutional), advocacy or issue, image, take-over bid and financial advertising.

2. Target audiences

Mostly such advertisements will appear in the business and financial press, and will be aimed at an AB but largely A (upper middle class) readership. Very occasionally, commercial television may be used. In the event of a crisis, such as a strike, disaster or the recall of a defective product, advertisements may be addressed to customers. Media such as *The Economist* will be typical of the institutional kind.

PRESTIGE OR INSTITUTIONAL ADVERTISING

3. Public relations

Prestige advertising includes the image-building ads (*see* Figure 15.1, Singapore Airlines) which are really a form of public relations, advertising space being bought to present controlled messages where, when and how the company wishes. Instead of issuing news in a broadcast fashion and hoping that editors will print it somewhere, some day, and reasonably accurately, the company takes space and is responsible for what is said in selected media on specified dates.

The word 'image' is one of the most misused words in the communication business. An image cannot be created or polished, although journalists are

> # THERE'S ONE DIFFERENCE WITH OUR FLIGHT SIMULATOR. IT ACTUALLY FLIES.
>
> It's one thing having to deal with a problem in a flight simulator that tilts up and down on the ground. It's quite another when the problem occurs at 45,000 feet above the South China Sea. That is why SIA pilots take their advanced training courses at the controls of a Learjet 31. They take off and land up to 6 times each day and, while they are in the air, they have to face emergencies prepared in advance by our somewhat exacting instructors. This is no quick refresher course. It lasts around two months, during which those who succeed will have taken the controls and the decisions on at least 50 separate flights. To some, this might appear to be excess caution. But it is simply our way of making sure that it's more than just our inflight service that other airlines talk about.
>
> **SINGAPORE AIRLINES**
> THE YOUNGEST, MOST MODERN FLEET IN THE WORLD.

Figure 15.1 A prestige advertisement from the business press

fond of such expressions. An image is the character of an organisation, how an organisation is perceived. It will depend on how well an organisation is known and understood, and how it is seen to behave. Image advertising is therefore concerned with improving knowledge and understanding of the organisation.

4. Style

Prestige advertisements may be produced in a very literary and artistic form in order to enhance the corporate image, but the modern tendency is to adopt the crisper, more precise style of persuasive copywriting, and to present the company's story, merits and achievements in a pungent and positive way. Figure 15.2 is an interesting example of a British Gas advertisement from *The Economist*.

ADVOCACY OR ISSUE ADVERTISING

5. Propaganda

This kind of corporate advertising is common in the United States, but it is used in the UK occasionally. In contrast to prestige or corporate image

---

**OUR SUCCESS
MEANS OTHER COMPANIES
CAN COMPETE IN THE
BIGGEST MARKET THERE IS.
THE WORLD.**

At British Gas, we're far from just being British Gas. In fact, we now operate in 45 countries.

Which is good news for us as well as good news for many other British companies. In the last two years, 400 companies have been awarded £100 million of contracts due to our expertise. They're now providing everything from central heating pipes to computers, from Argentina to Thailand. However none of our success abroad would be possible if it weren't for all the success we've had at home.

Since privatisation we've been able to bring down gas prices by as much as 20% in real terms to domestic users and by 25% to our industrial customers.

But with a world gas market estimated to grow in size by 40% by 2005, we're planning to play an even larger role in the world.

And, as a result of this, we are delighted to say, numerous other British companies are planning to do the same.

British Gas
A WORLD CLASS ENERGY COMPANY

Figure 15.2 A British Gas prestige ad from *The Economist*

advertising with its public relations characteristics, *advocacy* advertising is more often propaganda. It either presents a case for a business, or states its position in relation to a political issue. Reminiscent of the propaganda of a more political type are the costly campaigns (including sponsorship of a round-the-world yacht race) to promote Nuclear Electric and British Nuclear Fuels, both pets of Government policy. We are now in the realms of business politics, a company attacking policies or proposed legislation, or defending itself from antagonistic governments, political parties or pressure groups, or perhaps showing how it is being socially responsible by adhering to official policy and recommendations. The examples in **6** and **7** will demonstrate the use of such advertising.

Much of today's propaganda is conducted by pressure groups such as Friends of the Earth and Greenpeace. The latter caused a stir with their full page ad in the *New York Times*, headlined OZONE SHOCK – tell DuPont to stop destroying the ozone layer now. The ad pictured a happy family in normal dress and the same family wearing protective clothing in the future. The ad offered four response coupons, one to send to DuPont; one to Seagram (25 per cent shareholders of DuPont); one to the President of the USA; and one to Greenpeace.

There can be propaganda by organisations opposed to certain products, and propaganda for the criticised product group. Thus, the Infant & Dietetic Foods Association, representing makers of baby drinks, campaigns against pressure groups such as Action and Information on Sugars (supported by seven major health groups). The IDFA maintains that sugary drinks cause tooth decay only if the product is misused, and the AIS has succeeded in getting Farley Bed Timer ads to be modified to show a baby awake rather than asleep after drinking the product.

6. Defence

A company may have been criticised by the media or by politicians or other opinion leaders, and advertisements will be published to state the company's side of the story. It will present facts about itself to disprove the criticisms. For example, it may state the volume of employment it provides, the prosperity it has brought to a region, the taxes it pays, or the contribution it makes to exports and to the country's balance of trade. In TV commercials, British Airways has announced the millions of pounds its international services bring to the British economy. Some American multinationals, such as ITT and IBM, have used advertising to show that they, too, are contributing to the British economy when they have been accused of milking it on behalf of their American parent companies.

According to the opposing policies of Labour and Conservative governments, we have seen advertisements for companies threatened by either nationalisation or privatisation. This is very confusing when each of the two governments has contrary policies on these big issues, and the advertisement becomes little more than propaganda for opposing views, however justified it may seem to be to the opposing parties. 'Hands off' advertising was published by sugar, banking and insurance interests under Labour governments, and there was opposition to the privatisation of the highly profitable British Telecom. British Airways issued prestige advertising which could be read to mean either 'Why sell us off?' or 'Why not buy our shares when they are offered?' just as much as 'Aren't we successful?'

7. Positioning

The government may have declared its policy, with or without special legislation, on issues which affect the company. It may therefore be politic to announce publicly that the company respects this policy, and how it is complying with the requirements. There are many issues of this kind which concern companies either liable to, or deemed liable to, present a social problem. These can include:

(a) harm to the environment such as pollution;

(b) harm to the ecology, such as destruction of wildlife;

(c) waste of energy resources when conservation is required;

(d) health hazards, as with the use of certain ingredients in foods, cosmetics or medicines, and the alleged hazards to health related to genetically-modified crops;

(e) safety hazards, as with the design or use of certain materials in the manufacture of toys;

(f) road safety, and the design of cars to minimise fatalities in accidents;

(g) loss of money which can occur with investments, direct response marketing, or guarantees which are not supported by a trust fund in case a company goes out of business.

In recent years we have seen a number of 'green' campaigns ranging from the openly propagandist ones of organisations such as Greenpeace to attempts by commercial companies to jump on the 'green' bandwagon. Some of the latter have been sincere, other campaigns doubtful exploitation of a fashionable or topical theme. Eco-labelling may reduce the 'green bashing' exploitation of this issue.

Figure 15.3 is an example of an Esso advertisement which declares its position regarding pollution.

DIVERSIFICATION AND TAKE-OVER

8. Diversification

Some companies are believed to be monopolistic, or engaged in only one industry, and advertising may be used to correct this image and to show the true breadth of its activities. This sort of advertising may also be directed at the share market, since investors are likely to have greater confidence in a company which has a healthy spread of interests, and can sustain downturns in certain markets. Tobacco firms are nowadays involved in many businesses such as beer, foods and hotels and catering. Tate & Lyle are not confined to sugar. Chemical firms like ICI make insecticides, paints and plastics. These broader images are presented through corporate advertising.

Remember those hazy days of summer?

Esso are helping to put a stop to them.

How much would you give for a beautifully clear summer's day?

Millions? That's what we've spent so far on reducing pollution from escaped petrol vapours.

We call it vapour recovery. Basically, to stop any petrol evaporating we've designed sealed links between our depots and delivery tankers.

Then, as tankers unload at our major service stations, the vapours, instead of escaping, are stored and later chilled back into petrol.

Last year, using these methods, we stopped 850,000 gallons disappearing into the blue.

That's enough to run the average family car for the next 2,500 years. This is just one of the ways Esso lead the field in trying to reduce air pollution. As you can see, our aim is clear.

For further information contact Tom MacQuillan on 020 7245 2515.

Figure 15.3 Esso positions itself regarding pollution

9. Take-over bids

In the event of a take-over bid, when an apparently stronger company, known as a predator, buys up a large number of shares of a weaker company, and then tries to make the remaining shareholders a favourable offer, the two companies may become caught up in a battle of competing claims and offers. This is usually done by means of advertisements in the business press as well as in letters to shareholders. These financial struggles can be seen from time to time in newspapers like *The Times, Financial Times, International Herald Tribune* and *Wall Street Journal*.

CRISIS ADVERTISING

10. Crisis situations

Crises of various kinds can descend on companies, and urgent advertising may be necessary. The following are possible crisis situations requiring the use of special advertising that is different from the normal uses of trade or consumer advertising.

(a) A strike may require advertisements stating the employer's side of the dispute.

(b) An accident may need advertisements which state when normal services will be resumed.

(c) A product defect may require advertisements which identify the problem and ask customers to return the product for modification or replacement.

11. Example

Figure 15.4 reproduces a typical product recall advertisement.

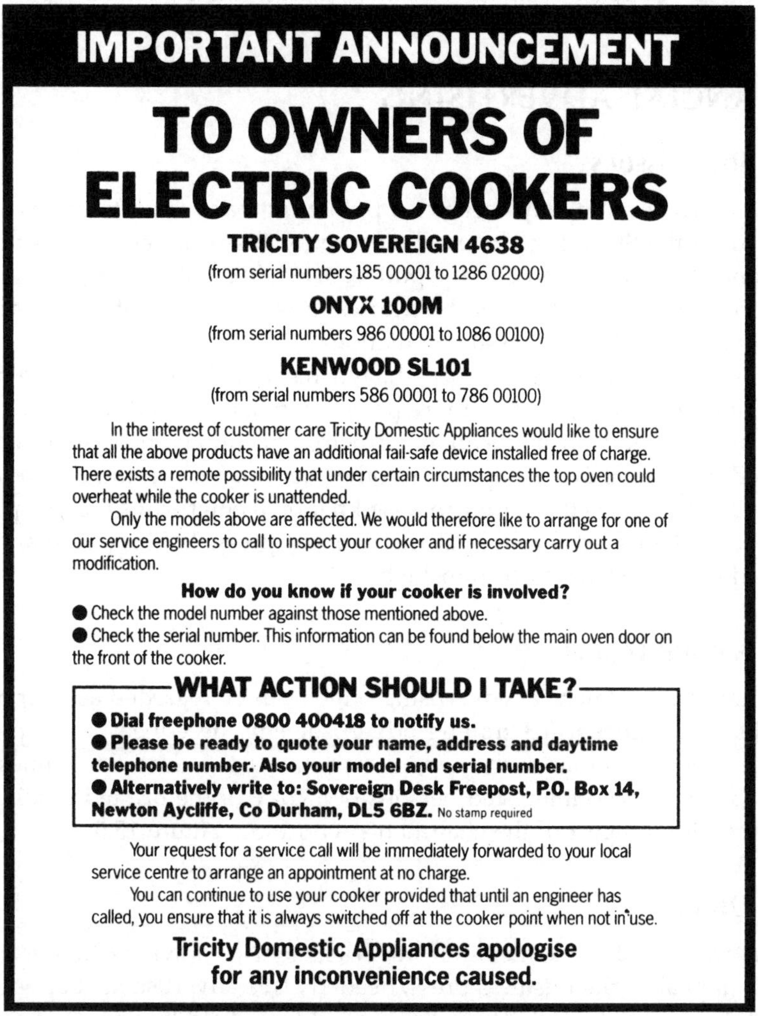

Figure 15.4 A typical product recall advertisement

271

The following is the copy which accompanied a brief statement of annual accounts for a Naples bank:

The total assets of Banco di Napoli exceeded Lit. 110,000 billion in 1992. In the course of the year the Bank opened 110 new branches, thereby achieving its objective of 750 branches in Italy. The strength of the Bank's balance sheet and the extension of its branch network enable it to meet the European challenge with confidence. Banco di Napoli also has many other branches throughout the world in order to maintain ever closer contact with its customers.

Figure 15.5 Copy from an advertisement concerning an annual report

FINANCIAL ADVERTISING

12. Share issues

When a private company becomes a public company, and its shares are to be sold on the Stock Exchange, when a nationalised undertaking is privatised and shares are offered to the public, or when a public company wishes to borrow money and offers debentures, a special form of advertising is required under the share issue regulations.

It takes the form of a *prospectus* which usually appears in full in the press, sometimes occupying two or more pages with background information on the company and an application form for the purchase of shares. Condensed versions may also appear in other newspapers. In the case of large share issues such as those for privatised national enterprises the prospectus is usually published throughout the national press. Millions of shares are offered on an instalment or tranche basis.

13. Annual report

Another form of financial advertising which can be regarded as 'corporate' (as distinct from normal trading advertisements described in Chapter 1) is that used to announce the annual report and accounts. Sometimes this includes an offer to interested persons of a copy of the printed report, and usually with a digest of the chairman's report. *See* Figure 15.5.

14. Others

There are also those rather dull advertisements, known as 'tombstones', which appear in the business press, headed 'This advertisement appears as a matter of record only'. These list the holdings held by various financial partners in an enterprise, and are a necessary public announcement so that there is no secrecy about the participations, or as a brief token announcement about a new share issue.

Progress test 15

1. Define corporate advertising. **(1)**

2. How can advertising be used for public relations purposes? **(3)**

3. What is advocacy or issue advertising? **(5)**

4. Give examples of the use of corporate advertising to 'position' a company. **(7)**

5. How is corporate advertising used to explain diversification? **(8)**

6. Explain the use of corporate advertising in the course of take-over bids. **(9)**

7. What sort of crisis situations require corporate advertising? What is meant by product recall? **(10, 11)**

8. How is corporate advertising used to announce a new share issue? **(12)**

16

Corporate identity

INTRODUCTION

1. Uses of corporate identity

Corporate identity is the way in which an organisation is recognised and distinguished, and this is achieved by a specially designed scheme that covers everything which creates physical identity. It can include major elements such as house colour, logotype, typography, livery and dress but also unifies the appearance of premises, is applied to everything printed, and to numerous items such as crockery, serviettes, employees' dress and badges. A hotel group like the Hilton may even design the shape of window frames, door handles and lampshades to give uniformity, while a store like Marks & Spencer will carry the sense of unity through both the exterior and interior of the store, the uniform of sales staff and the famous green plastic shopping bags.

It is difficult to find really distinctive colours – those of Gateway supermarkets and BP garages and forecourt shops are almost an identical green and yellow – but there are exceptions such as the brown Guinness label, the special shades of red and green of the Fuji film pack, and the two blues of British Gas.

Typefaces have to be chosen with care for four reasons:

(a) certain styles date;

(b) sans serif faces are less easy to read than serif faces when printed in small sizes;

(c) not every printer may have your chosen typeface, a problem with modern photo typesetting and desk top systems;

(d) some faces are attractive as display faces in large sizes, but are not very legible (especially if they have a low x-height, i.e. the size of the circular base of letters like 'b', 'p', and 'h') in small text sizes.

These considerations are very important with press advertisements, as when local newspapers are expected to set advertisements for local branches of a national firm such as large estate agents.

Figure 16.1 Logos used in recruitment advertisements; left to right: Institute of Legal Executives, Welsh Development Agency, Severn Trent Water, General Utilities

Figure 16.2 The revised logo introduced as a total new look, including that of shop layout

Figure 16.3 The revised Rentokil corporate identity, using a more refined typeface and incorporating the Royal Warrant for all environmental services. It occupies the side panels of vehicles

Corporate identity, by unifying physical appearance, reinforces advertising and helps to give it the repetition which helps advertising succeed. The use of the same colour scheme, the same logo, and the same typography, plus the repetition of this in packaging, on delivery vehicles, on point-of-sale displays and so on all make corporate identity a valuable contribution to advertising.

For this reason it is a mistake to change a corporate identity scheme without good reasons and careful thought. Nevertheless, they have occurred, as has been seen with KitKat, BT, Rentokil, BP, Shell, Our Price and electricity undertakings such as SWEB. Why is this? There are usually two reasons – to modernise or because there has been a fundamental change in the organisation such as privatisation.

Rentokil has retained its red, but there have been three versions of its corporate identity scheme since a number of companies were combined under the single name of Rentokil. The latest version, reproduced in Figure 16.3, incorporates the Royal Warrant which now applies to all Rentokil Environmental Services, and the classic lettering has been refined again. This new version is important to a company which has now moved into many new fields of business and has companies all over the world.

2. Origins of corporate identity

It is one of the oldest forms of designed communication, and it has always had a practical purpose. The basic idea has always been to create identification, doing so through uniformity. In fact, the 'uniform' is its simplest use and expression.

Centuries ago armies were led into war by their leader such as the king. Leaders did not hide away in safe bunkers. The leader identified himself, usually by a design on his shield. Even so, this was a dangerous practice, so all his knights carried similarly decorated shields. Eventually the troops were given uniforms, and different regiments were identified by colours and headdress.

Ships have long identified themselves from the Viking ships with eagles on their sails to the present day. When steamships arrived the funnels of each line were painted a different colour like the red ones of Cunard. Stage coaches, buses, trams, trains and aircraft have had their particular corporate identity schemes. So have shops as we walk down the high street and identify the different chains, and banks do the same.

Animals have featured in many logos, the most popular being the lion, but such logos can look very much alike as with those for Vauxhall and Peugeot. All over the world there are Lion brand beers, presumably representing strength. The Guinness label, while retaining its Irish harp symbol, uses additional animal symbols, a dog in Singapore and Malaysia, and a cat in Indonesia. If one asks a hotel waiter in Indonesia for a Guinness he knows what is wanted if one calls for a 'black cat beer'. Cats, especially black, feature in some symbols but the cat has different meanings in different countries, disliked in Nigeria, esteemed in Egypt.

The most famous and best loved animal in a logo is Nipper, the fox-terrier listening to an old Edison cylinder phonograph which first appeared in an HMV advertisement in 1900. The original picture was painted, without horn, by Francis Barrau who owned both dog and phonograph. At first it was rejected by the Edison Bell Company in America but later taken up by the Gramophone Company in Britain who paid £50 for the picture repainted with a horn, and £50 for the copyright.

At Christie's £715 was paid in July 1993 for a 3-inch silver model of Nipper. Earlier in the year, £1,120 was paid at Christie's for a papier maché model of Nipper. The only countries which disliked Nipper were Italy where bad singers are likened to dogs, and Egypt where dogs were thought to be unclean. Ruth Edge and Leonard Petts have catalogued 707 Nipper collectables.

The name His Master's Voice was probably derived from the fact that the phonograph, which could record and reproduce, probably played back the artist's voice, and Nipper was in fact listening to his master's voice.

Many overseas logos are based on the national bird or animal such as the golden ibis in Trinidad, the mouflon in Cyprus, the Kelantan kite in Malaysia, and the garuda in Indonesia. It was not appreciated when the elephant was once associated with Nigeria Airlines because it flew jumbo jets.

3. Some typical changes

KitKat, as has been mentioned, has sharpened the lettering of its name. British Telecom has had a revolutionary change since privatisation, replacing its well-known yellow-orange vehicles with pearly grey ones bearing the current BT logo. BP and Shell have both smartened up their petrol stations in line with new construction and the introduction of 24-hour forecourt shops.

Our Price has adopted a different logo as shown in Figure 16.2. This fits in with a new store layout with lower counters and new facias, but retaining the familiar red and white colours. A new store look and layout were tested in Richmond before being applied to the company's 310 branches. Design agency Carroll Dempsey & Thirkell were responsible for the Our Price changes.

Noticeably, the name of the company or of the product are nowadays incorporated in the logo. This was not always so, say, 25 ago when the fashion was to create a shape, such as British Rail's arrows, which did not, by themselves, identify the user. Too often they were expensive, clever but meaningless symbols. Having to guess what a logo stands for is poor communication.

4. Corporate identity scheme consultants

At one time the creation of corporate identity schemes tended to be the prerogative of American firms, but in recent years the call for new ideas has brought about the setting up of several corporate identity scheme specialists. Wally Olins wrote his famous book *The Corporate Personality* in 1978. Why has this happened? There are many reasons such as mergers and amalgamations, privatisations, changes in business activities, new products such as computers and other office machines, and the need to be more competitive as the retail scene has changed. Advertising depends more than ever on visibility, and the communications impact can be divided into 10 per cent written, 20 per cent spoken and 70 per cent visual. A logotype visualises the values, culture, behaviour and attitude of an organisation. A logotype identifies and an identity personifies.

Sampson Tyrrell have been responsible for many of the corporate identity schemes which we see every day, and not only in Britain. They have a philosophy of not just creating a new logo and associated physical iden-tification accessories, but of planning how the scheme should be applied, applied continuously and regularly. For example, the green and yellow colours of the BP shield logo are applied to the total design and decor of a BP petrol station so that it stands out as a green building which is unmis-takably a BP one, the logo being almost incidental.

According to Terry Moore of Sampson Tyrrell, the corporate identity scheme must be a top management commitment, not just an advertising, marketing or public relations aid.

Before designing a scheme, Sampson Tyrrell are concerned with six ques-tions which are concerned with articulating an organisation in order to project its efficiency and appeal to different audiences and media. These are:

(a) maximising existing identification – one does not always have to start afresh;

(b) creating a new identity if that is necessary;

(c) international aspects;

(d) national identity issues;

(e) how it will be implemented;

(f) commercial exploitation.

As will be seen from the following examples of Sampson Tyrrell's work, (e) and (f) are the practical ones which can make a company's advertising more effective.

5. Examples of Sampson Tyrrell's work

South West Electricity Board had a well-known symbol and orange colour scheme, but following privatisation and a changing business, Sampson Tyrrell were invited to re-think their identity scheme. It was decided to retain the core design but develop it to express the company's expansion of activities. The new logo was made less geometrical, and more contemporary, but it remained very similar to the original. The typeface was standardised. The well-known orange was complemented by grey, and each logo was given a descriptive line which identified the department such as engineer-ing or contracting. The house journal was redesigned. The vans were given orange tops and grey skirts. Orange and grey facia boards were designed for SWEB shops with the logo in orange.

An unusual assignment was for the South of Scotland Electricity Board (SSEB). In the past nationalised electricity undertakings did not have to answer to shareholders, but now it was a commercial public company. It has a new name, Scottish Power, and this required a logo representing power, but at the same time it needed to be open-ended because the new company could engage in a variety of interests such as gas, water, waste, or telecoms.

The problem was that there had to be a simultaneous launch of the corporate identity involving everything where it would be seen, but this had to occur within the space of a day while remaining secret until that day. The Scottish Power shops, for instance, were re-named Powerpoint. The old and the new had to be blended to maintain continuity in the minds of customers. Half of the vehicle fleet was re-liveried in three days and kept out of sight. New stationery and new sizes of literature were produced. The new symbol combined the two names SSEB and Scottish Power, and then within a year the old SSEB was dropped.

Another Sampson Tyrrell client was Castrol, a worldwide lubricant which had used a circular logo since 1974 and had adopted the colours red, green and white since the beginning of the century. There was no real control over how the colours and logo should be used, and numerous versions, using the badge, were implemented by marketing managers in the USA, Middle East, Africa and the Far East.

The red, green and white were retained, and it is important to remember that white is a colour which can be exploited like any other. Putting the name in a square box helped to get it used straight. The typography was cleaned up. A manual was produced showing how the scheme could be used as flexibly as possible by local marketing companies. There was no absolutely uniform design but the same standards. It was important to use colours suitable for satellite TV, and since red does not come out well on video the Castrol sponsored racing cars were painted green and white.

Shell has made great use of its red and yellow which are warm and friendly colours. A Shell petrol station really glows! The long-established shell symbol speaks for itself. The company required a world-wide standard decor for its 30,000 petrol stations which have been redecorated or reconstructed with Select forecourt shops over a six-year period.

Sampson Tyrrell redesigned the word 'Shell', and the legibility of the word links with the shell symbol. A design manual was produced for contractors building different petrol stations, each country having different-looking stations because they are operated by local companies. In other countries such as Singapore the tankers were given new liveries. Every possible part of the petrol station bears the red and yellow colours, even 'in' and 'out' signs.

The Royal Mail (see Figure 16.4) is one of the three businesses which make up the Post Office, together with Parcel Force and Post Office Counters. It employs some 210,000 staff, and handles about 5,475 million first class and 12,615 million second class letters annually. The mail market place has

Figure 16.4 Sampson Tyrell's logo to distinguish the Royal Mail from Parcel Force and Post Office Counters

changed with new technologies and new customer needs and services. Hence, a separate corporate identity was required for the Royal Mail. The brief was to create an identity which could be exploited, separating the Royal Mail from the other Post Office services.

The total scheme embraced 32,000 vehicles; 160,000 postmen's uniforms; 120,000 postboxes, collection plates; 4,000 forms; 1,500 signage systems for premises nationwide; and 1,200 letterhead variations for an overall print run of more than one million letterheads.

The former cruciform logo was given a new look which still reflected the heritage, quality and goodwill built up over generations of Post Office customers. The new powerful presence incorporated the privileged use of the St Edward and Scottish crowns, the Royal cypher, with destinctive double line lettering (and the colours red and yellow) as Figure 16.4. A set of Guidelines were produced for both internal marketing staff and external suppliers nationwide.

6. New television contractors

When the ITC awarded new franchises to television contractors some well-known companies such as Thames TV, Television South, Television South West and TV-am lost to other contenders under the new bid system introduced by the Broadcasting Act 1990. The new companies, which are consortiums set up for the purpose, had to create corporate identity schemes. Those for Carlton (London Monday to Friday), GMTV (breakfast TV), Meridian Broadcasting (South) and Westcountry Television (South West) are as reproduced in Figure 16.5. These identities have had to be established with both advertisers as well as viewers.

Carlton Television

GMTV

Meridian Broadcasting

Westcountry Television

Figure 16.5 Logos of new television contractors who replaced Thames TV, TV-am, TVS and TVW in 1993

7. Corporate identity in recruitment advertising

Logotypes help to identify employers in their recruitment advertisements, and to establish the status of the potential employer in the eyes of potential applicants. These logos may be unfamiliar to applicants but serve to suggest that they are reputable employers.

8. The Automobile Association

Newell and Sorrell designed the new-style vehicle livery and uniforms introduced by the Automobile Association in June 1993 and featured in the Summer 1993 issue of *AA Magazine* which is mailed to its 7.5 million

Figure 16.6 The distinctive corporate identity for AA vehicles and patrols

members (*see* Figure 16.6). Established 88 years earlier, this was the AA's first significant livery and uniform change in 25 years. A strong yellow has always been the AA's dominant colour, and many a stranded motorist has welcomed the approaching yellow rescue vehicle. Newell and Sorrell began planning changes in 1990.

The history of the AA's corporate identity goes back a long way since visibility was an essential factor of the service. Until 1909 AA patrolmen rode bicycles but then matured to motorcycles with yellow fuel tanks. To identify them the bicycle riding patrolmen wore an armband and a circular badge round their neck. The 1909 uniform was a peaked cap and yellow oil skins for wet weather, again with armband. In 1911 they wore khaki tunics. The uniform remained unchanged for 40 years.

Sidecars, bearing a winged AA logo and black Road Service lettering, took over in the 1920s and 1930s. But during the Second World War the sidecars had to be sprayed khaki to camouflage them from enemy aircraft crews. The black and yellow square logo was introduced in 1966. After the Second World War open-necked tunics with collar and tie were introduced. Olive coloured uniforms were worn from 1969 until the present change.

The logo appears for the first time on vehicle bonnets. The livery is made by the Halo Company of Burgess Hill. Elsewhere, such as on letterheadings or literature, the logo has a yellow background. The rooftop lightbar has been re-styled to show a larger, square AA Logo.

The uniform is worn by 3,600 patrol staff and consists of shirts, trousers, sweaters, ties, overalls, body-warmers, waterproofs, reflective jackets and trousers. The 250 inspectors have a suit for administrative duties, but are kitted out like patrol staff except for white instead of green shirts. The clothing was supplied by Company Image of Bradford.

The introduction of the new livery and dark green uniform coincided with press, poster and TV advertising. Whole page ads for the AA in colour magazines such as that of the *Independent on Sunday* were printed in black type on a yellow background. The amusing 'I know a very nice man who can'. TV commercials were replaced by the ingenious '4th emergency service' – fourth only to the police, fire brigade and ambulance service.

Progress test 16

1. What is the purpose of a corporate identity scheme? **(1)**

2. What are the essential elements of a corporate identity scheme? **(1)**

3. Why do typefaces have to be chosen with care? **(1)**

4. How did corporate identity originate? **(2)**

5. What are the percentage values of the communication impact of print, the spoken word and visual items? **(4)**

6. What six questions do Sampson Tyrrell require to be answered before producing a corporate identity scheme? **(4)**

7. Give some of the reasons for requiring a new or revised corporate identity scheme? **(1, 3, 6)**

8. Why can a logotype be important in recruitment advertising? **(7)**

9. Why were reflective colours used for the new Automobile Association liveries and uniforms? **(8)**

17

Advertising research

VALUE OF RESEARCH

1. Scope of advertising research

Advertising research is a branch of marketing research. It is both a sort of insurance to avoid wasting money on ineffective advertising and a means of monitoring the effectiveness of a campaign while it is running and after the campaign has ended. It is also possible and advantageous to link advertising research with other forms of marketing research which the company is undertaking. Today, the advertiser has the benefits of many sorts of research, and they are usually recommended and commissioned by an advertising agency. In fact, in its own interests a good advertising agency may insist on the use of research to ensure that it produces and conducts successful advertising. This applies particularly to copy-testing to establish the best idea, theme, selling points or presentation before entering into costly artwork or production of commercials and the buying of space and airtime.

Research is not confined to testing creativity. There is a wealth of independently researched statistical information on sales, readership and audience figures regarding all the principal media so that the most economic media can be used. In addition to this it is possible to control the duration of appearance of an advertisement by assessing when enough people have had the opportunity to see the advertisement a sufficient number of times.

This is in line with the IPA definition of advertising which refers to presenting 'the most persuasive selling message to the right prospects for the product or service at the lowest possible cost'. Advertising research can help to achieve this effectively and economically.

2. Reliability of research

How reliable is marketing research? The answer to this is that while it is better than crystal ball gazing or astrology, marketing research does not produce facts but only tendencies and indications which are open to interpretation. For example, the opinion poll technique is often applied to political

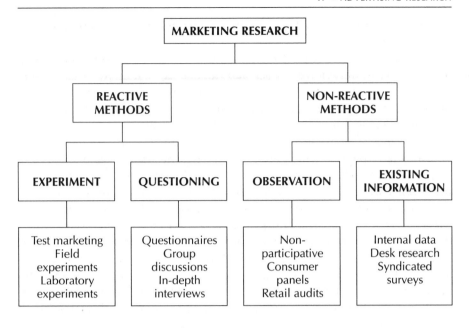

Figure 17.1 The anatomy of marketing research

surveys, but the accuracy of the figures tends to depend on how near to an election the poll was conducted, the final voting being the only true result. Much will also depend on the size or kind of sample interviewed. (*See* Figure 17.1.)

RESEARCH IN DEVELOPING COUNTRIES

3. Limitations

From this chapter's survey of the techniques and statistics available in the UK to advertisers, and especially to their advertising agencies, it will be appreciated that methods and information can be applied to the planning and creation of advertising campaigns which are both economic and effective. However, such a wealth of intelligence rarely exists in developing countries. Media may be expensive simply because of the costs of producing newspapers, magazines or television programmes for small readerships or audiences. Field research may be difficult or costly to conduct, although

285

a number of surveys have been conducted which have produced otherwise unknown data.

But statistics may not exist on which to base samples, and respondents may be wary of interviewers. Local taboos may make it impossible to interview women, or count children. Researchers may be thought to be tax investigators. Large rural populations, many languages and ethnic groups and long distances may all make researching difficult.

For instance, a media survey in Kenya revealed the number of people who 'listen to newspapers' which are read to them by literate members of the family. It has also been found in Nigeria and Zambia that radio may be less penetrating than is often believed, and that people living in remote areas use radio (and especially pop or 'high life' music) purely as a companionable background sound, and pay little heed to news from distant cities of which they have little knowledge. Major world events may not be of much concern to a villager whose interests are limited to his or her local community. On the other hand, the travelling film show and product demonstration will be more significant, and in Malawi the textile firm of David Whitehead has taken fashion shows to villagers to promote dress-making materials (*see* 5: **35**).

4. Social grades

The British system of social grades, also used in advertising research, especially readership and audience surveys, has been described in 3: **7**. It was seen that the three largest (C^1, C^2 and D) total 82 per cent or close on three-quarters of the adult male and female population. They form the mass market for FMCGs, the readers of the popular press (e.g. the *Sun*, *Daily Mirror*, *Daily Star*, *Daily Mail* and *Daily Express*) and the watchers of prime-time evening television.

Elsewhere in the world, other methods may be used to represent the different classes in a society, e.g. the socio-economic way of grading by income, or the educational status method. In a developing country, where most people are rural dwellers, 70 per cent may be classed as lower class, quite the opposite of the British experience.

RESEARCH BEFORE, DURING AND AFTER THE CAMPAIGN

5. Pre-campaign research

The aim of research before advertising appears is to:

(a) define the copy platform or theme;

(b) pre-test proposed advertisements; and

(c) plan the media schedule.

The marketing department will have researched other matters concerning the market, the product, the name, the price and the packaging. It will continue to research (or subscribe to surveys) regarding what, how and where consumers purchase (e.g. by means of consumer panels), and the movement of stocks and the brand share held (e.g. dealer audit research). Some of this general continuous marketing research may also assist in the creation of advertisements and the choice of media.

6. Defining the copy platform

What will make the most effective appeal – price, quality, something new, a special offer? Should the advertisement be serious or humorous? Should there be a lot of copy or mostly pictures? It is no use plumping for the first idea. When the presentation is made to the client there must be sound justification for the proposed advertisement or series of advertisements. Above all, it must meet in full the demands of the brief. The following kinds of research may be used.

(a) Motivational research. In this type of research, a number of clinical tests are used to discover the hidden motives for buying. If questioned by normal research techniques respondents may say they buy because, for instance, they like the new design of a car. Motivational research will probe deeper and produce the underlying motive that, for example, it is believed to be the safest car for family motoring, and will therefore satisfy the buyer's wife. It uses clinical tests and a small sample of people, and was pioneered in the USA by Dr Ernst Dichter. Motivational research was popular in the 1960s but has given way to more simple techniques such as the discussion or 'focus' group.

(b) Discussion group. Motivational research can be expensive, and a much less expensive method is to set up a discussion or focus group controlled by a chairman who poses questions, listens to the discussion which sparks off spontaneous ideas and comments, and summarises the answer. It is rather like brainstorming. A report is then written presenting the answers to the questions. These answers can indicate the copy theme which should be adopted by the creative department of the advertising agency. But while discussion groups are expensive the sample of perhaps no more than 25 people can be too small or too unrepresentative to produce a reliable survey.

7. Copy-testing

When the theme has been worked up creatively as a press advertisement, radio script or storyboard for a TV commercial, it will be tested on a sample of people representative of the market. One idea may be tested at a time, or different versions will be tested simultaneously. Press advertisements can be shown to respondents, then withdrawn and questions asked to test what is remembered. This is known as the folder technique, the different advertisements being inserted in the plastic sleeves of a cover, rather like a menu. Commercials may be broadcast or screened to an invited audience in a hall or private theatre. Reactions can be tested by recording which commercial would most encourage purchase.

A number of techniques are practised such as interspersing the commercial under test among others and comparing the responses. Does the new one achieve a greater willingness to buy than the others?

In some campaigns it may be necessary to go on testing until a version achieves the desired response rate. In one well-known press advertising campaign five versions were rejected before the agency was satisfied that the sixth was the one which could be presented to the client with confidence. The campaign, with annual refinements, ran successfully for three years.

8. Reading and noting

Another method is to place the advertisement in a limited regional edition of a national newspaper, and then to question a sample of readers of the newspaper next day. The sample is found by asking people in the street whether or not they read the previous day's paper, and whether or not they saw the advertisement. Those who did are then taken through every part of the advertisement and questioned to test what percentage of these readers remembered each item. Once the weaknesses and the strengths of the advertisement are established, the final advertisement is produced for the campaign proper in the full national edition of that paper and in the other publications on the media schedule.

9. Research during the campaign

When the advertising campaign is running, further reading and noting tests may be held, but probably a more simple next-day recall test can be best used to measure what percentage of readers or viewers saw and remembered details of the advertisement when it appeared the previous day or evening.

If the company is subscribing to a monthly dealer audit report, this information can indicate how the campaign is influencing sales. Other data such as the number of enquiries received or orders taken will also test the effectiveness of a campaign. If the advertisement contains a keyed coupon, that is one with a code such as ST1 for the first insertion in the *Sunday Times*, the response can be counted. If the cost of the space is divided by the number of enquiries, a cost-per-reply figure can be calculated, and this can be done to arrive at a cost-per-conversion-into-sale figure.

10. Testing the final result

When the campaign has finished some of the methods already described can be used again, especially in assessing the total number of enquiries or orders obtained (and the relative cost for each publication), while dealer audit – being a continuous study – can produce a graphical representation of the effect of the campaign over the period of its run. A target may have been set such as a given percentage increase in the volume of sales, or an improvement in the share of the market held by the product in relation to rival brands. For instance, has the brand moved up from third position to second or first? Or has the brand retained its previous position in spite of the efforts made by competitors? If it is a new product, what share of the market has the advertising campaign achieved? To be fair, any other influences must be considered too. The sales force may have been strengthened or there could have been a coincidental sales promotion scheme such as a money-off offer.

11. Continuous research

Two forms of continuous research need explanation here. 'Continuous' does not mean every day but regularly, say every month. The advantage of continuous over single or *ad hoc* surveys is that they record trends over time. They show how sales of a brand vary and compete with other brands, influenced perhaps by advertising or sales promotion campaigns.

The two main kinds of continuous research are the consumer panel and dealer (retail or shop) audit. Consumer panels are carefully recruited and consist of housewives or householders who agree to keep a diary of their purchases. The diaries are posted to the research company for tabulation. The final report will show what social grades buy which brands in which quantities, how often and where. Dealer audit requires a recruited cross-section of retailers who are visited regularly and their invoices and stocks checked to record the movement of brands and the shares of the market held by each brand.

MEDIA RESEARCH: SOURCES OF STATISTICS

12. Independent media surveys

A number of research organisations produce regular independent media studies. They are 'independent' in the sense that they have tripartite sponsorship representing the three sides of advertising through bodies serving the advertisers (e.g. Incorporated Society of British Advertisers), advertising agencies (e.g. Institute of Practitioners in Advertising) and the relevant media bodies (e.g. Press Research Council, Outdoor Advertising Association,

Commercial Radio Companies Association or the Independent Television Commission). Some surveys are conducted continuously, as with press and television, or periodically as with radio, or occasionally as with outdoor.

In addition, individual media owners such as publishing houses, television contractors and London Underground conduct their own surveys. There is, therefore, a wealth of statistical information concerning readerships and audiences.

13. 'Readership' and 'circulation'

These two terms are sometimes misunderstood or even wrongly used to mean the same thing. They describe entirely different press media data. 'Readership' is an estimate of the number of people who *read* newspapers and magazines, and the figures result from surveying a sample of the reading public. 'Circulation' is the average audited net sale, or the number of copies actually *sold* at the full cover price, other copies being deducted from the total number printed.

Readership is estimated by means of extensive readership surveys (*see* also **16**). Readership is *not* found by multiplying the circulation figure by a given number. This would be nonsense if only that journals read in waiting rooms and hairdressing salons have readership figures far in excess of newspapers. The new Computer Assisted Personal Interview System was applied by the National Readership Survey in 1993.

Circulation figures are based on audited net sales, *not* field research. In their absence there are sometimes 'publishers' statements' which have been likened to 'publishers' lies'.

14. Audit Bureau of Circulations

The ABC was founded in 1931 (and there are today similar bureaux in other countries) to inform advertisers and advertising agencies of true numbers of newspapers or magazines which are sold or, in the case of controlled circulations, have reliable distribution against requests. It was created because publishers were selling advertisement space on the basis of spurious circulation figures which were often total print orders irrespective of the actual number of copies sold. Today the ABC works closely with *British Rate and Data*, and no ABC figure can be claimed unless it has been certified by the ABC. The procedure is for the publisher's own accountants to complete audit forms showing the net circulation figures. After scrutiny the ABC issues an audited net sale figure based on an average number of copies sold per day, week or month as the case may be over the preceding six-monthly period prior to 30 June and 31 December. (The figures in Table 5.3 are based on ABC audits.) About 3,000 British publications quote ABC figures. Exhibition attendances are also certified under the COA system introduced in 1993.

Thus, ABC figures are actual figures and are not based on interviews as in the case of readership figures. Readership figures, however, take into account secondary readership and are therefore much larger. A problem with ABC figures is that when copies are lost as a result of strikes, a publication can suffer a loss of sales through no fault of its own, that is, not because sales have fallen. It also has to be realised that at certain times of the year, and on certain days of the year, the circulation may be greater or smaller than the average ABC figure.

At one time sales fell for Saturday editions of dailies, mainly because those not working on a Saturday, and who normally bought their paper on the way to work, did not do so. However, recent ABC figures show that those papers which have Saturday magazines, actually sell more copies on a Saturday and less on a Monday. The Saturday magazine has induced people to buy a copy of the Saturday edition, or to place a regular home delivery order with a newsagent.

The comparative costs of different publications can be calculated on the basis of a cost-per-thousand net sale. In the competition for sale of advertisement space, ABC figures become a major sales argument.

The ABC also publishes the *ABC Media Buyer's Guide* which details the breakdown of circulation data held on each ABC Business Press Certificate of Circulation. This includes information on cover prices and subscription rates for 'paid for' publications, details of controlled circulation readers, and counter claims of publishers who refuse to reveal audited net sales. (*See* Figure 17.2.)

15. Verified Free Distribution

This development in the auditing of circulation figures was made necessary by the rapid growth of free newspapers. Again, advertisers are entitled to know reliable figures, which is not easy when copies are delivered door-to-door, handed out to passers-by in the street, or delivered in bulk to distribution centres. Verified Free Distribution is a subsidiary company launched by the ABC in 1981, resulting in credible data in this difficult field.

Delivered newspapers, magazines and directories can qualify for VFD certification, while bulk supplies (e.g. copies distributed by hotels, shops and airlines) receive BVS (Bulk Verification Services) certification. Vast numbers of copies are involved and the first 200 free newspaper titles to be registered with VFD represented 10 million copies distributed of each issue.

The Croydon Post carries the VFD symbol beside its title and for one six-month period its VFD figure of free copies was 107,997 copies. This free newspaper has an interesting history. Originally it was sold as the *Mid-Week Post*, sister paper of the long-established *Croydon Advertiser*. When it failed to sell it was converted into a free newspaper and with saturation house-to-house circulation it was able to command profitable advertisement revenue.

291

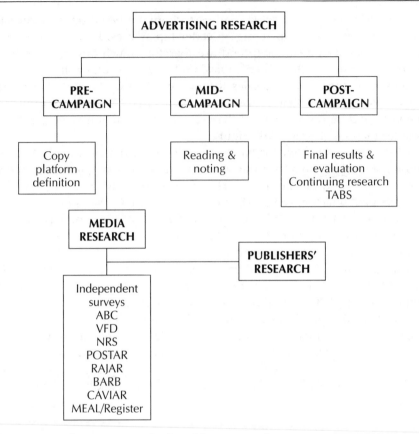

Figure 17.2 The anatomy of advertising research

Free newspapers are rather like controlled circulation magazines: guaranteed distribution on a big scale plus market penetration are big attractions for advertisers.

16. National Readership Surveys

The NRS took over from JICNARS in 1992. The constituent bodies of this tripartite independent research organisation are the Newspaper Publishers Association, the Periodical Publishers Association, the Institute of Practitioners in Advertising, and the Incorporated Society of British Advertisers.

Some 250 national newspapers and magazines are included in the readership survey, plus certain other specialist journals from time to time, and a sample of 35,000 people is interviewed. During the continuous survey, questions are asked about ITV viewing, listening to ILR, and cinema-going, in addition to many questions relating to readership. Using the A, B, C^1, C^2, D, E social grades which were devised specifically for JICNARS (the forerunner of the NRS 20 years earlier), demographic profiles are produced of the readership of each publication. As with ABC figures, NRS figures are issued every six months for the periods January–June and July–December.

There are three volumes. Volume 1 is a comprehensive one based on the fieldwork for the period July to the following June, and gives data on many topics including readership among special interest groups. Volume 2 carries similar data for the period January to December. Voume 3 has duplication tables. In addition there are various Bulletins such as monthly estimates for national newspapers, and early monthly estimates for journals which have undergone major changes, or are new publications.

These figures may be to the advantage or disadvantage of particular journals, but for advertisers and their advertising agencies NRS data provides revealing information about how many people of what kind read the 250 or so leading publications. Two papers with similar titles and circulations may appear to attract similar readers, but this may not be the case. Some journals may have large readerships because (like the *Financial Times* which has a small circulation) it is essential reading in business offices. Some magazines may enjoy large readerships because they are frequently passed on to other people, or they are read in doctors' or dentists' waiting-rooms or in hairdressing salons. These publications just go on being read and have long lives, like the *Reader's Digest*.

In selling space, NRS data can produce valuable support, and the following from an advertisement in the trade press for *Reader's Digest* is typical: 'Our readership is up by 60,000 to a massive 6,928,000. It's nice to know that the world's biggest magazine is still getting bigger.'

17. POSTAR

Structured poster audience traffic studies are carried out by POSTAR, Poster Audience Research, now the principal provider for the advertising industry. It supersedes both JICPAR and OSCAR. Both served the industry well in their time, but were overtaken by more sophisticated research methodology, as well as state-of-the-art computerisation and information technology.

POSTAR was set up in 1996 to provide independent on-going research into audiences for outdoor advertising. It operates as a joint industry body, addressing the needs of companies working in the outdoor medium, and the advertising industry as a whole.

The organisation was created, and is underpinned, by:

• OAA, The Outdoor Advertising Association;

• IPA, The Institute of Practitioners in Advertising;

• ISBA, The Incorporated Society of British Advertisers;

• COS, The Council of Outdoor Specialists – representing agency specialist outdoor media buyers.

293

POSTAR provides on-going data on poster audience traffic, coverage and frequency estimates. These indicate:

- how each site is located and panel positioned;
- how many people pass each panel;
- how they see it.

This information is obtained through:

- computer-modelled traffic counts;
- advanced visibility studies;
- extensive travel surveys.

The organisation indicates that POSTAR research not only counts those who pass a poster panel, and so have opportunities to see it. It also determines who looks at it. In one evaluation, for example, controlled-eye camera-photographed observations revealed what passers-by actually looked at, rather than what they said they looked at.

Applying this information, POSTAR provides data including:

- realistic and reliable cover and frequency data;
- Visibility Adjusted Impacts per panel (VAIs);
- panel numbers needed to reach campaign targets;
- how panel illumination and seasonal daylight changes affect cover.

These are applied across variables including:

- national, ITV area and conurbation campaigns;
- nine key demographic groups;
- three sizes of poster: 6-sheet, 48-sheet and 96-sheet.

In addition to JICPAR studies there have been those of the transport advertising contractors for buses and London Underground. One worth noting was the *See You In Barking* tracking study into awareness of bus advertising, carried out by the British Market Research Bureau for London Transport Advertising. About 70 different bus side campaigns were measured. Some 500 adults were interviewed at 40 sampling points and during home interviews. A test campaign was devised by London Transport Advertising consisting of a poster of barking dogs and a caption 'See You in Barking' which was placed on 750 T-sides for a month. After two weeks, the interviews revealed that 32 per cent recalled the poster, and after four weeks 37 per cent. Other campaigns scored from 8 per cent to 63 per cent awareness, but the majority scored 32–37 per cent awareness.

London Underground has its Tube Research Audience Classification (TRAC) research which bases its reports on information given by 5,000 Underground travellers who filled 28-day travel diaries. The TRAC database provides gross audience coverage and frequency for Underground advertisements. The data is reweighted to the latest Target Group Index (*see* also **22**).

18. Radio Joint Advertising Research

Radio audience research is carried out by RAJAR and this is commissioned and paid for by the individual ILR stations in membership of the Commercial Radio Companies Association. The five members of RAJAR are the Institute of Practitioners in Advertising, the Incorporated Society of British Advertisers, the Association of Media Independents, the CRCA and the BBC. It measures the percentage of UK adults (15+) population listening for at least five minutes in an average week. Average hours are the total hours of listening in a week, averaged across all listeners. The share of listening is the percentage of total listening time accounted for in the UK. A listening summary is issued every quarter.

From 1992 the BBC has been covered by the research. Data is collected continuously by means of random-location sampling, paid for by all the participating radio broadcasters. As before, there is personal placement and collection of a seven-day diary, with listening recorded on a quarter-hour basis, plus any other station category. For the first time, there is now comprehensive radio advertising research.

19. Broadcasters' Audience Research Board

Replacing JICTAR in 1981, and better known as BARB, it has an unfortunate title which is not easy to remember, and which encourages people to think that the 'B' stands for 'British' as in British Market Research Bureau (BMRB). The change came about with the combination of the television audience surveys of non-commercial BBC and commercial ITV. Previously, controversy had raged because the two services were subject to separate and very different weekly surveys resulting in conflicting figures.

For audience measurement, electronic meters are attached to a representative sample of television sets, and members of the household complete diaries to record their personal viewing, although this original JICTAR method has been modernised and developed to meet changed circumstances. There are now electronic methods of recording personal viewing, viewing on second sets in homes is now monitored, and there have been technical adjustments to cover the different viewing habits of viewers as between alternative channels (*see* also **5: 18**).

In February 1990 BARB appointed AGB Research and RSMB Television Research as joint contractors for television audience measurement with effect

295

from 1 August 1991. The new method was tested alongside the previous panel for three months prior to August 1991. A larger panel is used under the new contract, monitoring more TV sets and more channels, isolating timeshift viewing programme by programme from the playback statistics, and registering the age and sex of guest viewers instead of estimating them. The timeshift calculation takes into account the playing at a later date of videotaped programmes. Results are available, if required, on a daily basis, the basic method of receiving results being electronic instead of on paper as in the past.

BARB issues Top Ten TV Ratings and also measures satellite audiences.

20. MEAL/Register

The MEAL/Register is a combination of two former media research organisations, MEAL and the Media Register, the latter being formed originally to measure TV impacts and costs per thousand. The two now combine press and TV advertising expenditure. Figures tend to be higher than reality because they cannot allow for special deals. Their figures are widely quoted as sources of information on what advertisers are spending on advertising.

21. NTC Pocket Books

NTC Publications publish a series of compact pocket books on subjects such as Marketing, Regional Marketing, Media, Lifestyle and European Marketing. They are packed with statistics including breakdowns of advertising expenditure on most media, and by advertisers.

22. Target Group Index

This service run by the British Market Research Bureau takes a different approach to TV audience research, and the TGI panel of 24,000 adults questioned annually exceeds the number of homes in the BARB sample. It records the sample's demographic characteristics and media exposure and provides data covering 400 product fields. Questions on TV viewing are by hourly segments whereas BARB correspondents record quarter-hour segments. Respondents provide on-line data to the BMRB.

23. Advertising Statistics Yearbook

Published under the auspices of the Advertising Association, this annual publication is a comprehensive collection of advertising statistics.

The *Yearbook* covers advertising and the economy; cinema, direct mail, poster, national newspapers, regional newspapers, business and professional magazines, directories, radio and television advertising; advertising expenditure by product sector; top advertiser and agency statistics; and many other topics.

TRACKING STUDIES

24. Measuring the effect of advertising

Far more comprehensive than a next-day recall study is the system of tracking studies to measure the effect advertising has on target audiences rather than the incidence of impact or recall. This service is provided by TABS Ltd (Tracking, Advertising and Brand Strength), an independent market research company formed in 1976 to supply a national *continuous* weekly syndicated monitor to track 'brand health' and advertising effectiveness across all major media. The information aims to refine and optimise the advertising's creative execution and media planning and buying. With the growth of highly critical media independents whose services depend on media planning and buying skills, tracking studies can be a valuable means of increasing their efficiency.

25. Essential difference

Media planners and buyers seek to achieve maximum 'share of voice' for their clients. Traditional media research estimates 'opportunities to see' (OTS) or exposure to a campaign, but this is based on hypothetical analyses of what **might** have been achieved rather than what really happened. Because a certain volume of people of different categories saw or remembered an advertisement does not mean that they ultimately did anything about it. The reach of an advertisement may say something about which medium produced the highest numbers or percentages, and this may lead to the calculation of cost-per-thousand figures, but no more. It treats 'share of voice' in terms of share of *shouting*, whereas tracking studies go further and test the share of *hearing*. Measurement of OTS and cost-per-thousand remain important, but measurement of influence goes a long way further in testing the cost-effectiveness of advertising, and that is what advertisers (the agency clients) really need to know.

As POSTAR studies have demonstrated, it is now possible to research effectively beyond *opportunities* to see, into the more useful *likely to have seen*.

26. The TABS method

By combining computer technology and a very efficient self-completion questionnaire (*see* Figure 17.3), TABS monitors the *strengths* of reactions about advertised brands. The respondents place pencil ticks on scaled and other questions covering brand buying, brand usage, brand awareness, advertising awareness, brand goodwill, price image and detailed brand image. These pencil marks are read by an Optical Mark Reading computer, which converts them into scores and percentages among the target market for each of the various products or services covered. Responses are derived

SAINSBURY SUPERMARKETS		
Ever use nowadays? Yes ☐　　No ☐	Spend the most on groceries with them? Yes ☐　　No ☐	Never heard of this supermarket ☐ For me　Recently advertised a lot　Recently high priced
Mark ALL those boxes you feel fit these shops.	low prices ☐ foods are always fresh ☐ value for money ☐ friendly, helpful staff ☐ high quality products ☐	Not for me　Not at all　Low priced

Figure 17.3 Specimen page from a TABS questionnaire

from a representative sample in each of the ten main TV areas. The sample size is 500 adults each week, made up of 250 each of housewives and men, totalling 24,000 different adults a year.

27. TABS reports

Throughout the year subscribers receive 13 four-weekly reports. They cover FMCGs such as confectionery, drinks and toiletries, retailing, financial services, holidays and travel, durables (e.g. domestic appliances), clothing and do-it-yourself goods (e.g. decorating materials). This is an excellent example of continuous research. Moreover, the TABS measure is not a simple percentage awareness figure but is shown on a 10-point scaled score which is indexed 0–100. This picks up the different levels of a campaign's real impact on members of the target market which can range from very strong, clear and detailed recall through the many shades of grey to somebody who can scarcely remember a given campaign and may be confused about what they read, saw or heard and are not even sure about the brand.

28. Media covered

TABS scores for any given campaign are analysed not only among relevant subdivisions of the target market such as social class, age or with or without children but also according to the following *media consumption* criteria:

(a) readership of every named individual national daily newspaper;

(b) readership of every named individual national Sunday newspaper;

(c) weight of newspaper reading;

(d) readership of listing magazines (e.g. *Radio Times, TV Times, TV Quick, What's On TV*);

(e) readership of weekend newspaper magazines (e.g. *Sunday Times, Observer, Daily Telegraph, Mail on Sunday*);

(f) weight of ITV and other TV viewing (i.e. commercial television);

(g) Channel 4 TV viewing;

(h) breakfast ITV viewing (i.e. GMTV);

(i) listening to each of the named ILR stations;

(j) by all the different interlaced combinations of weight of ITV and satellite viewing, newspaper reading and ILR/INR listening.

29. Decay

The impact of advertising is subject to a deterioration or decay factor after advertising campaigns have ended, something which justifies sustained advertising and refutes the old argument about why advertise something with which everyone is familiar! Some campaigns are deliberately rested and it is important to know when advertising should be resumed. Brooke Bond PG Tips television chimp commercials are a case in point. TABS reports can reveal rates of decay and heritage effects where there is a halo effect from the company's other or earlier advertising. Associated with all this are media implications in terms of pattern and frequency when allocating the appropriation, whether to adopt regular 'drip' or sudden 'burst' tactics, and the best time to advertise cost-effectively.

30. Relation to media

When the information provided is married to data on media exposure, it is possible to separate the contribution made by the creative execution from that of the media spend and mix. TABS analyses then pin-points weaknesses in both creative and media aspects of the campaign by measuring real effects such as improved awareness, image or buying attitudes. The result is a £ for £ assessment of the quantitative contribution made by the press, TV and other media.

31. Cost

There is a set-up charge to prepare the study, and a rate is charged per brand per annum for either all adults or men or housewives only (some products may be bought mainly by only one sex). There are volume discounts for surveying 11 or more brands, which is an advantage to an agency handling many brands or a company with many brands. Costs are quoted for either women or men, or for all adults.

Note: The expression 'tracking' tends to be used very loosely to include various forms of recall and awareness testing, but the TABS example makes a very precise use of the term.

32. Evaluation

In evaluating media data it should be remembered that it concerns all three sides of advertising, the advertiser, the agency and the media owner. The first will judge the agency by its skilful use of media figures, the second will use the figures to plan media schedules, and the third will sell on the merits revealed by the figures.

Progress test 17

1. Describe some of the reasons for applying marketing research techniques to advertising. (1)

2. How reliable is research, and why should the resulting statistics be interpreted carefully? (2)

3. What problems or weaknesses are there concerning the evaluation of media in developing countries? (3)

4. How do social grades differ between Britain and developing countries? (4)

5. Name the three objectives of pre-advertising campaign research. (5)

6. What is motivational research, and how does it differ from other forms of research? (6)

7. How is a discussion group conducted? (6)

8. Describe the methods of pre-testing press advertisements and TV commercials. (7)

9. What is a keyed coupon and how can it be used to measure response? (9)

10. What are cost-per-reply and cost-per-conversion-into-sales figures? (9)

11. What is continuous research? (11)

12. Distinguish between 'readership' and 'circulation'. (13)

13. How are the circulations of free newspapers verified? (15)

14. Why are poster advertising statistics necessary? (17)

15. How do POSTAR studies help the media buyer? (17)

16. How does BARB measure television audiences? **(19)**

17. How can MEAL assist the advertiser? **(20)**

18. What is a TABS tracking study, and how does this technique provide data different from other advertising research? **(24–32)**

19. Explain the expression 'decay'. **(29)**

18

Law and ethics of advertising

LEGAL AND VOLUNTARY CONTROLS

1. Criticism of advertising

This book opens with the economic justification for advertising, and although the extent of advertising tends to reflect the prosperity and standard of living of a country, there are many critics of advertising. It is often accused by representatives of the intellectual left (including school teachers!) of being an immoral and parasitical force which exalts false values and induces people to buy things they either do not need or cannot afford. It is said to create expectations that cannot be satisfied. In fact, in Indonesia TV commercials were banned because they were thought to increase the expectations of poorer people! What these critics mean is that they would prefer to live in a primitive society, or at best the sort of medieval one which existed before the industrial revolution began to pioneer modern society.

Critics of advertising tend to make one very big fundamental mistake: they blame the *tool* and not the *user*. There is nothing wrong with *advertising*, but there are *advertisers* who abuse or misuse advertising, deliberately or unintentionally. Consequently, there are consumerist organisations, consumer protection laws, and representatives of the advertising industry who seek to control abuses of advertising. Note that we refer to abuses *of* and not *by* advertising. The distinction is vital to a proper understanding of this chapter.

2. Legal versus voluntary controls

Since the setting up of the National Vigilance Committee in 1926, the British advertising business has in its own interests sought to regulate advertising voluntarily. Various governments, but mostly Labour ones, have also sought to control advertising by imposing legislation. There are more than 250 statutes and regulations which are in some way relevant to advertising, and nowadays there are EC directives which concern advertising.

Some confusion exists over the merits and demerits of the two forms of control. Which is the more effective? Are both kinds of control necessary? These two questions invite very serious consideration for the answers are not simple beyond saying that both can be effective for different reasons, and both are valuable.

3. Characteristics of legislation

The main characteristics of legal control are as follows:

(a) There are written regulations which the advertiser should obey in the public interest, under penalty of fine or imprisonment if proved guilty of an offence.

(b) The law can be preventive in making known what is illegal.

(c) Some laws depend on interpretation by the courts, and may not be effective until a test case has occurred to set precedents.

(d) The law has to be invoked either by the plaintiff suing, or by the Crown deciding to prosecute, according to whether it is common or statute law. This can be costly and time-consuming, and it can take a long time for the case to come to court. By the time the case has been heard (and this might take three to five years) the original offence will have been committed, causing whatever harm it may, while the issue will have become history.

4. Characteristics of voluntary controls

These are different from those which apply to legal controls, and may be summarised as follows.

(a) There are written recommendations which the advertiser should obey in the public interest. An offending advertising agent risks losing his or her recognition status and right to commission, while the client risks damaging his or her reputation if a complaint is made to the Advertising Standards Authority (ASA) who publish their decisions in monthly reports which are widely quoted (*see* **38**).

(b) There are no penalties other than the above and the necessity to amend or withdraw an offending advertisement. The ASA has no power to impose fines.

(c) Voluntary controls are *self-regulatory* and are likely to prevent unethical advertising from appearing. The media act as censors, and advertising agents act as bulwarks, should an advertiser wish to advertise in a way likely to

303

offend against the British Codes of Advertising and Sales Promotion (BCASP). The media do not want complaints from readers and they have their own reputations to safeguard, while the agent does not wish to lose income by imperilling his right to commission. Once again, we see that responsibility for reputable or disreputable advertising rests with the advertiser, not with advertising.

(d) If there is a written complaint from any member of the public, and it is upheld by the ASA, action can be swift. The ad can be modified or withdrawn. In a very serious and urgent case, as when a complaint is made direct to the media, action can be instantaneous. This occurred on one occasion when an advertisement quite unintentionally caused offence by making a statement which coincided with a tragic event in the news – which was unanticipated when the ad was created – and the advertisement was withdrawn in a matter of hours. The offence was totally innocent but unfortunately the ad appeared to be in very poor taste to readers who did not appreciate that it had been produced many weeks in advance in order to be printed in a colour supplement.

There have been two instances where humorous ads have upset Islamic sensibilities, and the threat of trade sanctions brought about immediate apologies and withdrawal of the unintentionally offensive ads. One which implied that a sheikh had run out of oil for his car was intended to be funny, but it was regarded as being insulting by Muslims. A problem with many ads which provoke complaints is that the advertiser did not intend to cause offence. For instance, liquor ads provoke complaints from teetotallers!

(e) Generally, voluntary self-regulatory control can be more effective than legislation. It is interesting that in the past when the Advertising Association had its advertisement investigation department and administered voluntary controls, there was always the risk of incurring a libel action if an advertiser was criticised openly. The Advertising Standards Authority, however, was set up on a 'publish and be damned' basis to appease a Labour government which had accused the voluntary system of having no teeth, and wanted to introduce legislation which would be more effective.

(f) There is one exception where a code of practice is written into the law, and this is the ITC Code of Practice which was part of the Independent Broadcasting Authority Act 1973 and again forms part of the Broadcasting Act 1990. Although there are no prosecutions or penalties, the ITC does have the power of law in that certain categories of advertising are banned from commercial television and radio altogether, and all TV commercials have to be vetted before transmission. They can be rejected, or amendments may be required. The ITC Code is more far-reaching in its restrictions (which are not mere recommendations) and the viewer is well protected.

> We saw the successor to the Cortina in a different mould.
>
> Many people mourned the passing of the much loved Cortina. And, alas, they were not overjoyed with the replacement, the Sierra. 'A jelly mould' some have even been heard to say. Now at last a serious successor has arrived.
>
> The new Stellar 1.6 from Hyundai, the company that built Cortinas in the Far East. A car that makes other 1.6 saloons pale in comparison. At almost 2 inches longer and wider it makes a Cortina look small. With 5 speed gearbox, central locking, electric windows, headlamp washers, alloy wheels, and stereo radio-cassette the 1.6 GSL makes the nearest priced Sierra look rather basic.
>
> At £8,500 on the road the 1.6L even makes an Escort look expensive.
>
> 'Phone Teledata 081-200-0200 for a brochure and the name and address of your nearest dealer. HYUNDAI.
>
> The new Stellar 1.6. £8,500 to £9,500 on the road.

Figure 18.1 Example of 'knocking copy'

Television commercials are vetted by the Broadcast Advertising Clearance Centre (BACC) before transmission. Even so, the ITC may receive complaints after a commercial has appeared, and its rulings are given publicity in the press.

(g) There are certain aspects of advertising which are bad practice rather than anti-social or criminal, and the law cannot deal with them. Advertising is competitive, but there are limits. It does the industry no good if advertisers become too aggressive towards each other, and 'knocking copy' is a case in point. To denigrate a rival product is bad, but fair comparison is acceptable. Figure 18.1 is an interesting example of an advertisement which some people might consider derogatory, while others would accept it as making acceptable comparisons. It echoes the first Datsun ad in 1969 which made comparisons with the current model Cortina, and that caused a furore. *Marketing* (7 June 1984) referred to 'a provocative "new Cortina" platform', and said that 'the ads set a new standard in knocking copy'.

Doubtless the responsible advertising agents and the media found this copy acceptable, and doubtless Ford and Vauxhall were entitled to take a different view. The Advertising Standards Authority considered the Hyundai advertisement to be typical of the comparative ads which used to be common. Providing that substantiation for the claims is available and correct, the ASA would not question the ad. There would have been a question mark over the Hyundai ad if there had been any performance claims, but the copy was carefully phrased and there was no implication on performance. Readers may have been amused by the ad's audacity, but got the message, and the extent of the response received by Teledata would record the effectiveness of the ad.

305

Nevertheless, it was not as harsh as the one that appeared some years ago in the colour supplements, showing a rival make of car as a wreck on a scrap merchant's cart! We call this 'knocking copy', but the Americans have an even more apt expression – 'ashcanning'! If such advertising becomes too cut-throat, it does advertising no good, but occasionally the more piratical advertising can be ironically amusing and very impactive.

5. Common and statute law

There are two kinds of law. First, there is common law which is unwritten and largely based on precedent or what has been decided previously, and which requires the plaintiff to sue the defendant, the issue being decided on its merits by the judge. Aspects of common law relevant to advertising are discussed in **6–13** below. Second, there is statute law in which the rules and the penalties are set out in an Act (i.e. a Bill passed into law by Parliament and so placed on the Statute Book), and since an offence will be against the Crown, action can be taken by the public prosecutor against the accused. Examples of legislation which affect advertising are given in **14–29**.

LAW OF CONTRACT

6. Contracts

There are numerous occasions when advertisers, their advertising agents or their various suppliers are involved in contracts. To be legally binding a contract must have four elements, namely, an *offer*, an unconditional *acceptance* of the offer, and *consideration* in the form of some exchange or sacrifice while *consent* must be genuine and not wrongfully obtained. If the original offer is amended by the person to whom it was made it becomes a conditional acceptance which is now a new offer. This new offer has to be accepted by the other side. Thus, there could be an original offer to supply a brown bag for £5. If the offer is accepted, the £5 is paid, and the bag is supplied and there was no deceit, the contract is complete. But if the customer says he or she will pay £5 only if the bag is a blue one a new offer has been made, and the contract will be concluded only if the supplier now agrees to supply a blue bag, £5 is paid for it, and it is duly supplied.

A contract does not have to be in writing, provided the elements described above are adhered to, and verbal contracts often occur when orders are given on the telephone. If the order is completed in good faith the contract is valid, although should there be a dispute, written evidence is stronger and easier to prove in court than a conversation even if the work or service was carried out. Verbal contracts are therefore best confirmed in writing so that both sides are certain about their responsibilities. Advertisement space is often sold by telephone, especially classifieds with special telesales staff to either promote or receive orders. It is always wise to confirm in writing.

7. Definitions

It may be found useful to define the following terms:

(a) Simple contract. A simple contract is one that is not under seal, and as already stated above it can be made orally, in writing or implied.

(b) Express contract. This is one in which the terms are set out in words, either orally or in writing, by the partners.

(c) Implied contract. Here, circumstances tend to create the contract as when one takes a meal in a restaurant or occupies a room in a hotel, and the provision of the meal or room and its payment constitutes a contract although nothing is in writing.

(d) Executed contract. In this case, the contract is performed by one or both parties. Smith may agree to erect a fence if Jones pays the bill. If the fence is built and the payment is made the contract is executed. Usually dates are agreed for performance of the work and payment for it.

8. Contracts in advertising

An understanding of the law of contract is important to those engaged in all aspects of advertising. Contracts will arise in:

(a) the purchase of advertisement space and airtime;

(b) the hiring of outdoor advertisement sites and exhibition stand space;

(c) service agreements with advertising agents, public relations consultants and other professional consultants;

(d) the purchase of print, display material, photography and artwork.

The law of contract will also apply to many aspects of customer relations, and contractual obligations must be absolutely clear in coupons and literature which offer goods and expect payment. That is why direct response orders require a signature, as occurs in undertakings to buy so many books or CDs from a club.

9. Invitations to treat

If an advertisement (including a window display) merely offers goods for sale there is no obligation on the part of the seller actually to supply these on demand. Legally, there is only an *invitation to treat* and not an *offer*. An invitation can be withdrawn, and has no resemblance to an offer which is a

£100 REWARD

WILL BE PAID BY THE

CARBOLIC SMOKE BALL CO.

To any person who contracts the increasing Epidemic

INFLUENZA,

Colds, or any diseases caused by taking cold, AFTER HAVING USED the BALL 3 times daily for two weeks according to the printed directions supplied with each Ball.

£1,000

Is deposited with the ALLIANCE BANK, REGENT-STREET, showing our sincerity in the matter. During the last epidemic of Influenza many thousand CARBOLIC SMOKE BALLS were sold as Preventives against this Disease, and in no ascertained case was the disease contracted by those using the CARBOLIC SMOKE BALL.

One **CARBOLIC SMOKE BALL** will last a family several months, making it the cheapest remedy in the world at the price -- **10**s. post free. The BALL can be RE-FILLED at a cost of **5**s. Address:-

CARBOLIC SMOKE BALL CO.,

27, Princes-street, Hanover-sq, London, W.

Figure 18.2 Advertisement for the Carbolic Smoke Ball Company

single action to a *certain* person, otherwise the supplier would have to supply everyone who accepted the invitation irrespective of whether or not there was sufficient stock.

A leading case in consumer protection is *Carlill vs the Carbolic Smoke Ball Company*. Mrs Carlill saw the advertisement shown in Figure 18.2, bought the product, used it as prescribed, but contracted influenza within two weeks. She successfully sued the advertiser.

10. Void and voidable contracts

There are certain situations and conditions which can make a contract void or voidable, and these include the legal capacity of the parties.

(a) Mistake. This is not easy to prove, but if there is a genuine mistake a contract may be held to be void. A mistake could occur in the wording, or even the setting of the wording, of an advertisement. Usually advertisers are responsible for their own mistakes, but if the mistake applies to both parties, the contract is more likely to be void, as might happen if both sides held the same belief which proved to be wrong.

(b) Misrepresentation. A representation is a statement which, while not a term of the contract, nevertheless has an important influence upon acceptance. If this fact is proved to be untrue it becomes a misrepresentation, and the contract is void. A deceitful misrepresentation is a fraud.

(c) Privity. Only the parties privy to a contract, that is, aware of it and participating knowingly in the agreement, are affected or bound by it.

(d) Minors. Under the Family Law Reform Act 1969, the age of majority is 18 (instead of 21 as previously). Anyone below the age of 18 is, in law, a minor who has no capacity to enter into a legal contract.

(e) Persons of unsound mind and drunken persons. Contracts made by such people are void at their option if it can be shown that they were incapable of knowing what they were doing, and this condition was known to the other party, at the time of contracting.

DEFAMATION

11. Definitions

Damages may be sought if a person, organisation or product is intentionally or unintentionally brought into disrepute. Defamation takes two legal forms, spoken and transitory which is *slander* or *slander of goods* (which could occur in a derogatory advertisement), and *libel* which may be published or broadcast and can be permanent.

A libellous or scandalous statement must be:

(a) defamatory;

(b) false, unless the contrary is proved;

(c) understood to refer to the plaintiff;

(d) made known to at least one person other than the plaintiff.

It is therefore necessary to be careful about the use of pictures, such as ones obtained from a photo agency, if implications are made about people in them to which these people could object. One such case occurred when a picture of a queue of shoppers was used, and a balloon was attached to one person in which were drawn words which expressed the shopper's favourable opinion. This resulted in a successful libel action by the person who claimed not to be of that opinion.

309

12. Slander of goods

It is not often that the legal and voluntary controls coincide, but there are similarities between derogatory and therefore slanderous statements and knocking copy as prohibited by the BCASP. While the puffery of one product is obviously to the disadvantage of another, it is quite a different matter to savagely denigrate rival goods. Care has to be taken that comparisons are true, but it would be slanderous to publish, say, the results of tests which showed that named products were inferior. Comparisons have to confine themselves to indisputable facts such as brand A is available in five colours, brand B in ten colours, and not declare that the colours of brand A will fade but those of brand B will not.

An example of the difference between legal and voluntary codes was the case for libel made out by the Body Shop's lawyers in the High Court regarding Channel 4's 45-minute programme *Dispatches*. Body Shop won its case, but it took more than a year to bring it to court during which time it had to live with the smear that its claims and acts were insincere, and its profits fell by 4%. Damages of £273,000 were awarded for loss of profit, but this was less than half the loss Body Shop claimed in court that it had lost. An investigative programme of this kind can be costly for the victim, and it cannot be settled as quickly as one that comes within the BCASP.

It was a case of cynical media being unwilling to believe that a business can be socially responsible and still make a handsome profit. Body Shop had a reputation for selling products in its 950 shops world-wide which contained no ingredients until five years after they had been animal tested, but the programme said these claims were worthless. Help for the homeless, donations to the locality of a soap factory (although it operated at a loss), the sending of 60 volunteers to Romania, the recycling of large quantities of waste, environmental help, and aid for the Third World were discounted by the programme as a cynical mask which obscured the greed and hypocrisy of the company's founders Anita and Gordon Roddick. The Body Shop saw it as a degrading and inaccurate smear.

It is unfortunate that one of the penalties of having free media is that they will indulge in publishing or broadcasting libellous material of this kind, and even Esther Rantzen's *That's Life* was brought to court.

13. Passing off

This occurs when a product is packed in a deceptive package or 'get-up' which suggests it is a well-known brand, and it is bought on this misunderstanding. The injured party may sue for damages representing loss of business if:

(a) the trade name or get-up is associated with his or her goods in the public mind;

(b) the acts objected to have interfered with or are calculated to interfere with the conduct of business or sale of goods in the sense that there is confusion in the public mind.

Passing off has become a malpractice in a number of developing countries like Nigeria where famous imported brands have been impersonated in such a way that unsophisticated people have been misled by the similar-looking packs. The deceptions can be achieved by using the same colour, and by using a name which is spelt almost the same way as the original, e.g. Coka-Kola.

One British case concerned an original shaped container. When this was copied by a rival firm, and it was satisfactorily shown that lost sales had resulted from the deception, the owner of the original container won his case, even though it took a successful result in a House of Lords appeal to finally win the case.

STATUTE LAW

14. Typical statutes

There are far too many laws related to advertising to quote them all in a book of this size. Some statutes refer to particular trades, e.g. Pharmacy and Poisons Act, Fabrics (Misdescription) Act and the Fertilisers and Feeding Stuffs Act. In this book the reader will find it sufficient to be familiar with a selection of laws which are very much concerned with advertising.

15. Advertisements (Hire Purchase) Act 1967

This Act regulates advertisements giving hire-purchase terms which, for instance, must be correctly set out in a direct response advertisement so that the customer understands whether or not payment of instalments will incur payment higher than the cash price.

16. Consumer Credit Act 1974

Further regulations on the same theme are contained in this Act which also gives consumers the right to cancel a contract if 'oral representations were made in the presence of the debtor or hirer' in the discussion before the contract was undertaken. This usually refers to direct selling, and permits a 'cooling off' period of five days after the day when the customer received their copy of the agreement, e.g. an insurance policy sold by a visiting salesperson.

17. Consumer Protection Act 1987

This is one of the most important pieces of consumer legislation, and should be noted carefully by the student of advertising. It implemented in the UK the EC Product Liability Directive. Earlier Acts are amended by this Act. There are parts on Product Liability, Consumer Safety and Misleading Price Indications. All previous legislation on prices is repealed, and there are stringent controls on bogus prices. A general duty is imposed on producers and suppliers to sell safe products. Producers, importers and own labellers are liable for unlimited damages for defects which cause injury or death. No proof of negligence or contractual relationship is needed. Retailers must be careful not to sell dubious foreign products, e.g. dangerous Christmas tree lights or toys, but such products can be recalled urgently to avoid an offence.

18. Control of Misleading Advertisements Regulations 1988

This piece of consumer legislation implements a Council Directive of the EC and is an example of the harmonising of Common Market legislation under the European Communities Act 1972. The Director-General of Fair Trading gives powers to institute a High Court action for injunction prohibiting misleading advertising, always provided that the complainant has failed to obtain satisfaction from a voluntary body such as the Advertising Standards Authority. The regulations are not intended to compete with the British Codes of Advertising and Sales Promotion, but do provide a legal last resort if a complainant to the ASA has a complaint dismissed.

19. Copyright, Designs and Patents Act 1988

The Act restates the law of copyright as set out in the Copyright Act 1956; makes new provisions as to the rights of performers and others in performances; confers a design right in original designs; amends the Registered Designs Act 1949; makes provisions with respect to patent agents and trade mark agents; confers patents and designs jurisdiction in certain county courts; amends law of patents; makes provisions with respect of devices designed to circumvent copy protection of works in electronic form; makes new provisions penalising the fraudulent reception of transmissions; and makes the fraudulent application or use of a trade mark an offence.

Copyright subsists in original literary, dramatic, musical or artistic works; sound recordings, films, broadcasts or cable programmes; typographical arrangements of published editions. Copyright does not subsist in a work unless the qualification requirements are satisfied as regards the author, the country in which the work was first published, or, in the case of a broadcast or cable programme, the country from which the broadcast was sent.

Copyright does not subsist in literary, dramatic or musical work unless and until it is recorded, in writing or otherwise. Usually, the duration of copyright is for 50 years from the calendar year in which the author dies, film is released, broadcast is made or is included in a cable programme.

The first owner of copyright is the author of a work unless where a literary, dramatic, musical or artistic work is made by an employee in the course of his or her employment, when the employer is the first owner subject to any agreement to the contrary. Thus, an advertising agency will own copyright of advertising material produced for a client, unless in the service contract it is agreed to assign the copyright to the client.

A major change so far as advertising and public relations is concerned is that whereas under the 1956 Act the photographer owned the copyright of the negative he or she now owns the copyright of the print. Copyright can be assigned but this must be agreed when commissioning photography, or in the contract of service between a client and an agency or consultancy. The client (e.g. the advertiser) does not automatically own the copyright though having paid for the work.

20. Data Protection Act 1986

This is an Act of some importance regarding databases and mailing lists as used for direct mail and direct response purposes. Holders of computerised data have to register with the Data Protection Register. Copies of the Register are held in public libraries. Members of the public are entitled to apply for print-outs of data held about themselves, provided they know who holds the information and on which of their files it is held.

21. Fair Trading Act 1973

This Act has had a very significant effect on monopolistic practices in the advertising business. The Act provided for the appointment of a Director-General of Fair Trading and staff to study the effect upon consumers' interests of trading practices and commercial activities, and to advise on any necessary or desirable action. It is called the 'Consumers' Charter'. In November 1976 the Office of Fair Trading ruled that the traditional advertising agency recognition and commission system was an illegal monopoly under the Restrictive Trade Practices Act 1976 (see 4: 9).

Today a recognised advertising agency is guaranteed no standard rate of commission, but must negotiate commission rates with the media.

Under its new concept of *consumer trade practices*, that is, any method of undertaking the supply of goods or services, the Act refers to:

(a) the terms or conditions (whether as to price or otherwise) on or subject to which goods or services are or are sought to be supplied, or

(b) the manner in which these terms or conditions are communicated to persons to whom goods are or are sought to be supplied or for whom services are or are sought to be supplied, or

(c) promotion (by advertising, labelling or marking of goods, canvassing or otherwise) of the supply of goods or of the supply of services;

(d) methods of salesmanship employed in dealing with customers, or

(e) the way in which goods are packed or otherwise got up for the purpose of being supplied, or

(f) methods of demanding or securing payment for goods or services supplied.

The Director-General, if he or she considers a trade practice offensive, may propose an order for the control of the practice for consideration by the Consumer Protection Advisory Committee, and upon their recommendation the Director-General can ask the Secretary of State to place the proposed legislation before Parliament.

22. Lotteries and Amusements Act 1976

Advertisements relating to competitions or sales promotion schemes in the form of prize contests have to comply with this Act, the chief point being that a competition must contain an element of skill, otherwise it is a lottery. A lottery is a distribution of prizes by lot or chance.

However, matching numbers (as used in petrol promotions) are excluded because customers do not literally compete with each other or buy a scratch card. Two examples have been the Woolworth £1 million Family Game, store visitors receiving a free ticket or scratch card each time they visited a Woolworth/Woolco store irrespective of whether they made a purchase. Similarly, Esso had their Find the Tiger game, free scratch cards being given to drivers calling at Esso dealers, again with the proviso that no purchase was required. Although no skill was involved, there was no lottery since the players were virtually offered a gift which they might or might not be lucky enough to win. The two schemes sought to get people to visit the store or petrol station, but they were not obliged to buy anything and, in effect, purchase a lottery ticket. However, such promotions may be loosely termed 'lotteries' although they do not come within the provisions of the Act. A lottery requires an entry payment.

The National Lottery, established by Act of Parliament in October 1993, ensures that funds are distributed equally among arts, sports, heritage, charities and millennium projects – known as the Five Good Causes. In 1998, a further Act set up a Lottery Commission and a sixth Good Cause, the New Opportunities Fund.

23. Restrictive Trade Practices Act 1976

This could apply if a manufacturer tried to restrict supplies of goods because they were being offered as gifts. The Act also resulted in changes in the recognition and commission system (*see* 4: **9**).

24. Supply of Goods (Implied Terms) Act 1973

This Act amends the Sale of Goods Act 1893 to guarantee consumers' rights under the old Act, and combats unfair guarantees which claim to exclude consumer rights under the 1893 Act.

25. Trade Descriptions Act 1968

This Act is very important and its provisions must be observed when writing descriptions of goods in advertisements and catalogues and on labels, packaging or other descriptive or promotional material. It replaced the unworkable Merchandise Marks Act 1953 which required private legal action, and enforcement is now made through Weights and Measures and other officials. The Consumer Protection Act has taken over much of this Act. The three main offences are:

(a) false or misleading trade descriptions;

(b) false or misleading indications as to the price of goods;

(c) false or misleading statements as to services, accommodation or facilities.

The Act now applies to services as well as goods.

26. Definitions of trade description

The 1968 Act defines a *trade description* as an indication, direct or indirect, and by whatever means given, as to the:

(a) quantity, size or gauge;

(b) method of manufacture, production, processing or reconditioning;

(c) composition;

(d) fitness for purpose, strength, performance, behaviour or accuracy;

(e) any physical characteristics not included above;

(f) testing by any person and results thereof;

(g) approval by any person or conformity with a type approved by any person;

(h) place or date of manufacture, production, processing or reconditioning;

(i) person by whom manufactured, produced, processed or reconditioned.

(j) other history, including previous ownership or use.

27. Implications

An important effect of the Act is the ban on false sale prices in retail stores, and under the '28-day clause' goods advertised at a reduced price must have been on sale at the full price over a period of 28 days during the previous six months. There have, however, been certain abuses which the Office of Fair Trading has been powerless to control, when advertisements have offered goods at reduced prices although the higher price occurred at only one branch of a chain of shops. This seems to be a mockery of the Act.

The copywriter has to be very careful that the descriptions he or she writes are correct, and it is very easy to accept given information from merchandise buyers or suppliers. A number of prosecutions have occurred because of false or misleading descriptions which were in fact written in good faith and with no intention to mislead. Examples have been direct response catalogues and package tour brochures. The copywriter really has to be suspicious of claims that bedrooms have particular views, or that the hotel is only so many minutes from the sea. The Act imposes serious responsibilities on those making claims in promotional copy, and it is no excuse in law that another party's information was relied upon. People can make very optimistic generalisations, and some very famous companies have been heavily fined for their carelessness.

28. Imported goods

The Trade Descriptions Act 1972 concerned imported goods bearing UK names or marks, and names or marks which resembled UK ones. This Act was repealed under the Consumer Protection Act 1989 which took over the 1972 Act's provisions. However, the Trade Descriptions Act 1968 remains valid regarding, say, deceitful labelling and advertising of wines which have a recognised source of supply. One must say 'Cyprus' or 'South African' sherry, and not just sherry. The champagne shippers have prosecuted those misrepresenting champagne, including a British firm which sold elderflower champagne.

29. Trade Marks Act 1938

A trade mark includes 'a device, brand, heading, label, ticket, name, signature, word, letter, numeral or combination thereof'.

It is 'a mark used or proposed to be used in relation to goods for the purpose of indicating or so as to indicate a connection in the course of trade between the goods and some person having the right either as a proprietor or registered user to use the mark, whether with or without any indication of the identity of that person'. Sometimes, trade marks may be logotypes, but not necessarily, and a company may use both a registered trade mark and a separate logo. Briefly, a trade mark must have one at least of the following characteristics.

(a) Name of a company, individual or firm represented in a special or particular manner.

(b) Signature of the applicant for registration or some predecessor in his or her business.

(c) An invented word or words.

(d) A word or words having no direct reference to the character or quality of the goods, and not being according to its ordinary signification a geographical name or a surname.

(e) Any other distinctive mark, but a name, signature or word other than such as fall within (a)–(d) above is not registrable, except upon evidence of its distinctiveness.

30. Unfair Contract Terms Act 1977

This Act is important where guarantees and hire purchase agreements are concerned. When a consumer suffers loss or damage because goods are defective, no guarantee can limit or exclude liability if the manufacturer or supplier was negligent. The Act also protects the consumer from exclusion clauses in guarantees, as originally introduced in the Supply of Goods (Implied Terms) Act 1973.

31. Unsolicited Goods and Services Acts 1971 and 1975

The object of these Acts is to protect the consumer from *inertia selling*, that is the sending of goods which were not ordered but for which the recipient feels responsible. Such goods become the recipient's property if, during a six-month period starting with the day of receipt, the sender fails to regain possession, and the recipient does not unreasonably prevent repossession. However, this six-month period may be shortened if the recipient requests repossession by the sender within 30 days of expiration of the six-month period. If the sender does not repossess the goods by the end of the six-month period, the goods become the property of the recipient.

Even so, the recipient of unwanted goods must take care of them, and there was the case of a householder who had an unordered pot of cream deposited on the doorstep by the milkman. She left it there to deteriorate, but the Court held she should have put it in her refrigerator.

While the pot of cream example was no doubt a mistake, there are unscrupulous traders who exploit the fear of the recipient, especially when they receive strongly worded payment demands.

There are also other provisions. If a person is charged for unauthorised directory entries, he is not obliged to pay for them. The distribution of advertisements of a sexual nature are prohibited.

A variation of the directory entry racket is to send people invoices which offer a generous discount for immediate payment. But no directory has ever been published, and there is no entry to pay for. Such invoices are apt to be paid by accounts departments alert to discount offers.

32. Wireless Telegraphy Act 1984

This Act aims to combat pirate radio, that is the operation of commercial radio stations outside the authority of the Radio Authority and competing with the authorised independent local radio stations. The Act gives officers of the British Telecom Radio Interference Services the power to seize offending equipment. In 1983, for instance, there were 97 raids on pirates resulting in 40 people being convicted. Some broadcast copyright material such as Independent Radio News bulletins. Radio Jackie attempted to pay a fee to the Mechanised Copyright Protection Society, but it was not accepted. However, pirate stations do not normally make copyright payments for records played, nor pay trade union rates, and they exploit transmitter power and even usurp frequencies intended for authorised stations. The maximum fine for broadcasting without a licence is £2,000. While it is not illegal for advertisers to buy airtime on pirate radio, the medium is obviously a precarious one. Pirate stations have been killed by the competition from BBC and ILR stations.

VOLUNTARY CONTROLS

33. Codes of practice

There are several codes dealing with advertising in general (except radio and TV which are covered by the codes of practice of the Independent Television Commission and the Radio Authority), and certain specialised fields such as sales promotion, direct mail and transportation advertising. There are also the codes of conduct of the Institute of Public Relations and the Public Relations Consultants Association. The advertising control system is set out in Figure 18.3.

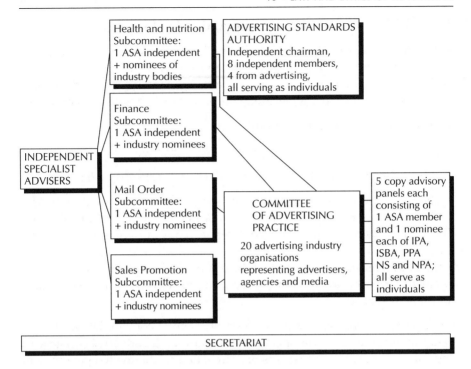

Figure 18.3 Organisation of the advertising control system

34. Historical development

The British advertising business has a long and creditable history of voluntary control beginning with the creation of the National Vigilance Committee in 1926, the pioneer efforts of the Advertising Association in the 1930s, the first joint industry code of 1948 known as the British Code of Standards in Relation to the Advertising of Medicines and Treatments, and today's comprehensive British Codes of Advertising and Sales Promotion.

35. Revisions to codes

Codes of practice are constantly under review. The latest British Codes of Advertising and Sales Promotion, published October 1999, became fully operational on 31 January 2000. There are new rules on political advertising, prices and protection policy; betting and gaming, following government deregulation; and a new section on the independent reviewer for ASA adjudications. An important amendment to the 'payments by results', clause 9, was made to the IPR Code of Professional Conduct. The following are general descriptions and the latest edition of each code should be obtained from the addresses in Appendix 1.

36. British Codes of Advertising and Sales Promotion

These are a set of rules by which the British advertising industry has agreed that the majority of advertisements it produces should be regulated. It is under the general supervision of the Advertising Standards Authority (ASA).

The codes require that advertisements and sales promotions should be:

- legal, decent, honest and truthful;

- prepared with a sense of responsibility to consumers and society;

- in line with the principles of fair competition generally accepted in business.

The codes are devised by the Committee of Advertising Practice (CAP). CAP members include advertising, sales promotion and media businesses. The CAP provides a free and confidential copy advice service for the industry.

If an advertisement or promotion breaks the codes, advertisers are asked to amend or withdraw it. If they choose not to comply, a number of sanctions are available:

(a) Adverse publicity. The ASA's monthly reports contain details of complaint adjudications. These include the names of the advertisers, agencies and media involved. The reports are circulated to the media, government agencies, the advertising industry, consumer bodies and the public. Published cases receive media coverage.

(b) Refusal of further advertising space. Media can be asked to enforce their standard terms of business, which require compliance with the codes. They may decide to refuse further space to advertisers.

(c) Removal of trade incentives. Advertisers and their agencies may jeopardise their membership of trade and professional organisations. This could result in the loss of financial and other trading benefits.

(d) Legal proceedings. Ultimately, the ASA can refer a misleading advertisement to the Office of Fair Trading (OFT). The OFT can obtain an injunction to prevent advertisers using the same or similar claims in future advertisements.

The BCASP establishes a standard against which advertisements and sales promotion may be assessed. It is a guide to those concerned with commissioning, creating and publishing advertisements and sales promotion activities. It is also available to those who believe they may have reason to question what an advertisement says or shows. In this capacity, it helps to protect the public against misleading and offensive advertising.

The CAP is the self-regulatory body that devises and enforces the codes. CAP's members include the following organisations that represent the advertising, sales promotion and media businesses:

Advertising Association
Association of Household Distributors
Association of Media and Communications Specialists
Broadcast Advertising Clearance Centre
Cinema Advertising Association
Council of Outdoor Specialists
Direct Mail Services Standards Board
Direct Marketing Association (UK)
Direct Selling Association
Incorporated Society of British Advertisers
Institute of Practitioners in Advertising
Institute of Sales Promotion
Mail Order Traders' Association
Mailing Preference Service
Newspaper Publishers' Association
Newspaper Society
Outdoor Advertising Association
Periodical Publishers' Association
Proprietary Association of Great Britain
Royal Mail
Scottish Daily Newspaper Society
Scottish Newspaper Publishers' Association

The codes apply to:

(a) advertisements in newspapers, magazines, brochures, leaflets, circulars, mailings, catalogues and other printed publications, fax transmissions, posters and aerial announcements;

(b) cinema and video commercials;

(c) advertisements in non-broadcast electronic media such as the Internet and computer games;

(d) viewdata services;

(e) mailing lists, except for business-to-business;

(f) sales promotions;

(g) advertisement promotions;

(h) advertisements and promotions covered by the Cigarette Code.

The codes do not apply to:

(a) broadcast commercials – these are the responsibility of the Independent Television Commission or the Radio Authority;

321

(b) the content of premium rate telephone calls, which are the responsibility of the Independent Committee for the Supervision of Standards of Telephone Information Services;

(c) advertisements in foreign media;

(d) health-related claims in advertisements and promotions addressed only to the medical and allied professions;

(e) classified private advertisements;

(f) statutory, public, police and other official notices;

(g) works of art exhibited in public places;

(h) private correspondence;

(i) oral communications, including telephone calls;

(j) news releases and other public relations material;

(k) the content of books and editorial communications;

(l) regular competitions, including crosswords;

(m) flyposting;

(n) packages, wrappers, labels and tickets, unless they advertise a sales promotion or are visible in an advertisement;

(o) point of sale displays, except for those covered by the Sales Promotion Code and the Cigarette Code.

37. Contents of the BCASP

The code is very extensive and covers many areas which are not covered by statute law. These include knocking copy and comparative advertising, the false use of the words 'free' if a direct cost is actually involved, and misleading testimonials. It also covers unacceptable practices connected with advertising and health claims. In particular the code deals with products or services for which misleading claims may be made such as collectables, slimming products, advertisements relating to children, credit and investment advertising, mail-order advertising, and advertising for cigarettes, alcoholic drinks and vitamins.

38. Complaints by the public

Advertisements appear in the media inviting members of the public to submit advertisements which they believe offend against the code (*see* Figure 18.4). The Advertising Standards Authority, which administers the code,

Figure 18.4 An ASA advertisement addressed to the public and inserted by publishers as a 'filler'

investigates complaints which are justified (some are frivolous, outside the code or concerning media such as TV/radio which do not come within its jurisdiction). An *ASA Monthly Report* is published on free circulation to anyone interested (including the press), and the following is quoted from an editorial in *ASA Case Report 177* (January 1990), headed *A Shade Less Green* which discussed the exploitation of green issues by advertisers:

> Six months has passed since the Authority last commented on 'green' advertising. A lot has happened in that time. The environment is still clearly the concern of the moment for many consumers and they continue to use the power of discretionary buying to make this known. In these circumstances the developing green tint of much advertising is not surprising. It is however reassuring that advertisers seem to be taking much greater care to ensure that 'green' claims neither mislead nor confuse.
>
> While we continue to receive public complaints about environmental claims an increasing number of businesses are presenting their 'green' claims in a comparative rather than absolute manner. 'Green' has given way to 'greener' and 'environmentally friendlier' has taken over from the much criticised blanket claim of 'environmentally friendly' (which only a few months ago headed many a misleading green advertisement).
>
> Industry is now offering products which are undoubtedly less harmful to the environment than those previously available and provided that any claims are accurate and clearly presented we do not object to their environmental advertising platform. We all know that cars cause air pollution but cars running on unleaded fuel will cause less. It was on this basis that we did not object to an advertisement for unleaded fuel which featured an illustration of rolling

countryside; the advertised product was unarguably more 'green' than normal fuel. We appreciated the complainants' point that pollution from cars can damage the countryside but the message of the advertisement was clear: a car which runs on unleaded fuel does less damage to the environment than one which does not.

When obvious inaccuracies are pointed out to advertisers corrective measures are generally swift. One car advertiser claimed that his unleaded petrol was 'good for the environment'. We took the view that this was too absolute a claim: unleaded petrol is certainly better for the environment, but claiming that it is 'good' is an exaggeration. Within days the advertiser agreed to make the necessary changes.

A leaflet advertising a new soap powder claimed that the product concerned was 'greener'; complainants maintained that any washing powder causes some harm to the environment and objected to the claim on this basis. The advertisement did not however claim that the product was green, only greener, and we felt this was reasonable.

We were not so sympathetic to claims by other advertisers that their products did no harm at all to the environment. If advertisers make this type of absolute claim they must be prepared to provide us with detailed substantiation in their support.

It should be noted that we have received several complaints about a recent series of 'green' advertisements placed by the nuclear power industry. As we have said many times before such advertisements are clearly putting forward arguments about a matter of public controversy/policy and the ASA would be straying beyond its terms of reference if it sought to censure debate on such matters. This may disappoint many an environmental pressure group but this is the position we must take (and it's also the position we take towards their advertising on the same subject).

Our Monitoring department has specifically targeted green advertisements since May 1989. While we have acted to stop unjustified use of the 'environmentally friendly' banner the majority of the advertisements sampled have been unobjectionable. With such a complex subject and such a diversity of claims it is necessary to undertake individual assessments of most advertisements. A claim for environmental 'friendliness' may be acceptable in an advertisement for a biodegradable adhesive tape product but it is most certainly not justified when linked to products still containing many elements which may be potentially harmful to the environment. The removal of one noxious substance alone is not sufficient to make an absolute 'green' claim.

Shortly after our first foray into the environmental arena, the Incorporated Society of British Advertisers discussed the development of 'green' claims in advertisements and shared our concern that some advertisers were showing a definite lack of restraint in their pursuit of the 'green' consumer. ISBA have now published a guidance booklet for their members on making environmental claims and this will usefully support the ASA's efforts to assist the business in this fast-moving area.

The upsurge in requests from advertisers for advice on the content of their 'green' advertising is encouraging and demonstrates the responsible attitude many have taken. Several major advertisers made significant amendments to their proposed advertising when possible problems under the Code were pointed out. It can be argued that with the complexity of environmental issues involved and the rate of increase of public awareness even the most careful advertisers can rapidly find themselves up against the thin line of acceptability.

As well as getting their facts *right* advertisers must ensure that facts are presented clearly. There is still a tendency amongst some advertisers to cloak claims that their products are beneficial to the environment in extravagant language. While this may present the claim as forcefully as possible it will most probably have the effect of confusing (and possibly misleading). Shaking consumers' confidence in advertising and provoking cynicism is not the way forward.

In the long term no advertising will be successful unless it is believable and proven to be true. Green advertising is no exception to this rule and generally advertisers appear to have realised that they will do themselves (and their customers) a disservice if they are not as scrupulous about the accuracy of 'green' claims as they would be about any other. The trend is unquestionably in the right direction. We intend to make sure it stays that way.

39. Typical ASA rulings

One might expect that the advertisers who offend against the BCASP, and about whom complaints are made to the ASA, would be obscure little advertisers who were unaware of the existence of voluntary controls. Yet every month the ASA publishes a report of complaints received, not upheld but in the main upheld against famous advertisers.

For example, the ASA Monthly Report 23 upheld complaints against Air Canada, Anglian Windows, Barclays Bank, Citroen, Co-operative Retail Services, Daihatsu, Forte, Haringay Council, Hospital Savings Association, Ingham Travel, International Distillers and Vintners, Jersey Tourism, Kuoni Travel, London Docklands Development Corporation, National Magazine Company, Private Patients Plan, Saab, Texas Homecare, and Whitbread Inns to name only some.

The previous month's Report 22 revealed that no fewer than six of the culprits were the publishers Express Newspapers, Manchester Evening News, Mirror Group Newspapers, News Group Newspapers, Newspaper Publishing and Scottish Daily Record. Not only is the British press notorious for its character assassinating editorials, and for flouting the law with its illegal lotteries, but it disregards the BCASP. Since the press trade associations are members of the Committee of Advertising Practice which is supposed to enforce the code it is a case of gamekeepers turned poachers.

The six cases reported by ASA provoked Torin Douglas to write a whole page feature article in *Marketing Week* with the headline *What the papers don't say*. Torin Douglas began by pointing out that 'Of all the people who ought to know the rules of the Advertising Standards Authority, you might think newspaper executives would be top of the list. It is their companies' money – raised by 0–1 per cent levy on their advertising revenue – that pays for the vast majority of the ASA's staff, premises and monitoring activity.'

The worst offender was, as usual, the *Daily Express* which had dared the public prosecutor to take legal action against its Duchess of Windsor necklace lottery, and proved to be above the law. It had had two previous complaints upheld by the ASA. The March 1993 complaint was sent to the ASA by the OFT, no less, under the Misleading Advertisements Regulations 1988. This time the complaint concerned a six-week competition in the *Sunday* and *Daily Express*. A car was to be won by matching the numbers on their game card to 'winning number plates', *but* the truth was that a significant number of cards had been issued with pre-determined losing numbers! This nullified the newspapers' claim that 'Every day there was a chance for you to win', but the so-called chance was negligible. The ASA's adjudication was as follows:

Adjudication: Complaint upheld.
The advertisers acknowledged that the promotion was a controlled scheme whereby the majority of game cards were pre-determined losers but stated that every person had an equal chance of receiving one of the potentially winning cards. While noting this, the Authority considered that in a controlled scheme involving repeat-entry devices, participants should not be given the impression that each day they had an equal chance with other participants of winning a prize. It requested the advertisers to avoid such an impression and to ensure that future promotional cards clearly indicated the precise nature of the scheme.

Two of the complaints were about front page offers which did not make it clear that further purchases were necessary. The *Manchester Evening News* made two front page offers for McDonald's 99p meal vouchers, but in both cases the actual voucher was not published until the next day, thus requiring purchase of another copy of the newspaper. The front page announcement read 'Big Mac Special Offer Voucher Details page 12'. In spite of the plea of a typographical error (sic!) the ASA's adjudication upheld the complaint in the following terms:

Adjudication: Complaint upheld.
The publications, with whom the advertisers had run a joint promotion, stated that the failure to indicate that only details of the offer were available inside was due to a typographical error. McDonalds had subsequently taken action to feature vouchers every evening to avoid confusion. The Authority considered that the publication should take care to ensure that any condition that may influence a consumer's decision to participate should be made clear and requested that the publishers exercise greater caution when running further promotions of this nature.

The similar complaint against the *Daily Mirror* (against whom there had been two previous complaints which the ASA had upheld) was about a front page flash 'Free! Soul hit tapes for every reader'. But inside the paper it was found that readers had to collect two tokens to qualify. In this case the ASA's adjudication was:

> Adjudication: Complaint upheld.
> The advertisers stated that the full conditions of the offer had been clearly indicated on the inside pages. The Authority considered that an indication that further purchases were necessary should have been made on the front cover and noted that similar complaints had been upheld against the advertisers in the past. The Authority was concerned at the advertisers' disregard for the Code and requested that future offers comply with its requirements.

News Group Newspapers, who publish the *Sun* and the *News of the World*, now had its fourth complaint in a year upheld by the ASA. Objections were raised to two national press advertisements for the *News of the World* headed 'Missing persons' which claimed 'An advertisement in the "Unclaimed Money" or "Missing Persons" category of the *News of the World* is read by over 12.6 million people (Source NRS July 92)'. One of the advertisements went on to state 'half the entire population of the UK'. One complainant questioned the first claim on the basis that general readership figures did not apply to specific advertising columns. The other questioned that half the entire population of the UK was 12.6 million. The ASA's adjudication was:

> Adjudication: Complaints upheld.
> The advertisers stated that the advertisements should not have been placed and accepted that both versions were misleading. Furthermore they stated that the reference to the population of the UK was an error. The Authority was concerned at the inaccuracy and that the NRS figure given had been used to imply that 12.6 million people read the advertising column. It noted the advertisers' assurance that such an approach would be avoided in future and greater care would be taken.

Surprisingly, the fifth complaint was against *The Independent* which had made a reader offer for the Filter Fresh water filter system which claimed 'Filter Fresh also reduces levels of chlorine and heavy metals in tap water which cause cloudiness. It does not, however, reduce the beneficial trace elements in the water, nor does it negate the effects of fluoridation'. The complainant objected on the grounds that:

(1) Chlorine and heavy metals did not cause cloudiness in tap water, and cloudiness in public supply tap water was rare in the United Kingdom, and

(2) the advertisement implied that heavy metals were found in tap water in quantities which were a serious problem to health, whereas most UK water complied with the EEC requirements.

327

In this case ASA's adjudication was:

Adjudication: Complaint upheld.
1. The advertisers confirmed that cloudiness in the tap water was often caused by organic matter, not by chlorine and heavy metals, as stated in the advertisement. The Authority noted that the advertisers had agreed to amend future copy.
2. The advertisers did not consider the reference to heavy metals to imply that these elements constituted a health risk. The Authority considered the inclusion of a reference to heavy metals implied that they were contained in tap water in sufficient quantities to constitute a health risk and that this had not been supported. It requested the advertisers to delete the claim.

Finally, there was the complaint against lack of stock to satisfy an editorial offer in the *Scottish Daily Record*. A Trading Standards Department complained about an offer headlined 'Don't get killed cutting the grass' and stating '*The Daily Record* today launches a campaign to help give protection for our readers and their families against the risk of electrocution . . .' and mentioned a recent fatality by electrocution. The editorial offered a voucher entitling the bearer to £5 off a circuit breaker. The complainant tried to obtain a circuit breaker using the voucher but found it was out of stock. He therefore challenged whether the promoters had adequate stocks to service the offer.

This is something of a cautionary tale, not unlike those numerous sales promotion disasters when a brand manager has failed to ensure that the supplier can meet a large and sudden demand. It is a case of bad management rather than unscrupulous promoting. The ASA ruled that it was a cock up and adjudicated as follows:

Adjudication: Complaint upheld.
The promoters stated that stock could not be immediately guaranteed as the offer had been made quickly in response to the fatality. Staff had been issued with instructions by their internal electronic message system to stamp the voucher if they were out of stock so that consumers could use it when new stocks became available. The promoters were, however, unable to provide details of these instructions, although it was noted that the information had been included in the following day's newspaper. The Authority was concerned that in the complainant's case the voucher was not stamped and that the information was not included in the original offer. It also considered that inadequate arrangements had been made to avoid consumer disappointment and in particular was concerned that insufficient stock had been available to fulfil demand.

Torin Douglas concluded his article with these critical remarks:

Six separate newspaper groups, six separate cases. Some may seem trivial – but the fact remains they were found to breach the Code of Advertising Practice and are not isolated incidents. In addition to these six, Associated Newspapers, *The Observer*, the *Sunday Sport* and the *Sunday Times* all had complaints upheld against them last year for editorial offers or promotions, and the *Daily Telegraph* was asked to clarify its promotional material. If newspapers want other advertisers to comply with the CAP, perhaps they should take greater notice of it themselves.

40. Avoidance of complaints

The recommendations of the code are open to interpretation, but it is surprising how many famous names appear in the monthly *ASA Reports*. Since the investigations are published it is poor public relations for the companies concerned, whether or not complaints are upheld. It is therefore wise for advertisers or their agents to discuss proposed copy with the ASA before publication and so avoid possible complaints. Usually, the media will be vigilant about this and will reject unethical advertisements. Moreover, it is part of the recognition awarded to agents by the media owners' organisations for commission purposes that they uphold the code, and they are liable to lose this recognition if they commit offences.

41. Public advertisement

The following are extracts from an ASA advertisement which appeared in journals such as *The Economist*:

DO SOME ADVERTISERS GIVE YOU TOO MANY FACTS AND TOO LITTLE INFORMATION?

It is not difficult to find yourself blinded by science.

Some advertisers are so wrapped up in their own jargon they fail to realise that to most people it's nothing more than mumbojumbo.

But how can you be sure the facts and figures you read are accurate? And how can you tell if an over-abundance of them is not just a whitewash to conceal the truth.

... Financial advertising is a good example. In essence the rules state advertisements must take into account that the complexities of finance may well be beyond the people to whom the offer appeals.

An investment ad inviting direct response has to include a great deal of explanatory wording.

For instance, past growth of 500 per cent in five years would have to be qualified by the exact five years to which it referred.

And all investment ads have to carry wording to the effect that the value of investments and the income from them, if quoted, can go down as well as up.

... We once received a complaint that a car with a 1,442 cc engine had been advertised as a '1.5'.

People 'in the know' apparently accept this as normal. But our complainant pointed out that his employer's mileage allowance for a '1.5' was for engines over 1,451 cc.

What meant little to the car trade meant a lot to him, and we were pleased that the advertiser amended the ad to include the exact engine size in the text.

It's not enough for a building society to promise 'worth 13.93 per cent to basic rate income tax payers' when the actual interest rate can fluctuate. This must be made clear.

A hi-fi manufacturer should not merely advertise that his equipment develops a certain number of watts.

Since there are several different ways of measuring sound output, he should state which method he used and give the reader a fair basis for comparison.

And as for computers it is not on to advertise what a piece of equipment will do and simply assume that the reader will know he needs several other items in order to operate it.

42. Political advertising

In 1993 the ASA introduced new rules on political advertising, but it does not apply to party political advertisements, and does nothing to meet the complaints that were made about Conservative Party advertisements during the 1992 General Election.

The new rules mean that the code requirement that advertisements should be honest and truthful has now been extended to 'public policy' and 'issue' advertisements placed by charities, pressure groups, trade unions, corporate advertisers and the like. They oblige advertisers to support factual claims within their advertisements.

Advertisers will continue to be able to express their opinions freely within an advertisement. There will also be an exemption for those advertisements whose function is party political.

The amendment enables the overwhelming majority of public policy and issue advertisements from whatever source to be treated under the BCASP in the same way as all other advertisements.

The full amendment is contained in a 16-page supplement to the 8th edition of the code.

Because of the peculiar and special natures of *government* and *political party* advertising, these differences as they apply to the code should be clearly understood. Advertisements by central or local government or those concerning government policy, as distinct from party policy, are subject to all the code's requirements on substantiation without exemption. But any advertisement, from whatever source, whose principal function is to influence opinion in favour of or against a political party or electoral candidate, or any matter before the electorate for a referendum, is exempt.

Until this amendment, the code precluded the ASA from investigating misleading claims in political advertisements. Unlike commercial advertisements, most non-broadcast advertisements placed by charities, pressure groups, trade unions and corporate advertisers could not be tested for accuracy.

43. IPR and PRCA Codes

The Institute of Public Relations (IPR) represents more than 5,000 individual public relations practitioners. The Public Relations Consultants Association represents more than 100 of the larger consultancies. Both have codes of practice which are very similar in their provisions. These codes have to be accepted as a condition of membership. In general terms, they set out recommendations concerning the professional and ethical behaviour of members in relation to one another, their clients or employers, the media and society.

The IPR's procedure is that a member may make a complaint about another member's breach of the code in writing to the executive director for consideration by the Professional Practices Committee. A breach of the code may then be submitted to the Disciplinary Committee for action to be taken which could take the form of a reprimand or suspension of membership. Most complaints are settled amicably at the Professional Practice Committee stage, but over the years there have been a few cases which have required legal representation on both sides and have resulted in a public reprimand or suspension.

44. ITC Code of Advertising Standards and Practice

This code, which relates only to British commercial television advertising (that is, not to other channels transmitted to British audiences) was published by the Independent Television Commission (ITC) in January 1991 as a statutory duty of the Broadcasting Act 1990. It broadly follows the original IBA and Cable Authority codes which were absorbed by the ITC. A copy may be obtained from the ITC, and the address is in Appendix 1.

Sponsorship rules and more detailed rules on the scheduling of advertisements are published separately in the *ITC Code of Programme Sponsorship* which lays down rules about credits for sponsored programmes and the *ITC Rules on Advertising Breaks* which refers to the maximum amount of time which may be allotted to commercials in any given hour. The sponsorship code also defines prohibited and restricted sponsors, these being political organisations, and manufacturers of tobacco products, pharmaceutical products available only on prescription, and (without special approval) any other product or service banned under the *ITC Code of Advertising Standards and Practice*.

The ITC Code is not unlike the BCASP in many respects but being part of an Act of Parliament it has legal and not voluntary power. Moreover, it refers to matters which are specifically to do with television such as banning *subliminal* advertising. With subliminals the photographic frames are so briefly screened that while the mind records them the eye does not, and the message could be deceptive. Another characteristic rule is that advertisements should not show children doing hazardous things which they might copy.

The code is mindful of the impact of television on the home, which differs from other media which are usually more selective. There are six important appendices covering children; financial advertising; health claims, medicines and treatments; charity advertising (which is now permitted provided free airtime is not already being given by the ITC for disaster appeals); religious advertising (now acceptable up to a point); while the sixth appendix lists more than 50 laws affecting television advertising.

The ITC Code also specifies products or services which are unacceptable, these being breath-testing devices and products which purport to mask the effects of alcohol; the occult; betting tips, and betting and gaming (including pools); all tobacco products (not just cigarettes); private investigation agencies; commercial advisory services (but not solicitors); guns and gun clubs, and pornography.

45. Radio Authority Code of Advertising Standards and Practices and Programme Sponsorship

The advertising and sponsorship codes for independent radio are contained in one volume. There are similarities between the RA Code and the ITC Code and BCASP, except where the particular conditions of radio prevail.

Presenters may voice commercials but must not:

(a) endorse, recommend or identify themselves with or personally testify about an advertiser's products or services;

(b) make reference to any specific advertisement when in their presenter's role;

(c) feature in an advertisement for a medicine or treatment.

A licensee must not discriminate for or against any advertiser. There must be no product placement, i.e. gratuitous reference to brand names in programmes. There must be no unkind or hurtful references to minority groups. The word 'free' must not be used unless there is no extra cost other than postage or carriage. Sounds likely to create a safety hazard to listeners such as motorists must not be used. This is but a brief sketch of typical provisions.

Sponsored commercial radio programmes may have taglines such as 'The Fashion Report, courtesy of Lever Brothers, makers of Persil'. Sponsors must be clearly identified. The frequency of credits is specified, and there must be one sponsor credit for every 15 minutes of programme.

46. Direct Marketing Association Code of Practice for Telemarketing

Since telemarketing is not covered by BCASP, this is the only source of professional controls for organisations which sell by telephone. Advertisers are expected to disclose their names and condemns sugging (selling under the pretence of research), requires calls to be made at reasonable hours, and that there should be a cooling off period. It seeks to control the malpractices of timeshare operators. Unfortunately, the majority of offenders are unlikely to be members of the DMA, but are more likely to be freelance salespeople for timeshare operators, photographers and home improvement firms who operate from home and are either unaware of rules or have been taught a drill by their employers which is unethical.

A new set of regulations came into force in May 1999; these too are operated by the DMA. It is important to check with them before embarking on a campaign which includes telemarketing. Their website is www.dma.org.uk.

Progress test 18

1. Distinguish between abuses *of* and abuses *by* advertising. (1)

2. What are the main advantages and disadvantages of both legal and voluntary controls of advertising? (2–4)

3. How are voluntary controls self-regulatory? (4)

4. How do the British Codes of Advertising and Sales Promotion differ from the ITC Code of Practice? (4)

5. Distinguish between 'knocking copy' and comparative advertising. (4)

6. What are the three essentials of a valid contract? (6)

7. Explain the difference between slander and libel. (11)

8. Explain the terms 'slander of goods', 'passing off', and 'get-up'. (12, 13)

9. Who owns the copyright of artwork produced by an advertising agency to illustrate a client's advertisement? (19)

10. How did the Office of Fair Trading rule on the question of the traditional advertising agency recognition and commission system? (21)

11. Why have certain advertisements, which appear to be lotteries, escaped the requirements of lottery legislation? (22)

12. What are the three main offences which may be committed under the Trade Descriptions Acts, unless the advertiser is very careful about the claims made in the advertisements? (25)

13. Name the characteristics of which at least one must apply to a trade mark if it is to be registrable. **(29)**

14. What legal control exists concerning pirate radio? **(32)**

15. What is the basis of the BCASP, and what media does it cover? **(36)**

16. Describe the procedure by which the Advertising Standards Authority invites, receives, investigates and reports on complaints about advertisements which appear to offend against the British Codes of Advertising and Sales Promotion. **(38–41)**

19

Planning and executing an advertising campaign

INTRODUCTION

1. Variations in procedures

Advertising agencies vary in size and structure. They may operate a plans board system (*see* 4: **49**), or have creative groups, or simply have discussions between departmental heads as required. Nevertheless, the general flow and control of work will be similar, with the account executive maintaining liaison between the client and the agency, and the production manager or traffic controller acting as progress chaser to see that each stage of the campaign is completed on time so that advertisements reach the media by the deadlines or copy dates. A number of different campaigns will be progressing through the agency at the same time so there will be a great variety of 'work in progress'.

In this chapter the plans board method will be used to discuss the total procedure from the initial briefing to the final assessment of results.

PRELIMINARY DISCUSSIONS

2. Initial briefing

Before anything can be planned an account executive from the agency must obtain from the client the fullest possible information about the client's company and the product or service to be advertised. It may be a regular client for whom the next campaign is to be prepared, or a potential client for whom a competitive proposition has to be assembled. In the latter case information will be required regarding the client about whom little may be known at this point.

Generally speaking, the sort of data required by the account executive, so that colleagues inside the agency can be properly instructed, are likely to be as follows.

(a) The budget. Usually, the advertiser will have decided how much to spend on advertising, and this will be part of an overall marketing budget. It may be divided into above-the-line and below-the-line media, and the agency may be responsible for some or all of this media. Thus, the agency will have to plan the campaign within pre-set financial limits. There can also be occasions when the agency will be asked what it will cost to undertake a campaign for a certain purpose, but it is more likely that the client knows what he wants to spend and the agency will have to do its sums, depending on whether it operates under the commission or the fee system.

(b) The company, product or service. The account executive has to understand the company, its background and how it operates. A copy of the annual report will provide some of this information. But every company has its own character. Nissan is different from Ford, Cadbury's from Nestlé, British Airways from Air France.

It is essential that the account executive gleans every possible detail, and this may include obtaining first-hand experience depending on the nature of the product or service. The product has to be sampled or studied until the account executive becomes utterly familiar with it, taking nothing for granted. If it is a product that can easily be taken back to the office, so much the better, but it might be something like a tower crane, a new holiday camp or a dish-washing machine. It could also be something institutional like a charity or comparatively intellectual like an election campaign. The account executive has to understand the product or service inside out. Moreover, to produce a motivating campaign, it has to be believed in, and even though he or she may never stay at a holiday camp its value to those who do or might has to be understood. Provided the product or service is not bad or devious, it will usually have its particular market, whether it be a cheap ball-point or a gold-plated gift pen.

(c) Market. So what is the market, or the market segment? At whom is the product or service aimed, who is likely to buy it? Was it created to satisfy a particular market? Does the client require marketing advice? Are buying motives known? Is the agency expected to conduct marketing research?

(d) Distribution. How will it reach the consumer? What is the distribution channel – wholesalers, retailers, brokers, agents, direct response?

(e) What is the name? Has this been decided, or is the agency to find a name, possibly researching a number of names? New product agencies get in at the birth of products whereas full service agencies may have ready-made new products thrust upon them. Ideally, an advertising agency of any kind should be consulted as early as possible.

(f) Price. Has this been decided or again, is research necessary to arrive at the best selling price? What is the pricing policy? Is it a psychological, market, bargain or competitive price? Or is the product pitched at a certain price bracket, allied to (c) above?

(g) Packaging. Has this been decided or does it have to be designed? Is research necessary? This may concern the actual container, its type or material, the labelling, and any other form of container as when a bottle is packed in a box.

(h) Competition. Is the product unique, or does it compete within an established product group? Or, if it is expensive, what sort of discretionary income expenditure does it compete with? In respect of the latter, a person might sacrifice a holiday in order to buy double glazing.

3. Marketing aspects

The above may seem an untidy list, and it may even seem extraordinary that some of these questions have to be asked at all. In this age of modern marketing it might be assumed that a manufacturer would have prepared a marketing mix, done all the research, and appointed an advertising agency to conduct the advertising campaign required as part of the marketing mix.

The fact is that business management is seldom as marketing-oriented as it should be although it is aware that advertising is necessary. Very often marketing is introduced by the advertising agency, and as already mentioned there are specialist product development agencies which start at the beginning. It is even possible for such an agency to recommend what sort of new product should be developed. Moreover, it is a good idea to bring in the agency at the earliest possible time so that the agency can advise throughout all the stages of the marketing mix, beginning with the new product which may be only at the prototype stage.

4 'Four Ps' marketing myth

In marketing circles the McCarthy/Kotler 'Four Ps' concept is often adopted as the basis of the marketing mix, but if it is taken too literally it can imply that Promotion (advertising, sales promotion, publicity (presumably meaning public relations!) and selling) is an isolated activity. Promotional activities should be introduced alongside the other considerations of naming, pricing, packaging, market segment, distribution and after-sales. Similarly we find that some approaches to marketing communication are limited to promotion.

Public relations specialists (whether in-house or consultancy) should be brought in right at the start, and overall marketing communications are essential. This could, for instance, include corporate identity. Naming a product has great public relations relevance, as have packaging and pricing.

Public relations is to do with creating knowledge and understanding whereas Kotler (and marketing people in general) tend to see public relations as a fringe activity concerned only with favourable images and favourable publicity, even with so-called 'free advertising', as product publicity is falsely termed.

The advertiser should seek or be entitled to all the specialist advice he or she can get. So without trying to promote any fetishes about advertising and public relations it is practical to have marketing, advertising and public relations working as a team as early in the marketing strategy as possible, simply to get the maximum benefit from all three. They are quite different disciplines, as different yet associated as medicine, dentistry and pharmacy.

5. Account executive reports to agency head

Having obtained all the information needed or obtainable, the account executive returns to the agency and reports to a superior who may be the managing director or, in a large agency, the account director in charge of a group of accounts and account executives. This meeting is essential for policy reasons. The senior director needs to know the progress of work, the take-up of agency services and possibly the need for additional staff, plus the financial implications of the new account or renewal business.

In addition to normal business considerations, however, it is necessary for the managing director or account director to examine the *suitability* of the new business. Is it ethically acceptable? It might be for a foreign government which was unpopular. Should the agency handle Indonesian paper-clips or Chinese sardines or an Iraqi airline? Apart from the considerations of personal conscience, would there be a risk of offending existing clients? Or is there likely to be a conflict of trading interests between the new and an old account? Sometimes the areas of conflict may be difficult to define. The account executive, eager to accept new business, may not see the possible conflict as keenly as the agency head. The problem will have to be resolved, perhaps by a top level agency decision, or by diplomatic talks with the two clients. It may be, in the case of conflicting interests, that one of these clients will fear lack of confidentiality, but on the other hand both may be delighted to use the same agency which either promises good service or is experienced in their industry.

6. Report to departmental heads

Assuming, however, that the account executive has the go-ahead to accept the account and to prepare a proposal for presentation to the client, a detailed report is now submitted to the departmental chiefs who comprise the plans board. Agencies are structured in various ways, but here it will be assumed that the team will consist of the agency's marketing manager, art director, copy chief and media planner. The production manager (or traffic controller) is not usually required at this stage. If the agency has a public relations manager, or there is a public relations subsidiary company, or the client employs an independent public relations consultant, a public relations representative may also be included. Each will study the account executive's reports, and there may be discussions among them.

DEVELOPMENT OF COPY PLATFORM

7. First plans board meeting

Under the chairmanship of the account executive, the departmental heads will attend the first plans board meeting. There will be a detailed discussion during which members will frankly express their views and ideas. Some may like the product, others will not, some will see one way of advertising it and others will have different ideas. Eventually, the account executive will call a halt to the discussion, and each member will go away to work up a scheme to present to the next meeting. The marketing manager may have to consider any necessary research, the copy chief and art director will create a copy platform and its visual presentation, and the media planner will select media and prepare a media schedule. There may also be television and radio commercials to think about. The agency may have a specialist TV producer who will prepare a script and storyboard.

8. Second plans board meeting

At this meeting, the department heads, who have been consulting with each other in the meantime, will present their ideas for the campaign. A theme or copy platform will have been devised, and copy drafts and rough visuals will have been prepared together with a media schedule. If TV is to be used there will be cartoon-like storyboards showing the sequence of scenes for the proposed commercials. The marketing manager will have studied the market, and will make his or her recommendations. As a result of copy-testing, various ads may have been discarded in favour of the one now adopted.

If relationships are good it can be sensible to invite the client's advertising manager or product manager to attend this meeting. This is a preliminary stage in the planning of the campaign, and it can be helpful to ask the advertising manager to express opinions on the way the campaign is shaping. The agency may have adopted a wrong approach which the client is unlikely to accept, or it may be a novel approach which has to be tried out on the advertising manager before a more complete and costly presentation is made to the company's chief executive and managers.

PREPARING THE CAMPAIGN

9. Preparing for the presentation

Once the ideas have been agreed, the campaign can be assembled for presentation to the client. Visuals will be worked up into near-finished layouts even though at this stage artists may not have been engaged for artwork, and the copy will be represented on the layouts and not actually typeset. This can be done in one of two ways – by ruled lines, or by meaningless 'Greek' wording to resemble typesetting. The media schedules will be plotted carefully, and it will be necessary to make tentative bookings in certain magazines like weekend colour supplements which have lead times of two or three months.

10. Presentation to client

This is the big day when the campaign has to be 'sold' to the client. In making the presentation the account executive must be able to justify the copy platform, the visual treatment, the choice of media and the dates, sizes and positions recommended. The client has to be convinced that the scheme will achieve the desired result, or at least contribute effectively to the sales target which may depend on other factors (e.g. good product, good public relations, good field salespeople, good trade terms, good distribution, good point-of-sale display, and perhaps a good sales promotion scheme) as well as advertising.

A common problem at client presentations is that approval may be required of a number of company directors and executives representing the board, marketing, sales, advertising and public relations. Some of these people will propose alternative ideas which are often ones considered and rejected in the agency during the early planning stages. If the advertising manager has worked closely with the agency he or she at least is an ally on the client side who can argue in favour of the agency proposals. With large companies and big accounts the presentation could take all day, especially if it is a complicated campaign covering perhaps more than one product and making use of a variety of media. It can be an occasion of great argument. Everyone thinks they know all about advertising.

11. Putting the scheme into operation

Once the client has given approval (which will involve a contract of service) the creative work and media buying can go ahead. The campaign is not the only one being handled by the agency, and it is necessary to plan the work allocated to each department so that the advertisements are produced, delivered and inserted correctly. This is where the production manager or traffic controller takes charge, preparing time schedules showing when each stage of the work must be completed, i.e. the finalising of copy, production of finished layouts, completion of artwork and typesetting, submission to client, return by clients, amendments made and final copy in the desired form being despatched to the media. A daily check will be made to see that all the work is being produced on time. Similarly, with the production of TV commercials, a routine has to be followed which will include appointment of director and film unit, casting, shooting, editing, approval by client, submission to the ITC and BACC for copy approval, and distribution to the television companies.

12. Liaison work of account executive

The account executive will work closely with agency departments to oversee the preparation and production of the campaign, and will act as the liaison between the agency and the client to present work in progress such as copy, artwork and proofs to obtain approval. The client has to be kept to the time schedule, but there may be amendments which have to be incorporated, and sometimes clients do not know what they really want until creative work has reached an advanced stage. Alternatives can create problems and pressures such as extra costs or extra work when time is running out. Often, the situation calls for the diplomatic skills of the account executive when dealing with both the client and agency staff. The client may be important, but is not the only important client whose work is being handled simultaneously by the agency. A typical client complaint is the size of production costs, but budgets may be exceeded solely because the client insists on last-minute expensive changes.

13. Approved advertisements to the media

When everything has been completed and approved the advertisements are despatched to the media. Even now a hitch can occur if advertisement managers of newspapers and magazines, or the television copy clearance officials, are worried that the advertisement may offend the BCASP or the television or radio code. Amendments may have to be negotiated. This does not mean that the advertiser or the agency has deliberately offended but that a statement or claim may have been made too zealously, or that something unethical can be read into the advertisement which was not intended. Occasionally, in a highly competitive business, a hard-selling advertisement, perhaps containing knocking copy, may have been created deliberately and there may be a dispute over its acceptability. This has occurred a number of times in the automotive industry. However, as the monthly reports of the Advertising Standards Authority show, offences against the BCASP do slip through or complainants think they have done so. British advertising is subject to both official and private watchdogs!

341

THE CAMPAIGN AND AFTERWARDS

14. Appearance of campaign

Both the agency's account executive and the client's advertising manager will study the actual appearance of the advertising. Has it reproduced well? Has it appeared in the right position on the right day? What are the audience ratings (TVRs) for the programmes when the commercial appeared on television? Fresh problems can arise. Insertions may have been made wrongly. Printing quality may have been poor. Perhaps the advertisements did not appear at all because of strikes! The campaign has to be monitored to make sure that the media schedules have been met. This is critical if a new product is being launched in the shops and its success depends upon coincidental advertising. The cost-effectiveness of the campaign could be in peril if something has gone wrong.

15. Recall research

There is still time to improve a campaign and next-day recall research can be conducted to test whether people saw, remembered and maybe responded to the advertising. A TABS tracking study (*see* 17: **24–32**) may be commissioned. Later, dealer audit research will record what effect the advertising had in moving stocks and also the effect it had on brand share and position in the product group.

16. Charging out

It is likely that since production of the campaign may have occupied weeks or months certain expenditures incurred by the agency will have been invoiced already. Agency cash flow demands this, and with technical accounts producing little commission the client may have to pay the agency an advance fund. Media expect prompt payment, and agencies have to invoice clients promptly too. An agency could not survive if it did not render accounts until the completion of a campaign which might run over a considerable period. Strict business accounting is therefore vital, and within the agency this requires the use of job numbers, clearly identified orders and suppliers' accounts, and time-sheets where service is charged on an hourly or daily fee basis.

It will be remembered that a condition of agency recognition is its creditworthiness. This can be maintained only if the agency is strict about charging out what is due to it from clients, and making sure that cash flow is maintained through prompt payment by clients. Long-standing credit cannot be sustained. In this the account executive may in a sense have to play the role of credit manager, certainly insofar as the client may query any bills. The client's advertising manager is responsible for checking and approving agency accounts.

17. Assessment of results

Have the objectives of the campaign been achieved? This may be less easy to assess if the marketing mix contains a number of influences upon sales. However, a new FMCG will either sell or it won't, and it is amazing sometimes how, say, a new chocolate bar will produce a tremendous response following television advertising, and this is quickly assessable in the shops. Long-term advertising, such as that of Brooke Bond PG Tips chimps or Nescafé Gold Blend TV commercials, has created and maintained the product's premier selling position. Some advertising can be measured by the response to offers as when Nescafé print a money-off offer in the press. Direct response marketers can easily measure the number of enquiries or orders received.

The pulling power of individual media can be calculated by keying coupons or addresses for replies, a different key (e.g. DM1 on a coupon in the first ad placed in the *Daily Mail*) being used for each advertisement. Thus it is possible to record the response to each advertisement, and by dividing the cost of the space by the number of replies a cost-per-reply figure can be worked out. This will show which media are the most economical. Similarly, cost-per-order or cost-per-conversion-into-sales can also be calculated. This important information will guide the future choice of media.

It may be desired to reach a certain volume of viewers, and weekly audience ratings (TVRs) can be totalled until the required number has been obtained. Then the commercial can be rested, which both avoids boring viewers, and is more economical than saturation advertising.

18. Agency/client relations

It will be realised from the foregoing description of the conception and birth of an advertising campaign that to maintain a good relationship between an agency and a client it is necessary for both sides to work together harmoniously. This is not easy. The pressures are great. Creative and executive people on both sides can be under great stress. A good relationship leads to good advertising, and this calls for both a skilled advertising manager representing the client and a skilled account executive representing the agency, and they need to operate as partners. Otherwise the relationship becomes soured, and the client starts looking for a new agency. It may take months of patient endeavour for agency staff to understand a client and their problems, and it can be very wasteful to change agencies too frequently.

Progress test 19

1. Describe how the account executive is briefed regarding a proposed advertising campaign. What does he or she need to know in order to report back to his or her agency? **(2)**

2. Why should the planning of an advertising campaign start as early as possible in the planning of a client's marketing strategy? **(4)**

3. For what reasons might the agency head consider a proposed new account to be undesirable? **(5)**

4. What is the function of the plans board? **(6, 7, 8)**

5. Describe how a proposed campaign is prepared for presentation to the client. **(9)**

6. How can co-operation with the client's advertising manager help to resolve problems during the presentation to client? **(10)**

7. Describe the external and internal liaison duties of the account executive. **(12)**

8. How can budgetary control be applied so that accounts can be rendered and collected efficiently and the agency's cash flow maintained? **(16)**

9. How can the results of an advertising campaign be assessed? **(17)**

10. Why are good agency/client relations essential, and what are the essentials of a good relationship? **(18)**

20

The advertiser and the Internet

THE INTERNET

1. Background

The dynamic growth of the Internet is producing dramatic changes in every corner of the business world. According to Martin Read, editor of *Mind Your Own Business* magazine, the number of Internet users doubles every hundred days. The marketing, commercial and trading potential of this growth has been recognised by marketers and advertisers in every field of endeavour. This is especially true in fields such as consumer, business-to-business, manufacturing and service industries and communications.

There is scarcely a business of any size in the industrialised countries which does not possess and use at least one computer. Many businesses have networks of users; examples are estate agents, banks, supermarkets, airlines, travel agents, freight hauliers and insurance companies.

The Internet is often described as the fastest-growing advertising medium, and it is rapidly becoming the most preferred. It depends from where you are viewing the situation. In Britain, for example, it could well be the fastest growing, but only when considered in relation to other media. These are relatively static and have been so for some time.

In the United States, this view of growth may be true. According to the Association of National Advertisers, advertising appropriations devoted to on-line promotion have tripled each year since 1997. Other experts predict that that advertising on the Internet is likely to grow to almost $8bn (£5bn) in the USA, and in Europe to approaching £1bn. There are indications that European households capable of accessing on-line advertising are approaching 10 per cent of total households, and rising. At the current rate of growth, the proportion could reach 40 per cent by 2002.

In Europe, householders are starting to take up on-line shopping, but more cautiously. According to informed opinion, Britain, France and Germany, the most advanced of the European e-business markets, are set to buy over £2.1 bn in products and services by 2002.

Whatever the reality, nobody knows for certain how fast Internet commerce is growing, or what the future holds for advertisers. What we do know is that everything is developing at high speed, including the technology. So too is the movement to curb Internet activities and control what until now has been an almost free market.

There seems little doubt that, if the current trend continues, the Internet will be the backbone of business, commerce and trade – locally, nationally and globally. As Intel chairman Andy Grove said in April 1999, 'All companies will be Internet companies, or they won't be companies.'

2. The nature of the Internet

The Internet is a huge global network of computers. Some computers are owned by individuals, such as householders; others by businesses, companies, corporations and organisations, many of them with internal networks.

Many of these computers are used for purposes other than surfing the Internet. Individuals use them for activities as diverse as education, research, entertainment, Email, scientific pursuits and household accounts. Businesses use them for every aspect of commercial life, including high-level decision-making and, of course, marketing.

With this in mind, it is easy to see how computers connected to the Internet are a source of revenue to anyone with a product or service to sell. Millions of customers are out there. The question is, how to reach and promote to them, quickly and cost-effectively. The Internet, Email and the World Wide Web are powerful tools in the hands of advertisers who want to reach consumers.

Many well-known marketing organisations are already using on-line advertising. Companies such as Ford, IBM, Hewlett Packard, Mitsubishi Electric, Pearson, Dell and Fidelity Investments use Internet advertising as part of their promotional portfolios. Smaller fry are beginning to adopt the medium, but more cautiously. Some, for example, are uncertain about the possible returns on the investment. Advertising on the Internet, like other media, costs money; budgets must be created and allocated. Others are confused by the rapid advances in the technology, or are waiting for more reliable methods of measuring response and media performance. Still others are uncertain of the awesome power of the Internet as a marketing tool, remaining passive until convincing case studies emerge.

Meanwhile, the growth of the Internet advances, and the technology continues to improve. Marketers and advertisers continue to warm to it – commercially speaking. They continue to deliver the right messages to the right

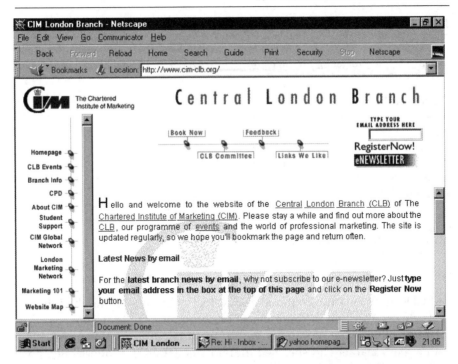

Figure 20.1 Website homepage. The Chartered Institute of Marketing's London Branch website. Simple, clear, uncluttered, totally oriented to the needs of its members and students. One day all websites will be as good as this

target audiences at the right time, efficiently measuring the results – indeed, just as they do with press, broadcast and direct response media.

Readers should remember that this chapter is a panorama of advertising in relation to the Internet. They – whether practitioners or students – must be sensitive to the changes taking place in the medium day by day, and constantly alert to the advertising opportunities they present.

3. The Internet as an advertising medium

As a medium, the Internet is just as capable of growth as any other medium. Its dynamic expansion over the period from 1993 to 1999 has encouraged marketers, advertisers and their agencies to exploit it. Many have already done so with success. Amazon.com, the US direct bookseller, for example, has taken up on-line advertising with enthusiasm. Although it is not the largest on-line advertiser using the Internet, it claims a sales turnover of over $550 million in five years. Amazon, clearly believing in the future of on-line advertising as a factor for company growth, has expanded into videos

347

Table 20.1 Media capability matrix

Media	Targeting	Response tracking		Message delivery	Flexibility	Interactivity
		A	B			
The Internet	5	0	5	5	5	5
Television	2	1	0	4	1	0
Press	3	5	0	4	3	0
Direct mail	5	5	0	5	5	5
Radio	2	1	0	4	4	0
Posters	0	0	0	2	1	0
Telesales	5	5	5	5	5	5

Key:
0 = nil   1 = poor   5 = excellent
A = by response other than direct in real time
B = by real-time interaction

and CDs. It looks set to continue to develop its business using the Internet as its chosen medium of communication, promotion and sales.

Unlike other communications media, the Internet is capable of reaching both a mass market and specified individuals within it. It offers huge possibilities for bringing sellers and buyers together on a worldwide basis. Moreover, on-line advertising differs from other media in one other important respect. It allows enquirers and consumers *to interact with advertisements direct and with immediacy*. With a key-stroke or a mouse-click, a 'visitor' can call up information about a product, resolve questions about it and then buy it – all this in the same 'visit'.

Some comparisons can be drawn between the Internet and other media – broadcast, press, direct mail and outdoor. However, its capability extends beyond all these because of its immediacy, flexibility and interactivity and its ability to reach target audiences on a truly global scale. (*See* Table 20.1.)

COMPARISONS

4. Television advertising

Television commercials enable advertisers to dominate television screens. They allow the advertiser to use all TV's capabilities: movement, animation, colour, sound and response-contact information. The most popular formats are 30-second, 45-second and 60-second slots.

Although TV cannot target individual consumers, it can address the interests, wants, needs and emotions of well-defined consumer groups. It does this up to and slightly beyond the geographical limits of transmission areas of individual stations, which is a crude form of targeting.

So far, on-line advertising has been less aggressive than that appearing on TV, and consumers have become accustomed to this low-key commercial environment. Advertisers, however, are gradually becoming more assertive in their on-line presentations, experimenting with and introducing videoed advertisements and animation.

There is an intriguing but important side-issue here. The downside for advertisers using TV is that consumers using the Internet cannot at the same time be watching TV. Prime-time TV in the UK is roughly 7 pm to 11 pm. There is some evidence that Internet usage peaks in the early evening, around 7.30 pm to 9 pm. For example, when people arrive home from work, one of the first things they do is check their Emails. This on-line activity, including surfing the Internet, may continue until bed-time, with a break for dinner. With 100m or more households expected to be on-line by 2001, this could represent unwelcome news for TV contractors.

5. Radio advertising

Some of the conditions outlined above apply to radio. You will find at least one radio set in every household in industrialised countries. Most of the time, listening to radio demands no concentration by the consumer. He or she can be occupied in other activities at the same time as listening to the radio: reading, bathing, ironing, designing, polishing diamonds. Indeed, radio is often described as audible wallpaper. When surfing the net, reading Emails or studying on-line offers by advertisers, the consumer needs to concentrate on the screen. On-line advertisers have therefore to make their presentations as interesting and motivating as possible – especially as the consumer may have the radio on in the background.

6. Press advertising

On a newspaper or magazine page, it is easy to distinguish advertising from editorial. Indeed, editors and advertisers are careful to design their presentations to emphasise this distinction. In the UK, some advertisers use an 'advertorial' technique. The design of the advertisements closely resembles that of the editorial environment in which they appear. This is deliberate, and permitted by publishers. Each advertorial insertion, however, must be clearly identified as such, and must carry the heading 'Advertisement' or 'Advertisement Feature'.

For on-line advertising, advertisements can be treated as such. In its way, editorial is also advertising. The usual divisions between advertising and editorial are virtually abolished, because advertisers can also be publishers. Anything on screen can be treated as an advertising element. The advertiser can use logos, headlines, body copy, product names, symbols and pack designs. Currently there are no restrictions such as those exercised in print advertising, except possibly those relating to legality, honesty and decency in the countries in which they are published. *See* **18** for further comment.

7. Direct response advertising

Advertisers using direct mail know the extent to which they can track response. The same applies to most other forms of direct marketing. Key numbers in press advertisement coupons are the best example of direct response tracking. With radio and television it is more difficult to achieve a traceable response, but key numbers and specially designated telephone lines help with tracking.

Detailed assessments of response to on-line advertisements are not only possible but essential. These enable advertisers to compare on-line advertising with the best results obtained from other direct-response methods. Some advertisers take the conventional direct response route to evaluation, basing it on cost of response or cost of enquiry. The real test for effective advertising, of course, is cost per sale.

ABC//electronic, a company in the Audit Bureau of Circulations group, carries out website auditing. Independent measurement of website usage, with directly comparable audit reports, allows marketers, media buyers and planners to take advertising decisions. These can be at their most effective when based on facts and figures. For a full description, *see* **14**.

8. Outdoor advertising

There is no foolproof way of determining how many passers-by look at a poster. Even on London Underground, where human traffic at poster sites can be estimated fairly accurately at various times of the day, there can be swings in either direction. Nobody has yet come up with a method of tracing actual response to poster advertising at individual sites. POSTAR has gone some way to remedying this situation overall. However, the nature of posters as an advertising medium does not lend itself to accurately relating exposure at the site to sales at the check-out.

Web users, on the other hand, can interact with on-line advertisements, and accurate results can be calculated. On-line banner advertisements are often compared to posters. Like a poster, a banner can refer users to a website where product information is to be obtained. But whereas posters are static, and may be changed infrequently, banners encourage users to interact at once and can be changed as frequently as the advertiser needs. A mouse-click or key-stroke links the user to an interactive source of data, pleasure, knowledge or product offer. Each click on a banner or website is recorded, and added to the cost-effectiveness calculation for that banner or site.

TYPES OF ON-LINE ADVERTISING

9. Web advertising

Most on-line advertising activity takes place on the web. The media effect is not unlike that offered by television: colour, movement, sound, graphics and animation. There is also opportunity for downloading advertisers' material to the user's computer, and printing it.

The unique advantage to advertisers, however, is the ability to offer products and services to consumers worldwide, take orders and receive payment, direct from a website.

10. Classified advertisements

As with newspaper classifieds, an advertiser buys lineage from the owner of the site. Popular directory and search sites, such as Yahoo!, offer this service. Lesser-known organisations offer similar services, often at cheaper rates or even free of charge. The advertiser therefore needs to establish the reach and track record of such sites before investing advertising money in them. With TV, radio and print-based advertising, this is standard practice; website advertising is no different. An advertisement rate card and media information should be obtained from each site being considered. (*See* Figure 20.2.)

It is always advisable to test sites selected for advertising before investing substantially in contracts with them. The tests should include evaluation of quality as well as quantity.

There are some advantages to be gained from using classified advertising on the web. Sites that charge fees are often of higher quality than free sites. They may also receive more visits from potential customers looking for particular products and services – if that is what the advertiser wants.

On the downside, some sites offering free classified advertising may be using the sites to collect Email addresses. If an advertiser takes classifieds on such sites, they may sooner or later be involved with multiple junk Email lists, which are bought and sold to all comers and at random. The practical quality of these addresses for the advertiser's specific needs may be questionable. It is especially important to bear this in mind when the advertiser plans to reach a specified target audience for a product or service on offer.

11. Banner advertising

A banner is a strip of advertising material on a web page, often appearing at the head or foot of the page. The page can be a 'home' page of a website, an advertiser's own or someone else's, or some other page which receives a great deal of visitor traffic. A banner can be any size – within reason. An over-large banner might as well be a half page, or most of it. However, as

351

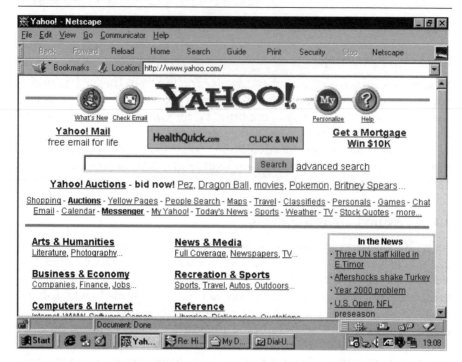

Figure 20.2 The Yahoo! home page with its top level menu. A subject-oriented guide to the web, it is packed with useful topics and links to where they can be found. Note the advertising banner just above the centre

with other media, appearing within editorial is to the advertiser's advantage. Banners are usually about 17 cm wide by 2.5 cm deep, with variations in height and depth for the requirements of graphics and typography.

The main function of a banner is to direct the visitor to a website where more information can be obtained. Once at the website, the visitor can be persuaded to purchase a product or service. A press advertisement can offer information, to be sent for by filling in a coupon or making a telephone call. The website, because its size is theoretically limitless, can hold all the information the visitor is likely to need for making purchasing decisions.

Banner designs vary widely, limited only by the demands of the brief, the budget and the imagination of the designer. However, nearly all banner advertisements have one feature in common: the request 'click here', click now' or an equivalent. Some banners are interactive, encouraging the visitor to carry out an action within the banner. An interactive banner can, for example, prompt the visitor to ask a question or series of questions, using a pull-down menu. Alternatively, a pull-down menu can refer the visitor to a specific page on the advertiser's main website. The visitor clicks on the menu strip he or she has chosen, or on 'click here'. The software

Informative advertising banners. You can see direct the benefit on the screen.

Typography is important in helping to motivate the visitor. Caveat: eccentric typography should be used with extreme care. It can render an advertising banner unreadable.

A banner in corporate style. Symbols and formality convey the authority and prestige of a powerful, institutional organisation.

Figure 20.3 Advertising banners. They can be motivating, informative or teasing. The only limitation is your designer's imagination. Careful typography is needed to ensure legibility on screen.

jumps straight to that page, where the full information or sales pitch is displayed.

Some banners are designed as self-contained units, interacting with the visitor without jumping to another page or website. They show what is on offer, and also take the order. The 'click here' button is replaced by 'order here' or 'buy here'. This is an ideal situation for the advertiser. Instead of spending substantial amounts of time and money constructing a complex website and building brand recognition to entice customers, the whole transaction is concentrated in a single banner. This also saves time and effort for visitors. It could be described as the electronic equivalent of the impulse purchase. (*See* Figure 20.3.)

With banners, as with all advertising material, there are a number of practical guidelines to be recommended.

(a) Host website selection. Some sites will out-perform others in terms of response activity. A banner advertisement may perform better when incorporated into a site which appeals to a predetermined target audience. This is pure common sense. It is also common sense to post a banner to a host website for a limited period as a test before entering into long contracts or substantial financial outlay.

(b) Positioning. It is important to test each host website for the best pages, and the best positions on those pages. The advertiser may discover, for example, that the best position on a poor site out-performs a poor position on a good site. The answer will show in the tests.

(c) Visitor monitoring. Monitor carefully and constantly. Experience indicates that visitors are most likely to take action on the first or second visit to a banner advertisement. After a second visit, response is likely to fall. *See* **15–17**.

(d) Seizing attention. As with other types of advertising, proven copy and design techniques should be used. These include the following:

(*i*) *Offers*. Make an offer, a proposal. Use a unique selling proposition (USP). Put a benefit or a promise into it. If the product or service helps to resolve a consumer or business problem, say clearly what it is.

(*ii*) *Copy*. Headlines do most of the work on a banner. Do not crowd a banner with text; it can confuse or mislead the visitor, so that no action is taken. Keep copy short, clear and simple. This encourages the visitor to go for the click-button.

(*iii*) *Typography*. Use bold, chunky type, especially for headlines. Use sans serif fonts rather than ones with serifs. Spindly type is often broken up or distorted by the lines or pixels on screen.

(*iv*) *Colour*. Use bold colours, and ones which make the banner stand out from the material round it. This will differ for each host site.

(*v*) *Animation*. Where the rest of the page is static, a banner featuring animation, blinking, sparking or other simple visual effect will grab attention, and divert attention away from other material on the page.

(e) Getting action. Where you want action from the visitor, feature a click-button or line of text saying 'Click here', 'Click now', 'Click to order' or giving a similar instruction. This should be organised to link with the advertiser's own website, or straight through to a ordering system.

(f) Incentives. Encourage the visitor to click on a banner by giving a compelling reason for doing so. This can be anything from a worthwhile discount or a closing date to a prize or free gift. If this is not incorporated, the visitor may leave the banner, and even the site, without taking any action.

12. Email advertising

Two main types of Email advertising are currently in use. First, straight, so-called 'push' techniques, of which the easiest to operate is ordinary Email. Electronic mailshots delivered in this way are sent direct to the user's mailbox, without waiting for him or her to go on line. The user receives it whether it has been requested it or not, just like a mailshot delivered by post. There are some constraints and controls on this type of advertising in the pipeline; *see* **18**.

A number of companies are currently offering free Email access to users. As always, there is a reciprocal element. The Email software displays paid-for advertising on the user's screen. Hotmail and Juno were among the pioneers of this useful arrangement. Hotmail operates in the way just described. Juno provides free software and dial-up connection in exchange for a demographic questionnaire completed by the user. The result enables Juno to compile and operate a highly detailed mailing list, based on the questionnaire. Its client advertisers can target users with great accuracy, using the demographic information provided by Juno. This can reach virtually any Email user with a Windows-compatible personal computer and a modem.

13. Email newsletters and discussion groups

Another route to target audiences is the sponsored discussion group. An advertiser can sponsor discussion groups by providing the software and the access free to users. In exchange, the advertiser benefits from a precisely targeted audience. Participants are those who have taken a decision to subscribe to that particular discussion group, rather than casual Internet surfers. This makes the sponsorship all the more valuable to the advertiser, and participation valuable to the user.

A discussion group comprises a number of individuals with a common interest. This can be anything from finance, marketing or computing to photography, bookbinding, babies or genetically modified foods. Users get together on the Internet for an exchange of ideas and advice, or merely to chat about their common interest. They are said to 'subscribe' to the group, although the subscription is free. Any subscriber wishing to contribute to the discussion sends a message to the Email address of the group, and this is read by all its subscribers.

An Email newsletter is a similar technique. Its content is material created by an organisation or individual, and distributed by Email to subscribers. Again, the subscription is free to participants. Advertisers can insert their copy to be read on screen by all subscribers.

An advertiser sponsoring Email discussion groups and newsletters benefits in several ways. First, the content is text-only, free from distractions and diversions offered by conventional websites. Second, because advertisements in group newsletters promote products and services related to the interests of the group, subscribers are more likely to respond favourably. For example, an advertiser promoting cameras, film and processing materials at worthwhile discounts is likely to receive an unusually high degree of attention and interest from subscribers. Provided that the offer is appropriate and viable, and the copy persuasive, this interest can be converted into orders.

There are many thousands of Email discussion groups and newsletters currently on line. Advertisers can sponsor them for as long as their budgets allow, and the sponsorships remain commercially viable. Usually, sponsorship is conducted on a weekly or monthly basis.

One major disadvantage to the advertiser is that discussion groups can come and go. They often arise spontaneously and decline or disappear without warning when they become stale or banal.

14. Promoting a website

There is little point in having a website to promote products and services if the world is unaware of it. An advertiser dare not rely on random visits if a website is to be commercially viable. For a website to be a cost-effective sales tool, an advertiser's target audiences must know both of its existence and how to access it.

The advertiser can implement a number of measures to gain and maintain awareness of a website. These include the following:

(a) Establishing the website's Internet address, commonly called the URL – uniform resource locator. The name of the company, organisation brand, product name or *raison d'etre* should appear within it.

(b) Having the URL present on company stationery, vehicles, retail outlets and other forms of routine company communication.

(c) Having as many banners on appropriate websites as the budget allows.

(d) Highlighting the company's URL in all Email communications.

(e) Featuring the URL in all the company's promotional, sales and corporate literature. House journals are particularly important for this purpose.

(f) Highlighting the company's URL in its press, TV, radio, direct mail and outdoor advertising.

(g) Preparing and implementing public relations campaigns both to launch the URL and maintain awareness of it. The URL should appear on every item of public relations material as a permanent feature.

(h) Creating and distributing as wide a variety of give-aways featuring the URL as budgets allow. These could include calendars, notepads, diaries, carrier bags, T-shirts, flags, playing cards, pens, badges, key-rings, bottle openers, calculators, drinking mugs and paperweights.

15. Monitoring website cost-effectiveness

To be cost-effective, advertising on the Internet must deliver against the demands of the brief. A website advertiser can install software to monitor the effectiveness of their own website. But the monitoring of banners and other advertising material on other websites needs more than the owners' statements of visitor traffic. The advertiser relies on independent third party audits conducted for other media, in order to estimate their cost-effectiveness. This is also possible with advertising on the Internet.

Most visitor traffic claims rely on 'hits'. This is a questionable measure for proving the effectiveness of the Internet as an advertising medium. This is because hits can be inflated at the site operator's whim without any real increase in traffic. Page impressions, where specific information and pages are requested, give a clearer picture. This has given rise to the establishment of independent auditing services.

For this purpose, ABC//electronic, an associate company of the Audit Bureau of Circulations, was formed in 1996 in response to demand by advertisers, publishers and media buyers. The company provides advertisers and Internet publishers with information, independently audited and reported, to agreed standards. This is a reliable aid to the buying and selling of advertising space on UK-based Internet sites.

16. Website auditing

The ABC//electronic auditing process comprises the following:

(a) A questionnaire, to gain as much information as possible on a website before auditing begins.

(b) An individual auditor assigned to each site.

(c) The use of census-based measurements reflecting actual total activity, rather than ratings or sampling-based research.

(d) For registration-based sites, two-way communication with web-users, allowing for validation of site visits by individuals.

(e) Audited web information is augmented by analysis and diagnosis, which helps with demographic profiling.

(f) Audit reports are designed to indicate not only the number of visits, but also the types of visitor. This takes place where the site captures the information, allowing for validation of the demographics of individual visitors.

17. The audit certificate

Ten steps are taken for the issuing of an ABC//electronic website audit certificate, as follows:

(a) The site is registered for ABC audit, and the site commits to ABC membership and first audit.

(b) An auditor visits the site to observe access logs and databases, taking sample segments of data.

(c) Interim fixes of record numbers and file sizes are also monitored.

(d) The auditor also observes the registration building for registration sites.

(e) Using Email, samples of registered visitors are checked.

(f) The site compiles the statistics it is claiming for the audit period; this is usually once a month.

(g) The site sends the information to ABC//electronic for verification.

(h) The auditor verifies the data claimed on site.

(i) Site statistics are checked to ensure that they have been compiled using ABC//electronic definitions.

(j) The ABC//electronic certificate is issued.

Each ABC//electronic certificate carries the following information:

(i) top level URL;

(ii) definitions;

(iii) audit opinion;

(iv) the period covered by the certificate;

(v) page impressions;

(vi) description of site content;

(vii) a breakdown of registered and non-registered traffic for sites declaring registration. To be claimed, a registrant must be contactable by the auditor.

18. Controls

It is widely supposed that the Internet is a free-for-all and completely unregulated. This is not the case. Also, it is due for substantial change in the near future, certainly within the life of this edition.

Several types of control are already in place, influencing the conduct of Internet advertisers. For example, all British law applying to general commerce also applies to the Internet. The ASA's British Codes of Advertising and Sales Promotion apply to Internet activity. These codes apply to 'advertisements in non-broadcast electronic media such as computer games' (1.1c). According to the ASA's information department, this includes Internet activity.

At the time this edition is being prepared for press, a number of other regulatory measures are either already in force or being considered. The main motivator for this is the European Union. Regrettably, many directives are issued without public consultation, democratic or parliamentary debate.

Some of the more important and far-reaching regulations should be noted:

(a) The Data Protection and Telecommunications Directive; currently in force. Article 12 applies to unsolicited faxes and telephone calls, but not to unsolicited Emails. This may change.

(b) The Data Protection Act 2000. Applies to all electronic commerce in the UK.

(c) The Distance Selling Directive. To be implemented in June 2000.

(d) The EU's Data Protection Directive. No specific application in place for Emails.

(e) The E-commerce Directive. Now being debated in the EU.

(f) The Electronic Commerce Bill. A UK parliamentary White Paper, tabled in March 1999.

The White Paper has been tabled by the Department of Trade and Industry (DTI). Two organisations have been given the task of accrediting e-commerce codes of practice: the Direct Marketing Association (DMA) and the Consumers Association. The DMA is a founder member of the Alliance for Electronic Business, and in this case is acting within the Alliance's initiative, TrustUK.

As part of this initiative, the DMA has established access to a global Email preference service (EPS). This is an opt-out scheme for unsolicited Email. Consumers wishing to register their Email addresses for the EPS need to access the DMA website and link to the EPS. Advertisers wishing to send unsolicited Email messages are required to purge their lists against the master EPS file. TrustUK provides companies using e-commerce with an e-hallmark. This enables consumers to identify at a glance companies signed up to codes or practice, which helps to guarantee high standards of customer service.

The White Paper states: 'For business, e-commerce will be the trade route of the new millennium.' It puts forward proposals for enhancing consumer protection and service to consumers, giving particular emphasis to electronic commerce. It looks to TrustUK to help raise consumer confidence in e-commerce by ensuring that UK websites subscribe to stringent codes of practice. These set out clear trading principles, respect data privacy, and ensure robust procedures are in place for cross-border resolution and redress of consumer complaints.

It must be remembered that, in Internet affairs, what is possible is not always legal. For example, the distribution of pornography via the Internet is a criminal offence in the UK. As use of the Internet as a commercial tool increases, governments across the world will inevitably strive to regulate it. That process is now under way. Practitioners and students of advertising and related disciplines are advised – and professionally obliged – to keep up to date with it.

Progress test 20

1. What is the predicted growth of the Internet in monetary terms, and in numbers of users? **(1)**

2. How does Internet advertising differ from other media? **(3–8)**

3. What is the extent of the Internet's capability as an advertising medium? **(3)**

4. What is demonstrated by the Media Capability Matrix? **(3)**

5. How does Internet advertising compare with the following:
   (a) Advertising on television? **(4)**
   (b) On radio? **(5)**
   (c) In the press **(6)**
   (d) Direct response? **(7)**
   (e) Outdoor? **(8)**

6. What are the advantages of classified advertising on the web? **(10)**

7. What is a banner advertisement? What is its main function? **(11)**

8. Why are host website selection and positioning important? **(11)**

9. Describe two main types of Email advertising. What are their pros and cons? **(12, 13)**

10. Describe eight basic techniques for promoting a website. **(14)**

11. Why do websites need to be monitored? **(15)**

12. Outline the ABC//electronic method of website auditing. **(16, 17)**

13. What controls are exercised on Internet advertising activity? What measures are in the pipeline? **(18)**

Appendix 1

Contacts

Bear in mind that addresses, telephone numbers, Email addresses and URLs change frequently, sometimes without notice. If you would like to suggest new entries or updates of existing ones, this would be very welcome and helpful to the next generation of readers. Please Email your suggestions and updates to the author at: danyad@cwcom.net

ABC//electronic
Electronic Media Audits Ltd
Norman House, 207–209 High Street,
Berkhamsted,
Hertfordshire HP4 1AD
Contact: Richard Foan
Tel: 01442 870 800
Fax: 01442 877 409
Email: raf@abc.org.uk
Web: www.abc.org.uk
An associate company of the Audit Bureau of Circulations.

A.C. Nielsen Media International
2nd floor, Kings Court, 185 Kings Road, Reading, Berkshire RG1 4EX.
Tel: 01189 569165
          or 0800 328 4477
Fax: 01189 596579
Web: www.ACNielsen.co.uk

Advertising Archives
45 Lyndale Avenue, London NW2 2QB
Tel: 020 7435 6540
Fax: 020 7794 6584

Advertising Association
Abford House, 15 Wilton Road,
London SW1V 1NJ
Tel: 020 7828 4831
Fax: 020 7931 0376
Web: www.adassoc.org.uk

Advertising Creative Circle
22 Poland Street, London W1V 3DD
Tel: 020 7734 9334

Advertising Standards Authority (ASA)
Brook House, 2–16 Torrington Place,
London WC1E 7HN
Tel: 020 7580 5555
Web: www.asa.org.uk

The 10th edition of the British Codes of Advertising & Sales Promotion came into force on 1 October 1999, replacing all previous editions. It became fully operational on 31 January 2000. There are a number of changes of substance since the previous edition. These include rules on political advertising, prices and protection of privacy. There is also a new set of specific rules on betting and gaming, brought in as a result of government deregulation; and a new section on the Independent Reviewer for ASA Adjudications.

Adwomen
18–24 Westbourne Grove, London W2 5RH
Tel: 020 7221 1819
Fax: 020 7221 2707

Agfa-Gevaert Ltd
Business Group and Graphic Systems
27 Great West Road, Brentford,
Middlesex TW8 9AX
Tel: 020 8231 4922
Fax: 020 8231 4957
Chromapress and IntelliStream digital
printing systems.

Association of Business Advertising
Agencies
Hammer Business Communications
23–28 Gt Russell Street, London
WC1B 3PX
Tel: 020 7753 0005
Fax: 020 7753 0036

Audit Bureau of Circulations Ltd (ABC)
Black Prince Yard, 207–209 High Street,
Berkhamsted, Herts HP4 1AD
Tel: 01442 870 800
Fax: 01442 877 407
Email: abcpost@abc.org.uk
Web: www.abc.org.uk

BARB. Broadcasters Audience
Research Board
Glenthorne House, Hammersmith
Grove, London W6 0ND
Tel: 020 8741 9110
Web: www.barb.co.uk

BMRB International
British Market Research Association
16 Creighton Avenue, London
N10 1NU
Tel: 020 8374 4095
Fax: 020 8883 9953
Email: admin@bmra.org.uk
Web: www.bmra.org.uk

British Association of Industrial Editors
3 Locks Yard, High Street, Sevenoaks,
Kent TN13 1LT
Tel: 01732 459331
Membership: editors of house journals.
Entry by examination. Journal:
BAIE News

British Library Business Information
Service
25 Southampton Buildings, London
WC2A 1AW
Tel: 020 7412 7454
Fax: 020 7412 7453
Web: www.bl.uk

British Market Research Bureau
Hadley House, 79–81 Uxbridge Road,
London W5 5SU
Tel: 020 8566 5000
Fax: 020 8579 9208
Email: mailbox@bmrb.co.uk
Web: www.bmrb.co.uk

Broadcast Advertising Clearance Centre
(BACC)
200 Grays Inn Road, London
WC1X 8HF
Tel: 020 7843 8000
Fax: 020 7843 8158
Checking and clearance of radio and
TV commercials.

Broadcasting Standards Commission
7 The Sanctuary, London SW1P 3JS
Tel: 020 7233 0544
Fax: 020 7233 0397
Email: bsc@bsc.org.uk
Web: www.bsc.org.uk

CACI
CACI House, Kensington Village,
Avonmore Road, London W14 8TS
Tel: 020 7602 6000
Fax: 020 7603 5862
Email: marketing@caci.co.uk
Web: www.caci.co.uk

CAM
Communication, Advertising and
Marketing Education Foundation
Abford House, 15 Wilton Road,
London SW1V 1NJ
Tel: 020 7828 7506
Fax: 010 7976 5140
Web: www.cam.co.uk

Certificate and diploma examinations. Vocational examination for those working in British communications industry. Holders of CIM Diploma exempt from Certificate, except PR, if they wish to take CAM Diploma in PR.

CAM Graduates Association
Abford House, 15 Wilton Road,
London SW1V 1NJ
Tel: 020 7828 7506
Fax: 010 7976 5140

Chartered Institute of Marketing (CIM)
Moor Hall, Cookham, Maidenhead,
Berkshire SL6 9QH
Tel: 01628 427 500
Fax: 01628 427 499
Web: www.cim.co.uk
Publications: *Marketing Business; Solutions.*
Professional body for 65,000 members worldwide. Professional and vocational qualifications. Activities include legal and other advisory services; library, information and research services; training in marketing, sales, strategy and associated techniques.

Chartered Institute of Marketing
Central London Branch (CLB)
Web: www.central-london.org
Publications: *CLB News;* e-Newsletter.
Activities include branch events with key speakers on professional issues and topics; CPD training events; social events; student support (CIM, MBA etc); 'Marketing 101' web-based professional discussion and information forum; business and career networking.

Cinema Advertising Association
12 Golden Square, London W1R 3AF
Publications: CAVIAR Cinema and Video Industry Audience Research; UK Advertising Admissions Monitor; Cinema Coverage and Frequency Guide.

Commercial Radio Companies
Association Ltd
77 Shaftsbury Avenue, London
W1V 7AD
Tel: 020 7306 2603
Fax: 020 7470 0062

Committee of Advertising Practice (CAP)
2 Torrington Place, London
WC1E 7HW
Tel: 020 7580 5555
Fax: 020 7631 3051
Web: www.asa.org.uk
Publications: The British Codes of Advertising and Sales Promotion

Confederation of British Industry
Centre Point, 103 New Oxford Street,
London WC1A 1DU
Tel: 020 7397 7400
Fax: 020 7240 0988
Email: enquiry.desk@cbi.org.uk
Web: www.cbi.org.uk

Council of Outdoor Specialists (COS)
Posterscope
55 North Wharf Road, London W2 1LA
Tel: 020 7724 7244
Fax: 020 7724 7620

Data Protection Registrar (DPR)
Wycliffe House, Water Lane,
Wilmslow, Cheshire SK9 5AF
Tel: 01625 545 745
Fax: 01625 524 510
Email: data@wycliffe.demon.co.uk
Web: www.dpr.gov.uk

Debating Group
196 Verulam Court, Woolmead
Avenue, London NW9 7AZ.
Tel & fax: 020 8202 5854

Department of Trade and Industry (DTI)
151 Buckingham Palace Road, London
SW1W 9SS
Tel: 020 7215 5000
Fax: 020 7222 0612
Email: dti.enquiries@imsv.dti.gov.uk
Web: www.dti.gov.uk

363

Direct Mail Accreditation and
Recognition Centre (DMARC)
Haymarket House, 1 Oxendon Street,
London SW1Y 4EE
Tel: 020 7766 4430
Fax: 020 7976 1886

Direct Mail Information Service
5 Carlisle Street, London W1V 6JX
Tel: 020 7494 0483
Fax: 020 7494 0455
Web: www.dmis.co.uk

Direct Marketing Association (UK)
Ltd (DMA)
5th Floor, Haymarket House,
1 Oxendon Street,
London SW1Y 4EE
Tel: 020 7321 2525
Fax: 020 7321 0191
Email: dma@dma.org.uk
Web: www.dma.org.uk

Du Pont (UK) Ltd
Imaging Systems Department
Wedgwood Way, Stevenage,
Hertfordshire SG1 4QN
Tel: 01438 734523
Fax: 01483 734522

Enterprise Identity Group
6 Mercer Street, London WC2H 9QA.
Tel: 020 7574 4000
Fax: 020 7574 4100

European Marketing Association
18 St Peters Steps, Brixham,
Devon TQ5 9TE
Tel: 01803 859 575

Independent Television Commission
(ITC)
33 Foley Street, London W1P 7LB
Tel: 020 7255 3000
Fax: 020 7306 7800
Email: publicaffairs@itc.org.uk
Web: www.itc.org.uk
Journal: *Spectrum*

Independent Television Network
Centre
200 Grays Inn Road, London WC1X 8HF
Tel: 020 7843 8000
Fax: 020 7843 8158

Indigo UK
Suite 1, Awberry Court, Croxley
Business Park, Watford, Hertfordshire
WD1 8YJ
Tel: 01923 242 402
Fax: 01923 242 412
Email: berneyp@indigo.co.il
Web: www.indigonet.com

Institute of Direct Marketing
1 Park Road, Teddington, Middlesex
TW11 0AR
Tel: 020 8977 5705
Fax: 020 8943 2535
Web:
http://tendou.corpex.com/users/idm

Institute of Practitioners in Advertising
44 Belgrave Square, London SW1X 8QS
Tel: 020 7235 7020
Fax: 020 7245 9904
Email: mark@ipa.co.uk
Web: www.ipa.co.uk
The professional representative body
for advertising agencies.

Institute of Public Relations
The Old Trading House, 15
Northburgh Street, London EC1V 0PR
Tel: 020 7253 5151
Membership by age and experience
plus CAM
Diploma or its equivalent. Journal:
Public Relations.
Annual Sword of Excellence awards.

Institute of Sales Promotion
Arena House, 66–68 Pentonville Road,
London N1 9HS
Tel: 020 7837 5340
Fax: 020 7837 5326
Web: www.isp.org.uk

IPSOS-RSL Ltd
Media research specialists
Kings House, Kymberley Road,
Harrow, Middlesex HA1 1PT
Tel: 020 8861 8000
Fax: 020 8861 5515
Web: www.ipsos.com

ISBA
Incorporated Society of British
Advertisers
44 Hertford Street. London W1Y 8AE
Tel: 020 7499 7502
Fax: 020 7629 5355
Web: www.isba.org.uk

JICREG
Joint Industry Committee for Regional
Press Research
Bloomsbury House, 74–77 Gt Russell
Street, London WC1B 3DA
Tel: 020 7636 7014
Web: www.jicreg.co.uk

Letraset UK
195–203 Waterloo Road, London SE1 8XJ
Tel: 020 7928 7551

London Chamber of Commerce and
Industry
Examinations Board
Athena House, Station Road, Sidcup,
Kent DA15 7BJ
Tel: 020 8302 0261
Fax: 020 8302 4169
Web: www.lccieb.org.uk
Third Level Certificate Examinations
in Advertising, Marketing, Public
Relations, Selling and Sales
Management (with Diplomas for passes
in three or four subjects taken at the
same time). Diploma in Management
Studies if three subjects passed at
different times.

London College of Printing
Elephant & Castle, London SE1
Tel: 020 7514 6500
A constituent college of the London
Institute.

London Management Training Centre
166 Upper Richmond Road, London
SW15 2SH
Tel: 01342 326704
Specialises in business training for
overseas management, including
business, marketing, advertising, public
relations, finance and human resources.

Maiden Outdoor
128 Buckingham Palace Road, London
SW1W 9SA
Tel: 020 7838 4000 and 7838 4040
Fax: 020 7838 4002
Web: www.maiden.co.uk

Mail Order Protection Scheme (MOPS)
16 Tooks Court, London EC4A 1LB
Operated by publishers of the national
press.

Mailing Preference Service
5 Reef House, Plantation Wharf,
London SW11 3UF
Tel: 020 7738 1625
Fax: 020 7978 4918

Market Research Society
15 Northburgh Street, London
EC1V 0AH
Tel: 020 7490 4911
Fax: 020 7490 0608
Email: info@marketresearch.org.uk
Web: www.marketresearch.org.uk

Marketing Society
St George's House, 3–5 Pepys Road,
London SW20 8NJ
Tel: 020 8879 3464
Fax: 020 8879 0362
Email: info@marketing-society.org.uk
Web: www.marketing-society.org.uk

Mintel International Group
18–19 Long Acre, London EC1A 9HE
Tel: 020 7606 4533
Fax: 020 7606 5932
Email: enquiries@mintel.co.uk
Web: www.mintel.co.uk

National Readership Surveys Ltd
42 Drury Lane, London WC2B 5RT
Tel: 020 7632 2915
Fax: 020 7632 2916
Email: anyname@nrs.co.uk
Web: www.nrs.co.uk

NOP Research Group
Ludgate House, 245 Blackfriars Road,
London SE1 9UL
Tel: 020 7890 9099
Fax: 020 7890 9744
Web: www.nopres.co.uk

Office of Telecommunications
(OFTEL)
50 Ludgate Hill, London EC4M 7JJ
Tel: 020 7634 8700
Fax: 020 7634 8943
Email: crs.oftel@gtnet.gov.uk

ONdigital
PO Box 4, Plymouth PL1 3XU
Tel: 0808 100 0101
Web: www.ondigital.co.uk

Outdoor Advertising Association
(OAA)
Summit House, 27 Sale Place, London
W2 1YR
Tel: 020 7973 0315
Fax: 020 7973 0318
Email: mcarrington@oaa.org.uk
Web: www.oaa.org.uk

Oxford University Press
Walton Street, Oxford OX2 6DP

POSTAR
Summit House
27 Sale Place, London W2 1YR
Tel: 020 7479 9700
Fax: 020 7298 8034
Email: info@postar.co.uk
Web: www.postar.co.uk

Public Relations Consultants
Association (PRCA)
Willow House, Willow Place, London
SW1P 1JH.
Tel: 020 7233 6026
Fax: 020 7828 4797
Web: www.martex.co.uk/prca
Corporate membership. Overseas
Associates
Publications: *Public Relations Year Book.*
What's Happening at the PRCA
(newsletters). Guidance Papers (training).
Briefing papers (legal).

Radio Advertising Bureau
77 Shaftesbury Avenue, London
W1V 7AD
Tel: 020 7306 2500
Fax: 020 7306 2505
Email: rab@rab.co.uk
Web: www.rab.co.uk
Marketing arm of the commercial radio
industry. Provides independent
information to advertisers.

Radio Advertising Clearance Centre
Radio House, 46 Westbourne Grove,
London W2 5SH
Tel: 020 7727 2646
Fax: 020 7229 0352
Email: adclear@racc.co.uk

Radio Authority
Holbrook House, 14 Gt Queen Street,
London WC2B 5DG
Tel: 020 7430 2724
Fax: 020 7405 7062
Email: info@radioauthority.org.uk
Web: www.radioauthority.org.uk

RAJAR
Radio Joint Audience Research Ltd
Collier House, 163–169 Brompton
Road, London SW3 1PY
Tel: 020 7584 3003
Fax: 020 7589 4004
Email: rajar@dial.pipex.com

Royal Mail Direct Marketing
Department
Room 221, Royal Mail House,
148/166 Old Street,
London EC1V 9HQ
Tel: 020 7250 2346
Fax: 020 7250 2366
Publications include: *The Complete
Guide to Advertising Your Business by
Post. The Direct Mail Guide. Postal
Services for Business.*

Standard Rate and Data Service
(SRDS)
1700 Higgins Road, Des Plaines, Illinois
60018-5605, United States of America
Tel: (847) 375 5183
Fax: (847) 375 5009
Monthly media directories, covering
newspapers, consumer magazines and
business publications.

Telephone Preference Service (TPS)
5th Floor, Haymarket House,
1 Oxendon Street, London SW1Y 4EE
Tel: 020 7766 4422
Fax: 020 7976 1886
Email: tps@dma.org.uk
Web: www.dma.org.uk

Training Resources and Courses
63 Cheyneys Avenue, Edgware,
Middlesex HA8 6SD
Tel: 020 8951 3732
Email: danyad@cwcom.net
Web:
www.TrainingResources.mcmail.com

A faculty of trainers, consultants and
practitioners, providing training across
the whole range of marketing,
management media and business
disciplines. Journal: *Training Resources.*

VFD
Verified Free Distribution
Black Prince Yard, 207–209 High Street,
Berkhamsted, Hertfordshire HP4 1AD
Tel: 01442 870 800
Fax: 01442 877 409
Web: www.abc.org.uk
Part of the Audit Bureau of Circulations.

Watford School of Business
Postgraduate Diploma in Advertising
West Herts College
Hempstead Road, Watford WD1 3EZ
Tel: 01923 812591/2
Web: www.westherts.ac.uk
Contact: Andrea Neidle

Winmark
Shakespeare House, 168 Lavender Hill,
London SW11 5TF
Tel: 020 7801 6247
Fax: 020 7801 6251
Email: research@winmark.co.uk
Market research and business analysis.

Women in Advertising and
Communications
Guardian Newspapers, 119 Farringdon
Road, London EC1R 3GR
Tel: 020 7278 2332
Fax: 020 7837 0651

Appendix 2

Further reading

Note: Check for revised editions and up-dates before you buy.

Advertising Budget, The, Simon Broadbent (NTC Henley, 1989).
Advertising Made Simple (5th edition), Frank Jefkins (Butterworth-Heinemann Made Simple Books, Oxford, 1992).
Advertising Statistics Yearbook (The Advertising Association).
Advertising Worldwide, Marieke K. de Mooij and Warren J. Keegan (Prentice Hall, Hemel Hempstead, 1991).
British Codes of Advertising and Sales Promotion, The (The Advertising Standards Authority).
British Rate and Data (Maclean Hunter Ltd, Barnet, Hertfordshire, monthly).
British Standard BS 5261: Part 2 1976. Copy Preparation and Proof Correction – Specification of Typographic Requirements, Marks for Copy Preparation and Proof Correction, Proofing Procedure (The British Standards Institution).
Concise Oxford Dictionary, The (Oxford University Press).
Confessions of an Advertising Man, David Ogilvy (Atheneum, New York).
Creative Handbook, The (Cahners Publishing Co., London, annually).
Creative Marketing Communications, Daniel Yadin (Kogan Page, 1998).
Designer's Handbook, The, Alastair Campbell (Macdonald Orbis, London).
Desktop Design, Brian Cookman (Blueprint Publishing, London).
Dictionary of Advertising, Frank Jefkins (Pitman, London, 1990).
Dupont Series on Print Production and Reprographics, The (Dupont (UK) Ltd, Stevenage, Hertfordshire).
Effective Advertiser, The, Tom Brannan (Butterworth-Heinemann, Oxford, 1993).
Effective Use of Advertising Media, The, Martyn P. Davis (Century Business, London).
Effective Use of Market Research (3rd edition), Robin Birn (Kogan Page, London, 1993).
European Sales Promotion, Alan Toap (Kogan Page, London, 1992).
Graphic Design for the Electronic Age, Jan V. White (Watson-Guptill Publications, New York).
Great Advertising Campaigns, Nicholas Ind (Kogan Page, London, 1993).
Guide to Sales Promotion, A (ISBA, London, 1992).
Hart's Rules for Compositors and Readers (Oxford University Press).
Hollis Sponsorship and Donations Year Book (Hollis Directories, Sunbury-on-Thames, annually).
How to Get Into Advertising, Andrea Neidle (Cassell, 1999).
ITC Code of Advertising Standards and Practice, The (Independent Television Commission).
Lifestyle Pocket Book (NTC, Henley, annually).

Marketing Handbook (Hollis Directories, Teddington, Middlesex, annually).

Marketing Pocket Book (NTC, Henley, annually).

Marketing Today, Gordon Oliver (Prentice Hall, New York and London).

Media Pocket Book (NTC, Henley, annually).

Modern Marketing (3rd edition), Frank Jefkins (Pitman, London, 1993).

New How to Advertise, The, Kenneth Roman and Jane Maas (Kogan Page, London, 1992).

Ogilvy on Advertising, David Ogilvy (Pan Books, London).

Planned Press and Public Relations (3rd edition), Frank Jefkins (Blackie Academic, Glasgow, 1993).

Printing Reproduction Pocket Pal (International Paper Co., Memphis TN 38197, USA; in the UK, Creative Services Association, London).

Print Production Handbook, The, David Bann (Macdonald, London).

Production and Creativity in Advertising, Robin B. Evans (Pitman, London).

Public Relations, Frank Jefkins and Daniel Yadin (Pitman, 5th edition, 1997).

Radio Authority Code of Advertising Standards and Practice and Programme Sponsorship, The (The Radio Authority).

Sales Promotion (2nd edition), Julian Cummins (Kogan Page, London, 1993).

Scientific Advertising, Claude Hopkins (MacGibbon & Kee, London).

Successful Advertising: Key Alternative Approaches, Martyn P. Davis (Cassell, London, 1997).

Understanding and Designing Marketing Research, John R. Webb (Harcourt Brace Jovanovich, Academic Press, London, 1993).

Appendix 3

Glossary of advertising terms

A la carte agency One which offers creative services but does not plan or buy media and consequently does not require recognition, making small firms feasible and not dependent on volume of billings.

A/B Split method Kind of split run media testing, a control and a test advertisement appearing in different editions of a journal on same day and in same position to measure response. Or different advertisements can be tested on different radio or TV stations at same time.

Above-the-line Sometimes called media advertising. Press, TV, radio, cinema and outdoor which traditionally pay recognised agencies commission on purchases.

Account Client of an advertising agency or public relations consultancy. *See* account executive.

Account executive, representative, supervisor Person who represents the agency and liaises with the client, conveying client's instructions and requirements to agency team. Generally has all-round knowledge of advertising and will be responsible for a number of accounts.

Account planner Some, but not all, advertising agencies have an account planner who integrates the work of agency functions. Works closely with account executive, prepares the creative brief, and co-ordinates departmental work on a campaign.

ACORN Acronym for A Classification of Residential Neighbourhoods. A marketing research database classification technique, built around the premise that people in similar neighbourhoods are likely to have similar lifestyle and purchasing patterns. Provides a tool for identifying and targeting consumers.

Ad click An advertisement impression a user has clicked on for the advertisement in question.

Ad impression A combination of one or more files sent to a user as an individual advertisement file, via that user's request, received by the server in question.

Adaptation Different version of original advertisement to fit different size or shape space.

Adequate distribution Situation where goods have been sold into the shops in readiness for advertising to break, and in order to meet demand created by advertising.

Address Email address: a unique address which identifies you to a distant computer. Web address: a unique address which identifies your website; usually referred to as a URL, uniform resource locator.

Advertorial Two kinds, the legitimate and the deceitful. When, as a reader service, a publication makes a special offer of a new product such as a lipstick or shampoo this is legitimate. The maker of the product buys no space. But when the manufacturer buys space and the publisher undertakes to make the advertisement appear to be independent editorial this is deceitful and both advertiser and publisher are involved in tricking the reader. Unfortunately, this racket has been conducted by some well-known PR consultancies and publishers, and they have been severely criticised.

Allocation Portion of the appropriation (*see*) set aside for a particular part of the advertising campaign, e.g. press advertising, TV commercials or exhibitions.

AltaVista An organisation with a huge search engine devoted to finding information on the World Wide Web (WWW).

Animatics 1. Use of video to pre-test advertisements, using a cartoon of visual ideas. Slides may also be used. 2. Animated or cartoon effects in TV commercial.

Answerprint Master print of TV commercial. *See* photomatics.

Applet A small computer program in the Java computing language.

Appropriation The budget of an advertising campaign, covering all production and media costs.

Arena advertising Advertising on board around perimeters of sports stadium.

Armchair buying Direct response marketing, the buying of selected goods from a catalogue while sitting at home.

Art director Specialist in a creative department in advertising agency. May work on visuals, layouts, typography and art buying.

Attachment A computer file attached to an Email message and delivered with it.

Audio Written description on storyboard of script, sound effects, music in proposed TV commercials.

Audit Bureau of Circulations Body of which most publishers are members, which certifies at regular intervals average audited net sales submitted by members, issuing an ABC figure. May conduct independent audit if submitted figures are doubted.

Audited net sale The circulation figure of a journal, as declared by publishers' independent auditors after deduction from original print order of free copies, returns, vouchers, and copies not sold at full cover price (*see* cover price).

Banner A small informational message or advertisement placed on a web page, linked to the advertiser's own website.

BARB Broadcasters' Audience Research Board. Researches TV audiences. Has panel of 4,435 homes with meters for recording programmes watched. Also measures watching of VCRs. Weekly, monthly reports. Weekly report gives hours of viewing for each channel and lists audiences for most popular programmes on each channel. Monthly report provides hours of viewing plus regional shares, and top 50 programmes for the month.

Below-the-line Non-commission paying advertising such as exhibitions, direct mail, sales literature, point-of-sale displays but not public relations.

Billboard (British) Poster advertisement on hoarding placed outside shop. (American) Outdoor poster advertising.

Billings Total amount spent by agencies on behalf of clients. May be quoted as 'declared billing' or 'Register-Meal billing'. The latter, based on estimates of agency expenditure, is usually a lower figure.

Bleed Printing of illustration or type area to extreme edge of page which is trimmed to give bled-off effect. Artwork has to be larger than page size so that it can be trimmed.

Bookmark   The address of a web page, grouped with others in a list, to which you may want to return frequently.

Bounce-back   Extra premium offer made to customer who has responded to sales promotion offer.

BRAD   British Rate and Data, a monthly media directory containing rate card data. BRADbase makes data available on line.

Brand   Name of product, originally derived from cattle branding to prove ownership. Branding makes it possible to advertise a product.

Brand share   Proportion of market held by a particular brand as recorded by dealer audit research which records purchases, stocks and sales of brands in a sample of shops.

Break bumpers   Credits during breaks or parts in a sponsored ITV programme.

British Codes of Advertising and Sales Promotion   Voluntary code covering all print advertising and administered by Advertising Standards Authority. For recognition (*see*) purposes advertising agencies must support BCASP. Public invited to make written complaints. Basic principle: advertising should be legal, decent and honest. One Benetton poster produced 1,000 complaints. Has no power to penalise but can recommend modifications or non-repetition of misleading claims in the future. Publishes monthly reports on its investigations, recording whether complaints upheld or not upheld.

Broadband cable   Cable television which provides 45 or more channels together with interactive facilities and telecommunications.

Broadsheet   (1) Large sheet newspaper compared with a tabloid. (2) Fold-up mailing shot, folding like a map.

Browser   A program which enables you to access and read information on the WWW.

Bulkhead   Advertisement spaces above windows of bus interior.

Bulletin board   Large specially constructed solus advertising site, sometimes with garden and lights.

Bullets   Graphic device as when dots, stars, squares used to highlight selling points in copy.

Burst advertising   Short dramatic advertising campaigns as distinct from regular drips advertising (*see* drip advertising).

Business press   Magazines and newspapers read by businesspeople such as the *Financial Times, Investor's Chronicle, Fortune, The Times* and the *Economist*.

Business-to-business advertising   Non-consumer advertising of industrial and business goods and services such as plant, machinery, raw materials, office equipment, business services.

Buzz words   Contemporary expressions which may be short lived. Clichés which make copy effective, e.g. now, unique, free, exciting.

Call report   *See* contact report.

CAVIAR   Cinema and Video Industry Audience Research. Run by Carrick James Market Research, it conducts research into cinema-going for the Cinema Advertising Association.

Certificate of Attendance   The COA was introduced in 1993 by the Audit Bureau of Circulations, and requires registered members to show proof of systems existing to reliably audit attendances at exhibitions and to provide accurate information for certification purposes.

CG Computer graphics.

Cheshire labels Specially prepared paper used to print names and addresses that can be mechanically fixed singly to mailing pieces.

Circulation Number of copies of a journal sold. Net sale after deduction from original print order of free copies, vouchers, returns and those sold at less than full price. *See* Audit Bureau of Circulations.

Classifieds The 'smalls'. Small advertisements, private or commercial, with run-on copy and classified under headings.

Click-through rate The number of visitors who click to and land on a website or page.

Clutter Excessive advertising which causes annoyance. Clutter Code (Code of Standards for Advertising and Business Premises, 1962) resulted in removal or modification of 4,662 unsightly facias, wallboards and headboards within six months. Problem arose again in 1993 with clutter of TV advertising as criticised at TV93 conference in Monte Carlo, and subject of report by Henley Centre. Such clutter consists of normal commercials, sponsorship coverage and sponsored programmes. Also problem of increasing number of channels. Even worse on ILR and INR with frequent sponsors' copylines.

Cold mailing Direct mailing to new prospects as when a mailing list is hired.

Commission system Method of recognising advertising agents by NPA, NS, PRA, ITVA, CRCA so that they may receive commission on media purchases. Agencies required to show proof of credit worthiness so that media bills are paid promptly, and to adhere to British Codes of Advertising and Sales Promotion.

Computergraphics *See* Harry, morphing, post production.

Condensed Characters of a typeface which are narrower than normal typeface, taking up less space, but less easy to read.

Contact report Essential agency or consultancy paperwork representing brief minutes of meetings. Usual to have right-hand column ruled off for instructions and responsibilities. Copied to those present at meetings, and to others on both sides who need to be informed. Should be limited to reports and decisions and avoid discussion. Also known as call report.

Contract of service Agreement between advertiser and agency which states conditions of service such as method of remuneration, required notice of termination, and conditions regarding assignment of copyright.

Controlled circulation A cc magazine is sent to a selected plus requested readership (the latter being required for ABC figure), and commands higher advertisement rate than one which relies on retail or subscription sales because it has greater penetration of the market. New magazines are sometimes launched on cc basis, and subscriptions sought when magazine is established.

Cookie A small text file stored on your computer, put there by a web site you have visited. Its intention is to give that site details about you on your next visit.

Co-operative advertising Three kinds: (1) manufacturer's support for dealer's local advertising, (2) joint advertising by members of a trade or industry, and (3) advertising for two related products, e.g. bread and butter.

Copy platform Theme for advertising campaign, usually devised by the copywriter.

Copyline Sponsor's statement accompanying sponsored ILR/INR announcement as permitted by Radio Authority's Code of Advertising Standards and Practice and Programme Sponsorship.

Copywriter   Writer of copy for an advertisement, including total wording consisting of display lines, text, slogan, strapline, coupon copy.

Corporate advertising   Prestige, institutional advertising as seen in business press, describing history, attributes or achievements of a company.

Corporate identity   Combination of logo, colour scheme, typography, dress, livery, etc. which identify an organisation visibly. Important element of advertising, packaging, print, vehicles. Not to be confused with corporate image (*see*).

Corporate image   Perceived mental idea of an organisation based on knowledge and experience. Can vary accordingly dependent on one's relationship with organisation, i.e. employee, shareholder, dealer, consumer may have very different perceived corporate image. Fallacious to seek to create a corporate image, although facts may be presented to establish a correct image.

Cost-per-thousand   Means of comparing media with different rates, circulations or readerships by dividing the rate by the number of thousands of buyers or readers.

Cover price   Retail price of a journal.

CPM   Cost per thousand impressions; the cost of a thousand visits to your website.

Cross-over test   Form of split-run or A/B split (*see*) testing of alternative advertisements except that alternative publications are tested. Different advertisements are placed in different journals, and then switched from one journal to the other when the next issue comes out.

Crown   Small poster measuring 500mm × 38lmm, or 20″ × 15″. Basis of measurement of larger posters, e.g. 16 sheet although this does not consist of 16 separate crown size pieces of paper.

Day after recall   Advertisement research method to test recall of advertisements read, seen or heard on previous day.

dc   Double column. Twice width of newspaper column. Expression used regarding advertisement space. Written in lower case.

DC   Double crown. Small poster size. *See* double fronts, rears. Written in caps.

De-duplication   Removing duplicated names from mailing list.

Denigration   Unfair comparison. Knocking copy or ashcanning.

Direct advertising   Door-to-door distribution of maildrops.

Direct mail   Britain's third largest advertising medium, mail shots being delivered by post.

Display face   Large, bold and often decorative type used for headlines and sub-headings in contrast to small text type.

Display outer   Point-of-sale display piece in form of carton for small unit goods which can be converted into a dispenser with a display panel when folded out of lid. Used for counter and shelf displays.

Displayed advertisement   Press advertisement with pictures and mixture of display and text type.

Dissolve   Slow transition from one shot to another in film or video, often denoting passing of time.

Distribution cycle   Time it takes for product to move from production to retailer including selling and delivery, which is important to know when planning an advertising campaign to avoid campaign breaking before goods are available in the shops.

Domain name   Part of the unique identifying name of a computer on the net. Example: cim.com.

Doormat media   Direct mail addressed to consumer at home. Not unaddressed maildrop (*see*).

Double crown   Popular small poster size as used for window bills, news bills, or double fronts/backs on double-decker buses. Measures 762mm × 508mm or 30″ × 20″.

Double fronts, rears   Pairs of double crown posters on front or back of upper deck of double-decker bus.

Double-head   In production of a television commercial when sound and vision are still on separate tapes. *See* married print.

Doublespread   Press advertisement occupying two facing pages.

Download   To copy a file or program from another computer to yours.

Drip advertising   Continuous advertising, such as reminder advertisements which occupy same space on same day in same medium. *See* burst advertising.

Duplication   Number of people who use the same medium and could be wasteful. Media may be chosen with least duplication. Also repetition in mailing, perhaps because of a difference in presentation of name, first name spelt out or as an initial.

Ear   Title corner advertisement space on front page of some newspapers, usually broadsheets (*see*).

Eco-advertising   Often form of corporate advertising (*see*) which seeks to gain credit for company's anti-pollution, wild life protection or other environmental activities. May be genuine, but could be cover up. Dubious eco-advertising, including that of supposedly 'green' products, known as greenwashing (*see*).

Effectiveness   Ability of advertisement to achieve advertiser's purpose, e.g. produce enquiries or direct sales, use cash voucher, visit store or simply remember.

Egyptian   Slab serif typeface such as Rockwell, Cairo, Karnak which have serifs and strokes of the same thickness.

Email   Messages delivered electronically via the Internet.

Emphatic full stop   A full stop (full point) at end of a sentence used as the headline of an advertisement.

Escalator panels   Advertisement panel on wall of escalator, as on London Underground.

Exhibition train   One which can be toured to different towns, remaining in station and siding so that visitors can see exhibition on board.

Facts book   Collection of contact reports (*see*).

Family   Varieties of typeface design such as light, medium, bold, extra bold, condensed, expanded, shadow, in roman and italic versions.

Finished artwork   Complete camera-ready or computer-generated copy comprising words and pictures. Also called mechanical artwork or mechanical.

Firewall   A security measure, usually a specially programmed computer, which allows only certain messages into and out of it.

Flexography   Form of letterpress printing, using flexible rubber plates and used for printing on delicate material such as foil. Used for newspaper printing and adopted at new *Daily Mail* plant, using improved photopolymer plates and inks and rivals offset litho. Flexo inks brighter than offset inks. Good picture reproduction.

Flighting   Use of burst advertising interspersed by periods without advertising.

Float   White space around an advertisement. Can occur when same advertisement is supplied for publications with different page sizes instead of producing adaptations to suit different spaces.

Flutter sign Outdoor poster site made up of spangles which flutter in the breeze and appear to be constantly moving. Seen in the East, e.g. Indonesia, but has been used in Piccadilly Circus and elsewhere in Britain.

Flyer A direct mail shot.

Folder technique *See* pre-testing.

Footprint Geographical area, covering many countries, which can receive TV programmes broadcast by a satellite station.

Fount Pronounced, and sometimes spelled, 'font'. Full set of characters, numbers and signs of a typeface design.

Free newspaper Usually weekly, a local newspaper delivered door-to-door free of charge. Revenue obtained from large number of advertisers who are given access to a very large circulation and saturation coverage of a town or area. Some towns have three or four such papers. Mostly owned by large regional newspaper groups. In some cases have replaced paid-for weeklies because of their ability to attract large volumes of advertising, largely from stores, motor-car dealers and estate agents plus classifieds (*see*).

Free standing insert A separate advertisement inserted in a publication. An insert or tip-in.

FTP File transfer protocol. A method of transferring files between computers via the Internet.

Fulfilment house One which deals with response to advertising, warehousing and distributing leaflets, brochures, catalogues, mail-in offers, cash vouchers and other items offered in advertisements, on-the-pack-offers and so on.

Full-out Setting of paragraphs without indents (*see*). Should be applied only to first paragraph of text.

Full point Full stop.

Gable end Poster site on side wall of house or shop.

Gatefold Page in a journal or piece of print which folds out to make extra page.

Generic advertising Co-operative advertising by competing companies in the same product group, e.g. a campaign to encourage people to watch more videos, to eat meat, or to consume dairy products. Such campaigns are usually financed by a trade association, e.g. British Videogram Association, the Meat and Livestock Commission or the National Dairy Council.

Generic products Usually unbranded, perhaps sold loose, such as aspirin, rice or soap.

Geo-demographic targeting Reaching target audiences (*see*) by use of geographic and demographic classifications of residential neighbourhoods. *See* ACORN, Monica, MOSAIC, PIN, Sagacity, Super Profiles.

Get-up Distinctive design or a package, resemblances or near-copies of which may be legally actionable as passing off.

Global advertising Few products are capable of global advertising or global marketing but exceptions are Coca-Cola, Pepsi-Cola, Fuji and Kodak films.

Glossy Originally referred to minority of up-market magazines, but with modern shiny offset-litho papers is commonly if wrongly used to describe many popular magazines.

Gondola Circular self-service display stand with five or more shelves.

Graphics Pictures, halftones, illustrations and diagrams, as distinct from lettering or typography.

Greenwashing   Advertising which exploits environmental issues.

Gross OTS   Measuring opportunities to see any type of advertisement in any medium in order to calculate coverage of a campaign.

Gutter   Space between pages, or between unruled columns of text.

Gutter crossing   Headline which extends across centre margins of facing pages (not necessarily centre spread), when it is best to avoid break words.

Halftone   Continuous tonal effect of a photograph or painting, created by imposition of a dot screen. The better the paper, the finer the screen. Coarse screens used by former letterpress printed newspapers, but finer screens and better picture quality with litho printing. Can be applied to letterpress, lithography, flexography and screen printing.

Harry   Digital compositor from Quantrel for adding creative effects to videotape productions.

Heavies   *See* quality press.

Heli-blimp   Advertising balloon painted with customer's name, design, message, or fitted with interchangeable banners.

Hoarding   A roadside poster site, mostly 16 or 48 sheet.

Home page   The first or main page of a website. This will usually contain links to other pages on the site. If the website operator is advertising and offering goods and services, menus of these items will be displayed.

Horizontal advertising   Co-operative advertising on behalf of a trade or industry whose members are levied to pay the cost. Usually organised by a trade association. or a special body may be set up to conduct joint advertising.

Host   A computer connected to the Internet. A host-name is the identifying name of that computer.

Hot shop   Small creative advertising agency which buys no media and does not require recognition. Some have become larger and are called à la carte agencies.

HTTP   Hypertext transfer protocol. A language which enables computers to transfer web pages to one another via the Internet.

ILR   Independent local radio. Over 250 stations in Britain, some with split frequencies broadcasting different programmes to different listeners.

Impact   Effect advertisement has on reader, viewer or listener. A TV campaign can be shown as many times as it is likely to achieve a given number of impacts per viewer, bearing in mind that the viewer will not see every appearance of the commercial.

Indent   To start a paragraph with a space as in books and newspapers. Makes copy more readable than the unindented block paragraphs of business letters. Useful way of introducing white space into text of advertisements.

INR   Independent National radio. First licences awarded to Classic FM (INR1) and Virgin Radio (INR2) by Radio Authority in 1992. Classic FM launched 1992. Virgin 1215 1992, broadcasting pop music.

In-theatre test   *See* pre-testing.

Internet   The global network of computers.

ISBA   Incorporated Society of British Advertisers. Trade body for protection and advancement of advertising interests of member firms. Advises on all forms of media and publishes useful guidance booklets.

ISP   Internet service provider. Any organisation through which you access the Internet, its information and facilities.

Italic   Type that slopes to the right. May be used to give emphasis. If copy is to be set in italics it should be underlined.

ITC   Independent Television Commission. Founded by Broadcasting Act 1990, replacing IBA and dealing with commercial television (ITV) only. Licenses ITV contractors. Has Code of Practice and rules regarding sponsored programmes.

ITVA   Independent Television Association. Trade body of ITV contractors. Recognises advertising agencies.

Java   A computer language, designed to create and deliver applications via the Internet.

Jingles   Catchy tunes used in radio and TV commercials.

Junk mail   Uncomplimentary name for unsolicited direct mail.

Key   Device printed on advertisement or in coupon to identify source of enquiry or order. Best if unobtrusive, such as number in corner of coupon, or as part of address.

Keyline   Outline used for positioning artwork in piece of print.

Kicker   Brief line of copy in smaller type above headline of an advertisement.

Knock down   Dismantling of stand at close of exhibition.

Knocking copy   Advertisement which denigrates or ashcans a rival advertiser.

Laminate   To apply plastic film surface to print, such as a wall chart or cover of a publication in order to protect.

Layout   Plan of a piece of print or an advertisement with exact measurements for display lines, illustrations, text, name, address, etc; usually marked up with names, sizes and varieties of typefaces. Produced from the rough visual by the layout man.

Letterbox marketing   Direct advertising. Door-to-door distribution of mail drops. Delivered with free newspapers.

Lifestyle   Form of research which places people in numerous interest groups. There are those symbolised by expressions such as empty nesters, baby boomers, crinklies, yuppies or other psychographic types. Lifestyle databases are based on answers to very elaborate questionnaires inserted in magazines and delivered door-to-door.

Light reader   Those who spend less than 4.5 hours a week on leisure reading. One third of all adults. Tend to be heavy viewers of TV.

Light viewers   Those of higher social grades or whose activities preclude watching TV who watch less TV than majority of viewers.

Link   A connection, in the form of text or pictures on a web page or Email, which connects you to another web page or website. It can also connect you to another part of the same page.

List broker   Supplier of mailing lists for direct mail campaigns.

Logotype   Logo. Part of corporate identity scheme. Visual presentation of company name, or distinctive shape, or a handwritten name as with Coca-Cola and Ford.

Lowercase   Small letters in typesetting. Originates from lower case in cabinet of individual type characters in days of typesetting by hand.

Mail Order Protection Scheme   MOPS. Reader protection scheme run by Newspaper Publishers' Association (*see* NPA) and Periodical Publishers' Association (*see* PPA). Advertisements are displayed in newspapers/magazines. Direct response advertisements are vetted before publication and advertisers have to contribute to pool which may be used to compensate a reader who loses money because a trader goes bankrupt. Excludes classifieds, goods supplied on approval and some other categories.

Maildrop   Advertisement delivered door-to-door. Direct advertising. Unaddressed.

Mailsort   Post Office service offering special postal rates for large mailings presorted by postal code. Uses distinctive mailsort printed badge instead of postage stamp which reveals that it could be a direct mail shot. This could be unfortunate if contents were otherwise and important to recipient who might be tempted to discard as junk mail. Three grades, 1st class, 2nd class and economy class with different delivery dates and discounts.

Marketing mix   All elements from research and development to the after-market, such as branding, pricing, packaging, distribution, selling, advertising, which constitute the total marketing strategy. *See* also media mix and product mix.

Married print   Film print or videotape combining picture and sound. *See* double-head.

Media   Plural of medium. Means of conveying advertising messages. Press, radio, television, outdoor, direct mail are media. The press (etc.) is a medium.

Media buyer   Agency executive who negotiates purchase of space with advertisement manager of publication.

Media independent   Advertising agency which plans and buys media but does no creative work. Some owned by service agencies, e.g. largest is Zenith owned by Saatchi & Saatchi.

Media mix   The combination of media used in an advertising campaign, e.g. press, TV, outdoor.

Media planner   Agency executive who proposes media schedule (*see*) for approval by client.

Media schedule   Plan of insertions of advertisements with names of publications, dates, positions, rates, etc.

Merge-purge   Weeding out of duplicate names when two or more mailing lists are merged.

Mobile   An advertisement which is suspended from the ceiling of a shop and is made to move by air currents.

Modem   An electronic device which enables one computer to communicate with another, or with a fax machine, via a telephone line or cable.

Modern face   Typeface with vertical thickness to sides of letters such as 'O'. *See* old face.

Monica   A marketing research database tool which predicts the likely age group of consumers on the basis of their first names. *See* ACORN.

Morphing   Special computer graphics effect often used in TV commercials, such as when a vacuum cleaner sucks up objects, and also in films such as *Death Becomes Her*. Derived from an effect called cross-warping as used by ILM in the film *Willow*. Morphing software is supplied by firms such as SoftImage, 50 Sollutions and Parallex. Creates bending and stretching or warping effects.

MOSAIC   Neighbourhood classification system which defines 58 lifestyle categories. *See* lifestyle, target audience. Developed by CCN.

Narrowband cable   Older cable television system which was limited to television programmes. *See* broadband cable.

National Readership Survey   Replaced JICNARS in 1992. Publishes results of 35,000 interviews a year regarding readership and demographics of readers of 250 national newspapers and magazines. Has replaced face-to-face interviews with computer assisted personal interviews.

Networking Placing of commercials on a network of local radio or regional TV stations. Also, working with an international network of advertising agencies or PR consultancies.

New product development agency One which plans advertising right from the initial stages of marketing research, branding, packaging and pricing right through to distribution, advertising sales promotion and, if applicable, after-sales service.

Newscaster Large electronically operated outdoor advertising site, message appearing as moving horizontal strip of lighted words.

Niche marketing Selling to special segments of the market as with sports cars, special interest holidays or health foods.

Nixie Direct mail shot returned 'gone away'.

NPA Newspaper Proprietors Association. Trade body of national newspapers. Recognises advertising agencies for commission purposes. *See* commission system.

NPD New product development.

NS Newspaper Society. Trade body of regional newspapers. Recognises advertising agencies for commission purposes.

Off-the-page Direct response marketing use of press advertising.

Offset-litho Printing process based on principle that grease and water do not mix so that excess ink can be washed off plate. Plate prints on blanket cylinder which offsets image onto paper. Sheet or web fed with machines of varying size capable of printing small jobs, sales literature, magazines and newspapers. Machines more compact than letterpress plants and economical for printing smaller circulation newspapers such as *The Independent*.

Old face Typeface with slanting sides to letters such as 'O'. *See* modern face.

One-piece mailer Mailing shot which is complete as folder or booklet, but usually consisting of single sheet of paper which folds down like a map.

Opportunities to see OTS. First applied to outdoor advertising but now applied to all visual media. Measure of number of people who have opportunity to see advertisement. Such as number of travellers on London Underground.

Opticals On TV, film and video-making, trick effects achieved by laboratory processes and camera devices such as fade-ins, dissolves and wipes. Super is lettering superimposed on a picture. Many effects now achieved by computer graphics.

Originals Artwork for reproduction.

Page A piece of information or a document, containing advertising, text, graphics, video material, sound files and so on, accessed via the WWW.

Page impressions The minimum currency of website auditing. A combination of one or more files sent to a user via that user's request received by the server in question.

Password A unique, secret electronic code, for preventing unauthorised access to a computer, program, application, file, piece of information etc.

Penetration Ability of medium to reach a certain proportion of readership or audience.

Perfect binding Method of binding many pages by glueing edges of pages to spine. Pages apt to burst free.

Perimeter advertising *See* arena advertising.

Photomatics Method of testing TV commercials, taping photographs of storyboard sequences. More expensive than animatics (*see*).

Photomechanical transfer (PMT) Paper negative used to produce positive print by chemical transfer.

PIN Pinpoint Identified Neighbourhoods. Analyses 130,000 neighbourhoods and 60 types of census neighbourhoods. Produces proprietory mapping system. Have compressed entire Census results on a single disc. *See* target audience.

Placement Supply of a product as a property for use in theatrical, film, TV or video production. Early use in plays when programmes acknowledged 'Stockings by Kayser-Bondor' and 'Cigarettes by Abdullah'. The 1950s TV show *Emergency Ward 10* had a Smiths clock. Most American and British police films and TV series use Ford cars. These items may be requested and paid for by TV companies. Advertisers are not permitted to pay for placements, so most items are supplied free of charge. Legitimate use of branded products like HP Sauce or a brand of whisky can make a scene look authentic. Recent development has been companies which specialise in placing products for clients. Some prefer the term product props.

Plans board Account executive and agency department heads who form a planning committee to consider client's requirements and jointly produce a proposed campaign for presentation to the client.

PMT Photomechanical transfer (*see*).

Post production After shooting on film or videotape, the adding of computer graphics and editing, using systems such as Paintbox, Harry, Hal and Henry, to complete the commercial or video, or Softimage systems for animated scenes.

PPA Periodical Publishers Association. Trade body of magazine publishers. Recognises advertising agencies. *See* commission system.

Premium house Special agency which buys and supplies goods used for sales promotion purposes, often buying on an international scale.

Presentation Setting up by agency of its proposals for an advertising campaign, usually with mocked up advertisements, and media schedule supported by statistics. Could be a competitive presentation when client is seeking new agency, or a scheme seeking renewal of contract with existing client. Can be elaborate and justify making a charge for its time and effort.

Presenter Actor or unseen commentator making sales pitch in TV commercial, or person making vocal appeal in radio commercial.

Pre-testing Testing of advertisements at an early stage to see which, or which elements, are remembered, and which advertisement is most likely to achieve the required response. The folder technique may be used to test a set of advertisements contained in plastic sleeves, a sample of people being interviewed, usually in the street. The reading and noting test uses an actual advertisement printed in a regional edition of a national newspaper. Respondents are questioned about each part of the advertisement, percentage ratings being calculated for men and women. The advertisement may be amended as suggested by the test. TV commercials are given in-theatre tests, a recruited audience recording its willingness to buy advertised product. The commercial may be shown and reshown with other material being screened in between.

Primary media Those which spearhead an advertising campaign, e.g. press or TV. *See* secondary media.

Product mix Range of products, especially of varieties such as flavours or colours, made and distributed by a company, e.g. range of Heinz foods or Dulux paints.

Product props *See* placement.

Production manager In an advertising agency or department person responsible for preparing final material for printer or publisher including typesettings and camera-ready copy or organising photography and artwork for reproduction. Despatches copy to printer or publisher. Deals with proofs. May also be print buyer. *See* traffic controller.

Progress report Essential agency paperwork in form of concise minutes of a meeting with a client, reporting topics discussed, decisions taken, and responsibilities of people on both sides concerning these decisions. Sometimes called call report. Filed in facts book.

Psychographic types Form of Lifestyle classification, e.g. baby boomers who have grown up since the baby boom of the 1960s, Crinklies or Wrinkles who are elderly people who were in their twenties during the Second World War, empty nesters who are married couples without children, and Yuppies, the young upwardly mobile professionals.

Pulsing Continuous advertising with additional occasional bursts.

Push-pull strategy Process of pushing products through distribution system by means of trade terms, trade advertising, point-of-sale displays and schemes, advertising and sales promotion being used to pull products by creating demand. Sometimes reversed as pull-push strategy.

Quad crown Size of poster seen on walls of London Underground. Measures 1016mm × 762mm or 40″ × 30″.

Quality press The AB nationals such as *The Times, Financial Times, Daily Telegraph, Guardian, Sunday Times, Observer, Sunday Telegraph, Independent on Sunday* and *Scotsman*. They have large business sections or supplements. Usually broadsheet but may have tabloid sections.

Quantel Makers of computer graphics system such as Paintbox (paint system), Picturebox (stills separation, presentation and storage), Harriet (dynamic graphics systems), Hal (digital compositing system), Henry (con-current editing system).

Quire Twentieth part of a ream, or 25 sheets. Newsagents buy publications in quires, which may be increased in number as a bonus.

Quotes Inverted commas used for direct speech or quotations. Publishers usually use single quotation marks.

Radio Authority Separate Authority for ILR (*see*) and INR (*see*) set up under Broadcasting Act 1990. Has Code of Practice and rules regarding sponsored programmes. Licenses contractors.

RAJAR Radio Joint Audience Research which, since 1992, has researched all radio audiences and produced quarterly listening summaries.

Reach Number of different readers, viewers, listeners who are aware of advertisement at least once.

Reading and noting test *See* pre-testing.

Ream Five hundred sheets of paper. Under metrication, also 100 sheet ream.

Recall (i) Product recall. When a fault has been found in a product, appeals to purchasers to return product to maker for adjustment or replacement. (ii) Aided recall. As in readership survey when respondents are shown titles of journals. (iii) Day after recall. When members of the public are questioned regarding advertisements/commercials they may have seen on previous day.

Recognition For purpose of claiming commission on media purchases, advertising agencies and media independents have to apply to NPA, NS, PPA, ITVA,

CRCA for relevant recognition. This is granted upon satisfactory evidence of credit worthiness (ability to pay media bills promptly) and acceptance of BCASP. Office of Fair Trading in 1979, under Restrictive Trade Practices Act 1976, ruled that it was monopolistic for media bodies to guarantee rate of commission which became negotiable between agencies and media owners.

Reverse out Reversing copy to read white on black or a second colour. Minimal use can give emphasis, but a lot of reading matter reversed out has far less legibility than if type is printed normally black on white. Said to reduce reading speed by 10.5 per cent, and cuts comprehension by 30 per cent. A reverse panel in glossy ink and shiny paper as with magazines printed by off-set litho is very difficult to read. Sometimes called reverse type.

Roman Upright typeface, as most type used in print. Written in lower case as 'rom'. Distinct from italic (*see*).

Roughcut Early stage in editing of a TV commercial.

Rule Printing word for a line, underlining copy or separating columns. Copy should not be underlined or it will be set in italics.

Run-of-paper Advertisement inserted anywhere in a publication at the discretion of the advertisement manager.

Saddle-stitching Binding of magazines or other print with staples, stitched from spine to centre-spread, so that pages lie flat when opened unlike perfect binding (*see*).

Sagacity System of life cycle grouping based on idea that people have different aspirations and behaviour patterns as they go through different age-groups. Also divided by income and occupation groups. Produced by Research Services.

Sans-serif Typeface without lines at ends of stems and arms of letters. Good as display faces, poor as text faces. Examples: Erbar, Gill, Univers, Helvetica.

Scamp, scribble Rough visual of a proposed advertisement.

Scene advertising Another name for sales promotion.

Screamer An exclamation mark.

Search engine A computer program designed to search for information on the web. Most search engines are highly structured, to enable information to be obtained easily by subject or classification.

Secondary media That which supports primary media, such as out-door, point-of-sale displays.

Serif Lines at ends of stems and arms of letters. Serif typefaces include Times, Goudy, Plantin. Easier to read in small sizes or on shiny paper than sans-serif (*see*) faces. Mainly book or text faces.

Session A series of page impressions to one user, which ends when there is a gap of at least 30 minutes between two page impressions for that user.

Share of voice Percentage of broadcast audience which sees, hears commercial.

Shopping basket A feature on a shopping website which enables the visitor to accumulate the advertised items he or she wishes to order. When the selection is complete, the shopper gives his or her credit card number, thereby paying for the contents of the shopping basket.

Shopping for an agency Process of short-listing, selecting and appointment of an advertising agency.

Snipe Overlay pasted to poster to give additional information.

Soap opera Popular TV series. Derived from American radio shows of the 1930s which were sponsored by soap advertisers. They produced entire programme and inserted commercial messages and announced that the programme was by courtesy of sponsors. Not adopted in Britain where programmes are produced independently by TV contractor even when sponsored.

Social grades Replaced socio-economic groups in 1970s when social grades (based on occupation instead of income) were applied to the National Readership Survey. Grades are A (Upper Middle class), B (Middle class), C^1 (Lower Middle class), C^2 (Skilled working class), D (Semi-skilled and unskilled working class), E (Those at lowest level of subsistence). Percentage breakdowns vary annually but available from National Readership Survey.

Softimage Producers of innovative, high-performance 3D animation and simulation software for film studios, animation houses, broadcasters, graphic artists, product designers, architects and engineers. Of particular value for post-production video computer graphics. Modules include Model, a range of sophisticated tools for creating objects; Motion, to create and control choreography; Matter to incorporate lighting, surface colours and textural qualities; Actor, animation with inverse Kinematics, flexible envelopes and dynamics; Tools, a Unix file manager, image processor and device driver.

Spectacular Very large outdoor poster such as a bulletin board or supersite, or above stairway on Underground station.

Split-run test *See* A/B split method.

Storyboard Sequence of scenes for a TV commercial, drawn like a cartoon in rectangles or shapes like TV screens. *See* also audio.

Strapline Slogan or signature slogan, usually placed at foot of an advertisement, e.g. The Ultimate Driving Machine (BMW).

Subliminal advertising Not permitted in Britain. Television commercial with such short sequences that message is not visible but is registered mentally.

Sugging Pretending to be making a marketing research study in order to lead up to a sales pitch.

Super Profiles Geo-demographic targeting system which links consumer life-style with postal geography. Uses 10 life styles and 37 target markets. Run by Credit and Data Marketing Services. *See* target audience, lifestyle.

TABS Tracking, Advertising and Brand Strength. A sophisticated form of tracking study research which, among other things, identifies media consumption, weaknesses in both creative and media aspects of a campaign, rates of decay (the wear out factor) and whether drip (*see*) or burst advertising (*see*) is advisable.

Tabloids Small sheet popular newspapers such as the *Daily Mirror, Sun, Daily Mail* and *Daily Express* with circulations from three to two million.

Tactical advertising Another name for sales promotion.

Target audience Prospective buyers at which advertising is aimed. May be selected on basis of age, sex, special interests or social grades (*see*). Geo-demographic and lifestyle data may be used, e.g. ACORN.

Target Group Index TGI Source of market including media data owned by BMRB. Based on information provided on-line by panel of 24,000 adults a year, covering 400 product fields, their demographic characteristics and media exposure.

Targeting *See* target audience.

TC Till cancelled. Usually applied to poster contracts.

Tear sheet   Page torn from a journal containing an advertisement which has appeared, and serving as a voucher copy or proof of insertion. May accompany publisher's invoice.

Third-agers   The 14 million or more people in the UK aged between 50 and 74. Expected to become 30 per cent of the population. Big market for overseas holidays and bulk of savings.

Through-the-line agency   Advertising agency which offers both above-the-line and below-the-line advertising. Very few such agencies.

Tracking study   Form of advertisement research which goes beyond recall testing and tests history of advertisement, extent of its effectiveness over time, and its wear-out factor. *See* TABS.

Traffic controller   May combine duties of production manager (*see*) in agency, sending copies of job instructions to agency department heads, and checking flow of work. Agency progress chaser.

Transportation advertising   Posters of various shapes and sizes on public transport vehicles and on transportation sites such as railway stations, Underground railway stations and trains, and at airports and seaports. Differs from ordinary outdoor advertisements with their brief messages because passengers have time to read longer copy, while posters on buses and trams (including all-over decorating of a tram for one advertiser as in Hong Kong) are seen by people along routes.

T-side   T-shape poster on side of double-decker bus.

Typeface   A design type such as Rockwell, Times or Univers.

Typographer   Person who selects typefaces for print work or advertisements, and marks up layout or copy with typesizes, measure (width of column), and varieties of type such as roman, bold, medium or light.

Ultravision sites   Outdoor advertising site consisting of a series of advertisements produced as revolving slats to provide a succession of advertisements.

Uni-poles   Tubular-shaped poster sites on pavements or in shopping precincts, especially in France although a similar version is to be found in some British shopping centres.

Unit   Set of printing cylinders, four-colour press having four units usually with drier between each unit which prints succession of colours in four-colour process.

URL   Uniform resource locator. A website address, using a universally recognised method of naming websites.

User   In website terminology, an individual IP address.

Vandal proof vinyl posters   Specially protected posters produced for 'pedestrian housewife' sites in shopping precinct.

Verified Free Distribution   Subsidiary of the Audit Bureau of Circulations (*see*) which certifies circulations of free newspapers.

Vertical advertising   Another name for co-operative advertising as when manufacturer assists distribution with their advertising by contributing to cost or supplying art work and camera-ready copy to which distributor adds his name and address.

Visit   A series of page impressions served in an unbroken sequence from within a website to the same user.

Visual   A rough layout of an advertisement.

Visualiser   Advertising agency designer who designs or interprets copy and produces roughs or scamps of proposed advertisements.

Voice   Ability of advertisement to reach target audience effectively. Media planners and buyers will seek to obtain maximum share of voice. Tracking studies (*see*) measure share of voice (*see*) achieved.

Voice-over   Commentary by unseen presenter on TV commercial.

Waistband   Advertisement band round bus, or rear waistband on single-decker bus.

Wash drawing   Monochrome drawing painted in grey and black.

Wear-out factor   Point at which advertisement ceases to be remembered and loses effectiveness.

Weasel   Statement in advertisement which deliberately implies product does something it may not always do.

Web   Reel of paper as used on rotary letterpress, offset-litho and flexography printing. Common in newspaper printing.

Web-fed   Printing from reel of paper instead of from sheets.

Weight   (1) Lightness or boldness of a typeface. (2) Weight of paper in grammes. (3) Volume of advertising.

White mail   Correspondence incurred in direct response marketing due to goods out-of-stock, claims for refunds, returned goods, complaints. Some white mail can be avoided if customer asked to state alternative choice.

Wire-stitching   As in many magazines. *See* saddle-stitched.

WWW   The World Wide Web. A global electronic system for holding and accessing information.

X-height   The mean line. Height of small letters without ascenders or descenders, e.g. a, e, i, o, u or of lower case part as in b, d, h. Letters with low x-height difficult to read as text types although in larger sizes can be an attractive display face.

Yahoo!   An organisation with a huge search engine devoted to finding information on the WWW (*see*).

Zapping   By means of remote control, changing TV channels to avoid commercials.

Zipping   Fast forwarding through commercials when watching video-taped programmes. Some recorders have device for zipping automatically.

Zoned campaigns   Advertising campaigns limited to certain areas.

Index